HOLY ROMAN EMPIRE

FRANCE

BURGUNDY

LOIRE R.

SAÔNE R.

Cluny

MILAN

Milan

Pavía

PO R.

VENICE

Venice

AQUITANIA

LOIRE R.

RHÔNE R.

Avignon

GENOA

Genoa

Florence

TUSCANY

PAPAL
STATES

Toulouse

Montpélier

RENEES

ARAGÓN

Barcelona

CORSICA
(TO GENOA)

Rome

MRS. JOHN EDWARD CAHILL
2 MADRONE AVENUE
KENTFIELD, CALIFORNIA 94904

SARDINIA
(TO ARAGÓN)

MALLORCA

BALEARIC ISLANDS
(TO ARAGÓN)

MEDITERRANEAN SEA

SICILY
(TO ARAGÓN)

ALGERIA

Tunis

D0916005

MILES

0   100   200

palacios

The Portugal Story

Books by

JOHN DOS PASSOS

The Portugal Story:

Three Centuries of Exploration and Discovery

JOHN DOS PASSOS

1969
Doubleday & Company, Inc.
GARDEN CITY, NEW YORK

Library of Congress Catalog Card Number 69-12227
Copyright © 1969 by John Dos Passos
All Rights Reserved
Printed in the United States of America
First Edition

ACKNOWLEDGMENTS

So many people were helpful during my last trip through Portugal to check on the materials for this book that it is hardly possible to thank them all. There were the boys who led us through vineyards up in the valley of the Douro on that long search to find the cave that had prehistoric paintings in it. There was my old friend Dr. Cintra who took us to that lovely clear cove in the flank of the Serra da Arrabida and introduced me to the *conventinho* up the hill. There was Senhora Acabado at the National Archives who found me reprints of the books in the Torre do Tumbo collection. There was a very well-informed gentleman named Alarcón who showed us about the excavations at Conimbriga. The pleasantest law student took us through the university at Coimbra. My friend Lieutenant-Colonel Afonso do Paço brought me up to date on the recent excavations. His running commentary as he guided us through the archaeological museum at Belém was an education in Portuguese pre-history. His monograph on the excavation of the battlefield at Aljubarrota, with his personal explanations and impromptu sketches, gave me a fresh picture of the tactics of that battle. The trip with him up to the citânia of Sanfins was unforgettable. To all these ladies and gentlemen many thanks.

Samuel Eliot Morison's detailed report on ships and navigation in the fifteenth century in his *Admiral of the Ocean Sea* was essential. Two other American publications were particularly useful. Francis M. Rogers' careful researching of John of Avis' son Pedro's actual travels dispelled the fantasies these travels were enveloped in by nineteenth-century historians. Charles Wendell

David's fine edition of the low Latin text of *De Expugnatione Lyxbonensi* furnished the vividest picture of twelfth-century siege warfare I found anywhere. Though my quotations from the writings of these scholars are trifling I owe them a debt of gratitude. Many thanks, too, to Tarcísio Beal for his careful overhaul of my Portuguese spellings.

CONTENTS

PART FOUR

Peak of Empire

PART FIVE

Portugal in America

LIST OF ILLUSTRATIONS

A NOTE ON PRONUNCIATION

Portuguese names present certain problems to the English-speaking reader, but for the purposes of this book he needs only to worry about a few Portuguese sounds. *Lh* like *ll* in Castilian has the sound of *lli* in million. *Nh* is equivalent to *ny* in canyon. Ç reads *s* as in French. The nasal diphthongs are difficult but the reader can get by if he pronounces the Portuguese João as something between the French Jean and plain English John; *õe* as in Camões sounds something like *oi* in joins, i.e. Camoins.

To try to English all the proper names would have been confusing, so I have only used the English form of the most often mentioned cities and the most prominent historical characters. Thus Lisboa is written Lisbon. *O infante Dom Henrique* comes out Prince Henry. The most important Joãos of the Houses of Avis and Bragança are written John, but for the Spaniards I have kept the Castilian Juan since the pronunciation comes easily to most Americans: Hwan.

J.D.P.

PART ONE

How Portugal Began

I

THE HILL PEOPLE

Between beds of petunias in the main square of the village of Murça in Portugal's northeasternmost province there stands on a pedestal a rudely carved stone boar. In front of the ancient hilltop fortifications of Bragança, some fifty miles further inland, another forms the base of an ancient pillory which has been ascribed to Visigothic times. These ornamented stone pillars to which criminals were tied up for punishment were the symbols of authority in every Portuguese town. Other boars have been found incorporated into Roman family altars. Stone boars turn up in Galicia and in the walled city of Ciudad Rodrigo in Spanish Leon. In Portugal they are simply known as *porcos* or *porcas*. In Spain they are called *verracos* and some people try to imagine that they are bulls. The country people still regard them with a certain half humorous awe. Through the ages they have been dimly associated with fertility, authority, power. Scholars tax their imaginations speculating about their origin.

The most popular theory is that these stone boars were the work of some of the Celtic peoples who started drifting into the Iberian peninsula across the western passes of the Pyrenees toward the latter part of the tenth century before Christ.

The Celts and possibly Germanic groups that came along with them, all speaking languages of the Indo-European family, seem to have brought in a more advanced agricultural culture than had prevailed among the shellfish eaters of the coast of what is now Portugal. In early days some of them may have been food gatherers who lived largely on acorns and chestnuts, but long before the Carthaginians and the Romans arrived to trouble them they were cultivating wheat for bread, barley for beer and flax for clothing. They seem to have passed their lives in a state of continual warfare, raiding and counterraiding. For defense they huddled in villages of round stone houses—the foundations that have been excavated give a little the impression of stone igloos—set in a tangle of defensive walls on the most imposing heights they could find. Traces of them are turning up on almost every mountaintop in northern Portugal.

They raised horses from very early times, and kept cattle, sheep, goats and pigs. Swine rated high: in Roman times the northwestern part of the Iberian peninsula was noted for its hams. They worked stone and, along with their cousins in Gaul and Britain and Ireland, developed a highly unique and intricate style of decoration. They understood the principle of the wheel. Small hand mills for grinding grain abounded in their villages. They are supposed to have introduced the peculiar squeaking cart, with an axle that turns with the wheel, used in parts of Galicia and Portugal to this day.

While Celts and associated peoples were seeping down through the Pyrenees, Phoenician traders were exploring the southern coast of the peninsula where they found the population in a stage of civilization which the Greeks later described as Iberian. The Phoenicians broached the Pillars of Hercules, rounded Cape St. Vincent and probed the Atlantic shores, trading manufactured articles for silver and bronze and tin. They established settlements for fishing and for drying salt out of seawater to salt down their catch with.

As soon as bronze was invented tin became an important commodity. There was very little tin in the Mediterranean basin. Deposits in riverbeds in northern Portugal and Galicia seem to have been placered out at an early date. Eventually the tin trade established contact between the Celtic and Iberian tribes in the northwest of the peninsula and their kinfolk in Brittany and the British Isles where tin was in plentiful supply.

4

The beginnings of written history find a flourishing trade in metals enriching the people of the region between the Guadalquivir and the Guadiana rivers along what is now the border between Spain and Portugal. This region was known as Tarshish which means smelter or refinery in Phoenician Hebrew. This may have been the *tarshish* where Hiram of Tyre procured precious metals for King Solomon. To protect their trade route the Tyrians founded Gadir, the present Cádiz, in the ninth century B.C.

Hard upon the Phoenicians came the Greeks. Ships from Rhodes, Samos, and Phocaea in Asia Minor scoured the shores of the peninsula as far as a semi-mythical settlement called Ophioussa on the Tagus. The Greek for Tarshish was Tartessos. With the weakening of Tyrean influence the alliance between the Phocaeans and the rich king of that country became proverbial. This Arganthonios loaned specie to the Phocaeans to help pay for the fortification of their city against a threatened invasion from Persia.

Bands of Ionian Greeks harried out of their homes by the Persian invaders took refuge in the western Mediterranean. There they were challenged by a new Semitic power. Carthage was founded as a Phoenician colony in 814 B.C. and, as the mother cities fell into the hands of the Babylonians, outweighed Tyre and Sidon in power and influence.

By the middle of the sixth century the Carthaginians had united with the Etruscans to defeat a Phocaean fleet off Corsica. In subsequent years they destroyed the Greek city of Mainaké and built up in its stead their own colony of Malach (meaning salting place) which became modern Málaga. The gold and silver mines and the tin trade were now in their hands. Their fleets sealed off the Straits of Gibraltar and furnished a core of truth to the legends spread by the Greeks of sea monsters and nameless terrors barring the way into the Atlantic.

The Carthaginians profoundly influenced the development of the southeastern half of the Iberian peninsula. Along the distant Atlantic shores their penetration was more sporadic. Still Celtiberian mercenaries from the hill towns were an important factor in the wars of the Carthaginians against the Greek states in Sicily. When these mercenaries returned home they brought with them seeds of a generalized Mediterranean culture. In the Punic Wars Hannibal recruited and impressed Galicians, Lusitanians and Celtiberians into his armies. His defeat was hastened by the resistance which the peoples of the interior, fortified in their lofty villages, put up against his press gangs.

When the Romans consolidated their rule over the Iberian peninsula during the second and first centuries B.C. they recognized a cultural difference between the matriarchal peasantry of the coastal fringes and the cattle herders of the tableland, who traced descent through the father. Already there was something conservative and withdrawn from the main stream about the inhabitants of the rainy coastal valleys.

The Roman legions overran all Gaul in seven years but it took them almost two centuries to subdue the Celtiberian peoples. The struggle was long and bloody. In a last burst of defiance a leader known to history as Viriathus led the ancestors of the modern Portuguese in a triumphant campaign against the Romans which only ended in his death at the hands of hired assassins. The Lusitanians, defeated and leaderless, retired in small groups to the hill villages of the northwest, where they kept up a resistance, punctuated by occasional raids on the settled territories, well into the reign of Augustus.

Augustus founded military colonies to keep the country pacified. His chief centers in what is now Portugal were Braga in the north and Evora in the south. Lisbon was first heard of as a fortification established by the Consul Decimus Junius Brutus in his campaign against Viriathus.

The Romans set to work to spread their extraordinarily standardized civilization. Roads linked the military colonies. The Latin language and Roman law superceded every local tradition. Forums, temples and lawcourts sprung up in the cities. The architecture and layout of Mérida was exactly the same as the architecture and layout of some distant Asian or African outpost. Large-scale agriculture was conducted with slave labor under the villa system. Efficient networks of irrigation were established in the dry lands south of the Tagus. The plow was introduced everywhere.

2

OUT OF THE RUINS OF EMPIRE

When the Romans succumbed to bureaucratic paralysis, hungry peoples of Germanic origins and speech began to pour down through the passes of the Pyrenees. Of these the Alans and Vandals merely looted the countryside and moved on into richer lands in the south, but the Swabians and the Visigoths came to stay.

The Swabians, known as Suevi to the Romans, who occupied a good part of what is now Portugal and Galicia, came from Saxony and Thuringia. In the course of their migration south they mixed with Celtic peoples along the River Main, with the result that their culture was not too different from that of the Celts who had originally settled the country. They blended easily with the Romanized peasantry. Basically the Swabians were a people of small landowners who lived in detached houses separated from the villages. They found the soil and rainfall suitable to the crops they were accustomed to in Central Germany. Their great addition to the culture of the region was an improved iron plow.

The Visigoths on the other hand were a pastoral race. They came from the grazing lands north of the Black Sea. In their trek westward they had become so thoroughly Romanized that the desperate administrators who were superintending the disintegration of the empire invited them in to keep order. After a number of wars between the various invaders, in which the Latin-speaking peasants seem to have taken very little part, the Swabians established a kingdom which included Galicia and northern Portugal. Their capital was Braga. Meanwhile the Visigoths became the overlords of the central tableland and made their capital at Toledo.

The lives of the serfs bound to the land who produced the food were hardly changed. Such traces of the Roman administrative framework as subsisted were largely ecclesiastical. The church became the most powerful social bond. After the conversion of the Swabian Rechiarius to Christianity around 447, (some fifty years before the conversion of Clovis the Frank), Braga became a powerful religious center. A Bishop Martin of Braga left an important compilation of Roman philosophical writers, through which much of the younger Seneca's work was preserved. Even after the absorption of the Swabian kingdom by the Visigoths, Braga remained a center of churchly learning.

The Visigothic empire lasted not much more than a century. By the year seven hundred the wave of proselyting and conquest launched by Mohammed from Mecca and Medina had reached Morocco. After sweeping like a brush fire through the civilized communities of North Africa the conquerors found their path blocked by the Atlantic. Mohammedan warriors began to look greedily northward across the Straits of Gibraltar. In the course of a row over the succession to the Visigothic throne, the defeated parties in 711 invited a Berber chieftain named Tarik to cross into Spain to bring them help. This Tarik, with a small band of Berbers, routed the army of the Visigothic king so easily that the next year a large force of mixed Berbers and Arabs crossed the straits and penetrated as far north as Lugo in Galicia. Traveling over what was left of the Roman roads, the Moslems subjugated the peninsula with incredible speed. By 715 they were ravaging the Atlantic coast. The Algarve was already Moslem. It was the Arabs who gave that region its name, which means "the West." They conquered Alcácer do Sal, Evora and Lisbon. Only north of the Douro did they meet any resistance. Portucale (now Oporto), and Braga showed fight and were laid waste. The same fate overtook Tuy, Orense and Lugo in Galicia.

8

No more than the Romans did the Mohammedans show much interest in the rainy lands to the north of the Douro. Within a couple of generations they had pulled back south of the Mondego River. Moslems from Egypt settled Faro and Beja. Yemenite Arabs built the walled city of Silves in the Algarve. Others fortified Lisbon and started the palace at Sintra which remains the most visible monument of the Moorish occupation in Portugal. The waterwheels in the valley of the Mondego below Coimbra are said to be left over from the irrigated estates of settlers from Persia.

After their drive into the Frankish kingdom was permanently checked by Charles Martel in the vicinity of Poitiers the motley armies of Islam settled down to the enjoyment of their Iberian domain. Large numbers of the inhabitants embraced the faith. The invaders married into the population. After a long period of instability, when warring Arab tribes, bands of Berbers and converted and unconverted Iberians fought for supremacy, a despotic military government was established at Córdova.

The century of the caliphate was a period of cultural effervescence. The Arabs brought with them into the peninsula all the debris of Greco-Roman civilization they had acquired during their long march of conquest. The restless Arab mind found new facets in the philosophy of Aristotle and the geography of Ptolemy and in Greek notions of science and cosmology. Through the Arabs the ancient astronomy of the Mesopotamian peoples filtered into Europe. The invention of zero made mathematics possible.

Córdova became a metropolis in an expanding world. There was travel and interchange of goods and ideas between the valley of the Guadalquivir and the remotest corners of the vast Moslem empire.

There seem to have been Jewish communities in the Iberian cities since Carthaginian times, but the two major waves of immigration into the peninsula came after the destruction of Jerusalem and during the period of the caliphate. The Visigothic kings had made a great show of legislating against the Jews but they still formed a prominent part of the population of the Visigothic capital at Toledo. They dominated the lettered class. Even the antisemitic Bishop Julian, Christian theologian and grammarian of the seventh century, was reported to be of Jewish origin. Now

9

the caliphs not only tolerated the Jews but cherished their scholarship. Though Mahomet, who had borrowed so much of his religion from Jewish sources, first applied his maxim of "plunder the infidel" to Jewish tribes, there was a Moslem tradition of respect for "The People of the Book."

The Jews influenced the cultural tone of the caliphate with their special type of fervent religious literacy, their saturation in the Hellenistic traditions of Alexandria and their knowledge of the chemistry and medicine of the ancient world. Though they had forgotten their Greek they brought with them Arabic translations of Aristotle and of compendiums of classical literature that came into Arabic through the Syriac. Especially they produced physicians and astrologers.

The Alexandrian technology was widely disseminated. The works of irrigation left over from Roman days were restored and perfected. Even provincial Lisbon had many public baths. The use of linen paper made the multiplication of books much easier than in the days of parchment rolls. Literacy was widespread. Córdova became a hive of copyists and booksellers. The caliph's library was said to amount to four hundred thousand volumes.

A local architecture was developed from a combination of the horseshoe arch with gesso decoration based on Persian and Byzantine styles. Metallurgy and ceramics flourished. It was a period of interpenetration of cultures.

The Atlantic coast, bordering on what the Arab geographers, parroting the Greeks, called the Ocean of Darkness, remained a backwater. The Arab geographer El Idrisi described the excellence of the harbors and fortifications of Lisbon and Alcácer do Sal, and the pinewoods and the shipyards on the river at Setúbal. He extolled the richness of the orchards around Silves and the purity of the Arabic spoken by its inhabitants. The figs of the region were, in the words of his Spanish translator: "good, delicate, appetizing and delicious."

In Lisbon El Idrisi collected a strange tale that may reflect memories of some early expedition to the Canaries. "It was from Lisbon that the adventurers set sail who went to find out what the Ocean of Darkness contains, and what its boundaries were," he wrote. He added that in his day there was still in the city, near the hot springs, a street named the Street of the Adventurers.

Eight men, so the tale was told to the Arabian geographer, all close cousins, got together to build a ship and victualed it with food and water for many months. At the first breath of the east wind they put to sea. After sailing west eleven days they found themselves in an ocean where the waves exhaled a fetid odor and hid numerous reefs which they discerned with difficulty. Terrified they changed their course and sailed south for twelve days until they found an island occupied by innumerable flocks of sheep. There was a spring of fresh water under a wild fig tree but no human inhabitants. They killed several sheep but the flesh was so poor they couldn't eat it. All the good they got out of them was the skins.

They sailed south another twelve days and made port on an island which was inhabited and cultivated. Boats put out from the shore. They were surrounded and made prisoners and taken to a town populated by men of great stature whose skin had a reddish tone and by women of rare beauty. They lay in prison for three days but on the fourth a man appeared who spoke Arabic. He announced that he was the king's interpreter and that they must tell him who they were and why they had come.

When they told him their story he took them before the king. The king told them that his own father had sent out a ship, manned by his slaves, that had sailed for a month into the west, until all light faded out of the sky and they had to abandon their vain enterprise. He assured the adventurers that they would not be harmed and sent them back to prison to await a wind out of the west.

When the west wind rose he had them bound and blindfolded and placed in a ship. "We sailed," they said, "for three days and three nights and arrived on an unknown shore. The islanders left us there with our hands tied behind our backs and blindfolds over our eyes." When morning came they heard laughter. People hearkened to their cries and cut them loose. They were Berbers. They told the adventurers that this was the westernmost port in all the world. They were two months journey from home. The name of the place was Asafi, which signified "Alas."

El Idrisi traveled as far as the Mondego, where he praised the well-watered gardens. Of the north all he had to say was that the inhabitants made a business of raising horses and raiding their neighbors.

3

THE BEGINNINGS OF
CHRISTIAN KINGDOMS

In the confusion of the Mohammedan conquest and the ruin of
the Visigothic empire, a young man named Pelayo escaped to
the Cantabrian mountains. Pelayo was supposed to be the son of
a member of the Visigothic royal family murdered at Tuy.
Pelayo remained in hiding for several years, which some researchers
claim he spent gathering adherents among the Swabians of the
Gallego-Portuguese coast. Then somewhere between 721 and 725
he and his mountain men, in a deep valley at Cangas de Onís
near the Picos de Europa, surprised and defeated a Moslem force
sent to destroy him. This engagement became legendary as the
Battle of Covadonga with which Castilian history begins. According to the story Pelayo was elected King of Asturias on the
battlefield.

His tiny kingdom became a refuge for Christian fighting men
from all over the peninsula. Their life was hard in the Asturian
mountains. Raiding the lowlands was the most convenient source
of money and goods. Pelayo's son-in-law, the first Alfonso, took
advantage of a Berber revolt against Arab rule in Africa which
set off a civil war between Arabs and Berbers on the peninsula,
to lead raids as far south as Astorga, León, Salamanca and Avila
and as far west as Braga and Portucale, the old Roman port at
the mouth of the Douro.

The policy of Alfonso I, which became that of his successors, was to resettle localities considered safe from Moorish raids. Grants of land and feudal privileges were an inducement to men-at-arms to settle the frontier. To the south of the resettlement the policy, only sporadically enforced, was to destroy everything that could give shelter to an invader. Trees were cut down and crops carried off. Captured cities were razed, their infidel inhabitants slaughtered and the Christians brought home to populate the Asturian valleys. Incessant raiding and plundering back and forth made settled life impossible on a broad band across the peninsula which fluctuated with the fortunes of war.

The next Alfonso sought aid from the mighty Charlemagne. In the course of consolidating his empire Charlemagne was trying to create a Spanish mark in the eastern Pyrenees which would include the Christian settlements in Navarre and upper Aragon and the duchy of Barcelona. Charlemagne's expedition against the Moors at Zaragoza failed and, returning north through the pass at Roncesvalles, his rearguard suffered the defeat made glorious by the *Chanson de Roland*. With or without Charlemagne's help Alfonso II managed to penetrate as far as Lisbon in the West but had to withdraw without occupying the city.

Alfonso II called a council of local counts and bishops at Guimarães, which seems to have been one of the few towns still populated, to consider the restoration of Braga, but he died before the plans they elaborated could be put in effect. As early as 841 the term "Provincia Portucalence" began to appear in documents. From then on the name Portugal was used to denote the lands reconquered from the Moors between the Douro and the Minho rivers.

During the following century Christian settlers ventured further into the depopulated region. The Asturians moved the seat of their monarchy to the abandoned Roman city of León. From León as a base parties were sent out to build castles on the table-lands to the south and east. It was these castles that gave their name to Castile.

While, amid continual bloodshed over conflicting claims to the throne of León, the Christian chieftains strengthened their hold over the central uplands, the Portuguese counts were left very much to their own devices. They had to defend themselves and their farms and vassals not only from the Moors but from the Northmen who were pushing ever further down the coast, robbing and burning wherever they landed their black ships. Another factor which contributed to the isolation of the county of Portugal was that contact with León and Castile was largely roundabout through Galicia, since the rivers were not navigable inland and the direct road east led through mountains of tedious passage.

The division between Portugal and Galicia, two regions of similar language and customs, came about through the development of Santiago de Compostela. Around 830 a Roman tomb was uncovered in a cove on the Galician coast and some local ecclesiastic decided it must contain the body of St. James the Apostle. According to the legend, after his martyrdom at Jerusalem in the early years of the Christian era, St. James's body had been miraculously transported in a bark without oars or sails to the shores of Galicia. The bones, probably for protection against the Northmen, were moved up to Compostela, which seems to have been a religious center from prehistoric times.

Compostela became the most important pilgrimage site in Europe. A legend arose that God had put the Milky Way into the sky simply to guide the pilgrims to Santiago. By the end of the century the cult of Santiago and of his symbol the scallop shell was in full flower. Popes, kings, knights, ecclesiastics, many of them barefoot in their shirts, made the pilgrimage from every corner of Europe. While Portugal consisted of some forgotten counties vaguely dependent on the kingdom of León, the pilgrimage road tied in Galician Compostela with the Spanish kingdoms of the plateau and with Cluny, the great French center of religious reform.

The abbey of Cluny was founded in the hilly country between the Saône and the Loire by a pious Count of Auvergne in 910. By the end of the century it had become the focus of a movement for the reform of the Christian church. The Cluniacs believed in rigorous monastic rule, ascetic living for the clergy and meticulous performance of the liturgy. They encouraged pilgrimages. They urged the knights and feudal princelings to fight the infidel instead of fighting among themselves. The religious revival that radiated from Cluny set off the wild enthusiasms that launched the crusades. In the tenth and eleventh centuries

Cluny outshone Rome as the religious center of Western Europe. In the Hispanic peninsula as in Italy and France it was influences from Cluny that stimulated the great developments in romanesque architecture.

While the monks of Cluny were electing popes and spreading their rule from monastery to monastery to consolidate Christendom, Hugh Capet and his heirs were consolidating the French monarchy. Starting with a few castles on the Ile de France a series of able rulers built a kingdom out of the Frankish part of the chaotic dominions left over by the fragmentation of the heritage of Charlemagne. Hugh Capet, the founder, died in 996. When his grandson Henry came to the throne he had to appease the ambitions of his younger brother Robert by turning over to him what was left in France of the old Burgundian realm.

This younger branch of the Capet family were profoundly imbued with the enthusiasms that emanated from the monks of Cluny. Through the marriage of Constance of Burgundy to Alfonso VI of Castile they became interested in Hispanic affairs. This Alfonso was the crusty king of the *Poema del Cid* which, as recited in inn yards and castle halls was the Castilian answer to the *chansons de geste*, and nascent Spain's first literary expression.

During the early part of Alfonso's reign he won victories on every side. Already his father Ferdinand had subjugated enough of the peninsula to revive the Visigothic title of Emperor. Now Alfonso reconquered from the Moors a large slice of Portuguese territory, including Montemór and Coimbra. He occupied Lisbon and Santarém and in 1070 restored the ancient bishopric of Braga. In 1085 he captured Toledo. The Cid seized Valencia in his name. The whole Hispanic world, Christian and Moslem, paid him tribute.

These Christian victories caused such alarm among the contending Moslem princes who had taken over the territory of the old caliphate that they called to their aid a fanatical Berber sect of reformers of Islam which had just conquered Morocco. The Almoravids were serious fighting men. Under Yusuf ibn Tashfin they inflicted such a severe defeat on Alfonso's forces that the king barely escaped with his life.

Immediately he sent messengers to his wife's Burgundian brothers and cousins imploring their aid. Count Raymond, whose brother was the Cluniac Pope Calixtus II, Count Eudes and Count Henry of Burgundy rode across the Pyrenees and assembled at Burgos, each with his troop of adherents. With them they brought the enthusiasms of the Cluniac reform which were soon to culminate in the First Crusade.

To consolidate their support, Alfonso's legitimate daughter Urraca was given in marriage to Count Raymond. His cousin Henry had to be content with an illegitimate daughter named Teresa. The Cluniac reforms were instituted in the Castilian churches.

Placed in charge of the Portuguese counties, Raymond did no better than his father-in-law against the Almoravids. In 1094 they occupied Lisbon and Santarém. To bolster Raymond's failing fortunes Henry was sent to Portugal as Duke of Coimbra. Soon he was being styled Count of Portugal in the documents.

Henry held court in Guimarães, where, to facilitate the growth of commerce, he opened a street for the residence of foreign merchants. He started rebuilding the cathedrals of Braga and Oporto in the magnificent round-arched style encouraged by the monks at Cluny. Though he favored the Cluniac clergy in churchly matters he surrounded himself with mozarab and Portuguese barons. He consolidated his control over the rich farmlands of the Minho and the ancient city of Bragança.

With Raymond he signed a pact, drawn up by a certain Dalmatius, representing the powerful Abbot of Cluny, promising to support Raymond's claim to the throne of Castile. In return Raymond would grant Henry, among other considerations, the Kingdom of Galicia.

This pact became worthless when, after Constance's death, Alfonso VI took a Moslem princess for his fourth wife and produced an heir named Sancho. Raymond died leaving an infant son known as Alfonso Raimundez. Sancho was killed at the age of ten in a skirmish with the Moors. King Alfonso never forgave Count Henry, who was in command of the troop with which he rode. Forever after there was bad blood between them. Before Alfonso died he recognized Raymond's son as his heir.

There followed a family row over the succession hardly equalled in history. As mother of the heir presumptive, Raymond's widow Urraca declared herself queen of Castile and León and arranged a marriage with Alfonso *el Batallador*, the aggressive Aragonese monarch who was carrying his own conquests as far as the Mediterranean. On the strength of this marriage Alfonso of Aragon assumed the title of emperor.

The Battler and Urraca got along very badly. He was reported to have been seen beating her in public. Urraca herself was something of a termagant. She was widely believed to have had an incestuous relationship with her brother Alfonso VI of Castile. The bishop of Toledo now declared her marriage with the Battler to be incestuous by canon law. When Urraca took steps to leave him the Battler tried to carry her off into Aragon by force, but she escaped and joined her Castilian supporters.

The Galicians and Portuguese had risen in arms against any union with Aragon. Young Alfonso Raimundez was proclaimed King of Galicia by his guardian Pedro Froilaz, Count of Trava. Meanwhile Henry of Portugal, whose wife Teresa had produced a boy named Afonso Henriques, traveled to France to beg his Burgundian relatives to back up his claim to the Castilian throne. He returned disappointed, but Alfonso of Aragon enlisted his help and between them they defeated Urraca's Castilians. Urraca promptly offered Henry the command of her army, but Henry, under the influence of his wife Teresa, demanded such exorbitant terms for his support that Urraca patched things up with the Battler. Henry and Teresa as a result made common cause with the Galicians and little Alfonso Raimundez. Urraca couldn't stand the Battler so she left him again and joined the troops supporting her son in Galicia. When Henry of Burgundy died in Astorga in 1112 any claim he may have had to the throne of Castile was considered extinguished, but his five-year-old heir Afonso Henriques was recognized as Count of Portugal and taken in charge by the Portuguese barons.

When the Almoravids, again on the warpath, laid siege to Coimbra, Pedro Froilaz sent his son Fernando Peres with a force of Galician knights to help Teresa who was ruling during her boy's minority. Fernando Peres found the widowed countess shut up in the keep. Their association led to his abandoning his legal wife and taking up with Teresa as her consort. She bore him a daughter.

Fernando Peres was unpopular with the Portuguese. Countess Teresa's authority was negligible. As soon as he reached the age of seventeen Afonso Henriques armed himself knight in the cathedral of Zamora. When Urraca died Alfonso of Castile confirmed her half sister Teresa in the possession of her Portuguese territories, but when Teresa refused to do homage for them the Castilians invaded her county and laid siege to Guimarães. The defenders capitulated and did homage in the name of Afonso Henriques. The young count refused to abide by the terms and started to take possession of the government. When Teresa and her paramour raised an army to oppose him he captured them both and sent them off packing into Galicia.

Meanwhile his cousin Alfonso of Castile was setting out to emulate the deeds of their grandfather. When his Castilians defeated the Aragonese, the old Battler slunk away to die. Alfonso called an assembly of his vassals in León. The new king of Aragon, the king of Navarre, the counts of Barcelona, Toulouse and Montpelier and the dispossessed Moslem ruler of Zaragoza presented themselves to do homage. Afonso Henriques stayed home.

Afonso Henriques was now in his early twenties. He was represented by the chroniclers as a man of gigantic stature with flowing beard and enormous strength. It is obvious that he had a shrewd and calculating mind. When his mother died he made peace with Fernando Peres, but peace changed to war when Afonso Henriques tried to assert his claims to certain Galician fiefdoms north of the Minho. Alfonso of Castile entered Galicia in martial array and after elaborate negotiations Afonso Henriques was compelled to make token submission to the authority of Castile and León. A hundred and fifty of his vassals were called on to ratify the pact between the cousins.

This setback merely turned his struggle for independence into other channels. The Portuguese churches had been trying to free themselves from the domination of the archbishoprics of Santiago and Toledo. Their claim was that the see of Braga was much older. A Cluniac ecclesiastic named John Peculiar, who had considerable influence in Rome, where a Cluniac pope sat on the throne of St. Peter, cooperated with Afonso Henriques in a campaign to free these churches from Castilian influence. When the bishop of Oporto, whose see had depended on Compostela, died, Afonso managed to get Peculiar installed in the episcopal chair. A couple of years later, he got him named Archbishop of Braga. After long and patient intrigues, the Archbishop of Braga and Afonso Henriques secured the practical independence of the Portuguese churches. For the kingship Afonso Henriques had to bide his time.

A fresh invasion led by members of a new Mohammedan sect which had originated among the mountaineers of the Atlas gave Afonso Henriques a chance to show his mettle. The Almohades overran Morocco and North Africa and established their capital in Seville. Afonso Henriques and his Portuguese men-at-arms routed their army at a place known to history and legend as Ourique. The position of Ourique on the map has been hard to identify. According to the royal chronicler the Portuguese were immensely outnumbered by the Moorish host, but Afonso Henriques, encouraged by the prophecies of an ancient hermit, and by a vision of Christ the Savior that appeared to him in a dream the night before the battle, accomplished their defeat. It was in 1139, on July 25, the feast of Saint James.

Wherever the battle was fought the results were impressive. A new Christian stronghold was established by the military order of the Knights Templar at Soure south of Coimbra. The Moslems at Santarém were forced to pay tribute. Afonso Henriques seized the occasion to declare himself King of Portugal. He renewed his connection with the House of Burgundy by marrying Mafalda the daughter of a count of Savoy.

He was formally proclaimed king at a Cortes of the realm held in the church of Santa Maria de Almacave in the town of Lamego—so the chronicler tells the tale—in the presence of the Archbishop of Braga, of the bishops of Viseu, Oporto, Coimbra and Lamego, of the members of the royal court, and of representatives of the cities of Coimbra, Guimarães, Lamego, Viseu, Barcelos, Oporto, Trancoso, Chaves, Castelo-Real, Vouzola, Paredes-Velha, Ceia, Covilhã, Montemor, Esquera and Vila del Rei . . . "besides a great multitude of monks and clergy." All Portugal north of the Tagus was already in his realm.

Recognition was another matter. It took all of Afonso Henriques' understanding of men and their motives and all of his archbishop's ecclesiastical diplomacy to get Portuguese independence recognized. In the end Afonso Henriques had to declare himself liegeman of the pope and to promise a tribute of four ounces of gold a year to the Holy See. A papal bull eventually confirmed him in his titles and possessions as King of Portugal.

4

DE EXPUGNATIONE LYXBONENSI

Along the frontier, when Afonso Henriques began to reign, an uneasy half-peace prevailed. The walled towns, both Christian and Moslem, were strong enough to hold off the customary summer raids back and forth to carry off cattle and crops. If beset by a regular army there was a growing tendency to capitulate on terms and to promise an annual tribute to the aggressor.

Afonso Henriques kept himself well informed of happenings in the Moorish zone. Though theoretically the Portuguese Algarve and the Alentejo were governed by the Almohade princes in Seville, practically the populations were ruled by independent sheikhs and caids. Taking advantage of uprisings and dissensions in the Moslem South, Afonso Henriques, in 1140, with the help of a fleet of belated crusaders bound for Palestine, many of them Englishmen from Southampton and Hastings, laid siege to Lisbon and sacked one of the city's suburbs. When the rulers of the city offered to pay him tribute the Portuguese king went off home to Coimbra, leaving the crusaders to extricate themselves from the siege as best they could. The English seamen and adventurers held it against him in later years.

In 1147 the Second Crusade was proclaimed by the pope and preached by Bernard de Clairvaux. Early that spring, Afonso Henriques, always ready to snatch at any opportunity to enlarge his realm, denounced a truce he had made with the Moors of Santarém on the Tagus and, with the help of the Templars, surprised its defenders and reduced the city. Now he was ready for a fresh try at Lisbon. The arrival of a second crusading fleet in the mouth of the Douro offered him his opportunity.

A manuscript in medieval Latin which gives the common soldier's view of this most important event in Afonso Henriques reign came to light years ago in the library of Corpus Christi College at Cambridge, England. It was undoubtedly composed by an English member of this band of crusaders. He was a priest of Anglo-Norman stock, most likely chaplain to Hervey de Glanvill, leader of the East Anglian contingent. The manuscript is in the form of a letter addressed to someone whose name is abbreviated to Osb. by someone whose name is only represented by the initial R.

Whether R.'s name was Rupert or Ralph, it's obvious from the text that he was a sturdy fellow, a fighting priest, loyal to his liege lord, almost laughably English in his horror at the wicked ways of foreigners and in his self-righteous demand for fair play.

He starts his tale with the assembling of men of varied nations, customs and speech in the port of Dartmouth in Cornwall. There were a hundred and sixty-four ships manned by shipmen and men-at-arms. Some were from the Holy Roman Empire under a Count Arnold of Aerschot. Another group consisted of "Flemings and men of Boulogne" under Christian of Ghistelles. The Normans and Englishmen were led by four constables. The ships of Norfolk and Suffolk were under Hervey de Glanvill; those of Kent under Simon of Dover; those of London under a certain Andrew, and all the rest under Saher of Archelle, a Norman from the vicinity of Dieppe.

Their first step was to enter into an association for the crusade. They pledged solemn oaths to preserve peace and friendship among them. Their law was to be a life for a life and a tooth for a tooth. There was to be no display of costly garments; their women were not to be seen in public. The laity and clergy should meet separately in weekly chapters. Every ship was to have its priest and to be organized like a parish church; everyone must go to confession and take communion every Sunday. For

every thousand men two judges should be elected, called con-
jurati, who would settle disputes and attend to the fair distribution of loot.

They set sail on the Friday before Ascension (May 23, 1147)
and by Sunday were in sight of the coast of Brittany. Four days
later with the wind favorable and the sea heavy they sighted the
Picos de Europa.

At that point a storm scattered the ships. The seamen gave
way to despair. In the howling of the gale they thought they
heard the song of the sirens, "a horrible sound first of wailing,
then of laughter and jeering, like the clamor of insolent men in
camp . . . Many a man repented of his sins that night."

Next day the storm subsided and they made port on the coast
of Asturias about ten miles from Oviedo. From there they coasted
westward until they reached the great lighthouse tower which
the author attributes to Julius Caesar who, he suggests, built it as
a center through which the revenue of all Britain and Ireland
and Spain, and "the interminable lawcases" might pass to and
fro. This harbor (now Ferrol) was the first landing place for
travelers coming directly over from Britain.

They rounded Finisterre and lay to behind an island in the
Tambre River, which was then the landing for the shrine of
Saint James at Compostela. There they saw an electric eel, "which
stupifies the hand that holds it" besides a wealth of other fish.

Father R. as he traveled was laboriously checking what he saw
and heard with a geographical compendium by one Solinus, which
seems to have been a garbled rehash of Pliny and other ancient
geographers. Father R.'s Latin though lively was none too good:
he somehow got the notion that an island they visited further on
down the coast, which they found full of rabbits and snakes,
was one of the Balearics. Solinus and the Holy Bible, so far as
one can learn from his narrative, comprised the extent of the good
priest's erudition.

On June 16 at about the ninth hour they beached their ships
in front of a city which he calls Portugala in the mouth of the
Douro. He adds that some eighty years had gone by since it
was rebuilt after its destruction by the Moors.

The bishop and clergy came out to meet them, and the bishop,
after making them welcome, "each according to the custom of

his own people," read a letter from King Afonso Henriques. "If perchance the ships of the Franks should come to you, treat them with every kindness and the most meticulous courtesy. . . ." The bishop was to strike a bargain with them to help the king. If need be he was to offer his own person as security and to journey with them to Lisbon.

The leaders replied cagily that they would wait till all the men on the ships had been informed of the king's letter and make their reply in the morning.

Next day the crusaders gathered on a knoll in the cemetery since they were so numerous the church wouldn't hold them all. The bishop delivered a long sermon in Latin on the justice of warring against the unjust and unbelieving. He called on them to help free the Christians of this land from the outrages of the Moors. "Our dear son, your brother and fellow in tribulation, our King Afonso has already departed ten days ago with all his forces against Lisbon." If they would help him capture that city the bishop promised them all the money the resources of the royal treasury would permit.

The crusaders were still suspicious. After the bishop wound up his sermon and performed the mass they decided to wait for some ships scattered in the storm and for the arrival of John Peculiar from Braga. Meanwhile "through the king's good will," a fair market for wine and victuals was provided them. The archbishop put in an appearance and consented to go along with them to Lisbon where they could hear the king's proposition from his own lips.

After a ten days' rest they ran down the coast, catching sight of castles and forests as they sailed and spending a night on Peniche Island which Father R. considered "the farthest limit of the known world." At the mouth of the Tagus a squall struck with such violence that several of the small boats were sunk with all aboard. In this squall they read a portent. A white cloud from the sea seemed to be engaged in combat with black clouds from the land. The white cloud pressed toward the city glittering on its hills, leaving the sky behind it the purest blue. The crusaders cried out that God was putting their enemies to flight.

The Tagus, wrote Father R., partly from his own observation and partly from his gleanings from Solinus, flowed down from the region of Toledo. Gold was found on its banks after the spring freshet. Fish were so plentiful that the natives declared the river was two parts water and one part fish. Shellfish abounded. All the fish was of marvelous flavor. To the south of the river the land was so fertile you could harvest two crops from a single seeding. There was good hunting and plentiful honey.

On the north bank of the Tagus the city of Lisbon stood on a round hill. Its walls zig-zagged down to the riverbank. The city, supposed to have been founded by Ulysses, was the richest in the trade of all Africa and of a great part of Europe. The surrounding country yielded fruit and vines. The olive flourished. Figs were so abundant that the crusaders could eat only a fraction of what they picked. There was gold and silver and iron to be mined. Magnificent hunting in the back country; no hares but many kinds of birds. The air was healthful. There were natural hot springs in the city. On the green upland pastures mares conceived from the wind.

The city contained sixty thousand families that paid taxes besides many more in the tax-free suburbs. At the time of the siege Father R. figured the population to be a hundred and fifty-four thousand men without counting women and children. This included refugees from Santarém and the castles of Sintra and Almada and Palmela. The buildings were so packed together that, outside of the merchants' quarter, there was hardly a street more than eight feet wide, and the lanes leading out of the city were so steep they hardly needed to be defended by fortifications.

The idea of religious toleration did not appeal to Father R. He ascribed the city's great population to the flowing together of the wickedest men of all nations, as into a cesspool, because there was no proscribed religion there and every man was a law unto himself, with the result that the city was the seedbed for every lust and abomination.

The people of Lisbon had only lances and shields for fourteen thousand fighting men, so the soldiers had to be armed in rotation according to the decree of the governor.

The crusaders arrived in front of Lisbon the afternoon of June 28, a little more than a month after sailing from Dartmouth. After dinner some of the English disembarked on the shore under the walls. The Moors made a sortie but were beaten back.

Saher de Archelle recalled the English from the pursuit for fear of an ambush, but cried out that, Thank God this was better than the last attempt on Lisbon. He said that the English and Normans should not give up the ground won and ordered tents to be pitched on a hill that overlooked the city "at a stick's throw." Everybody assented but by the first watch of the night only two tents appeared, those of Saher and of Hervey de Glanvill. "So we, with a small force of thirty-nine men, and not without fear, lay out on guard that night," wrote Father R. "We celebrated the solemn vigils of St. Peter with our corslets on."

Next morning the rest of the tents were pitched in a hurry. The bishops went to fetch King Afonso Henriques, who had been lurking in the neighborhood while he awaited the arrival of the fleet. The crusaders crowded out to meet him, rich and poor mixed up together in great disarray. The king made a speech. He suggested that their piety more than the promise of money or booty should drive them to the task of freeing the city from the infidel. His advice was that, lest their conference be broken up by the shouting of so many people, they choose whomever they wished to talk his offers over quietly with him.

The whole mob assembled in a council with the result that there was much loud talk and no decision. It was proposed that they eat dinner before reaching an agreement. After dinner it was discovered that the Flemings had already agreed to the king's proposal. William and Ralph Veal, of a powerful English seafaring family, and the men of Southampton and Hastings, who had taken part in the last unsuccessful siege, declared that the king's proposals were sheer treachery. Much easier money was to be made by piracy among the merchant ships in the straits. Besides why lose the favorable season for voyaging to Jerusalem?

Their talk threw everybody by the ears. Some wanted to besiege Lisbon and others to press on. Hervey de Glanvill made an impassioned speech and ended by prostrating himself in tears at the feet of the Veals begging them not to betray the compact they had all sworn to. The Veals and their men lifted him to his feet and everyone started chanting the crusader war cry: "Deus adiuva nos."

A covenant was drawn up with the king and his bishops that

afternoon: if the Franks would go ahead with the siege, Afonso yielded any claim to the possessions of the enemy, and offered to divide up the city and its lands among them, retaining only the overlordship. Further he would exempt anyone who joined him in the siege, and his descendants forever, from taxes on merchandise brought in or out of the Portuguese realm. He offered hostages as testimony of the honesty of his intentions. This covenant was confirmed by both sides and hostages were exchanged in pledge of performance.

The next step was to call on the people of Lisbon to surrender. Signals were exchanged for a parley. The alcaïde appeared on the wall with the mozarabic bishop and the chief men of the city. The Archbishop of Braga, John Peculiar, made a long speech, calling on the Moors to depart in peace, with their women and children and their money and goods, from the city which they had unjustly held for so many years. The Moors answered that they had beaten off previous attacks, that they would hold their ground and that God would judge the result. The royal forces withdrew to a hilltop to the north of the city and the Franks retired to their tents.

The next day the Frankish slingers began to harass the enemy. The first attack was made on a suburb adjacent to the tents. The Moors tried to fend off the attackers by throwing stones from the rooftops. By sunset the Franks had broached the parapet that surrounded the suburb and made their way up the hill behind the houses. Some turned to looting and almost disrupted the attack. In the confusion you could not tell friend from foe. Lord Saher and his knights took up a position in a Moslem cemetery above the suburb and, while houses burned all around them, stood guard all night.

In the morning the Moors tried to drive the Franks out of the suburb but, with the help of the Portuguese royal guard, the Anglo-Norman contingent held its ground. As a result they were comfortably lodged in the suburb right under the city wall for the rest of the siege. They found immense supplies of wheat, barley, millet and lentils in caves dug into the hill. They set up a nightly watch of five hundred men, with eight boats to protect them from the river side. The Flemings were so envious of their snug situa-

tion, wrote Father R., that they captured themselves another suburb on the opposite side of the city.

So the siege went on. The Franks built themselves two churches
for the burial of their dead, one on each side of the city. When
the blessed bread was divided up after the mass—men carried it
with them as a protection in battle against the blows of the enemy
—it was found to be bloody like meat. There was discussion
among the religious of the meaning of this portent. Some said,
noted Father R. wryly, that it meant that this fierce race, greedy
for the goods of others, even under the guise of a religious pilgrimage, had not yet put away their thirst for blood.

After a fortnight the besiegers set to work to build engines. The
Flemings and the men of Cologne constructed a "sow," a ram
and a movable tower. There was considerable jeering among the
English and Normans when these engines were set afire by the
enemy. The ram was barely saved. The catapults proved a failure.

The English and Normans on their side built a tower ninety-
five-feet high, but they hardly had better luck with it, as it stuck
in the sand while they were trying to move it toward the wall.
The enemy hammered it with stones. Hervey de Glanvill's men
suffered losses trying to protect it and finally it was burned.

After the siege had continued for many weeks the crusaders
intercepted a Moorish skiff trying to cross the river with a letter
to the ruler of Evora begging for help. A few days later the
corpse of a drowned man was found under one of the ships. A
letter was tied to his arm. It was from the king of Evora saying
that on account of his truce with the king of Portugal he could
not send help. He advised them to ransom their city with all the
money they had.

This news so encouraged Afonso Henriques that he sent most of
his own troops home and shipped such of his supplies as he hadn't
sold to Santarém. The English and Normans distinguished themselves by taking the town of Almada on the south bank of the
river. They returned with two hundred prisoners and eighty heads
of slain Moors. These they impaled on pikes. They set them up
where the defenders might see them from the walls. Men came
out from the city as suppliants and begged to be allowed to take
the heads away for burial. When the crusaders consented they
carried the heads back through the gate "with grief and wailing."

Father R. noted with pride that because of the daring of this exploit his comrades were held in greatest terror by the enemy and in honor by the men of Cologne, the Flemings and the Portuguese. Now the Breton fishermen could haul their seines in peace on the shelving beach on the south shore of the Tagus, to catch fish for the army.

The stench of corpses was becoming a torment to the enemy because there were no burial places in the rocky foundations of the city. The people of Lisbon were starving. Moors sneaked out at night to collect the refuse the tide piled on the beach under the walls. The Flemings, finding that some Moors had crept up to snatch at half-eaten figs they threw out from their sentry posts, set snares for them and, to the enormous amusement of the besiegers, caught three.

The siege had dragged on into the autumn. The time had come to make an end of it. Two "Balearic mangonels" were set up, one on the riverbank operated by the seamen and the other, in front of the Iron Gate, worked by the knights and their table companions. Teams of a hundred men worked these catapults in rotation so that in the space of ten hours five thousand stones were hurled at the enemy. Meanwhile Glanvill's men tried to undermine the wall near the gate, but to no avail.

The Normans and the English together were feverishly building a new siege tower under the direction of a Pisan engineer. The Flemings and the men of Cologne dug at their own mine, much higher up on the hill. When, after a month's work, an enormous chamber was ready under the city wall, they filled it with inflammable material and set it afire, with the result that some two hundred feet of wall came down.

The hill was so steep that when they tried an assault through the breach they were thrown back. This repulse gave the defenders a chance to stop the breach with wooden beams. The Flemings shot so many arrows at the defenders on the wall that they looked like hedgehogs but still they couldn't budge them. When the Flemings and men of Cologne retired exhausted to their camp the English and Normans marched up ready for a new assault but the leaders of the Flemings and of the men of Cologne said, "No, let them assault their own breach." Every day there was more bad blood between the two contingents.

When the movable tower was completed and covered all around with osier mats and oxhides to ward off stones and firebrands the archbishop came to sprinkle it with holy water and to pronounce his benediction.

Someone, referred to as "a certain priest," who may well have been the author of the narrative, preached a rousing sermon. Waving a relic of the True Cross, he called on his comrades to have no fear: each man was protected by his guardian angel. As voluntary exiles sworn to poverty they were invincible under the sign of the cross. "Brothers," he cried, "I will join you in your labors and tribulations. . . . With God's help, as guardian and protector of this sacred piece of wood, I shall remain with you in this engine while life shall last." He called on the Lord to fill them with courage and strength, and, rank on rank, they fell on their faces before him, repenting of their sins with groans and tears. He ordered them to their feet and made the sign of the cross over them in the name of the Father, the Son and the Holy Ghost.

Shouting the crusaders' battle cry they put their shoulders to the tower and moved it fifteen cubits toward the wall. It was already late. One man was killed by a stone from a sling and they gave up the enterprise for that day. It took them all of another day to get the tower in position near the Iron Gate. When night fell they left it in charge of a hundred knights and a hundred Galicians. Most of these were driven back during the first watch by the unexpected rising of the tide. The Moors sallied forth and attacked the machine. From the wall they threw down burning flax and pitch and oil to set it afire, keeping up all the time an intolerable hail of stones. The only protection the defenders had was a kind of penthouse of plaited osiers, known as a Welch Cat, which was handled by seven youths from Ipswich. Under this the crusaders, with the help of those inside the towers, kept beating out the flaming firebrands. Others in the upper stories poured water on the hides. All through the night they defended the tower in hand to hand combat until they had driven the Moors back into the city.

On the following day, which was the twenty-first of October, the battle continued just as hotly. The Pisan engineer was severely wounded by a stone. A fresh rise of the tide so discouraged the Galicians that most of them fled, either wounded or pretending to be wounded, some of them even throwing away their arms. When the tide ebbed again the enemy retired exhausted and the knights who had defended the tower for two days and a night without putting down their arms, were able to get some relief.

By the tenth hour the crusaders had managed to move the tower to about four feet from the wall. When the defenders saw that they were ready to let down the bridge for an assault the cry went up for a truce if only till morning.

Fernando Captivo was summoned on behalf of the Portuguese king. He was joined by Hervey de Glanvill on behalf of all the Franks. They arranged a truce and took five hostages as a guarantee that the defenders would not damage the tower or repair their defenses during the night. The fact that Glanvill delivered the hostages to the king caused dissatisfaction in the ranks of the crusaders.

Early next day the four constables of the Normans and English and the leaders of the Flemings and of the men of Cologne went to the king's camp to hear the terms of surrender. The proposal was to turn the city over to the King of Portugal. All the gold and silver and other property of the citizens would be distributed among the Franks. The people should go free. A council of the crusaders was called to consider these terms.

Meanwhile "the old enemy," as Father R. called Satan, made one last effort to cause dissension among the victors who already had the prize in their hands. He inspired a wicked priest from Bristol to stir up a mutiny among the seamen who were incensed at Hervey de Glanvill for having turned over the hostages to the king. The mutineers raised such a tumult that the hostages, hearing the shouting and deciding that the Franks were about to fight among themselves, began to hold out for better terms.

Afonso Henriques threatened to abandon the siege altogether unless the leaders of the Franks could control their men. Another council was called which degenerated into a row between the Normans and English, who were in favor of sparing the inhabitants and peacefully dividing their goods, and the Flemings and the men of Cologne who thought there would be more profit in taking the place by storm. At last after bitter debates it was agreed that the alcaïde would be allowed to leave with his victuals and possessions, except for a famous Arabian mare much coveted by the

Count of Aerschot. While this was being debated the rank and file of the Flemings and the men of Cologne were surrounding the royal tents with arms in their hands clamoring that the hostages must be turned over to them.

Though he was described as falling into a terrible temper, Afonso Henriques behaved with a great deal of dignity. He refused to make any move until the leaders of the Franks disciplined their forces. Next day the leaders of both crusader factions in penitent mood swore allegiance to the King of Portugal, for themselves and their men, for as long as they should remain in his dominions. They accepted the original terms offered by the Moors and agreed that a hundred and forty armed men from the English and Normans and a hundred and sixty from the Flemings and from the men of Cologne should enter the city first to occupy the keep of the upper castle. The inhabitants should bring their money and valuables to the castle and thereafter be allowed to leave the city. Anyone who tried to hold anything back would pay with his head.

So the Archbishop John Peculiar and his fellow bishops, carrying the crusaders' banner of the cross, led the way into Lisbon followed by the king and the leaders of the Franks. The banner of the cross was flown from the highest tower. While the clergy and the people entoned *Te Deum laudamus* King Afonso Henriques made on foot the circuit of the castle walls.

The men of Cologne and the Flemings had by a ruse managed to be the first to march in. Hordes of their fellows sneaked in through the breach in the wall, broke the agreement and started to pillage. They beat open doors, ransacked houses, abused the inhabitants, insulted women and began hiding valuables for themselves instead of taking them to the castle for allotment. They cut the throat of the aged mozarabic bishop and dragged the alcaïde out of his house with all his furniture. The Count of Aerschot siezed the alcaïde's mare with his own hands, and such a struggle ensued with representatives of the king and of the English and Normans that the mare began to bleed and lost her foal.

For five days thereafter the despoiled multitude poured out of the gates of the city. In the mosque "which rises aloft in seven rows of columns surmounted by as many arches" they found two

33

hundred dead and more than eight hundred sick and wounded lying in their own filth.

Since the season was too late for navigation eastward the crusaders stayed in the city all winter. It is likely that Father R. spent his time writing down his account of the siege. After the mosque had been purified by the Archbishop of Braga, assisted by four other bishops, an English cleric, Gilbert of Hastings, was chosen Bishop of Lisbon. John Peculiar saw to it that Gilbert swore an oath of allegiance to his see of Braga.

To add to the miseries of the war a pestilence broke out. "Throughout the desert wastes, in vineyards, in villages and squares, and among the ruins of houses, unnumbered thousands of corpses lay exposed to birds and beasts." Most of them must have been mozarabic Christians because Father R. described them as grasping for the cross before they died and most pitiably crying out: "Maria bona, bona Maria."

5

ROYAL ENTREPRENEURS

Afonso Henriques set to work to repopulate his conquered lands. Crusaders who were willing to settle received grants around Lisbon. Such of the mozarab peasants as had survived the plague were ceded along with the land they worked. Bishop Gilbert established a confraternity of English settlers in one of the churches built as a memorial to those who died in the siege. A monastery was founded at the other for the cultivation of the land. The Templars were given a castle on the Rio Tomar as a base for the defense of the Tagus valley. Most of the great stretch of territory between Obidos and Leiria was turned over to a group of Cistercian monks from Burgundy. They established the monastery of Alcobaça and threw themselves so effectively into the improvement of their crops that their hundred thousand or so acres became the richest farmland in the kingdom and to this day grow the finest fruit in Portugal.

The Cistercian monks brought their church plans with them. Their projects were ambitious. In the early eleven fifties Afonso Henriques, in accordance with a vow he made when he was besieging Santarém, ordered the foundations laid for the great church at Alcobaça. The architects followed the plan of the abbey at Clairvaux. It remains the largest church in Portugal. The high romanesque style with its sculptured portals and individually carved capitals was in full flower. In Compostela a new cathedral was going up under the influence of Saint Sernin in Toulouse. In Coimbra and Braga the restoration of cathedrals was employing a host of stone carvers and masons, many of them Moslems or mozarabs whose training in abstract design gave a special character to their work. In spite of wars and pestilence, towns, monasteries and knightly orders threw an immense amount of treasure and invention into their public monuments. The king was expected to take the lead in encouraging these projects.

Afonso Henriques inaugurated a policy of fostering agriculture which his successors continued in good times and bad, so that occasionally a successful farmer would be ennobled and welcomed at court. Charcoal burning was wreaking havoc with the coastal forests. The Portuguese kings early caught on to the need to preserve pine trees for resin and ships' timbers; according to one of his chroniclers it was this first Afonso who issued the decree that every man who cut down a tree must plant another in its place. Later a statute was passed: "If a man cut down a pine tree let him hang." Timber must be saved for shipbuilding. From the beginning subsidies and indulgences were granted to the builders of ships.

Through the whole of Afonso Henriques' long reign raiding and counterraiding went on between Christians and Moslems. When the Christian princes weren't fighting the Moors they fought each other. Cities were taken, lost and retaken. There were treaties and marriages with the royal houses of Castile and León which broke down into quarrels and skirmishes and sieges. A sort of Portuguese Cid appeared, known as Geraldo Sem Pavor, whose exploits bore the same relationship to Afonse Henriques' campaigns as the Cid's had to his grandfather's. When Geraldo was besieged at Badajoz Afonso Henriques came to his aid against Afonso's own son-in-law, Fernando of León. In a scrimmage at the city gate the portcullis dropped on Afonso's leg. The bone was so badly fractured he was never able to ride again. He suffered the humiliation of being captured by Fernando's retainers and lay two months in durance, while his vassals raised money for his ransom. As part of the ransom agreement he was forced to renounce any claim to Galicia.

Afonso Henriques' son Sancho was sixteen. In 1170 he was knighted at Coimbra and thereafter took his father's place as leader of the troops. After the old king died Sancho carried on his father's plans for driving the Moors out of the lands south of the Tagus. When the Third Crusade brought a new fleet of Flemings and Germans and English to Lisbon, Sancho made an agreement with them to reduce Silves, the chief city of the Algarve. He already had a fleet of his own; the Portuguese are listed as having furnished thirty-seven galleys and "ships of high freeboard" to the expedition, as well as a number of *setias*, or pinnaces. When the city fell Sancho encountered the customary difficulties with the crusaders about the distribution of the loot.

A couple of years later Richard Coeur de Lion showed up in Lisbon on his way to the Holy Land. Richard detailed one of his ships, carrying a hundred men-at-arms from London, to help Sancho defend Silves against a counterattack by an army of Moroccans. At the same time another crusader band forced a Moorish expedition to lift the siege of Santarém. As soon as the crusaders had departed, a fresh Moslem army, still imbued with the frenzy of the Almohade reformers, landed from Africa and retook every city the Portuguese had captured south of the Tagus.

In spite of the ebb and flow of the fortunes of war, Sancho I died one of the wealthiest monarchs on the peninsula. His will was the center of family squabbles for a generation. He had interests beyond conquest and settlement. He encouraged the Flanders trade and the establishment of a trading post by Portuguese merchants in the Low Countries. His court was the first center for lyric poetry in the vernacular. The homely Gallego-Portuguese was beginning to challenge Provençal as the language of the court poetry of the peninsula.

The knights and their ladies, preoccupied with martial expeditions all summer, found themselves with little to do in winter, shut up during the bad weather in their keeps and castles. They were glad to be entertained by ballad singers and troubadours. At first the highly formalized prosody that grew up in Languedoc and Provence was the rage. Later the Hispanic courts began to cultivate a taste for the folksongs of Galicia and northern Portugal. The *jograes*, minstrels roving from tavern to tavern and fair to fair, sang simple chanties known as *cossantes* in the language of the

37

peasants and fishermen. In form the cossantes were a secular version of the Hebrew psalms sung in church. Noble knights began to turn their hands to the people's style of poetic composition. King Sancho himself was reputed to be the author of one of the earliest lyrics that came down in the collection called *Cantares de Amigo*.

The age of the Crusades was a time of the growth of cities, especially in Flanders and England and the Hanseatic North. Church architecture was in a brilliant phase of transition from the round arch style to the ogival. The conversion of the Northmen to Christianity had cut down on their piracies. Commerce was discovered to be more profitable than freebooting. In spite of wars between Christian and Moslem, trade continued for the products of Africa and the Far East with Moslem merchants in Morocco and the Algarve. Sugar and oranges were already being exported from the region of Ceuta. Merchant ships followed in the wake of the crusaders' fleets, selling supplies to the armies, and bringing home silk and spices from the Levant.

Portuguese shipmasters traded in London and frequented the great fair at Bruges. Sparto grass for weaving mats and baskets, raisins, wine—there were already vineyards in the valley of the Douro—oil, figs, honey, beeswax, hides and sea salt were listed among their exports. Flemish merchants bought English wool to be woven into cloth on the looms of Bruges and Ghent and Ypres. This was the best cloth available in Europe and much of it was shipped south to be exchanged for the silks and sugars of the Moslem world.

The successors of Afonso Henriques were as keen to expand trade and shipping as they were to expand the territory that paid them tribute. The monarchs and the *fidalgos* of their courts made no bones about engaging in commerce. Kings had their own shops in the markets, invested in shiploads of produce, built ships for profit, and constructed dwellings and warehouses for sale and rent. The Jewish community was bound to furnish each of the king's ships with an anchor and cable.

Royal diplomacy was involved in the promotion of trade. A series of royal marriages improved relations with the Low Countries. Afonso I's daughter Teresa married Count Philip of Flanders.

When Philip lost his life on a crusade she married a duke of Burgundy, and arranged for the wedding of her nephew, who would become Afonso III of Portugal, to a Burgundian cousin who was heiress of the county of Flanders.

Trade with England was already considerable enough to stimulate projects for courtly alliances. When Richard's brother John succeeded to the English throne he tried to arrange a marriage with one of Sancho's daughters. The negotiation fell through but another daughter, Berengaria, became Queen of the Danes.

Intermarriages continued with the ruling families of Castile and Aragon. Though these marriages were intended to promote peace they produced a great deal of haggling and warfare over the succession to the various kingdoms. Each of the royal houses was in a position to lay claim to the thrones of the others.

These contests, added to a long tussle with Rome over the right of the Portuguese kings to appoint their own bishops, almost reduced the country to anarchy until Afonso III, who had acquired by his marriage the French title of Count of Boulogne, returned from Paris and made himself master of Lisbon. As soon as this Afonso had consolidated his regime by winning the support of the merchants of the towns and the knights of the military orders, he raised an army and subdued the last Moorish strongholds in the Algarve.

The merchants were gaining political power. In the Cortes which Afonso called at Leiria, the representatives of the towns bargained with him on equal terms on the question of the coinage. They induced him to allow them to replace for seven years the royal right to clip the coinage by a cash subsidy.

Afonso III's son, Dinis, who inherited the throne in 1279 at the age of eighteen, was the ablest of his line. Dom Dinis was so bent on improving the crops in his kingdom that he became known as el Rei Lavrador, the Farmer King. He worked tirelessly to increase the production of barley and wheat. He encouraged the improvement of the native homespuns of the Minho. He tried to induce the great nobles and the endowed monasteries either to cultivate their lands or to allow them to be distributed among the peasants who would put them into crops. He excluded from the land tax all those who brought new acreage into cultivation. Tenants who raised proper crops were to become owners after from six to ten years. He tried to convince his courtiers that there was nothing degrading about farming. Beside building a chain of castles to protect the country from raids from Castile, he interested himself in the mining of tin and in the construction of irrigation canals. The fame of his accomplishments reached as far as Florence, where Dante made a laudatory reference to him in the *Paradiso*.

Dom Dinis was educated by his father's French tutor. He spent some time as a boy at the court of his grandfather, Alfonso X of Castile, known to his subjects as the Learned. Alfonso X was one of the great men of his age. He was a literary monarch in the style of the erudite caliphs. He codified the laws of Castile and preserved his country's history in the Cronica General. He respected the learning of the Jews and the Arabs. He was renowned as an astronomer. As a statesman and soldier he was more or less of a failure, though his fame for wisdom was so great that at one point he was elected to the throne of the Holy Roman Empire. The election was contested and he never got to rule.

The literary reputation of Alfonso the Learned rests as much on his Gallego-Portuguese poetry as on his Castilian prose. He may have spent his youth in Galicia. Though he did write poems in the mannered Provençal still fashionable in the Hispanic courts, he preferred the rustic language of Galicia and Portugal for his lyrics and for his canticles celebrating various minor and very rural miracles of the Virgin Mary.

It may well be due to his grandfather's precept and example that when Dinis turned to poetry he relied on the lilting language of the jograes. The hundred or so poems attributed to him have an earthy naturalism that have caused critics to compare him to Robert Burns.

These lyrics, attributed to the king and the ballad singers he entertained at his court, constituted a racy popular literature which disappeared from sight soon after Dom Dinis' death and was forgotten until it was rediscovered lying in manuscript in various European libraries by nineteenth-century scholars. The cossantes and *cancioneiros* are now recognized as forming the headwaters of the main current of Portuguese poetry.

Though essentially a poet Dom Dinis encouraged men of letters to develop the first Portuguese prose. He saw to it that Alfonso X's legal treatise and his chronicle were done into the vernacular. He sponsored the first purely Portuguese chronicles. He superintended the translation of an important treatise on Roman law which became the basis for legal reforms in subsequent reigns. Deeds and official documents were now written in Portuguese. Indeed it was due to the prose and poetry which Dom Dinis encouraged and wrote that Portuguese became firmly established as a separate language with literary roots.

It is likely that the first versions of the Arthurian tales were done into Portuguese in Dom Dinis' literary circle. Through the Galician popular lyrics the vernacular poets had long been in touch with the cloudy legends of blameless knights and hapless loves that drifted south from Brittany and Cornwall. *Amadis of Gaul,* the most popular of the romances of knight errantry, the book which even Cervantes himself was willing to have saved from the flames when he wrote of Don Quijote's friends the barber and the priest burning up the library that had encouraged the poor knight's delusions, saw the light during Dom Dinis' reign in its Portuguese version.

Portugal had spread to the borders which, so far as Europe was concerned, were to contain the nation throughout its history. Increased area demanded improved administration. Dom Dinis felt the lack of trained men. Though there had been Latin schools for many years in the monasteries of Alcobaça and Santa Cruz in Coimbra, Portuguese youths had to travel to Paris or Montpellier or Salamanca or Bologna for higher education. With the help of his old French tutor, now bishop of Coimbra, he set up in Lisbon a school called *Estudo Geral* for the study of grammar, logic, cannon and civil law and medicine. According to the chronicler, the students raised such cain that a few years later the Estudo was removed out of the capital to become the University of Coimbra.

With the king's approval the first *bolsa de comércio* was created in Lisbon. For years members of the shipmen's guild had paid a premium on each ship that went to sea. The money was collected in a fund to be used to reimburse shipmasters despoiled by pirates or by foreign customhouses. This soon developed into a primitive form of marine insurance.

The king chartered fairs, some of them free trade areas, all over the country. He entered into a series of agreements with the English and the Flemish for the mutual protection of merchants engaged in the import-export business.

The commercial cities such as Lisbon and Oporto were to a certain extent self-governing. The first commercial treaty on record between Portugal and England was signed by a burgess of Oporto in behalf of the merchants, mariners and shipmasters of Oporto and Lisbon. A royal alcaïde ruled them with the advice of local *conselhos*, or councils. Continually challenged by the great feudal lords, royal authority depended on the merchants and artisans of the towns working through their *homens bons*, "good men and true," as the representatives of the guilds and parishes were known.

Further support for consolidation of royal power was furnished during the reign of Dom Dinis by his policy of turning the military orders of knighthood into national organizations under his direct control. His father had already made the Order of Calatrava into a national institution and bestowed on it the walled town of Avis. Now Dinis procured an independent status for the knights of Santiago and settled them at Palmela. He took advantage of Philip le Bel of France's brutal suppression (through his puppet pope Clement V) of the Knights Templar to turn their order in his country into the purely Portuguese Order of Christ. To constitute a defense against incursions from the Spanish kingdoms, he established their headquarters at Castro Marim on the Guadiana. In each case the grand master was appointed by the crown.

Dom Dinis' interests were as diverse as his learned grandfather's but he was a far more practical man. As much as a sound agriculture the country needed trade with England and Flanders. The king had his own shipyard and encouraged shipbuilding by exemptions from taxes. To replenish the country's supply of timber he planted a pine forest along the sandy shore in the vicinity of Leiria. This forest was to have the added advantage of protecting the coastal farms from the encroachment of sand dunes. The story was told that Dinis' queen, Dona Isabel, known to the people as Santa Isabel for her many virtues, brought out an apronful of pine seed imported from France, to make the first plantings. Whether or not the queen's seed was responsible, since Dom Dinis' time the aboriginal stone pine of the Portuguese coast has gradually been replaced by the faster growing cluster pine found on the *Landes* of Aquitaine.

Dom Dinis had made a good marriage. Isabel was the daughter of Pedro III of Aragon. Her grandfather had, with the help of the shipmen of Barcelona, conquered the Balearic Islands, bearded the Moors in their dens in Tunis and Tlemcen, and established Aragon as a Mediterranean power. Isabel's mother was Constance, daughter of Manfred, the bastard heir to the Hohenstaufens. The years after Isabel's marriage to Dinis, her father took advantage of the chaos that followed the war to the death between the Emperor Frederick's various heirs to get himself elected to the throne of the two Sicilies.

Dona Isabel was considered a saint in her lifetime. According to the chronicle of Rui de Pina she performed the daily offices of the church with punctilious care, restricted herself to one meal of bread and water on fast days, avoided the sin of idleness by keeping herself and her ladies constantly at work on embroidering and weaving, and gave away most of her income to the poor. Every Friday in Lent she washed the feet of twelve poor men, "the most leprous that they could find," states the chronicler. Miraculous cures were attributed by the sick to her blessing. She was formally canonized in the fifteenth century and as patron saint of Coimbra filled a very special niche in the Portuguese pantheon.

She bore Dinis two children, Afonso, his heir, and a daughter. According to Rui de Pina, though King Dinis lived with Queen Isabel in amity and concord and she was as youthful and charming as any man could want, he couldn't help letting his fancy stray. He so far forgot his royal dignity as to beget seven bastards on seven different ladies. Queen Isabel never let anyone know that his infidelities gave her the slightest pang. She saw to it that clothes were furnished the nurses of these children and that every care was taken by their tutors. Her attitude, in spite of her youth, was so unlike the jealous attitude of other women that the king, said the chronicler, became ashamed of his weaknesses. "From

43

fear of God" he renounced all such frivolities "and placed himself in the straight and true path which he followed to the time of his death."

In the hundred and seventy-five years that had passed since Afonso Henriques first aspired to the title of King of Portugal, his kingdom had been consolidated, linguistically and politically. Portugal's separateness from the rest of the peninsula had been established. Along with Catalonia, Portugal in King Dinis' reign was the most prosperous of the Hispanic realms.

The beginning of the long war in which France, England and the Low Countries were involved for most of the following century gave the Portuguese, who managed to remain neutral in the conflict, a chance to send their trading ships further and further into the north. Dom Dinis managed to obtain favorable concessions for his merchants from both Edward II of England and Philip IV of France. At the same time new trade routes with breathtaking possibilities for profit and exploration began to open to the southward.

6

THE OCEAN OF DARKNESS

It was the Genoese who first braved the curse that had been thought since the days of the Carthaginians to hang over the open ocean off the Pillars of Hercules. As early as 1162, when the Portuguese Algarve was still in Moslem hands, a Genoese vessel made a successful trading journey to Sale on the Atlantic coast of Morocco. A Genoese trading post, permitted by treaty with the local rulers, which exported sugar, elephant tusks and gold dust was a going concern in Ceuta by 1191. After the expulsion of the Moslems from the Algarve and Seville in 1248, the Genoese played an important part in the building up of the new shipping centers which developed under the control of Castile in the mouths of the Guadiana and the Guadalquivir, and in ancient Cadiz. In 1253 a Genoese merchant reached Safi, perhaps the Asafi of El Idrisi's tale of the adventurers, on the western bulge of Morocco. Meanwhile a Genoese colony flourished in Lisbon. The Zaccharia and Pessagna families, using Lisbon as a way station between Genoa and London, became so important in the English trade that a member of the Pessagna family became Edward II's banker and was granted the usufruct of certain customhouses until his loans were repaid.

The era of Atlantic exploration began with unrecorded trading ventures by Genoese ships searching for ivory, gold dust and spices among the small ports of the Moorish coast. After the collapse of the Western caliphates, and the fading of the religious frenzies which had destroyed them, the local sheikhs were quite willing to trade with the Christians. The Genoese were soon followed by Catalans, by ships from the Andalusian ports and by ships from Lisbon and Oporto.

In 1291 a fleet of Genoese and other Italians, under the brothers Vivaldi, whose name has a Venetian sound, set out to find a passage to India and was never heard of again. A rumor lingered on that they had touched at the Fortunate Islands. Around 1312 a Genoese named Lanciloto Malocello actually landed on one of these islands, soon to be known as the Canaries, and was reported to have built a castle there.

During these years Dom Dinis kept increasing the royal fleet. His galleys were used to protect merchant shipping from pirates, for leasing to other monarchs for use in their wars, and, when there was no fighting to be done, for mercantile ventures on the king's behalf. When the first commander died Dom Dinis appointed the brother of Edward II's banker, whose name came out in Portuguese as Manoel Peçanha, to be grand admiral of Portugal.

So great was the prestige of the Genoese in matters of navigation that Peçanha could lay down his own terms. The contract was signed February 1, 1317. He was to hold the office for life and to hand it down to his heirs forever. He was to receive 3000 *libras* a year and to have the monopoly of the trade with Genoa and a few other specified ports. In return he was to bring in thirty Genoese captains to command the king's ships. He was to maintain the ships at his own expense except when they were in the king's service.

Again Dinis was following in the footsteps of his grandfather Alfonso the Learned. A generation before Alfonso had put one of the Zaccharia family in charge of his galleys based on dockyards in Seville that were to patrol the coast against Moslem raiders. With the appointment of a Genoese admiral Portugal formally took its place among the maritime powers of Europe.

In spite of the saintly abnegation of Queen Isabel, the result of Dom Dinis' marital infidelities proved the bane of his later life. The last years of his reign were tormented by revolts and raids and the seizures of towns and castles by the adherents of Prince Dom Afonso who was obsessed with the notion that his father was about to hand over the succession to one of his bastard half brothers. Each time the queen rode out with her ladies to interpose herself between the contestants and to arrange a truce.

In the winter of 1324–25, on his way from Lisbon to Santarém, King Dinis was taken ill. He was carried into Santarém in a litter strung on poles across men's shoulders. When he found his illness was mortal he arranged that his body should be buried in the Cistercian monastery of São Dinis at Odivelas which he had endowed and where his tomb was already prepared. Having completed his last will and testament he confessed his sins "with great contrition" and, "entrusting his soul to God, ended his life on January 7, 1325 at the age of sixty-four, of which years he had reigned forty-six."

The death of King Dinis marked the end of the Gallego-Portuguese lyric. No more court patronage for the authors of the *cantigas de amor* and the *cantigas de amigo* and the *cantigas de maldizer*. The cossantes were heard no more. Troubadours and jograes, the versifiers and ballad singers male and female, who had been treated as the king's peers and associates in the realm of poesy, and had found a welcome in his lofty summer palace in the castle at Leiria, and wine and fat capons and roast kid and suckling pig in the royal kitchens, crept away into the cold. One jogral tuned his grief into a refrain:

> "*When Dom Dinis drew his last breath*
> *Rhyming and poesy too met their death.*"

47

7

THE RISE OF
A MIDDLE CLASS

Dynastic wars and the turbulence of the barons threatened the growing commercial prosperity of the seaport towns. The reign of Dinis' son Afonso IV was embittered by endless infighting between Portuguese aspirants to the throne of Castile and Castilian aspirants to the throne of Portugal. Only when shocked in the fall of 1340 by the sudden threat of a Moslem invasion from Morocco, backed up by raiders from Granada, did the rancorous factions unite. Then it was only for a single campaign. The united chivalry of Portugal and Castile routed the Moorish host so decisively on the Rio Salado in Andalucia that the Moors never invaded again.

A few years later Portugal was visited by a disaster far more dreadful than a Moorish invasion. The Black Death, which seems to have been a more virulent form of earlier pestilences, made its appearance and, so the chroniclers claim, wiped out a third of the population in a single summer. This sudden mortality was to have profound social repercussions in the years to come. The working force was so reduced that serfs and peasants started to demand wages and better conditions generally for working the crops. A new class of proprietors appeared, enriched by the piling up of inheritances from their dead relatives. So much land was let go to waste that Afonso IV promulgated a law by which if the owner left his land uncultivated it would be expropriated by the crown.

The warrior barons round the court spent their spare time in love-making and intrigue. There was bitterness between the feudal lords who tended to favor Castile and the new rich from the cities who were developing a fervent Portuguese patriotism. Whenever they were challenged by the nobles the king and the townspeople found themselves on the same side.

When the heir apparent, Dom Pedro, took up with Inês de Castro, a daughter of the High Chamberlain of Castile, who was reputed to be of marvelous beauty, she became suspect to the patriotic faction as a center of Castilian intrigue. She was murdered, by King Afonso's orders so it was claimed, in her garden near Coimbra. Pedro's retainers devastated the Minho.

The story was spread that Pedro and Inês had been secretly married. Her body was taken to the monastery of Alcobaça where a magnificent tomb was carved for it out of the local limestone by some wandering French sculptor. When Dom Pedro became king six years later he had himself built a matching tomb across the chancel with his feet toward the feet of his beloved so, as the story was told, that when he rose in response to the last trump, the first thing he would see would be the resurrection of Dona Inês.

Pedro never rested until he laid hands on her murderers. He had his executioner cut their hearts out of their bodies while he sat at dinner with the fidalgos of his court. The remains were then burned at the stake in the square in front of his palace.

Pedro was a man of violent rages. He was obsessed with the punishment of criminals and was sometimes seen with a scourge hanging from his belt. In court circles he was known as "the Cruel" but the townspeople called him "the Just." He was popular with the merchants and artisans. He encouraged trade and commerce as vigorously as he manhandled wrongdoers. He welcomed to his court the Jewish leaders who had escaped from the massacre of their people in Navarre. One of them, ennobled under the name of Moise Navarro, became his court treasurer. He protected the *juderia* in Lisbon and beheaded two nobles for killing one of its inhabitants. He castrated another for adultery and had a bishop whipped for the same offense.

In lighter moods he loved to dance to the sound of the trumpet. The people of Lisbon got used to seeing him come capering through the streets followed by a long line of courtiers. His chronicler wrote rather wryly that Portugal never saw another ten years as the years of Dom Pedro's reign.

In spite of Pedro's devotion to the fair Inês, he consoled himself after her death with a lady of humble birth named Teresa Lourenço. She bore him a son out of wedlock who was to become, as Master of Avis and John I, the third founder, after Afonso Henriques and Dom Dinis, of the Portuguese kingdom.

Pedro's legitimate son Fernando was described as a handsome man, but as a ruler he lacked resolution and was supremely unlucky. He was shrewd enough in commercial matters. In the Cortes held in Lisbon in 1373 there were complaints that the king requisitioned wheat at five soldos in order to sell it again for five libras at a profit of a couple of thousand per cent. He owned his own merchant ships which had priority in loading over those of his subjects. Grumbling was heard from the conselhos about this practice, and it was further pointed out that the king and queen, the masters of the military orders, bishops and knights and palace officials, all exempt from paying taxes, were competing unfairly with merchants and shipowners, who did.

Lisbon, with four or five hundred ships a year loading there, was by this time one of the busiest marts in Europe. The streets were full of English, Flemings, Hanseatic merchants, Lombards, Genoese, Milanese, Catalans, Mallorcans, Aragonese, shipmen from Cahors and Bayonne. The city had become the chief waystation between the Mediterranean and the Channel and North Sea ports. "King Fernando's revenues were so great," wrote the chronicler "that it is now hard to believe."

Wealth accumulated. Profits were huge from the North African trade. Adventurous spirits felt their blood tingle as rumors spread of a visit of Portuguese and Italian ships to the Fortunate Islands. Not only were the clergy and nobility following the king's example by speculating in ships' cargoes, but the humble *villeins* were leaving the land for the seaports.

King Fernando tried to remedy this by a series of ordinances, reinforcing earlier agrarian laws. Every man who owned land must see that it was tilled. All land fit for grain must be sowed in wheat, barley or millet. Every landowner must raise enough oxen to till his land and failing that, the officers of the concelhos must furnish oxen at a reasonable price. Land fit for grain and not planted in grain should be distributed by the conselhos to those who were capable of cultivating it. Every man who had been a farmer or the son or grandson of a farmer, unless he was master of 500 libras, must work on the land. If he had no land of his own he must be given land to work, or hired out for wages to a landowning farmer. No man should feed cattle unless he already had put so much land in grain.

The cultivated area of Portugal was small, squeezed between the sea and the mountains, but the population was small too. As the attractions of the seafaring life lured more and more young men away from the farms, the crown was embarking in what was to prove an endless and losing battle to see that enough food was produced to feed the Portuguese people.

In economic matters Fernando was a farsighted administrator, but when he dealt with foreign affairs he became weirdly lightheaded. He fell under the spell of a Galician noblewoman named Leonor Telles de Meneses. To marry her he jilted a Castilian princess, thereby setting off a train of diplomatic and military reverses. The people of Lisbon were so incensed by his marriage with a foreigner who was not of royal blood that a mob led by a tailor named Fernão Vasques besieged the royal palace.

The tailor lost his head but during the sixteen years of his reign King Fernando remained profoundly unpopular. There was something strange about Fernando. It may be that he was impotent. Rumors began to fly about that the queen had a lover, another Galician, named João Fernandes Andeiro. Fernando ensconced Andeiro in one of the royal palaces. He was generally thought to be the father of the royal children.

Andeiro first appeared at court as proctor for John of Gaunt, Duke of Lancaster, when, after his marriage to the heiress of the murdered Pedro of Castile, the Plantagenet prince assumed the style of King of Castile and León and started negotiating treaties with Portugal and Aragon.

Portugal was already involved in the web of military alliances, diplomatic treacheries and royal betrayals that was part of the backwash of the Hundred Years' War between France and England. When Henry of Trastámara, one of the bastard sons of Alfonso XI of Castile, revolted against his half brother Pedro who, like his Portuguese namesake was called the Cruel—and with equally good reason—Charles V of France sent troops to aid the Trastámara faction. The English countered with an expedition under Edward III's eldest son, known from his armor as the Black Prince, who crossed the Pyrenees and defeated Henry's army at Nájara.

The victory at Nájara proved a milestone in the military history of the peninsula. It was the first important trial there of the Black Prince's tactics, successful at Crécy and Poitiers, of fighting dismounted and relying on pikes and squads of highly skilled archers to turn the charge of knights on horseback; but its practical results were almost nil. The Black Prince frittered away his advantage. He retired to Bordeaux in ill health after failing to receive the fiefdoms from Pedro which were to repay him for the expense of the expedition.

Henry fled to Aragon and raised a new army which carried all before him in Andalucía. After enticing his half brother to a parley at Montiel he killed him with his own hands in his own tent. A few years later the Duke of Lancaster, the Black Prince's younger brother, married Pedro's heiress Constanza who had fled for safety to English Bayonne, thereby reinforcing the Plantagenet claim to the Castilian throne. Among the small fry of the legitimist faction received at the court of the Pretender was this Galician knight Andeiro who became the architect, in its early stages, of the alliance between the Plantagenets and the Portuguese kings.

John of Gaunt (so named because he was born in Ghent) was Edward III's fourth son, but by marriage to Blanche of Lancaster he had taken title to the Duchy of Lancaster which was the richest fief in England. His wife was the fair Blanche of Chaucer's "Book of the Duchess." John of Gaunt was a lanky stiff-necked nobleman, full of pride and ambition, but he had a capacity for friendship and an appreciation of letters. He fostered young Chaucer's career as part of his entourage in war and peace. He protected that premature Protestant, John Wycliffe. His court at the Savoy Palace in London rivaled the king's in splendor. When

Blanche died, leaving him with three girls to bring up, he was stricken with grief. Chaucer's elegy on the dead duchess, in spite of being a young man's poem full of imitations of the courtly French romances, is animated by a certain human warmth which emanated from John of Gaunt's court.

In Portugal João Fernandes Andeiro so improved on his position as English diplomat and the queen's bedfellow that before long he was managing not only the queen's affairs but the king's. Fernando's complacent cuckoldry rankled with his subjects, particularly with the energetic citizenry of the seaport towns. In defiance of scandal Fernando ennobled Andeiro and bestowed on him the rich county of Ourém.

His treaties with the English Pretender to the throne of Castile brought on a short war with the Trastámara faction in which Fernando was ignominiously beaten. Even Lisbon capitulated. He was forced to sign a humiliating peace at Santarém. Among the terms was a commitment to send Portuguese galleys to help the powerful French and Castilian fleet which had wrested command of the Channel from the English. In spite of his renouncing the English cause and with it the cause of the Roman pope—the French and the Castilians backed the "schismatic" pope at Avignon—Fernando continued to encourage trade with England. Andeiro was sent on a secret mission to assure the English that if they landed an expeditionary force, Fernando would go over to their side. Meanwhile Fernando threw every resource into strengthening the fortifications of Lisbon.

The English had their hands full in the north. French and Castilian galleys under a Genoese admiral had already destroyed a Plantagenet fleet at La Rochelle and French armies were steadily whittling away at English possessions in Gascony. It wasn't until the summer of 1381 that an expedition of English and Gascons was ready to sail for Portugal under John of Gaunt's younger brother. Andeiro led a small contingent. The Earl of Cambridge proved an incompetent commander. Fernando, ever unfortunate in military affairs, sent out the Portuguese galleys under Queen Leonor's brother to convoy the English in, only to have them badly cut to pieces by a much smaller Castilian flotilla out of Seville.

Fernando tried to make up for this defeat by the extraordinary pomp with which he greeted the royal earl. Bulls of Pope Urban from Rome were promulgated to the effect that war against the schismatic French and Castilians was as holy as a crusade against the infidel. To please his English allies Fernando publicly renounced his adhesion to the cause of the Avignon pope. This announcement was immediately followed by a ceremony of espousal between the Earl of Cambridge's young son Edward Langley, who was all of six, and the ten-year-old Portuguese Princess Beatriz. The children were placed together in a highly ornamented bed and blessed by the bishop of Lisbon. Meanwhile the king's agents scoured the country to find mounts for the English and Gascon troops.

Henry of Trastámara had gone to his reward. Luckily for the Anglo-Portuguese allies his successor, Juan I of Castile, was not the man his father was. Though he made warlike passes along the frontier, he kept delaying an attack on Lisbon for fear that a new English army, rumored to be embarking under John of Gaunt, might land in Asturias.

A serious situation was developing in Portugal between the Portuguese and their English allies. Horses for the cavalry were not forthcoming. No pay arrived from England for the troops. Fernando was slow getting his army ready for action. The Plantagenet soldiery whiled away their time plundering the countryside. Cambridge moved his camp across the Tagus, ostensibly to protect the Portuguese frontier, but his troops, instead of waging war on the Castilians, raided the towns and villages of their allies. The Portuguese resisted. Casualties mounted on both sides.

The king and queen were holding court in Evora that winter where they were at last busy with preparations for next spring's campaign. Word had gotten out that the queen was pregnant. The whole country was convinced that Andeiro must be the father. Merchants and townspeople were outspoken in abuse of the adulteress. Queen Leonor began to suspect that Fernando's bastard half brother, John, who had been made Grand Master of the Order of Avis at the age of seven and had been brought up in holy orders, was secretly leading the agitation against the court. He was a promising young man of twenty-two and as popular with the people as Fernando and Leonor were unpopular. Leonor

THE RISE OF A MIDDLE CLASS

had him arrested and held in chains in the castle at Evora. Fernando hurried out of town so as not to be mixed up in the affair. The story went around that the queen was having letters forged to implicate John in a treasonous plot. The popular outcry was such that the Earl of Cambridge feared John's execution would endanger the success of the coming campaign and insisted on his release. John of Avis was ever afterward convinced that the Englishman had saved his life.

By June the armies of Portugal and Castile were moving in a leisurely way toward the frontier. Fernando declared he wouldn't fight a battle until the queen was brought to bed. A boy was born but died in four days. The people suspected foul play. Soon the armies faced each other in martial array at a prearranged field of arms, but both turned tail and retired without a clash. It came out that Fernando and Juan I had been privately arranging a truce all along.

In some things the Portuguese got the better of the negotiations. The Castilians promised to evacuate several frontier fortresses they had seized and to furnish ships to take the unruly English and Gascons back where they came from. To Portugal's detriment was a secret clause only published after the departure of the Earl of Cambridge by which Princess Beatriz, instead of marrying the Earl of Cambridge's son, was to marry Juan of Castile's younger son, so cementing an alliance between Portugal and Castile and assuring the reversion of the Portuguese throne to a prince of the house of Trastámara.

The Earl of Cambridge wearily marched his remaining troops back to Almada on the Tagus to await the Castilian ships which were to take them to England. More than forty ships had been needed to bring the expedition to Portugal. Little more than a dozen sufficed to take the survivors home.

Fernando the Handsome died in Lisbon October 22, 1383. According to the terms of the secret agreement with Juan I, Leonor assumed the regency in the name of her daughter. She was assisted by a council made up largely of Castilians. Andeiro was the actual ruler.

Juan I rashly assumed that the moment had come to make Portugal his. News that a Castilian force had entered Beira touched off a smoldering social revolution in Lisbon. The *arraia miúda*, as Fernão Lopes called it, the mob of small artisans, sailors, fishermen, laborers, poured out into the streets.

There seems to have been a conspiracy of sorts led by the retired chancellor of the court of Dom Pedro, Alvaro Paes, who was in contact with leaders among the merchants and townspeople. At first the Master of Avis refused to lead the revolt. The odds seemed too much on the side of the feudal lords who favored the queen and Andeiro, backed up as they were by an army advancing from Castile. He accepted the queen's orders to take a post on the frontier. Then suddenly, a few miles out, he changed his mind and led his small band of retainers back into Lisbon.

Fernão Lopes, who was born about the time of this revolution, wrote down the story from the recollections of people who had been actors in the events he described when he was in charge of the archives in the castle in Lisbon in the latter part of John of Avis' reign.

The queen, as he tells it, with her ladies seated about her on the dais, was in her chamber in the royal palace and Andeiro was standing in the middle of the room talking to them in a low voice when there was a knocking at the outer door. The porter explained to the Master of Avis and his retainers, who had ridden up demanding to be let in, that since the queen was in mourning for the late king he had orders to admit no one without special permission.

"Who are you to say that?" cried the Master and forced his way through the door with his followers. They crowded into the queen's chamber. The queen and her ladies rose to their feet. The Master bowed deeply before the queen. She told him to be seated.

She asked him why he had come back, addressing him as "brother" because of his relationship to her late husband. He replied that he needed more vassals than had been assigned him if he were to play his part with honor in the defense of the frontier against the Castilians. The queen promptly sent for her chief notary to bring the book where the vassals in that part of the country were listed. He came with his scribes and they checked off a list of names to the Master's satisfaction.

Andeiro suggested that the Master and the queen's brother, the

Count of Barcelos (who was in on the plot), stay to dinner. The Master replied that he could not accept any invitation because he had sent orders home for a meal to be prepared for him. Then he whispered to Barcelos that the count mustn't stay either because he was going to kill Andeiro. The count whispered back that he would help. The Master said, "No, go and wait for me for dinner. With God's help as soon as this is done I'll come and eat with you."

Andeiro became suspicious. He privately sent word to his retainers to go home and arm themselves.

"By Saint Mary," cried the queen, "the English have a good custom. When there is peace they don't carry arms. They dress in nice clothes and wear gloves like ladies. Only in war do they carry arms, and everybody knows how well they use them."

"Lady," said the Master, "this is very true, but the English are always at war. We on the other hand are usually at peace. If we didn't get in the habit of carrying arms we couldn't bear them in battle."

Dinnertime came. The Count of Barcelos left, and several others. Andeiro was looking for a pretext to leave the room.

He became insistent. "At least you will eat with me. . . . While you are talking I'll go out to order the meal."

The Master repeated that he had dinner waiting for him at home.

Andeiro insisted that he would go and give orders for dinner.

"Don't go," said the Master. "I have to talk about something with you before leaving and then I'll go because it's already time to eat."

Then he took leave of the queen. He seized Andeiro by the hand and they left the chamber for a big room across the hall. All the Master's retainers followed. The two men stood talking in the embrasure of a window. Their words were so low and so few that nobody really heard what they said, but some claim they heard the Master say: "Count, it is a surprise to find that you, a man whom I very much liked, are working for my dishonor and death."

"Sir," said Andeiro, "whoever told you that told a very big lie."

The Master pulled out his long dagger and gave Andeiro a blow in the head. Seeing that the blow was not mortal the Master's retainers drew their swords. Andeiro tried to run back toward the queen's chamber but Rui Pereira who stood nearest ran him through and he fell dead.

The Master gave orders to close all the doors and sent his page off to run crying through the streets, "They are killing the Master."

The uproar and the sound of running feet was heard in the queen's chamber. The queen rose and told her ladies to go see what was happening. They came back saying that the Count João Fernandes was dead.

The queen took fright. "By Saint Mary," she cried, "they have killed a very good servant of mine." She swore to God that tomorrow she would have a great fire built and hold her hand in the fire to prove her innocence of adultery. (The chronicler added in a quaint aside, "She hadn't the slightest intention of doing it.")

Her courtiers, both men and women, were struck with panic and began to run away. They didn't dare go out through the doors so they fled through the windows, some of them over the roofs, others by obscure stairways. The notary and his scribes took flight as best they could.

The queen sent a trembling lady out to ask the Master, who stood on a great terrace in front of the queen's chamber, whether she must die too.

"God protect me from evil," he said quietly. "Tell the queen to remain quiet in her chamber. I did not come here to do her harm but to do this to this man who has richly deserved it."

She sent back word begging him to leave her palace. As they prepared to go Lourenço Martins brought the Master a sum of silver he had found on a table in front of the kitchen.

"I say, Sire, here you have enough for the day's expenses."

The Master answered angrily to take the money back where he found it. He hadn't come here for that, but to do what he had done. Lourenço Martins did as he was told.

Meanwhile the Master's page went galloping through the streets crying out that they were killing the Master in the queen's palace. He never stopped shouting till he arrived at the house of Alvaro Paes which was a long way off. As he passed, people kept coming out of their houses to see what was going on. Paes was already armed with "the kind of helmet on his head they used in those days." Though old and rheumatic he climbed on a horse "which he hadn't ridden for many years" and his retainers followed calling on whomever they met to go to the help of the Master because he was the son of Dom Pedro.

The people crowded after Alvaro Paes in such a multitude that the main thoroughfares became filled and people had to hurry along the bystreets. Everybody was trying to get there first. When anybody asked what was going on, the answer was that Count João Fernandes was killing the Master by the queen's orders. When they reached the palace the uproar was so great no one could decide what to do. The doors were all closed. Some brought wood and bundles of kindling to set the palace afire to burn up the traitor and the adulteress.

The Master appeared in a window and declared that he was alive and well. Some of the people were so confused they wouldn't believe it was he. Others burst into tears of joy. When the word went around that the Master really was safe and that Andeiro was dead, people began to tell each other that the Master had done wrong. He should have killed the adulteress too.

The Master and his retainers mounted their horses and rode out into the street. "What do you order us to do, Sire?" the people cried. "What do you want us to do?" The Master thanked them and said that now he had no further need of their help but the uproar was such he couldn't make himself heard. He rode through the streets to the admiral's palace where Count Barcelos with whom he was going to dine was staying. As he passed the ladies called out from the windows, "God bless you, Sire. Blessed be the Lord who saved you from the treason that was being prepared for you."

The notables of the town met him at the entrance to the Rossio, praising him for having saved them from so great a danger. They led him to the palace where the Count of Barcelos was staying.

When they were about to sit down to the table word came that the townspeople were going to kill the Bishop of Lisbon who was a Castilian and an adherent of the Avignon pope. "Don't worry about that, Sire," said the Count of Barcelos. "There are plenty of good Portuguese bishops who'll serve you better."

After they had thrown the bishop out of the bell tower of the cathedral the townspeople began to argue among themselves about what they ought to do next. Their first idea was to plunder the Jews. The Count of Barcelos and the Master rode out to the judería to dissuade them. The Master told the chief judge to announce in the queen's name that no one must go into the judería or do harm to the Jews. The people shouted that they wouldn't take orders from the queen. The only orders they would take would be from the Master of Avis.

The Master and his friends had a hard time persuading the mob not to massacre and plunder the Jews. Someone got the idea that the best thing to do was to ride away. If they moved off the people would follow. They did. The mob followed the cavalcade up the Rua Nova crying out that they would take this man for their master and raise him up to be king. At the cathedral the Master dismounted and went in to hear mass.

The queen had fled to the castle of Alenquer. Alvaro Paes was sent on a mission to suggest that since the people were determined to have the Master of Avis for Regent and Defender of the City, the best solution might be for her to marry him. Another faction wanted to make the Dom João king who was the elder of Dom Pedro's two sons by Inês de Castro, but they were both held in close custody by Juan of Castile since they had pretensions to his own throne as well as to that of Portugal. The Master of Avis let it be known that, to remove himself from the controversy he was outfitting a ship to take him to England where he would offer his services to Richard II. Meanwhile the people had met in the monastery of São Domingos and elected John of Avis king by acclamation. Whenever he appeared in the tortuous streets of Lisbon people shouted after him, "Isn't Portugal worth London?"

Finally to meet the popular clamor the notables of the city consented to meet in council. The Master of Avis, convinced at last that he had the support he needed, announced that he was accepting the people's choice. Now it was up to the council to confirm the powers the people had bestowed on him.

According to Fernão Lopes the answer was silence. Nobody dared speak. Here and there a man whispered in the ear of the man beside him. They were afraid of the queen and of the advancing armies of Castile. They were remembering the fate of Vasques the tailor. In the streets around crowds of people were listening to every rumor that came from the council chamber. A cooper named Afonse Anes Penedo appeared in the doorway with his hand on his sword. He cried out to the councillors that they weren't good Portuguese. This way they would all soon be in the power of the king of Castile.

The crowd backed him up with such a threatening roar that the councillors in fear and trembling gave their consent. It was written and signed by their hands that the Master of Avis should be Regent and Defender of the Realm.

PART TWO

Heirs of
the Adventurers

I

PORTUGAL, PORTUGAL
FOR THE MASTER OF AVIS

Fernão Lopes called the reign of the Master of Avis the Seventh Age of the World. Having listed the epochs of history from the creation of Adam to the coming of the Savior he found that there were five. The sixth age, in his opinion, lasted 1443 years, "reckoned by the era of Caesar according to which this chronicle is compiled." The seventh which "began with the deeds of the Master . . . will last to the end of the centuries, or whenever God wills who brought them all into being."

Fernão Lopes was himself of humble rustic stock. He had risen to be the king's confidential notary and keeper of the archives in the tower of Lisbon Castle. He was writing as a man whose career had been made by a successful social overturn. Similar risings of the populace had failed in Castile and Aragon and even in England, where Richard II so neatly outwitted the rebels under Wat Tyler. In France the nobles massacred the Jacqueries. Only in Portugal did a new monarchy attain power, based on the support of the artisans and merchants and shipmen of the seaports uniting with the johnny-come-latelies of the countryside who, as vassals of the new king, took over the strong places of the dispossessed feudal barons.

"There appeared a new world," wrote Fernão Lopes enthusiastically, "a new generation of people, because sons of men of such low condition that it is hardly to be spoken of, on account of their good services and hard work, were made knights, calling themselves thereafter by new lineages and names. Others seized hold of ancient titles of nobility, which had been forgotten, so that by dignities and honors and offices of the realm—in which this lord was Master and afterward King—forged so far ahead of their peers that their descendants today call themselves fidalgos and are held in high esteem. Just as the Son of God called his Apostles, saying that he would make them fishers of men, so many of those whom the Master made great, fished so well for themselves through their great and honorable estate that some rode out escorted by twenty or thirty men on horseback; and, in the wars that followed, were accompanied by three or four hundred lances and even by fidalgos of ancient blood."

At first the prospects of the Master of Avis seemed bleak indeed. In sympathy with Lisbon popular revolutions did take place in Oporto and Beja and Evora and Portalegre where the burghers rose and seized the castles, but the whole north remained in the hands of the feudal faction. The old chivalry sided with the Trastámara kings as protectors of their privileges. Juan of Castile was raising an army. By January 12, 1384, his vanguard reached Santarém. Queen Leonor opened the gates to him and resigned the regency in his favor. At the same time more than fifty towns and castles acknowledged his sovereignty.

In Lisbon John of Avis reorganized the city council to give representation to the trade guilds and enlisted the whole population in his measures of defense. "Like a city widowed," wrote the chronicler, "Lisbon chose the Master for her defender and spouse."

The strength of the new fortifications King Fernando had built gave the people a certain confidence. A mission was dispatched to England to ask help from the Plantagenets. Since no man of title could be found to serve, the first mission consisted of John's squire, light-fingered Lourenço Martins, and a Bristol cloth merchant, Thomas Daniel, who had an establishment in Lisbon. Though Richard II stalled on permitting the Portuguese to recruit troops in England, the British merchants were sympathetic.

Trade between the two countries was profitable both ways. King Richard's officers continued to treat Portuguese ships as friendly.

The vigor and discretion of John's rule began to attract defectors from the old nobility. Important court officials, appalled by Juan I of Castile's manifest intention of taking the Portuguese crown for his own, fled from Santarém and offered their services to the Master of Avis. Along with them came one of the great feudal barons, the master of the Portuguese branch of the military order of Santiago, Fernão Afonso de Albuquerque. Since John didn't have too much confidence in any of them he packed Albuquerque off to the Plantagenet court as ambassador.

In return for permission to levy troops in England he was to offer a squadron of Portuguese galleys to help the English, who were hard pressed by the combined fleets of France and Castile. The Plantagenets were still trying to fight their tubby merchant ships that were no match for the swift and maneuverable galleys developed in the Mediterranean by the Genoese. Guns and bombards using gunpowder to shoot stone balls were making the galleys still more formidable. Even so the English court continued to procrastinate about allowing the Portuguese to raise troops in Great Britain.

In the spring of 1384 John welcomed another adherent. This was a young nobleman named Nun'Alvares Pereira, already famous for his blameless life and reputed to be a passionate addict of the Knights of the Round Table. Nun'Alvares immediately proved his mettle as a commander by defeating a superior Castilian force at a place known as "the Marshes." There was nothing Arthurian about his tactics. Copying the Black Prince, he relied heavily on bowmen and dismounted his men to receive the charge of the Castilian knights.

Juan of Castile was losing support among the Portuguese barons. Even Queen Leonor repented of having resigned her regency. Juan caught her in a plot to have him murdered and sent her off under guard to be confined in a convent. The Castilian king used up all the resources of his kingdom for the army he raised to besiege Lisbon.

He built a great fortified camp in front of the city. Contingents marching down the valley of the Tagus were met by a fleet from Viscaya which joined the Castilian galleys blockading the mouth of the river. The city's defenses withstood all assaults but by midsummer the population was on short rations. By September the situation would have been desperate if the Castilian host hadn't been so decimated by an outbreak of plague that the besiegers were in almost as bad shape as the besieged.

There were two hundred deaths a day. Among the two thousand or more men at arms who perished under the walls of Lisbon was almost the entire leadership of the Castilian army. Both of Juan's marshals died and his accomplished admiral, Fernan Sanchez de Tovar.

Fernão Lopes described the straggle of pack animals carrying the dead home over the mountains to Castile, coffins draped in black, vassals in mourning stumbling under the furled banners of their liege lords, one after the other in single file on long stretches of the trail, "a procession most grievous to see."

When the Castilians lifted the siege the people of Lisbon saw it as the hand of God working in their favor.

Juan of Castile had not given up. His determination to conquer Lisbon was as strong as ever, but his retirement to Seville gave the Master of Avis a much needed respite. That winter Nun'Alvares took the offensive against the Castilians in the Alentejo while John reduced the castles in the neighborhood of Lisbon. His army was largely made up of artisans and townspeople. Their war cry was "Portugal, Portugal for the Master of Avis!"

In Evora the mob that seized the castle was led by a tailor and a goatherd. "It was a marvel," wrote Fernão Lopes, "to see the spirit that God gave them and the cowardice He instilled in the others; so that castles that had not given in when besieged for long months with great force by the ancient kings, were taken by storm in less than half a day by ragged commoners —with their bellies to the sun—badly armed and without leaders."

By the end of March 1385 the Master of Avis was strong enough to call a Cortes in Coimbra to confirm his popular mandate.

The election in the Cortes was not without opposition. One faction still wanted John to continue serving as regent in the name of Dom Pedro's elder son by Inês de Castro. Nun'Alvares offered to kill the leader of the opposition, but John of Avis' level head prevailed. A valuable adherent had appeared in the person of a doctor of laws not long home from Bologna. João das Regras was a profound student of Roman law and a supporter of Pope Urban as the legitimate vicar of Christendom. He carried everything before him in the Cortes by reading a letter from a previous pope, Innocent III, which may or may not have been a forgery, in which the pope refused to legitimize King Pedro's relations with Inês or to remove the bar sinister from the escutcheons of her sons. April 6, 1385, the Defender was proclaimed King of Portugal.

At about the same time the news arrived that two English ships carrying food and troops, equipped by money raised by pledging the credit of the Portuguese merchants in England, had beaten their way to Lisbon through the squadron of blockading galleys and that other ships had arrived in Oporto and Setúbal. Immediately King John sent off the six galleys he had promised to help protect the English coast and instructed his ambassadors to negotiate a formal alliance. Further he wrote them to whisper in King Richard's ear that the Portuguese would gladly further John of Gaunt's aspirations to the throne of Castile.

While Juan of Castile was raising a new army for a fresh expedition to Portugal, John and Nun'Alvares, who now bore the title of Constable of the Realm, hurried through northern Portugal, driving the Trastámara faction out of Braga, Guimarães, Viana do Castelo and Ponte de Lima. In June a Portuguese force countered a Castilian raid out of Ciudad Rodrigo with the same tactics that Nun'Alvares had found so successful before. At Trancoso Portuguese foot soldiers and dismounted knights withstood the Castilian charge in the middle of a plowed field. The Castilians were routed with serious losses.

A new Castilian army marched into Portugal to besiege Lisbon once more. To intercept them John of Avis and his constable had a force of some seven thousand men including several hundred English and Gascon bowmen. Though the exact size of the Castilian army is hard to figure it was probably twice as numerous, backed up by swarms of footmen and light cavalry and a battery of sixteen guns.

The Portuguese took up carefully chosen positions in a valley near Aljubarrota not far from the present site of the great abbey of Batalha which John I built later to commemorate the battle. Nun'Alvares commanded the van. The main body was formed in a hollow square under the personal supervision of the king. The Gascon and English bowmen were deployed on the flanks.

Instead of attacking through the valley as the Portuguese had hoped the Castilians performed a tedious flanking movement which forced Nun'Alvares and the king to shift the ground of their defense. The slowness of the Castilian advance gave the Portuguese time to turn their army around so as to face the enemy. They still had a watercourse on either flank. The Castilian march took all day. Nun'Alvares had his men dig two ditches on the slope in front of him and built a broken row of palisades of brushwood to protect his lines. The lines were further protected by a scattering of foxholes, which the Portuguese called *covas de lobos*, wolf burrows.

The main disadvantage to the Portuguese at that moment was that they only carried one day's rations, while the Castilians were known to be amply supplied. Their desperate digging in the sun and dust was hard on them, but the long march through the hot afternoon was even harder on the Castilians, who had already plodded seven miles to reach the battlefield that morning. It was nearly sunset before they began to attack. Their vanguard advanced on foot.

Juan of Castile was so ill he could barely ride an ambling mule. His more levelheaded advisers had convinced him that it would be folly to fight that day, but, with the lack of discipline typical of Trastámaran armies, before he could hold them back, independent companies of horsemen were already harassing the guards of the Portuguese baggage train from the rear. The result was, according to Fernão Lopes, that the least dependable Portuguese troops couldn't have run away if they had wanted to. The Castilian bombards began to toss stone balls into Nun'Alvares' van, causing some alarm but few casualties. The Castilian men-at-arms marched straight forward into the trap prepared for them. They were met by stones thrown from slings. In spite of the palisades and the ditches they pushed back Nun'Alvares' advanced line, but the king quietly advanced his men-at-arms in their hollow square to hew at the attackers with sword and battle-ax. The bowmen on each flank moved forward and shot at their leisure into the struggling mass in the wedge-shaped tract of land between them. On account of the ditches and the watercourse the Castilian wings were unable to reach the battlefield.

In a little less than an hour the Castilian standard had fallen. Don Juan was placed on a swift horse and fled through the dusk toward Santarém. The most ardent knights of the Castilian chivalry lay dead.

Almost every one of the Portuguese barons who had joined the Trastámara faction met his end that day. The bodies of two of Nun'Alvares' brothers were found on the field. The survivors fled into the darkness. In the days that followed most of them were butchered by peasants who were in no mood to put up any longer with the pillage and arson and rape of invading armies. It was reported that the baker's wife in the village of Aljubarrota killed six of them with the long iron scoop she used to push bread into the oven.

In the agony of waiting for the Castilian attack, when only the insistence of his young constable convinced him that he must do battle that day, John made a number of vows. He vowed that he would restore the old church of the miraculous fig tree at Braga. There he deposited the magnificent triptych and the silver angels found in Juan of Castile's tent. Near the site of the battle he founded an abbey.

Alcobaça had been almost purely French Cistercian in style. In the great church of Batalha, which was building all through John's reign, French and English elements are intermixed to form the first purely Portuguese version of the flamboyant gothic. The carving and the stonework reflect the dash and enthusiasm of the foundation of a new dynasty. Architects point out that the huge unsupported vault of the chapterhouse, which has withstood all the earthquakes, was one of the most daring constructions of its sort since Roman times.

The victory of Aljubarrota put the burgher-backed monarchy of the House of Avis on an equally firm base. John I proved a hardheaded statesman. He pressed his advantage to the full. While his namesake of Castile was ordering his subjects into mourning and appearing draped in black, in a strange mood of self-humiliation, before the Cortes at Valladolid, John I was building up the English alliance and trying to speed the long-delayed invasion of the peninsula by John of Gaunt.

John of Gaunt at last got on the move, but another year went by before he could collect the necessary funds, marshal his vassals and assemble enough shipping to transport his enormous household. Outside of men-at-arms the expedition included carpenters and masons and miners from the Forest of Dean for siege work. Since he was planning to set up his court in Castile, Doña Constanza, as heiress to Don Pedro, and her troop of attendants must come along, and also his daughters by Blanche of Lancaster. The Lancastrian court included chaplains and all manner of officials, domestics, craftsmen, tailors, goldsmiths, painters, embroiderers, cooks and scullions and even some minstrels. Pope Urban declared the expedition a crusade against the schismatics and authorized the Duke's agents to solicit contributions at the church doors. Richard II loaned his uncle thirteen thousand pounds and presented him with a gold crown to use at his coronation at Burgos.

Meanwhile the Portuguese ambassadors, negotiating at Windsor with Richard's chamberlains, were drawing up a new treaty, by which the English guaranteed their support of the Master of Avis against any attempt from Castile to overthrow his revolutionary government. Commercial interests were much stressed. Each country was to allow freedom of travel and residence to the merchants of the other. Ten large Portuguese galleys were to serve Richard II for six months at the expense of the Portuguese treasury. Each galley was to be manned by a master, three lieutenants, from eight to ten sailors, thirty bowmen and not less than a hundred and eighty rowers. May 17, 1386 the Portuguese envoys affixed their seals to the document in the Star Chamber at Westminster.

About a month later a fleet of a hundred vessels set sail from Plymouth. They were escorted by Portuguese galleys under Afonso Furtado. They made port at Brest where an English garrison was sorely beset by the French. After driving off the besiegers they continued to Coruña.

On July 25, the day of Saint James, the Lancastrian fleet made a safe landing in the beautiful Galician harbor, well-known to English shipmasters as the port of debarkation for pilgrims bound for Compostela. Furtado's galleys had a stroke of luck. They found the Castilian squadron, which had been hovering about them without daring to attack during the crossing of the Bay of Biscay, drawn up at the head of the *ria* at Betanzos. There was nobody aboard but the rowers. Furtado's men captured them easily. Convinced that John of Gaunt's fleet was headed for a Portuguese port the men-at-arms and the sailors had gone up to Compostela for the fiestas.

Neither did the castle at Coruña offer any resistance. A week later the English fleet was on its way home to cope with the immediate threat of a French invasion, and John of Gaunt, flying a banner on which the castles and lions of Castile and León were quartered with the arms of France and England, was receiving the submission of the legitimists of Galicia. Within a few weeks the Pretender's forces had occupied the coast as far south as the Minho and set up their headquarters in the city of Orense.

Santiago de Compostela surrendered without a blow and the canons of the cathedral, whose archbishop was in command of a Castilian army at Zamora, meekly admitted that the Avignon pope was an imposter. The city's hospices and monasteries provided comfortable billets for the English troops. Remembering the fate of his brother's unlucky expedition, the duke wooed the Galician peasantry by commanding that food, horses and supplies should be paid for at market prices and decreeing that any soldier caught looting or molesting the country people should be executed forthwith. Strong points were peaceably garrisoned. Supplies were easy to come by. All went well until, with the advent of the rainy Galician autumn, the plague put in an appearance.

Messengers scurried back and forth almost daily between John of Gaunt's chancery in Orense and John of Avis' court. They were planning a joint expedition against the Castilians in the spring. Negotiations were in progress for a marriage between John of Avis and one of John of Gaunt's daughters. After refusing to consider an alliance with Constanza's daughter Katherine which would involve him in dynastic conflict with the Trastámara family, John of Avis chose instead to ask for the hand of Lancaster's eldest daughter, Philippa. Philippa by that day's standards was already a hopeless spinster at twenty-eight. November 1, 1386, the Duke of Lancaster met the Portuguese king for the first time

73

at Ponte de Mouro on the Minho border. Each sovereign was accompanied by a bevy of dignitaries and men-at-arms. Their private discussions were held in the magnificent pavilion John had captured from his namesake of Castile at Aljubarrota. It was decided that the campaign must start in the late winter and that the marriage between John and Philippa should take place immediately.

It was John of Gaunt who insisted on an early date. John of Avis tried to delay the marriage. This was due less to a rumored distaste for the match than to the suspicion that something had gone wrong with an application he had made to Pope Urban to be released from his vow of celibacy. Overruling John of Avis the duke sent his daughter off to Oporto with an imposing escort. There in the episcopal palace John met his bride-to-be for the first time. Wearing cloth of gold and golden crowns, they rode on white horses amid much singing and bandplaying and public rejoicing, to the cathedral. They were married on St. Valentine's Day. Two weeks later John was on his way, with an army of some nine thousand men, to meet the Lancastrian troops near Bragança. Queen Philippa took up her residence with the court at Coimbra.

Already the alliance with the Duke of Lancaster was turning out less auspicious than John of Avis had hoped. The court gossip had it that, even from the time he first settled in Orense, the duke had been bargaining for terms with the king of Castile. When he joined forces with the Portuguese plague and garrison duty had much reduced his troops. Though Nun'Alvares was complaining in private of his disappointment with the English contingent, John fulfilled every commitment. In planning the campaign he treated the wishes of his father-in-law with a deference which seemed to his subordinates to be thoroughly unwise.

The campaign in León proved a painful exercise in futility to the Portuguese. Juan of Castile, whose realm had not yet recovered from the losses suffered in previous invasions of Portugal, was determined not to risk another pitched battle. His castles and walled cities were well supplied and well garrisoned by free companies sent to his aid by Charles VI of France. All the English and Portuguese armies accomplished was the ravaging of the wheatlands of the plain of León.

The Easter holidays found the two armies besieging the fortress of Benevente. The Lancastrians, who recognized among the defendants on the walls old opponents in many chivalric battle in the wars in France, were happy to arrange a truce. The Lancastrians and the French engaged in jousts and festivities while the Castilians and the Portuguese, who felt their quarrel was being taken too lightly by their allies, stood around with furrowed brows.

The jousting was broken up by a real set-to, but it was already obvious to John of Avis and his constable that John of Gaunt was more interested in negotiation than in serious warfare. When a few small towns were occupied the usual problems arose between allies over the division of the loot. By mid-May, having failed to provoke the Castilians to an engagement and having taken no city large enough to provide supplies for a base of operations, John suggested to the Duke of Lancaster that they call the campaign off. Lancaster was to make what terms he could. All pretense had now been dropped that the Lancastrians were not bargaining with the Castilian king.

The Lancastrian army was no longer a fighting force. Both marshals and most of the leadership had succumbed to dysentery or the plague. Many of the surviving chieftains made private truce with the Castilians and rode home under safe conduct to Gascony. The discomfited pretender and his queen retired with the Portuguese army toward Bragança.

In his quarters at Trancoso John of Gaunt accepted the original terms which Juan of Castile had sent him by secret messenger to Orense the winter before. John of Gaunt and Doña Constanza's daughter Katherine would marry Henry, Juan of Castile's son. The pair would be guaranteed the succession as Prince and Princess of Asturias. John of Gaunt would give up all pretensions to the Castilian throne and the Castilian treasury would repay him for his renunciation by an annuity of forty thousand francs. To indemnify him for the costs of the campaign he was to be paid, in annual payments delivered to him in Bayonne during the next three years, another six hundred thousand francs in gold. To show that he had no further use for it John of Gaunt amiably sent his crown to the Castilian king.

Though the campaign was a military defeat, financially it proved a bonanza. The French chronicler Froissart quotes the Count of Foix as exclaiming when he heard the terms, "By my Faith, the Duke of Lancaster is a smart man!"

John of Avis sent his vassals and men-at-arms home from Bragança. There the frustrations and fatigues of the campaign nearly made an end of him. He fell desperately ill. In the nick of time a plot by a Castilian spy to poison the Duke and Duchess of Lancaster was discovered. The would be poisoner was burned in the market place. Queen Philippa hurrying from Coimbra to her husband's bedside was so shocked by the terror and confusion of the court that she suffered a miscarriage.

John and his queen both recovered and conveyed their quasi-royal guests to Oporto. There the Duke and Duchess of Lancaster took ship to Bayonne.

Though the wars with Castile continued to turn the border country into a desert for another twenty years they were no longer the main preoccupation of John of Avis. The futile campaign in León had taught him a lesson. When next he turned to expansion it was against the infidel to the southward. It was along the sea lanes he expected his Portuguese to find their destiny.

2

THE COMING OF AGE OF
THE PORTUGUESE KINGDOM

John of Avis found the royal treasury empty when he took over the throne. Fernando's wars had exhausted the country's resources. One of his first acts was to devalue the currency. A mark of silver had represented 195 libras under Fernando. In John's reign it was reckoned at 29,000. It was a tribute to his personal popularity that this inflation seems to have been accepted with hardly a murmur by the Cortes and the conselhos.

Philippa of Lancaster set to work to reform the morals of the Portuguese court. Though her father had kept a mistress (whom he faithfully married when the queen died) during his merely political marriage with Constanza of Castile, the decencies had always been preserved at the Savoy palace. In fact Katherine Swineford acted as a governess for the children. Philippa now insisted that more than a hundred couples whom she found living in open sin get married immediately. According to Fernão Lopes these forced marriages turned out remarkably well. Philippa's austerity in these matters coincided with the Constable's. Nun'Alvares' wife died at an early age, leaving him two small children. According to the court chroniclers he never looked at another woman. John, whose vow of celibacy had not stood in the way of a little venery in his early days, enforced the queen's wishes with all the fury of a reformed rake.

When one of his favorite courtiers was laggard about taking a friendly hint that he should marry his *enamorata* and instead of taking her to church was discovered in her bedchamber, the king jumped up from his siesta in a fit of rage and ran out "in his drawers" to apprehend the culprit, who fled to sanctuary in the church of St. Elói. In the scuffle to escape the royal guard a statue of the Virgin was overturned. The king had the young man burned alive for sacrilege next day in the Rossio. After that when ordered to marry the courtiers went meek as lambs to the altar.

Philippa bore him six sons. The eldest died in infancy. The second, born in 1391, was Dom Duarte, the philosophical brooder and man of letters who succeeded John I on the throne. The third born in 1392 was Dom Pedro the traveler. The fourth in 1394 was Prince Henry, known to the nineteenth-century English as the Navigator, Master of the Order of Christ and organizer of the enterprise of the Indies. The fifth, born six years later, became Master of the Order of Santiago. The sixth, Dom Fernando, who was to suffer an untimely fate as captive of the Moors, saw the light in 1402. Isabel, the only daughter who survived, formed through her patronage, after she married the Duke of Burgundy, a link between the painters and sculptors of the Low Countries and the emerging Portuguese schools of art. It was to paint her portrait that Jan van Eyck, supposed by some to have been the master of Nuno Gonçalves, first came to Lisbon. Each of Philippa's children was to show quite special talents.

The education of their sons became the chief preoccupation of John and Philippa. John of Gaunt's daughters had been among the first English noblewomen to learn to read and write. The Duke of Lancaster himself was one of the most civilized men in England. Philippa was brought up by her mother, the lovely Blanche of Chaucer's elegy, in the early dawn of the humanist revival. There is a legend that it was Chaucer who taught her the use of the astrolabe. She became thoroughly Portuguese without losing touch with her Anglo-Saxon background. Particularly after her brother possessed himself of the English throne as Henry IV there was interchange of scholars and churchmen between London and Lisbon. One of her children's tutors was

78

Robert Payn, who became a canon of Lisbon cathedral and translated Gower's *Confessio Amantis* into Portuguese.

John of Avis himself, though hardly a scholar in the tradition of Alfonso the Learned or Dom Dinis, wrote a good plain Portuguese prose. In his spare time he composed a treatise on the hunting of bear and wolves, wild boar, deer and hares, which along with falconry were the main sports of the noblemen of the time. He expounded in his matter-of-fact way the proper care of horses and the training of hunting dogs. The *Livro de Montaria* exhibits a profoundly utilitarian mind; the king recommends hunting as a school of good health and a way of keeping fit for the trials of battle. He was thinking of his sons. From the time the three eldest were small boys he associated them in every way he could with the business of government.

John was a practical man. Though so long as he reigned he did not allow himself to forget that he owed his throne to election by the Cortes and to the Lisbon populace, imperceptibly the powers of the monarchy multiplied. Royal monopolies made the king all-powerful in the import-export trade. It was in his reign that grain had first to be brought in from the Channel ports to feed the population. Through the influence of such legalists as João das Regras, Roman law, as set forth in Justinian's code, formulated at the height of imperial absolutism, replaced the old customary law of the Swabians and Visigoths. Every reform brought about by the demands of efficiency in administration gave the monarchy greater powers over the guilds and brotherhoods, the merchants' organizations in the towns, the conselhos and ecclesiastical jurisdictions, and the fiefs of the feudal barons, all the contending privileges and exemptions that had formed the loose tissue of society during the Middle Ages. A sign of the times was the change, following the example of Castile and Aragon, from the old Hispanic chronology which dated the years from the birth of Caesar, to the more modern "Pisan chronology" which dated the years from the birth of Christ.

Though there were royal palaces and castles scattered through the country, the idea of a formal capital had not yet developed. The court still roamed from town to town, lodging, at vast expense to its hosts, in monasteries and in the castles of the king's vassals. The old fortified palace of the Moorish *walis* at Sintra became John I's favorite residence. Since many Moorish artisans still lived peaceably in the land, when he decided to restore the ruined halls it was the most natural thing in the world to use the Moorish style. The mozarab work of the palace of Sintra, with its tiled walls and carved doorways and *artesoado* ceilings, and the flamboyant gothic of Batalha became the two fountainheads of the indigenous Portuguese architecture which developed during the great days of the house of Avis.

The unconverted Moors were the artisans and stonecarvers of the new order. The Jews were its bankers, financiers and physicians, and also its manufacturers and small merchants. Though many of the Mohammedans formed a slave class and were restricted to special quarters, and the Jews had to wear the star of David on their breasts and were forbidden to leave the judería after curfew, the religious and racial hatreds that were already brewing in other parts of the peninsula had hardly reached Portugal. Moors were listed on the rosters of artisans who worked on the churches and monasteries that were rising everywhere for the glory of God and the Virgin and of *El Rei Dom João*. The Jews still retained their own courts and tribunals, as they had under the caliphate, and held offices of responsibility under the royal administration. Even as late as the middle years of the fifteenth century when Nuno Gonçalves executed his great panels, which constitute the chief glory of Portuguese painting, the grand rabbi of Lisbon, with an open torah in his hands, is represented, along with King Afonso VI and Prince Henry and the bishops and dignitaries of the realm, among the throng adoring Lisbon's patron saint.

In 1411 a permanent peace was signed with Castile. Trade with Flanders was put on a new firm basis by a charter of liberties and privileges granted to the Portuguese merchants who maintained a trading post at Bruges. At the same time rumors were heard of a civil war in Morocco in the course of which the rebel leader who held Ceuta, which for a hundred years had been the most flourishing port on the southern shore of the Straits of Gibraltar, had fled to Granada with his fleet. That left Ceuta undefended.

The king, who had been suggesting to his sons a great tournament to celebrate the successes of his reign, called them into secret council. Duarte was twenty. Pedro was nineteen and Prince Henry was seventeen. Afonso, Count of Barcelos, the bastard son the king had legitimized some years before and married to the daughter of his dear friend Nun'Alvares the constable, was about thirty. The princes were unanimous in declaring that a tournament would be a waste of money. Some great military victory against the infidel would be a more fitting capstone to their father's reign.

Ceuta was the obvious objective. Possession of Ceuta would give the Portuguese control of the straits and make it easy to eliminate the Moorish corsairs who harassed trade into the Mediterranean. Ceuta had become the terminal of the African caravan routes. In the eastern fringes of the Mediterranean the Ottoman Turks were already threatening the traffic in silk and spices with the Orient that had so enriched the Italian city-states. The Genoese had harvested rich profits from the voyages along the African coast. Now the Lisbon shipmasters, who had already participated with Italians in an expedition to the Canaries, were excited by the possibilities of fresh discoveries to the southward. Ceuta would be the first step.

John I was a cautious ruler. Although he was in his early fifties, his health had been undermined by what was described as the results of the bite of a mad dog. The chroniclers report that he took a great deal of convincing but that once he had made up his mind he threw himself into the preparations for an expedition to seize Ceuta with the enthusiasm of a young man.

His first act was to send off a Prior of the Knights Hospitalers, on the pretext of sailing to Palermo to see if a marriage could be arranged between Prince Pedro and the widowed Aragonese queen of Sicily. To spy out the land the prior managed to stop off in Ceuta both on the outward and return journeys without alarming the Moors, who seem to have received him hospitably enough. Landing in Lisbon the prior followed the king to Sintra where he found John and his sons in the small tiled council chamber.

Eannes de Azurara, who had succeeded Fernão Lopes as royal chronicler, described the interview in some detail. On being questioned about Ceuta the prior astonished everybody by refusing to answer. Instead he asked for two sacks of sand, a roll of ribbon, half a bushel of beans and a porridge bowl. With these he constructed a relief map in an adjoining room. He showed the twin peninsulas of Ceuta on the south side of the straits and of Gibraltar on the north. A pile of beans marked the houses of the city. The ribbon indicated the circuit of the walls and the sand represented the beach at the head of a splendid anchorage where landing should be easy for the troops.

He went on to describe, almost in the words of the old Arab geographer El Idrisi, the wealth of the place, the orange and lemon groves, the fields of sugar cane, the abundance of worked coral in the bazaars, the teeming fisheries. According to Azurara, while the others plied the prior with questions, Prince Henry stood thoughtful with his arms crossed on his chest. Maps were to be his whole life.

The secret had to be confided to the queen and to the constable. The queen approved of the expedition for the young princes. They had to win their spurs, but she begged the king to remember his age and his bad health. In his younger days, the chronicler quotes him as pleading, he had sullied his hands with much Christian blood, now he must do penance by washing them in the blood of the infidel.

The queen was so profoundly devout she could find no reply to that argument. Next Nun'Alvares, the king's closest councillor, must be consulted. For fear of setting tongues wagging by summoning the constable to court, a hunting trip was arranged in the Alentejo. The constable joined the king and his sons near Montemór. As soon as he heard of the plan he exclaimed that it was a direct inspiration from God. Next the conselhos and the Cortes had to be convened. Money had to be raised. The mint worked overtime coining currency. At a council in Tôrres Vedras, the plan was acclaimed with enthusiasm. Old warriors, white headed now, who had fought at Aljubarrota, crowded around to offer their services. "White heads to the front!" became a sort of war cry.

To make the task of organizing an army easier John divided up the government of the kingdom between his sons. Scholarly Dom Duarte was to deal with justice and home administration. Prince Henry was sent to Beira to levy troops, the Count of Barcelos to Viseu. Dom Pedro was put in charge of the region south of the Tagus. An emissary was sent to England where the recruiting of seven hundred and fifty lancers and certain other men-at-arms was authorized by Henry V. The king himself kept an eye on the shipyards where a new fleet was building in the seamen's suburb of Restelo outside of Lisbon.

The preparations took three years. Rumors of an immense Portuguese fleet preparing for war flew about the peninsula. Castile and Aragon and even the Moslem rulers of Granada sent ambassadors to inquire whither the expedition was bound. They were assured that no harm was meant to them. To throw all Europe off the scent a threatening mission was dispatched to the Duke of Holland demanding reparations for the despoiling of some Portuguese merchants by Dutch pirates. Meanwhile the northern levies were arriving in Lisbon from Oporto.

Along with the soldiery came the plague. The court which was summering in Sacavém hurriedly moved to the upland monastery of Odivelos which was considered healthier. Queen Philippa was already showing the fatal symptoms. As she lay on her deathbed she had three swords brought her which she had had made for her sons. The king was to use them in dubbing them knights after the conquest of Ceuta. Before she called for the sacraments she insisted that her death must not be allowed to delay the sailing of the fleet. According to Azurara, while she was in mortal agony, she pulled a golden reliquary from her breast which contained a splinter of the True Cross, broke it into four pieces, gave one to her husband and one to each of her sons. Then she closed her eyes and pulled the sheet up over her face. John stormed out of the chamber, roaring like a wounded bull.

Queen Philippa opened her eyes again and hearing the wind whistling in the roof tiles asked which way it was blowing. "From the north," she was told. "That will speed your journey," she whispered smiling to her sons. She received Communion, was sprinkled with the holy oils and gave up the ghost while the priests intoned the service for the dead.

She was buried that same night. The princes rode off to Restelo. The plague had appeared in the fleet. As if the death of the queen were not enough of an evil omen, it was followed by an eclipse of the sun. According to Azurara the king was ready to abdicate. It was Prince Henry who ordered an end to public mourning. He had the trumpets sounded. His ships raised their square banners, emblazoned with the red cross of the Knights of Christ, to the masthead, and the pennants with his motto: Talent de Bien Faire.

On June 23, 1415, the fleet of two hundred and forty sails put out to sea. There were twenty-seven galleys with three banks of oars, thirty-two with two banks of oars, and sixty-three supply ships of high freeboard. The rest were small vessels of all types. The king, all the royal princes and the constable were aboard. Rounding Cape St. Vincent they dipped their sails in honor of the sacred promontory. It was not until they were anchored in the ample bay of Lagos that the king let it be known that the destination was Ceuta. A papal bull was read bestowing on them the privileges and indulgences of a crusade.

First calms and then bad weather delayed them. After a slight skirmish on the western beaches of Ceuta, it was decided that the city could be more safely assaulted from the east. A gale sprang up and half the fleet made sail for Algeciras. The defenders decided that the attack had been abandoned. The king himself was undecided.

Another week was lost. The plague was taking its toll. It was late in August before King John finally got his courage up to risk a landing. The fleet slipped across the straits in the dark and anchored before Ceuta before dawn. The king, who had a game leg, was rowed through the fleet in a pinnace giving the orders.

Prince Henry's men were supposed to be the first to land, but some retainers of the Count of Barcelos managed to get ahead of them, causing bad blood between the half brothers.

After a short scuffle on the beach Prince Henry and his men broke down one of the gates. By the time the king, who came along painfully limping, and the constable, had walked up from the beach the Moorish defenders had fled and with them most of the city's population. The Genoese who had a trading post there had taken refuge in the castle. It was they who delivered it to Nun'Alvares. The Christians lost eight men killed.

The sack of the city began. Ceuta was the richest emporium in the western Mediterranean. The chroniclers described with distress the havoc wrought in the bazaar by the rude Portuguese bowmen from the back country who broke open jars of oil and honey and ripped up sacks of pepper and of expensive spices looking for gold.

The principal mosque was consecrated as a church. A *Te Deum* was sung, accompanied by all the trumpets in the army. There, in front of the improvised altar, the king knighted his three sons with the swords their mother had given them. Though Prince Henry was appointed governor of Ceuta with general supervision of the African trade, Pedro de Meneses was left in command of the defenses with a force of twenty-six-hundred men.

These bade their comrades a tearful goodbye when the fleet set sail, laden with spoil to the gunwales, on September 2. When the king first stepped on Portuguese soil at Tavira in the Algarve, he bestowed the title of duke upon two of his sons. Prince Henry, to whom he gave most of the credit for the success of the expedition, became Duke of Viseu. He was already Grand Master of the Order of Christ. Dom Pedro became Duke of Coimbra. Dom Duarte, the heir apparent, shy and retiring as always and distrustful of his own powers, demanded no further honors. The Count of Barcelos had to content himself with the six thousand marble and alabaster columns he was credited with having hacked out of the Moorish palaces of Ceuta.

The chronicler Azurara summed up the speed and success of the great achievement when he wrote of the Portuguese troops. "Many left the grain stored in their granaries and returned in time for the vintage."

3

TALENT DE BIEN FAIRE

The fame of Prince Henry of Portugal spread fast through Christendom. The taking of Ceuta aroused echoes of the doughty deeds of the early crusaders. Tales of the chastity, the sobriety, the devotion, the knightly virtues of the Master of the Order of Christ were told in every court. The pope suggested that he be put in charge of the forces of the Emperor Paleologos who was struggling with the Turks on the Bosphorus. His cousin, Henry V of England, who himself had just won a resounding victory over the French at Agincourt, offered him a command in an army he hoped to lead for the recapture of Jerusalem.

Prince Henry had other ideas. He took his African mission in dead earnest. Already he was collecting maps and portolanos and every traveler's tale that dealt with the African trade and the realm of Prester John, Christian ruler of the East, and the Asian lands where the spices came from. Azurara wrote: "His palace was a school of hospitality for all the good and highborn of the realm, and still more for strangers; and the fame of it caused a great increase in his expenses: for commonly there were to be seen in his presence men of various nations so different from our own, that it was a marvel to wellnigh all our people, and none of that great multitude could take his leave without some gift from the prince." As Duke of Viseu and Master of the Order of Christ he had large revenues at his disposition. Ships under his banner were already patrolling the straits to protect the Algarve from Moslem raiders.

The Prince seems to have been the first man to understand the strategic importance of Gibraltar. On the way to Ceuta he had begged for his father's permission to assault the Moorish forts on the Rock but that cautious ruler had considered the enterprise too risky.

In 1418 an energetic king of Granada known as Mohamet the Left-handed allied himself with the Wali of Fez to oust the Christians from Ceuta. According to an informant of Azurara's (who undoubtedly exaggerated the numbers) they raised an army of a hundred thousand men, well-furnished with siege engines and artillery. Pedro de Meneses sent home urgent pleas for help.

This Moslem counterattack came at a bad moment, because the troops of the royal princes were posted along the frontiers to ward off a threatened invasion from Castile. The king, again in bad health, had retired to his retreat at Sintra. Dom Henrique hurried south from Viseu and was put in command of a thousand men. He took along his younger brother Prince John. They sailed from the Algarve and reached Ceuta in three days. It was in the nick of time because the assault on the city had begun. At the sight of the Portuguese ships the Moors gave up the siege and retired. Prince Henry had another easy victory to his credit.

Sailing home he again made a try for Gibraltar, but as he was getting his troops ready for the assault a messenger came from his father forbidding any attempt on the Rock. The rules of the Order of Christ were chastity, poverty, obedience. With fury in his heart the prince obeyed his father's orders and trimmed his sails for Lagos.

Henry was now twenty-four. Azurara who knew him in later life describes him as being "of good height and stout frame, big and strong of limb, the hair of his head somewhat bristling, with a complexion naturally fair but which by constant toil and exposure had become dark. His expression at first sight inspired fear in those who did not know him and, when angry, which was not often, his countenance was harsh." It is remarkable how exactly this description corresponds with the portrait painted by Nuno Gonçalves. The chronicler went on to describe the prince's manner as being calm and dignified, his speech and address gentle. He spoke of his enthusiasm "for the labor of arms, especially against the enemies of the holy faith."

After the relief of Ceuta and the frustration of his hopes of being allowed to take Gibraltar Henry lost any taste he may have had for life at court. His older brother Pedro must have felt the same way. Still fuming from his disappointment at not having been allowed to join the second expedition to Ceuta, Pedro was planning to leave Portugal for his years of travel which were to become so legendary. Instead of traveling himself Prince Henry dedicated his life to promoting travel and exploration by his squires and henchmen.

He must have a headquarters of his own. He picked on a spot for a fortified village far out on Cape St. Vincent. First it was called Terecena or Terça Naval—a Portuguese corruption of the Venetian term Darsena Navale, but soon it became known simply as *Vila do Infante*, the prince's village.

The first plan was to make it a special mart for foreign merchants. The location was well chosen because it commanded a deep cove that formed a safe anchorage against every wind except the southerly. So strategic was the location that the Genoese were said to have offered a large sum of the money for a license to establish a trading post there: "and the Genoese," noted Azurara, "are known not to spend their money foolishly."

The prevailing winds in summer were from the north. The British still call them the Portuguese trades. The cove had from time immemorial been an anchorage for ships coasting out of the Mediterranean and bound for England and the channel ports. Sometimes ships had to wait weeks for the Portuguese trades to moderate enough to let them beat around Cape St. Vincent. The skippers would be at the mercy of whoever held the strong point on the hill. Prince Henry saw a chance to pump them dry of their sea lore in exchange for provisions and water.

"All ships that passed from the east to the west," wrote Azurara, who visited the place late in Prince Henry's life, "should be able to take their bearings there, and be furnished with provisions and pilots. There ships find shelter against every wind, except what we in this kingdom call a crosswind, and by the same token can sail out on every wind in whatever direction the seaman desires." A perfect base for expeditions down the African coast.

The place had other attractions. The prince was profoundly pious. Since prehistoric times Cape St. Vincent had been known as the Sacred Promontory. It is a vast arid outcropping of bare rock thrust miles out into the Atlantic. The surf thunders against the boulders hundreds of feet below the northern cliffs. There are strange blowholes where the sea spurts up hissing in fountains of spray with each oncoming wave. El Idrisi tells of a "church of the ravens" out on that cape where Christian priests watched over the relics of St. Vincent. So awesome was the place that they were tolerated by the Moslems. So rich were their revenues that no traveler, Moslem or Christian, was allowed to leave the shrine without partaking of a meal. A flock of ravens, which the Christians claimed had accompanied the bones of their saint from the place of his martyrdom at Zaragoza, continually perched on the ridge of the roof. After the reconquest the bones of St. Vincent were removed by the Portuguese and transported to Lisbon with great ceremony. He became that city's patron saint.

The awesomeness of the spot suited Prince Henry's austere religion. He had dedicated his life to two purposes: discovery of the lands and peoples of Africa and spreading the true faith among the infidel. His first care on establishing his naval arsenal was to build a chapel where his seamen could say their prayers before starting out on their voyages. As the years went on he became more and more ascetic in his personal life. According to Azurara, though he had drunk a little wine as a youth, he gave it up completely by the time he was a man grown. He had no interest in personal comforts or possessions. Though it would have been easy to get the pope's release, as his father had, from his vow of celibacy, he was determined never to marry. He scrupulously observed the fasts of the church. His chronicler wrote that he fasted half the days of the year. Often he wore a horsehair shirt under his clothes. It was not for nothing that the name by which his settlement was finally called was Sagres, which is a Portuguese corruption of the Latin *sacrum*, which meant holy or tabooed.

Along with the knightly devotion of a Don Quijote, went a flair for commerce, a shrewd instinct for the management of men and a passionate desire for knowledge for its own sake. Sagres, as well as having an aura of holiness about it, was a perfect place to observe the stars. Fog was rare. The nights were dry and crisp. Though no one at his time had completely put away astrology, his chief interest in the stars was as guides to navigation. From the beginning he collected maps and subsidized mapmakers. He kept up with the improvements on the Genoese compass and helped develop a new type of vessel which made Atlantic exploration possible.

In the early years of the fifteenth century the caravel, a stout-decked round-bottomed vessel with a high poop and lateen sails, began to come into its own. The Portuguese ports and the ports at the mouths of the Guadiana and Guadalquivir, of which the chief one was Palos, under Castilian hegemony since the ousting of the Moors from Seville, had for the past two hundred years been centers of shipbuilding and seamanship. Their first development was the oversize galley which evolved from Genoese prototypes. Portuguese triremes with three hundred rowers were the admiration of Europe during the Hundred Years' War. On account of the immense amount of food and water that had to be carried galleys were impractical for navigating the open ocean.

A type of sailing ship capable of breasting the Atlantic rollers took form slowly. The dragonships of the Vikings may have influenced the design of a type of Moorish fishingboat called a *carib* or *carabo*. The word caravel is used in the commercial legislation of Afonso III in the middle thirteenth century but the ship had certainly not attained the design and rigging for which it later became famous. The popular vessel for coasting work was then the *nao*, a broad-beamed cargo ship with a square sail. The *barcha* and the *barinel*, which are mentioned in the records of the early fourteenth century, were partially decked little ships stout enough to withstand heavy Atlantic seas. Some of them may have used the lateen rig of the Venetian carracks in the eastern Mediterranean. What made the caravel of the fifteenth century an achievement in the history of navigation was a combination of the sailing qualities of the lateen rig with improved modeling of the hull. The caravels could sail close-hauled into the wind. With the wind on the quarter or aft they could develop speeds of from six to ten knots. Their chief inconvenience was that they were hard to tack and that it took a large crew to handle the immense boom which was hoisted to the masthead. At that they needed about a tenth of the men needed to propel a galley.

The first recorded voyage of the classical caravel was Nuno Tristão's journey down the African coast in 1441, but it is hard to believe that the type was not developing among the vessels anchored in the deep cove at Sagres when Prince Henry first established his naval arsenal there.

According to Azurara—and to John de Barros who some years later compiled the history of the Portuguese explorations out of a number of different chronicles in his *Asia*—the first voyage out of Sagres to bear fruit was launched soon after Prince Henry's second return from Ceuta. His frustration at Gibraltar seems to have thrown him into a deep depression. He woke from it suddenly one morning with a resolution fully formed: someone must be found bold enough to sail down the African coast and round Cape Bojador.

Barros wrote that he had already been sending two or three ships a year to the vicinity of Cabo Não, a desolate spot on the coast of the Sahara which was a good three hundred miles southwest of Safi, the port of the caravan routes which for centuries had been frequented by the Genoese and by ships from Lisbon and Palos and Barcelona and Mallorca. Não, as its name implied, had up to now been the point beyond which seamen dared not venture. They had put their fears into a jingle:

> If you round Cape No
> You may return or no.

Somehow, on some unrecorded voyage, Prince Henry had coaxed his seafarers into rounding Cabo Não. Always in his mind was the passage in the younger Seneca's *Questionum Naturalium*, which epitomized the conjectures of the Romans about a sea route to India. "How far is it from the furthest shores of Spain to India? A very few days if the ship has a fair wind." Whether Seneca's imaginary ship was to sail west across the Atlantic or south around the stubby continent of Africa shown in the ancient maps was the problem that had to be resolved. Vivaldi's ships had gone south and never returned. A Catalan shipmaster named Jaime Ferrer was supposed to have sailed out of Barcelona for the River of Gold in 1346, but had not been heard of again. Better seamen might succeed where these had failed. Cape by cape the prince was bent on exploring the African coast until it turned east toward India. Não had been tamed. The next cape was Bojador. Who would tempt the fates round Bojador?

Two young men among the prince's retainers responded instantly. They were John Gonçalves, nicknamed Zarco for his blue eyes, whom he had ennobled for hard fighting at Ceuta, and Tristão Vaz Teixeira. Barros's account gives the impression that the vessel they sailed was an open barcha. After setting their course for Cabo Não they were caught in a storm out of the southeast and had to run before it out to sea. "The ship was so small and the seas so great they were about to swallow them as they ran under bare poles at the will of the wind."

They found safe harbor in an island. There were no inhabitants, no wild beasts, the place was well watered and had fertile air. They sailed back to tell their story to the prince.

Prince Henry seems to have already heard from a Spaniard recently ransomed out of Moorish captivity whom he picked up at Ceuta, the story which an English fellow captive had told the Spaniard of an English ship wrecked many years back on a magnificent island in the same vicinity. All the maps of the period showed islands, variously named and placed, out in the open Atlantic. The following year he sent Zarco and Teixeira back with a group of husbandmen and the equipment needed to establish a settlement on this island which they named Pôrto Santo. With them went a gentleman of young Prince John's household named Bartolomeu Perestrello, whose father had emigrated to Portugal from Piacenza. Perestrello brought along a pregnant doe-rabbit in a cage. All on board considered it a good omen when she produced a litter at sea. As soon as they landed they put the rabbits ashore. Perestrello went back with the ship, which they loaded with the gum of a fruit tree which produced a dye much esteemed at the time under the name of "dragon's blood," but Zarco and Vaz stayed to colonize the island.

Everything was fine on Pôrto Santo except for the rabbits. They bred so fast that they ate up the settlers' crops. A couple of years later Zarco and Teixeira determined to explore further.

They had been perplexed by a perpetual cloud that hung over the horizon to the southwest. Some of the settlers decided it must be the limits of the overcast which was supposed to hang eternally over the ocean of darkness. Brushing their fears aside they set out in a couple of stout boats they had built out of the excellent timber they found on the island. As they proceeded the mist became dense fog. Ahead they heard breakers which the rowers feared were the legendary boiling seas where no ship could live. They were about to turn back when they broke out of the mist into a sunny blue bay backed by a great green mountain crowned with cloud.

Again they found no inhabitants, no wild beasts, only trackless forests or enormous trees. They called the island Madeira which means wood. When the news of their discovery reached Prince Henry he divided the governorship of the island between Zarco and Teixeira. He sent Perestrello back to Pôrto Santo with a load of cattle to take over the management there.

After Iceland and Greenland Madeira was the first Atlantic island to be colonized by Europeans in historic times. The soil proved unbelievably fertile. The climate was perpetual spring. Every crop flourished there. Wheat yielded sixtyfold. Cattle thrived. Prince Henry sent vines he procured from Sicily and sugar cane. Within twenty-five years four towns had been established on the island with a population of some eight hundred, "of whom a hundred rode their own horses." The settlers prospered mightily from the sugar, hides, honey and beeswax, cedarwood and yew they shipped to the mainland.

The prince, when his brother Dom Duarte came to the throne, was invested with the sovereignty of the three islands. The tiny group called the Desertas, though hardly inhabited, were kept stocked with cattle. The fifth of the produce of Madeira, which was his share, helped mightily in financing expeditions to the southward. The ecclesiastical revenues went to the Order of Christ. Madeira became an essential way station and outfitting port for expeditions to the southward during the next thirty-five years.

So encouraged was Prince Henry by the successful colonization of the Madeira group that in 1424 he got ready an expedition to occupy the Canaries. The moment seemed propitious because the

93

French admiral Jean de Bethencourt had given up his settlement there and sold his rights of discovery, which the Portuguese claimed to be antedated by their own, to the Niebla family that formed a powerful seafaring clan situated along the banks of the Guadiana under the rule of Castile.

Occupation of the Canaries was being made difficult by the resistance of a Stone-Age people known as Guanchos, whose origins are still veiled in mystery. The Guanchos lived in caves on the larger islands. Their only arms were clubs and stones. The prince had boundless confidence in the ability of his Portuguese to beat down any heathen opponents, no matter how numerous. His idea was that, in the dispute over prior discovery, which would eventually have to be settled by the pope, possession would prove nine parts of the law. The chronicles are vague as to whether his ships actually occupied any of the islands, but it is certain that cautious old John I, fearing trouble with Castile, discouraged the project and that it had to be abandoned.

To compensate for this bitter reverse more islands fell under the prince's rule. One of his navigators, Gonçalo Velho, whom he sent to search for a hypothetical island to the northwest marked on a map he had procured from Catalonia, discovered Santa Maria in the Azores. Again the prince sent out a shipload of cattle. From Santa Maria, São Miguel was sighted and then Terceira, "the third," and so on until all the Azores were accounted for. In a little more than a decade the murk and the mystery that had barred the way of Portuguese seamen into the Ocean of Darkness was pushed far beyond the horizon.

4

DOM PEDRO'S TRAVELS

Pedro and Henry seem to have been the most congenial of the five brothers. They differed greatly in appearance. Where Henry took after his swarthy father, Pedro, lanky, blond and blue-eyed, had, according to Azurara, "a reddish beard like an Englishman's." He favored his grandfather, John of Gaunt. They shared with their brothers a burning ambition to distinguish themselves in the world, but they developed between the two of them a particular cult of Portuguese expansion.

Inland they figured, as their father had, that the country was hemmed in by the growing power of Castile to the east and the north. The outlet for Portuguese energies was overseas. Ceuta had proved a disappointment as a trading port. As soon as the city fell into the hands of the Christians the Moslem caravans ceased to frequent it. Strategically it was a boon but economically it was a drain on the resources of the kingdom. Pedro and Henry wanted to find new trade routes which might funnel the traffic in spices and oriental goods into the Portuguese ports. Henry was particularly interested in the caravan trade across the Sahara. The chief aim of Henry's exploration of the African coast was to find the source of the gold brought in by Moorish merchants. Then there was the enigma of Prester John. As eager Christians they yearned to discover whether there really was a powerful Christian ruler in the east whose aid could be sought against the conquering Turks.

Turkish armies had already besieged Constantinople. They were ravaging the Danube Valley. Christian power was crumbling in the eastern Mediterranean. All Christendom was in danger. How could the infidel flood be stemmed? These were the questions which, each in his different way, Pedro and Henry were setting out to answer.

In the division of powers by which John of Avis distributed the cares of office among the sons, Henry had charge of the exploration of Africa and the Atlantic islands; Duarte administered the kingdom, and Pedro conducted Portugal's relations with the European courts.

Even before the relief of Ceuta Pedro's fame as a man of learning, a warrior and a Christian prince had brought him to the attention of Sigismund of Luxembourg. Sigismund, an ambitious German prince who had gotten himself elected King of the Romans, was awaiting the appearance of a pope he considered worthy of crowning him Emperor. Meanwhile he was devoting his life to the elimination of the unholy schism which bid fair to ruin the Christian church. Under his management the Council of Constance had deposed the anti-pope at Avignon, caused the abdication of another pope at Rome, burned John Huss at the stake as a heretic, and finally brought about the election of Martin V of the powerful Roman Colonna family as sole spiritual lord of all Christendom. The Christian courts considered the emperor-elect the hero of the Council of Constance.

With the church reunited Sigismund's first duty was to protect Europe against the advancing Turks. He was in the front line of defense, since by marriage with the sore-beset queen he had become King of Hungary. With his brother Wenceslaus on the point of death Sigismund was about to inherit another troubled kingdom. In Bohemia the followers of John Huss, outraged at what they considered the murder of their leader, who had traveled to Constance under the Emperor Sigismund's own safe-conduct, were organizing a first rate army and taking over the country. The prospect of war on two fronts would tax the imperial resources to the limit. Sigismund was in sore need of glamorous crusading leaders to captain his armies.

The Portuguese ambassadors to the church council were also attached to Sigismund's court at Constance. At that moment the chief of them were Alvaro Gonçalves de Ataíde, the head of Dom Pedro's ducal household, and Fernando de Castro, who had succeeded another Ataíde, killed saving his young master's life during the assault on Ceuta, as Prince Henry's chief executive. It was undoubtedly after consultation with these direct representatives of the Portuguese princes that early in January 1418 the emperor named Pedro of Portugal as Markgraf of Treviso. Sigismund had attempted rather unsuccessfully to detach the Treviso region from its Venetian overlords a few years before in his capacity as King of Hungary.

This appointment, though it was highly complimentary and may have entailed a certain revenue, could hardly have brought much joy to the Portuguese diplomats. John I made a point of remaining on good terms with the Venetians who had a much better claim to Treviso than did the King of Hungary, and the whole foreign policy of the House of Avis was based on discouraging wars between Christian governments. The only action Pedro took to secure his rights in Treviso was to appoint Alvaro de Ataíde as his deputy.

The more attractive side of the overtures of the Emperor Sigismund was the opportunity offered Pedro to take part in the war against the Turks. Philippa of Lancaster had brought up her boys in the belief that a Christian's first duty was to drive back the infidel. Possibly because he knew that Sigismund had signed a truce with the Turks, Pedro was in no hurry to start on his crusade. While he let it be known that he was planning a pilgrimage to the Holy Sepulcher he busied himself with the composition of a philosophical treatise based on Seneca's *De Beneficiis* and with the construction of a memorial chapel to his mother in the monastery of Odivelas. His last extant letter written in Portugal, dated Lisbon in June of 1425 deals with this chapel.

Several prominent Portuguese had traveled on Venetian galleys to the holy places while Pedro was growing up. His half brother the Count of Barcelos was grandly entertained by the Venetians on his journey in 1406. He was said to have brought "a pagan" home with him when he returned two years later. A bishop of Lisbon visited Jerusalem. After the close of the Council of Constance Alvaro de Ataíde himself made the pilgrimage. Plans for reconquering the holy places, and particularly for alliances with Christian leaders in the east, were common talk at the court of John I. Before Dom Pedro could deem himself worthy of this pilgrimage he must perform some knightly deeds against the Turks.

During these years the court officials were exercised over the problem of royal marriages. The sons of John and Philippa were reaching their thirties and none of them had yet found a suitable wife. As early as 1417 Pedro had empowered Alvaro de Ataíde to enter into negotiations for his marriage to the daughter of some foreign prince. The first to marry, suprisingly enough, was the youngest. In 1424 by special dispensation Prince John married his niece Isabel, daughter of his half brother the Count of Barcelos.

In the late summer of the following year Dom Pedro finally set out on his travels. His father had arranged for him to finance his expedition from the interest on twenty thousand gold florins he had invested with the Medici bankers in Florence.

Like his half brother twenty years before, Pedro seems to have sailed directly to England. In the fall of 1425 various chronicles report him in London helping patch up a quarrel between the Duke of Gloucester, who governed England during the minority of Henry VI, and his uncle Henry Beaufort, John of Gaunt's son by Katherine Swineford, who was then Bishop of Winchester. According to one chronicler, the Duke of "Quymber" and the Archbishop of Canterbury rode eight times between the warring factions before they could induce them to put away their weapons. So successful was the Portuguese prince in averting bloodshed in the streets of London that two years later he was awarded the Order of the Garter.

That Christmas he was entertained by the municipality of Bruges. The public account books report the purchase of "24 cruchons, tout en amer," for a *vin d'honneur* in the prince's honor. Bruges was then the chief trade mart of the Hanseatic league, and the banking center in Western Europe for the Florentine Medicis. Pedro struck up a warm friendship with the Duke of Burgundy, and arranged the duke's marriage with his young sister Isabel. He spent much of the winter of 1426 at the Burgundian court. In the course of it he wrote a long letter to his brother, Dom

Duarte, who was ruling Portugal in their father's name, advising him on various phases of good government from the education of the clergy and the division of the university into colleges, as at Oxford and the Sorbonne, to the raising of horses and the discouragement of idlers around the court.

In February of that year Pedro traveled up the Rhine and attended a wedding in Cologne. He and his retinue worshiped at the shrine of the Three Kings in the cathedral. The three kings from the east who brought gifts to the infant Jesus at Bethlehem were the starting point of the legends of St. Thomas's Christians and Prester John. It was they who had converted the Hindus to Christianity. The story told was that the Empress Helena of Byzantium brought their bodies back from India. She entombed them in Santa Sophia where they remained until a Byzantine ruler presented them to a bishop of Milan. A Holy Roman emperor took advantage of a rebellion of the Milanese to have them brought to Cologne. Their cult was celebrated by a popular devotional work by John of Hildesheim, which the Portuguese princes could hardly have escaped reading, that described the conversion of the Eastern Christians, and the establishment of the rule of Prester John. It became the habit of traveling Portuguese to pay particular devotion to the Three Kings.

Pedro passed through Nuremberg in early March. By the middle of the month he had made his way as far east as Ratisbon on the Danube. A chronicler there is quoted as noting: "It was said that the afore-mentioned Pedro, son of the King of Portugal, had killed a certain soldier. His father wished to punish him. Due to the intercession of the nobles, however, he was freed and required, as a punishment, to travel through foreign lands for three years, at the end of which he might return to his native land."

On Holy Thursday, which fell on March 28 that year, the Portuguese prince arrived in Vienna with a suite of three hundred men-at-arms. The local chronicler reported that he knew no German but spoke Latin well. He was put up at an inn and a ball was given in his honor.

Soon after he joined the forces of the Emperor Sigismund in the Danube Valley. He probably reached the imperial camp at about the same time as news of the defeat of the emperor's vassal, Dan, Veovod of Walachia, and of the destruction of his army by the Turks. By winter the imperial headquarters was established in a castle in the mountains of what is now Rumania. That winter Pedro is supposed to have led an expedition eastward to raid Turkish territory south of the Danube. For a man brought up in the mild climate of Portugal a winter campaign in the snowy mountains of what was known to the Portuguese as Russia (Roxia) and crossing the Danube on the ice must have been severe indeed. The Italian biographer of the Condottiere Pippo Spano, in describing the fight with the Turks at a ford of the Danube where his hero met his death during the same campaign, refers to a son of the king of Portugal among Spano's battalions, who "had come from the furthest parts of the world with eight hundred men-at-arms all clothed in white, each with a red cross on his arms, almost all of whom were killed."

However it happened it is certain that by the end of the year 1427 the Turks had occupied all of Walachia and that Sigismund and his queen were retreating to their castles in Hungary.

Whether it is due to discouragement with the war against the Turks, or a disinclination to join in Sigismund's forthcoming campaign against his Hussite subjects in Bohemia; or perhaps on account of the news that reached him on the Danube of his brother Duarte's imminent marriage with an Aragonese princess, in the spring of 1428 Dom Pedro took leave of the Emperor Sigismund and led his surviving retainers through the Mark of Treviso to Venice.

Francesco Foscari, who was then doge, was informed by his ambassador to the Hungarian court of the time of the arrival of the Portuguese prince and decided to entertain him in the high style of the Venetian republic. The chroniclers speak of Pedro's being accompanied by three hundred horsemen. Emissaries met him at the Venetian border and he was received by the doge aboard the famous state galley, Bucintor. After two weeks visiting San Marco, San Giorgio, Murano—the sights of Venice were much the same then as they are now—he was accompanied on the road to Florence by a splendid cavalcade. Among the gifts he carried away was a jewel estimated at upward of four hundred gold ducats, a manuscript of Marco Polo's travels—probably the same manuscript which turned up in the inventory of King Duarte's library after his death—and one of the latest world maps by some Venetian cartographer.

In Florence Pedro was greeted so royally that his entertainment cost the city more than two thousand florins. He was put up at the Albergo de la Corona and later at the palazzo of his father's banker. A joust was held in his honor where the prize was carried off by one of his own suite. Literary works were dedicated to him. Since the Portuguese diplomats had as close relations with the literati of the city as with the bankers the Portuguese prince was made much of by the humanists. A historian of the time described him as "a very well brought up and valorous knight, the most charming, the best looking that ever sallied forth from the Spanish countries."

In May Pedro was in Rome. His audience with Pope Martin V was noted in a bull issued by that worthy on May 18 authorizing the heir apparent of Portugal to wear the royal crown when associated in the government by his father and extending to the Portuguese royal family the same privileges in the use of the holy oils which had been extended to the French and English kings. On June 16 Pedro drew on his bankers at Pisa for his expenses and somewhere around the end of the month sailed for Barcelona. There he was well received by the Catalan nobility. Barcelona and the Balearic Islands were the center of the cartography of the period. Pedro can hardly have gone through without collecting what portolanos and sailing charts he could for his brother Henry.

In late July he was entertained in Valencia by the "magnanimous" Alfonso V of Aragon. There were bullfights, banquets and fireworks. On the feast of Saint James bulls were baited all day in the market square. Again on August 1 a fiesta was held in the Mercat. The square was decorated with white and crimson canvas and plays were performed on specially constructed stages known as *castillos*. There was method in all this mad expenditure by Alfonso, for which he was forced to borrow twenty thousand gold florins from the City Council. Alfonso had already arranged the marriage of his daughter Leonor to the heir apparent of Portugal. He had hopes of marrying Pedro who was next in line to the succession, to another Aragonese princess. The two Hispanic maritime kingdoms shared the need to keep the haughty Castilians in their place. The very next day Dom Pedro entrusted to two of his squires the task of discussing the matter of his marriage to a noble lady whose name was not specified.

A further topic of Pedro's conversations with his royal host must have been the visit to Barcelona in the preceding year of a delegation from the Christian kingdom of Abyssinia. In the early fifteenth century, the tale of the Eastern Christians was beginning to turn from myth into reality.

From Aragon Dom Pedro and his suite followed the deep valley of the Douro to Aranda. A cavalcade of Castilian grandees including Alvaro de Luna, the constable of the kingdom with whom Pedro established a warm friendship, and the *adelantado* Pedro Manrique, whose death was to be celebrated by his son in the greatest elegy in the Castilian tongue, rode out a half a league to meet them, and even King Juan II advanced "a distance of one or two crossbow shots" from his lodging to do him honor. For five days the King of Castile entertained Dom Pedro at every meal. On his departure for Penafiel the king and his royal officials presented him with jewels, a pair of mules, four horses and letters of transit for the castles and towns through which he would have to pass.

September 1 he was in Valladolid. It was in a castle near Valladolid that the Count of Urgel, the defeated pretender to the throne of Aragon, was kept in perpetual prison by the Castilians by arrangement with the Aragonese. Actually his imprisonment was a sort of house arrest. He was surrounded by a large court and at liberty to receive whomever he wished. It is not known whether Dom Pedro rode out to see him from Valladolid, but that same day he announced his intention of marrying the count's daughter Isabel. He was marrying an Aragonese princess like his brother, but a princess of the losing faction. Bitterness between the two women was to go far toward destroying the family unity of the House of Avis in the years to come. Riding hard Pedro arrived in Coimbra in time to attend his brother's wedding with Dona Leonor.

Dom Pedro's travels became so legendary that historians have been trying to untangle fact from fiction ever since. The chief source of confusion was a popular work in Castilian published about ninety years later by a German printer in Seville. Printing had spread fast over Europe from Guttenberg during the fifteenth century. Reading, from being a monopoly of the courts and monasteries, became a common accomplishment. One of the first commercial successes in the popular literature that immediately burgeoned was a volume called *The Travels of Sir John Mandeville* published in Dutch in the Low Countries. To reach this same market Jacob Cromburger brought out a book called *El Libro del Infante Don Pedro de Portugal*, supposedly written from the recollections of one of the prince's companions.

The volume purported to be an account of Dom Pedro's travels to the Holy Land and to the seven parts of the world. It was translated into Portuguese with corrections that gave it more verisimilitude and went through hundreds of editions. In the earliest Spanish text Pedro's journey is confused with the actual pilgrimage of his elder half brother the Count of Barcelos. Pedro and his twelve companions are described as starting their journey from the town of Barcelos. His actual visit to Valladolid appears at the beginning instead of at the end of his journeyings. The prince and his retainers are credited with visiting Troy and Jerusalem and Babylonia and even with riding on dromedaries as far east as the court of Tamberlaine. Facts reported by actual travelers are ingeniously intermingled with all the tall tales of the day. After endless adventures the pilgrims reach the city of Luca, "where the giants are located," and are conducted to the court of Prester John. Everywhere they are introduced as vassals of "the Lion King of Hispania." The volume ends with a rehash of the famous bogus letter of Prester John to the peoples of the West which had been circulated in various forms throughout the Middle Ages.

The narrative has the devotional flavor popular at the time: "And as Prester John saw that we wished to take leave of him and his lands, he sighed and spoke thus: 'What a favor God our Lord would do us if we had our brother the Lion King of Hispania near to us, so that the power of the enemies of Jesus Christ might be diminished, for we are at all times much belabored by these cruel peoples. But tell my beloved brother the Lion King of Hispania to endeavor as a good man with the grace

of God, to maintain Truth and Justice in his realms and to act
in such a way that God may be served, and that we may all
appear without shame face to face with Jesus Christ on the very
formidable Judgment Day. Now go with the blessing of Jesus
Christ: and may he see fit to keep you, body and soul, from
the perils of this world.'"

Pedro and his twelve companions make their way to the Red
Sea where they find three hundred pillars set up on the shore
to represent each tribe and family of the Jews who crossed it
in their flight from Pharaoh, and thence journey through the
kingdom of Fez back to Castile. The story was reprinted with
a number of variations. A final echo appeared in Guillaume Apol-
linaire's haunting verses written in the early nineteen hundreds
which Poulenc set so liltingly to music:

> *Avec ses quatre dromadaires*
> *Dom Pedro d'Alfaroubeira*
>
> *Courut de monde et l'admira.*
> *Il fit ce que je voudrais faire*
> *Si j'avais quatre dromadaires.*

Dom Pedro married Isabel of Urgel early in 1429. The same
year Isabel of Portugal married Philip Duke of Burgundy who
was the most flamboyant ruler in Europe. The Portuguese royal
family was now allied to the most powerful kingdoms in the
Western world. Its ties to the Lancastrians in England were
cemented by a number of appointments of high-ranking Portuguese
as Knights and Ladies of the Garter. By Duarte's and Pedro's
marriages they were linked to both branches of the House of
Aragon, which was just on the point of extending its rule to
the two Sicilies. Peace with Castile seemed assured by Dom Pedro's
personal friendship with Alvaro de Luna, who, though Juan II
was king in name, was the real ruler of that kingdom. France,
in a state of chaos from which she was only to be rescued by
the appearance of Joan of Arc, hardly needed to be considered
at the moment.

Pedro's Isabel promptly bore him a son who was named for
his father. So far Duarte's marriage had borne no fruit. Throughout his travels Pedro had been received with the splendor due to
an heir to the throne. He can hardly have avoided feeling that

the high position of his tiny country was due in part at least to his knightly fame. His brother Duarte was a retiring man, ailing and neurasthenic. In his youth his doctors had remonstrated with him for carrying chastity to the extreme. Hardly a man to father children. Pedro and Isabel had reason to look forward to inheriting the throne after his death. Pedro was a man of vigorous passions. As a boy he had chosen the word "Désir" for his motto. All his desire was dashed when Leonor and Duarte produced a son, to everyone's surprise, and the following year another.

Portuguese life was changing. Though the merchants and artisans of the cities were prosperous the nobles on their great estates were regaining their political power. The generation of the victors of Aljubarrota was passing away leaving behind them a thriving seafaring kingdom and a wealth of gothic architecture.

The constable, Nun'Alvares, having devoted the latter part of his life and most of his revenues to building the Convento do Carmo in Lisbon, renounced all his titles, distributed his possessions and entered the monastery he had endowed as Frei Nuno de Santa Maria. Prince John became constable in his stead. Frei Nuno died eight years later in 1431, leaving behind him a memory of such sanctity that he was beatified by the church.

John of Avis only survived his bosom friend and companion at arms by two years. According to Rui de Pina, when the king was stricken with his fatal illness at Alcochete, a little country seat on the Tagus, he insisted on being carried to Lisbon so that he might die "as befitted a king," in the royal splendor of his Alcaçovas palace.

The chroniclers loved to linger over the details of a royal demise. On reaching Lisbon they have him insisting on being first carried to the cathedral in his litter and left to pray before the tomb of Saint Vincent. Work on the capela major was still in progress. He gave orders for money to be brought immediately to finish that chapel. Then he had himself taken to the church of Santa Maria da Escada which he had just ordered built. Having satisfied himself that construction was progressing he allowed himself to be laid on his bed in the castle. He called for a barber to shave him, took the last sacraments and died. He had reigned more than half a century. He died at the age of seventy-seven on his birthday which was also the anniversary of the battle of Aljubarrota.

Four of his sons were at his deathbed. Of the other two, Dom Pedro was on his way from Coimbra and the Count of Barcelos was on his lands in the north. The dead king's body was placed in a tightly sealed lead coffin and carried that night to the cathedral. The poles on which the coffin were slung were shouldered by Prince Duarte, Prince Henry, Prince John and Prince Fernando, all in black sackcloth, followed by all the nobles of the land carrying torches in solemn procession. Masses were sung for many days. Then the coffin was transported to Batalha and laid beside that of Philippa of Lancaster in the tomb which had been prepared for them in the royal mortuary.

Duarte was crowned king next morning by the bishop of Evora. His Jewish physician, Mestre Guedella, who was a notable astrologer, begged him to put off the ceremony until afternoon, because the stars would be more propitious then, but Duarte told him that God was more powerful than the stars. He received the unction with extraordinary humility and refused to let the bishop kiss his hand. When Pedro arrived from Coimbra the brothers all swore allegiance to the baby Afonso as King Duarte's heir.

5

BEYOND BOJADOR

Prince Henry's eyrie at Sagres was a simple oblong of defensive walls enclosing a few plain stone buildings. Recent excavations have uncovered a "rose of the winds" built into the paving of the courtyard. The tiny settlement perched over the Atlantic on the extreme southwest corner of the European continent became a hive of energies during the reign of Dom Duarte. The accounts which Dom Pedro brought back from his wanderings, certainly far different from the farrago of nonsense later published under the name of his retainer, surely added a great deal to his brother's geographical knowledge. Marco Polo's travels, which King Duarte himself is said to have translated, sketched out many details of the shape of the world and of the trade routes beyond the eastern confines of the Mediterranean. To add to the maps Pedro brought home, Prince Henry was accumulating all the sailing charts and mathematical treatises he could beg borrow or buy in Barcelona and Genoa. He did everything in his power to stock his household with skilled seafarers and astronomers. Many of his astronomers were Jewish physicians. The Mestre Jacome who worked for him as a cartographer, whom he attracted from Majorca to Sagres by the offer of an immense salary, according to the chroniclers, was supposed to be the son of the Abraham Cresques who made the famous Catalan world map of 1375.

Cape Bojador was still unconquered. Prince Henry's forbearance with his skippers when they came back with one excuse or another for not having pushed beyond it became proverbial. At last, the year after his father's death, he sent off his squire Gil Eannes, who had failed in his last attempt to accomplish anything better than a routine visit to some of the Canary Islands, to try again.

Azurara reports a conversation with Eannes when the prince tried to laugh him out of his fears of what might lie beyond the cape. "There is no peril so great," he told him, "that the hope of reward will not be greater." He made light of stories brought back by some sea captains whom he said had no other experience then the established courses of the Flanders trade, and knew nothing of the improved compass and modern sailing charts. "If the dangers you fear were based on any substantial evidence I wouldn't blame you. . . . Go along and pay no attention to old wives' tales."

Gil Eannes gritted his teeth and jollied his crew along by telling them of the immense rewards the prince had waiting for them if they doubled the cape. They found fair winds and sailed past "the bulging cape" without mishap. They landed on an uninhabited desert shore some leagues beyond. To prove that he had landed, Eannes brought back in a barrel a plant his men had dug up on the shore. It was a succulent known in Portugal as the rose of Santa Maria. Prince Henry was delighted. The conquest of Bojador was hailed with thanksgiving throughout the kingdom. According to Barros it was to celebrate that achievement that King Duarte invested his brother with the sovereignty of the Madeira Islands.

Henry immediately sent off his personal cupbearer, Afonso Gonçalves Baldaya, on a swift barinel, with Gil Eannes in his own barcha to lead the way, to see how much further south they could go. They reached a bay they called *Angra dos Ruivos* from a great catch of red mullet they made there. On the sandy shore they found footprints of men and camels. The barinel made all possible speed home to bring this report to the prince. He was convinced that they must have reached the borders of inhabited country beyond the Sahara.

The next spring he sent Baldaya off again. Baldaya sailed some seventy leagues further and found himself in an inlet which he thought was the mouth of a river. He had brought along two noble youths of seventeen with their horses, to act as scouts.

So that the horses wouldn't be weighed down in the great heat Baldaya made the boys leave their defensive armor behind. They only carried lances and swords. After riding some leagues inland they fell in with a group of nineteen men armed with assagais. They fought them until sundown with no harm to themselves except that one lad was wounded in the foot. The natives took shelter behind some rocks. As there was no way of getting at them the Portuguese rode off. It was dawn before they found the ship.

The same day Baldaya took the ship's boat and rowed up the inlet to the scene of the fight. The natives had run away, leaving behind them "only a few poor belongings." These the Portuguese took aboard to show to Prince Henry.

Sailing out of the inlet they came upon a great herd of seals on a rock in its mouth. They killed many seals and skinned them for their fur. The carcasses they tried out for oil. The manufacture of soap was one of Prince Henry's perquisites: seal oil and whale oil were in great demand at Sagres.

On that trip they pushed fifty leagues further before turning homeward. Their farthest point south was a river, which later came to be known as the Rio do Ouro. The landmark was an outcropping of rock in the shape of a galley. There they found a net made from unfamiliar palm fiber. The only booty they brought back was this net and a few barrels of seal oil, a slender return for the great sums of money the prince laid out in outfitting his ships.

For the next few years exploration was suspended except for an occasional voyage by fishermen after sealskins and oil. Henry's every effort and all the resources of his naval arsenal were concentrated on an attempt on Tangier.

The Portuguese Algarve was the Prince's bailiwick. Across the straits was another Algarve, for the Moors also gave that name to the northwest corner of Africa. For years he had been planning an expedition to open up the hinterland behind Ceuta and to take over the trading towns of the Moroccan coast, but always he had been held back by his aging father's caution. Now his scholarly brother Duarte, diligent in the writing of laws and in public administration, but somewhat irresolute in action, was king. Duarte could be convinced. The success at Ceuta must be repeated.

In talking up an expedition against Tangier Henry was supported by his youngest brother Fernando who was now Master of the Order of Avis. After a sickly youth Fernando had grown up a deeply religious monastic sort of man. He was burning to perform a feat of arms against the infidel and threatened, unless some worthy task were found for him, to leave the kingdom and offer his sword to a foreign prince. Fernando spoke for all the restless young bloods in the realm. Peace with Castile had left them unemployed without hope of military glory or the accompanying loot which was the chief source of income of the Hispanic nobility.

Duarte, whose studious habits had left him little time for women before his marriage, was slavishly devoted to his wife Leonor of Aragon. Henry got her on his side by promising to adopt her second son, Fernando. Since he would never marry, the boy would inherit vast estates. Between them they induced King Duarte to give his consent to the expedition and to dispatch an ambassador to Rome to obtain a bull authorizing the crusade.

The matter was made urgent by a gradual worsening of relations with Castile. The long dispute as to whether the Castilians or the Portuguese had a prior right to the Canaries, which Henry had tried to settle by buying the claims of several Castilian grantees, was still unresolved. Now the Castilian kings, as heirs of the Visigothic empire, were beginning to lay claim to Ceuta and to the whole Moorish Algarve and to threaten a descent of their own on the Moroccan ports.

A royal council was called. Prince Pedro and Prince John, who now had authority to military matters as constable thought the plan too risky. The Count of Barcelos concurred with their opposition. Their argument was that the population of Portugal was too small to support further conquests and that the people's energies had better be turned to developing the uncultivated lands in their own country. King Duarte overruled his brothers and called a Cortes which backed him only halfheartedly. Somehow troops were levied and funds raised. The royal mint was put to work. The shipyards and the armorers' shops started to hum.

When Prince Henry's contingent sailed out of Lisbon, after setting the king and his court up to a banquet on his flagship, beside the red crosses of the Order of Christ, his galleys and transports flew pennants with the letters IDA. This was the prince's new motto. The initials stood for Ifante Dom Anrique (Prince Henry), but they also spelled the word *ida:* departure.

When the ships rendezvoused at Ceuta, he suffered a disappointment. Instead of the fourteen thousand men he had originally asked for, the troops at his disposal only amounted to something like two thousand horse, a thousand crossbowmen and three thousand foot soldiers. Time was lost putting the army through its paces at Ceuta. This gave Sala ibn Sala, now Caïd of Tangier, the same Moorish chief whom Henry had driven out of Ceuta, who certainly had old scores to settle, an opportunity to prepare his defenses and to call on the King of Fez and all the chieftains of the hinterland for aid. Prince Henry, a man of great strategy and poor tactics, turned out to lack the cautious attention to detail which had laid the groundwork for the victories of his father and Nun'Alvares. A council of war, alarmed by reports of the immense numbers of troops the Moors were collecting, advised him to call off the attack, but he was determined to take Tangier at any cost.

He led a column of mounted men overland from Ceuta to Tangier while the fleet sailed to blockade the port. Young Fernando, to his great distress, fell so ill he could not ride his horse and had to go with the galleys.

The first assault failed, though Henry's men managed to break down two of the city gates. Dom Pedro's great friend and fellow Knight of the Garter, Alvaro Vaz de Almeida was wounded, as were several nobles of the royal blood. A second assault was beaten back. The Portuguese built themselves a fortified camp and settled down for the siege. In spite of King Duarte's admonition to make sure that their camp had secure access to the sea, sufficient measures were not taken to keep open a line of retreat. There were no wells within the ring of palisades. In a third battle Henry's horse was killed under him and the prince was with great difficulty rescued by his squires and retainers. With each engagement the Moors could count on more troops. For once their armed bands worked together. As news spread that the Christians were sore beset Bedouin and wandering Berbers gathered like jackals for the kill. After twenty-five days of besieging Tangier Henry's men found themselves besieged in their camp.

They held out for twelve more days. They lived on horsemeat which they cooked by burning the wood and straw off the baggage saddles. Their water ran out. "Many died," wrote Azurara in his chronicle, "with mud between their lips, trying to suck a little moisture out of it." In the end a truce was arranged.

The Portuguese must give up their horses and artillery and everything in the camp. They would be allowed to go peacefully back to their ships, but with only the clothes on their backs. Furthermore they must promise to evacuate Ceuta and to return all the Moslem captives held there in bondage. They must swear to a hundred years of peace. As hostages for performance Sala ben Sala would deliver his son to the Christians but they must leave Prince Fernando as his captive until the city was handed over. Henry put in a fervent plea to be allowed to stay in his brother's stead. He was overruled by the council of war.

Though the Portuguese had only lost five hundred men, it was the most distressing defeat in the history of their country. On their way to the shore they were set upon by bands of Berber horsemen so that they had to fight their way to the boats with what arms they had managed to conceal. The Portuguese leaders declared that this attack released them from their promise to evacuate Ceuta. The Moors said no. From that moment on, through many painful years, negotiations dragged on for the ransoming of Dom Fernando.

Back in Ceuta Prince Henry threw himself down on his bed. His retainers feared he would never rise again. He was ill for four months. From his sickbed he tried to bargain with the Moors for his brother's release while his brother John, who had set out with a few ships from the Algarve, tried to work through the authorities at Arzila. The Moors were obdurate. They must have Ceuta or they would hold Dom Fernando.

Henry went back to Sagres in despair. In spite of invitations from his brother Duarte he could not face the prospect of appearing at court. There had always been a large party opposed to his projects for Africa. He could not bear to see his enemies gloat over his disgrace.

Dom Fernando remained captive for eleven years. He suffered hideous humiliations. His devoted secretary, Frei João Alvares of the Order of Avis, who shared his sufferings, wrote an account of his patience and constancy which became a classic of Portuguese devotional literature. When he died in Fez the Moors had his body carried through the streets on a board by Christian captives and hung head down from the city walls for all the people to throw stones at. Somehow Brother Alvares managed to have his liege lord's heart and entrails embalmed in a jar and when he was ransomed carried them piously back to Portugal for burial at Batalha.

News of Duarte's failing health forced Henry out of hiding. They met almost secretly at Portel. Henry called for another army to smite the infidel and rescue their brother. Duarte had no heart for it. His spirit was broken. A month or so later he died at Tomar in the lovely valley guarded by the monastery fortress of the Knights of Christ Prince Henry had done so much to embellish. One of the king's physicians said that "the excessive grief and continual suffering caused by the unhappy consequences of the siege of Tangier" brought about his death. The fever that carried him off came from remorse that he had not given his brothers proper advice and had allowed them to go against the opinion of so many great ones of the realm.

King Duarte's death was the occasion of a clash of interests that split the House of Avis into factions. Both Pedro and the Count of Barcelos wanted the regency during the minority of Duarte's son Afonso. Passions were exacerbated by the hostility between Queen Leonor and Pedro's wife Isabel of Urgel. Then there was the shame of Tangier and the captivity of their brother Fernando.

When Duarte's will was read it was found that he had left both the guardianship of his heir and the regency of the kingdom to his wife, Leonor of Aragon. Dom Pedro immediately objected. A Cortes was summoned at Tôrres Novas which was attended by all the counts, dukes and princes of the royal blood. It was decided that the business of the realm would be conducted by a royal council which would include delegates from the Cortes. The queen would preside. All decisions must be approved by Dom

Pedro who would bear the title of regent. The Cortes would meet annually henceforward.

This time the queen refused to consent. She retired to her castle at Alenquer and sent off messengers begging for help from her brothers the princes of Aragon. The Count of Barcelos sided with the queen. Prince John and Prince Pedro called on Prince Henry to mediate between the factions. He rode posthaste to Alenquer and induced Dona Leonor to return to Lisbon to present the young king, to whom they had all sworn allegiance in his cradle, to a new Cortes. The queen consented. The Cortes confirmed Pedro as regent. The Count of Barcelos sulked in his estates in the north. To soothe his hurt feelings Pedro made him Duke of Bragança.

Prince Henry was at liberty to return to Sagres. Exploration of the African coast was proceeding apace. In 1441 he sent his chamberlain, a very young man named Antão Gonçalves, to take on a cargo of sealskins and oil in the inlet marked by a great rock shaped like a galley. After loading their ships Gonçalves' men did a little prospecting inland and managed to capture a naked man with an assagai and a woman whom they figured was a slave. Returning to their ship they found that one of the fine new caravels commanded by another young servitor of the prince's, Nuno Tristão, had just dropped anchor in the bight. Tristão had brought along a Moorish slave he hoped to use as an interpreter. It was a disappointment when the Moor and the captives couldn't understand each other.

The young skippers put their heads together as to how to secure more captives. Gonçalves had spied a large group of natives on a faraway hill. They mustered twenty picked men out of the crews of their two ships and, landing at night, managed to surprise a native camp. They killed three men and captured ten, among them a man named Adahu, whom they decided, from his air of authority, must be a noble.

Their Moor was able to converse in Arabic with Adahu. From him they learned that the rest of their prisoners could only speak "Azeneguey." They probably belonged to one of the Tuareg tribes that controlled the slave trade in those parts. Nuno Tristão was so delighted with the success of their adventure that he insisted on dubbing Antão Gonçalves a knight then and there.

Next day the Moor and one of the women were put ashore to try to induce the natives to ransom the captives or at least to come down to the shore to trade. Instead the natives, a hundred and fify strong, assisted by horsemen and camel riders, tried to lay an ambush from which the Portuguese barely escaped. Their Moor remained in the hands of the natives.

Taking Adahu and half the captives Gonçalves sailed for home. Meanwhile, "as cool as if he were on the sands of the Tagus," Tristão careened his caravel at low tide to clean her bottom and prepared for further discoveries. When Gonçalves reached Sagres the prince was so pleased with him that he made him his private secretary. Adahu kept declaring that if the Portuguese would take him home he would ransom himself and two other young men among the captives for ten Negro slaves. Henry consented to the deal, telling Gonçalves to be sure to collect what news he could of the Indies and of the realm of Prester John. Gonçalves provisioned his ship and set out again.

When they reached a point on the shore Adahu indicated as near his home, Gonçalves, trusting to his word as a fidalgo, put him on the beach wearing all the fine clothes Prince Henry had given him. That was the last they saw of Adahu. Gonçalves swore he would be less gullible next time.

However a week later, when they were anchored in the inlet they had visited before, a Moor on a white camel appeared on the shore. This time negotiations were conducted by the *alfaqueque*. That was the official of his household who made a business of handling the ransoming of prisoners from the Moors. The alfaqueque reported after some conversation in Arabic with the Moor on the white camel that, as a ransom for their three captives, the Portuguese were to be allowed to choose ten out of a group of a hundred men and women, some black, and some brown-skinned with European-type features, who were marshaled on the beach. The Moor threw in a little gold dust, the first procured on these explorations—from which the inlet immediately took its name of Rio do Ouro—an oxhide shield and three ostrich eggs. With these Antão Gonçalves sailed home in triumph. According to Azurara, though it is hard to believe when you think of the heat of the African coast, the ostrich eggs were served up to Prince Henry at his dinner table in Sagres, "fresh as hen's eggs."

In 1443 Prince Henry sent Nuno Tristão off again with special orders to explore the hinterland behind Cabo Branco, which was the next promontory to be doubled. Tristão found an inhabited island named Arguim about twenty-five leagues south of the cape. He hauled fourteen naked men out of a dugout canoe and caught fifteen more on the island. An adjacent island was full of royal herons "in which our men found great refreshment." Arguim became the first focus of Portuguese trade with the Arabs and Tuaregs and the slave-raiding Negro kings of the Guinea coast. Five years later Prince Henry had a fort built there.

So great was the enthusiasm in the Algarve over the appearance of gold and slaves at the prince's naval arsenal that many, who even after the settlement of Madeira had been critical of the waste of public funds on his exploring voyages and scornful of his defeat at Tangier, now, wrote Azurara, began to hail him as "the new Alexander." In 1443 young Henry VI of England showed the interest of his cousins of the Lancastrian court in his doings by awarding the Order of the Garter to Prince Henry of Portugal.

In 1444 the revenue officer of Lagos, Lancerote de Freitas, and a number of merchants of that port formed a trading company which equipped six caravels and applied to Prince Henry, who as well as being suzerain of Madeira and of the nearer Azores, held the monopoly from Dom Pedro of trade with West Africa, for a license to traffic at Arguim and the islands beyond. The prince furnished each ship with a banner of his Knights of Christ. They didn't do much discovering but they came back with two hundred and thirty-five captives.

Azurara gives a graphic description of the distribution of the slaves in Lagos. Since many of them had been much weakened in transit it was decided to make the distribution to the various owners before day in the morning. "Some were white enough, fair to look upon and well proportioned, others black as Ethiops. . . . Some kept their heads low and their faces bathed in tears, others stood groaning grievously fixing their eyes upon the height of heaven, crying out loud, as if asking help of the Father of Nature; others, with their faces in the palms of their hands, threw themselves at full length on the ground." In order to divide them into equal portions, "fathers were parted from sons, husbands from wives, brothers from brothers."

Prince Henry was there, mounted on a powerful horse and accompanied by his retinue. He immediately distributed among his retainers the forty-six souls that fell to him as his fifth. "His profit," wrote Azurara, "lay in his purpose, and he reflected with pleasure on the salvation of these souls which otherwise would have been lost."

The Negroes proved more docile than the Moors. "And certainly his expectation was not in vain, since, as soon as they understood our language they turned Christian with very little ado; and I, who put together this history in this present volume, saw in the town of Lagos boys and girls, children and grandchildren of those first captives, born in this land, as good and true Christians as if they had been directly descended, from the beginning of the dispensation of Christ, from those who were first baptized."

"As our own people," Azurara added, "saw how they came into the law of Christ with good will, they made no difference between them and their free servants, born in our country: but those whom they took when still young they caused to be instructed in the mechanical arts and those they saw fitted for managing property they set free and married to women who were natives of the land. I never saw any put in irons like other captives, and scarcely any who did not turn Christian and were very gently treated."

Slave-raiding, even as a method of converting the heathen, was not among Prince Henry's chief objectives. The next expedition under Gonçalo de Sintra had strict orders to continue on to the Guinea coast without stopping in Arguim.

Gonçalo disobeyed these orders and so lost his life. The people of the islands south of Cabo Branco were by this time thoroughly aroused. They were convinced the captives were being taken to Portugal to be eaten. When Gonçalo and his men tried to assault a village on the island of Naar they fell into an ambush. The captain and five men were killed.

The same summer Antão Gonçalves and two other of the prince's servants in command of his caravels were finding the natives so suspicious they could no longer do business with them. Before sailing home from a rather fruitless voyage, they left a squire of the prince's named João Fernandes, who had learned several African languages during years of captivity in Morocco, to spend a season among the barbarians and find out what he could of the geography to the southward. At the same time, an old Moor who expressed a desire to visit Portugal was taken to Sagres to tell his story.

Trade between Arguim and Lagos was becoming continuous. The Lagos Company sent down wheat, cloth, carpets and silver to be exchanged for slaves, gold and ivory. In this same busy year of 1444 the enterprising Nuno Tristão sailed his caravel far south of Cabo Branco to the land of the true Negroes, where the beaches were fringed with palms and the hills beyond had a green and forested look.

The following year Dinís Dias passed the mouth of the river of Senegal, where he found the water sweet and muddy far out to sea, and reached Cabo Verde. He named it the Green Cape on account of the tall trees and the fragrance of dense vegetation that wafted out on the land breeze at night, so delicious after the hundreds of leagues of desert shores he had coasted to get there. That same season Nuno Tristão tacked in and out along the beaches between the Rio do Ouro and Cabo Branco on the lookout for João Fernandes.

João Fernandes turned up in good health near Rio do Ouro. He declared he had lived off fish and camels' milk, lodging with wandering tribesmen who pastured herds of sheep and camels along the coast. Some were Berbers, some Tuaregs, some Arabs. The Berbers and Tuaregs used a sort of writing different from the Arabic script. Their chief wealth lay in the Negroes they captured and traded with the Moroccans for wheat. There was also a lively trade with the interior. Wool and hides were exchanged for amber, civet and resin. These Bedouin guided themselves over the trackless deserts by the stars and the winds, "like mariners," and by observing the flights of birds. Fernandes noted that the swallows that left Portugal in the fall wintered on these sands, but that the storks passed overhead in the direction of the land of the Negroes. He saw an abundance of ostriches, deer, gazelles and partridges. Gold, which was fairly plentiful among the head men, came from the south.

A couple of years later a great expedition was assembled at Lagos. Twenty-three caravels, fourteen of them from Madeira under the two governors of that island, Zarco and Teixeira, and a number from Lisbon, with all the master mariners of the realm aboard, put out from Lagos with instructions to meet at Cabo Branco. Henry's orders were not to raid for slaves, but to show the might of Portuguese arms to the Moorish inhabitants of the island of Tider and to explore the river of Senegal, which according to the current cosmogony was considered to be the western branch of the Nile. Azurara in his pompous way tells of the capture of some Negroes on that river as a glorious victory for the prince, because it was so far from home and so near the land of Egypt.

Madeira, besides being invaluable as a source of timber for ship-building and supplies for the African expeditions, was breeding navigators of its own. The caravel that went farthest that summer was captained by Zarco's son-in-law, Alvaro Fernandes. He brought home to the prince a pipe of the water of the Senegal, which the explorers still spoke of as the Nile. Not even Alexander, wrote Azurara, drank water brought from such distance.

It was this Fernandes who won, on another voyage, the prize for farthest south. Having doubled Cabo Verde he landed at a new landmark to the southward which they called the Cape of Masts because it bristled with palm trunks that had been stripped of their tops by the wind. The only notable thing he found there was a pile of elephant dung "as high as a man's head." He made the encouraging discovery that the coast had begun to deflect to the southeast, and reached the great river which is now known as the Gambia and another vast stream a hundred and ten leagues south of Cabo Verde. He was driven out of this river by the poisoned arrows of the natives, with whom he had been given strict orders not to engage in combat. Reaching Portugal he received a hundred gold dobras from the prince and a hundred from Dom Pedro the regent as a bounty for the ship that went farthest south.

These frequent voyages were alarming the natives. Efforts to induce them to trade were fruitless. The indefatigable João Fernandes did manage to establish contact with Arab traders at Messa not far from Cape Não. There he exchanged eighteen captured Moors for fifty-one Guinea Negroes, plus a lion. Azurara here lets drop a bit of information that casts light on Portuguese sailing routes to the northward. Prince Henry shipped the lion off as a gift to an Englishman who had been a retainer of his in the old days. The Englishman lived in Galway in Ireland. Customhouse records reveal a lively trade between the Portuguese ports and Galway and Bristol. Bristol would soon be the British port which sponsored most of the exploring voyages into the Western Atlantic.

The poisoned arrows of the Negroes proved the undoing of Nuno Tristão in 1446. Among the early explorers he was closest to the prince's heart for his courage and resourcefulness. Sixty leagues south of Cabo Verde he sailed up a great river which came to be known as the Rio Nuno. In reconnoitering a native town he was set upon by Negroes shooting poisoned arrows. Tristão and twenty of his crew were killed outright. The rest were so weakened by the poison they didn't have the strength to raise the anchors. They cut their cables and made for the open sea. Only five sailors, some of them mere boys, were unhurt. The wounded men died by inches. The ship's boys sailed the caravel northeast for sixty days out of sight of land, throwing the bodies of their comrades overboard as they died, "to be entombed in the bellies of the fish," until they were finally hailed by the pinnace of a Galician freebooter who told them they were off the Alentejan port of Sines. The loss of Nuno Tristão and his crew brought particular grief to Prince Henry because they had all been raised in his household. "But," wrote Azurara, "he was convinced their souls had found salvation and took particular care of their wives and children."

6

THE LAST VOYAGES
UNDER PRINCE HENRY

After 1448, when Azurara's Chronicle of Guinea ends, there is a gap in the records of Portuguese exploration. Azurara promised to write a continuation, but if he did it has disappeared.

Prince Henry still had very little to show for thirty years of work and the expenditure of vast sums of money. He had added to be sure some fertile and delightful islands to the skimpy Portuguese kingdom. He had established a fortified trading post on the African shore. His men had charted two thousand miles of coast, but every new discovery there had pushed further beyond the horizon that sharp turn to the east marked on so many world maps of the time that indicated a sea route to the Indies and to the lands of Prester John. He had failed in all his efforts to put the Canaries under Portuguese rule. There was the lasting misery of the defeat at Tangier. The only tangible profit he had to show after so many years of struggle to establish the Guinea trade was a few handfuls of gold dust and some miserable slaves.

Prince Henry's greatest achievements were still intangible. They were the information João Fernandes had collected about caravan routes, the improvement in design of his caravels, the merging of the techniques of the Genoese and Catalan mapmakers and instrument makers with the practical know-how of the Portuguese shipmasters. His school at Sagres had trained a body of young seamen who had thrown off the superstitions of the past and learned to deal with the shoals and currents and tricky winds of the African coast. They had learned to shorten the return journey by long tacks to seaward. A great deal of sea lore went into the successful course set into the north, that Azurara tells about, by the survivors of Nuno Tristão's crew with only a ship's boy at the helm. These men had learned the basic skills which were to make possible the breathtaking voyages of the next generation.

Another reason for the hiatus in the records was a sudden flareup in the discords smoldering in the royal house of Avis which had been smoothed over by the summary action of the Cortes of Lisbon in 1441. Dona Leonor, never reconciled to the assumption of power by the commons or the regency of Dom Pedro, had retired to the court of Castile where her sister was queen. Her son Afonso, now seventeen, was eager to kick over the traces of his uncle's tutelage. Although he was married to Dom Pedro's daughter, his first cousin, Afonso V fell under the influence of the Duke of Bragança who set himself to fanning all the resentments against Dom Pedro's rule among the great nobles of the court. The teen-age king succumbed to his flattery. The result was a short and tragic civil war.

After a series of pronouncements and counter pronouncements the king's party raised an army in the south which was commanded by the Duke of Bragança, and Dom Pedro raised an army in his dukedom at Coimbra. Pedro had already resigned the regency at the king's request. His chief adherent was his old comrade-in-arms Alvaro Vas de Alhama, the Count of Abranches, who had showed such courage and steadfastness in the dreary weeks before Tangier. The two armies advanced slowly until they were facing each other across the ravine of Alfarrobeira a little north of Santarém.

Dom Pedro had made the fatal mistake of calling on his old friend Don Alvaro de Luna the constable of Castile, for help. Calling in the foreign enemy alienated the merchants and towns-people who were the backbone of the Cortes which had supported him. To make his situation worse no Castilian troops appeared. Efforts at mediation failed.

Historians have blamed Prince Henry for not throwing himself bodily between the armies of his brother and his nephew. If he made any such attempt the chronicles did not record it. Possibly he did not believe that their confrontation would result in bloodshed.

Dom Pedro rejected repeated demands that he surrender. The situation in his camp became desperate. His vassals and adherents faded away. The story went the rounds that Dom Pedro and the Count of Abranches had sworn an oath that they would die together.

The fatal clash was almost accidental. Somebody on Pedro's side discharged some bombards in the direction of the king's camp. The royal forces were infuriated by seeing a cannonball fall near the king's tent. Immediately a group of crossbowmen hidden in a wood overlooking Dom Pedro's camp started shooting. Dom Pedro was killed in the first flight of arrows. King Afonso's men immediately charged the camp. Seeing that the time had come to sell his life dearly, so Azurara tells the tale, the Count of Abranches went coolly to his tent. There he drank a little wine and ate a little bread while he was being armed by his squires. Then he walked out to meet the attackers. He fell cut to pieces by a dozen swords. The skirmish was over almost before it began.

Henceforward Dom Afonso ruled as absolute monarch. Alfarrobeira was a victory for the court party. As the Cortes lost power prospects became dim for the future of representative government in Portugal. This was at a time when the English parliament was taking advantage of the wars and discords that heralded the last days of the House of Lancaster to consolidate its strength.

If there had been any break in relations between Prince Henry and young Afonso V on account of Alfarrobeira they were drawn together again by the shock of the fall of Constantinople to the Turks in 1453. Afonso agreed with his uncle that fresh blows must be aimed at the infidel. When the pope called for a crusade Portugal was the only nation in Europe that responded wholeheartedly.

A year after the fall of Constantinople African exploration was resumed, this time by a highly intelligent and inquisitive Venetian named Alvise da Ca' da Mosto. He came of a patrician family—a palace on the Grand Canal still bears their name—but his father had been banished as a result of some unlucky lawsuits, so young Cadamosto, as the name is usually written, had to scratch for a living as a merchant. In August 1454 Alvise and his brother Antonio enlisted under a Venetian grandee on a trading fleet bound for Flanders. They were forced by the usual adverse winds to anchor in the bight of Sagres. Prince Henry promptly sent his secretary aboard along with the Venetian consul, who was on his payroll, with samples of Madeira sugar and "dragon's blood" and other products of his subject lands. This consul was the son of a famous Venetian traveler named Nicola de' Conti. They told the Cadamosto brothers that shipmasters working for the prince in the Guinea trade made sixfold or even sevenfold profits.

The upshot was that Alvise turned over to his brother his interest in the shipment to Flanders and entered into an agreement with Prince Henry. When the Venetian fleet put to sea he joined the prince's maritime court where he was entertained in high style.

The following March he sailed with a new caravel of fifty-five tons which Prince Henry outfitted for him and put under the command of a skipper named Vicente Dias who was already experienced in the African trade. The arrangement was that Cadamosto and the prince would share equally in the profits of the trip, but that if there were no profits the prince would bear all the expense.

The caravel reached Pôrto Santo in three days. Now the African journeys all started from the Madeira islands. Cadamosto, who later published a most useful journal of the trip, noted that Pôrto Santo produced wheat and barley sufficient for its population and abounded in cattle, wild boars and rabbits. The coast was a magnificent fishing ground. There was a good anchorage but no harbor. The exports were the best honey in the world, beeswax and dragon's blood.

Before the end of the month they were in Madeira. He described the island as mountainous like Sicily and very fertile, extremely well watered. The land produced an immense amount of wheat. Though originally wheat had yielded sixtyfold it now yielded only thirty or forty times the seed planted. Sawmills in the streams supplied planking for shipbuilding and for frame houses for all Portugal. There was a lovely fragrant cedar-like cypress and a handsome red-colored yew. The sugar gave a high yield when it was refined. The wines were remarkable considering the youth of the vines. Already more was being produced than the population could drink. The Malvoisie vine which Prince Henry had imported from Sicily, produced as many grapes as leaves, in bunches two and three and even four palms in length. There were wild peacocks in the hills, quail, wild boar and immense numbers of pigeons, so tame they could be lassoed off the trees. Plenty of cattle. The towns abounded with fine sweetmeats. Many of the settlers were wealthy. The four settlements could if need be put eight hundred men in the field of whom a hundred and twenty would be mounted. The whole country was a garden.

From Madeira they sailed to the Canaries. They found four of the islands inhabited by converted natives, but the pagans still held out on Teneriffe, Palma and Grand Canary. Ferro was full of wild asses. The Christian islands were under the rule of a nobleman of Seville who was subject to the king of Castile. The Christians lived on barley bread, meat and goats' milk but had neither wine nor wheat. There were many figs. Each Christian island spoke a different language so that the people could hardly understand each other. The exports were goats' leather and a dye plant called orchil which was exported to Cádiz and Seville.

The inhabitants of the pagan island went naked except for an occasional goatskin. They ran nimbly as their goats up the steep mountainsides. They painted their skins with the juice of certain herbs, green, red and yellow and esteemed their colors as much as the Europeans did fine clothes. They were cave dwellers. They had no religion except a worship of the sun, moon and planets. Their chiefs had the right of the first night. Cadamosto esteemed them "the most nimble and dextrous people in the world. With a few blows they can shatter a shield."

From the Canaries Dias and Cadamosto set their course direct for Cabo Branco. From that landfall they sailed south to the island of Arguim. The waters around were shallow, full of treacherous currents. "One navigates only by day and with lead in hand, and according to the state of the tide."

On Arguim they found European-style houses and a fort. No one could trade there, they were told, without license from Prince Henry. He had made an end of raiding the native villages for slaves. The slave traffic was to be left in the hands of Berber and Arab traders who procured their slaves from the Negro kings to the southward. Every effort was being made by the Portuguese to remain at peace with the coastal people.

The prince's merchants brought in wheat, silver, silk handkerchiefs and carpets which they exchanged for slaves and gold dust with the Arabs. These Arabs brought in Barbary horses across country from Morocco to trade for blacks. A good horse brought from nine to fourteen slaves. Other items were silk fabrics from Granada. Pepper and gold dust came in by caravan from Timbuctu.

Arguim had become a port of shipment for the caravan routes to the south and east. Already the Portuguese were shipping a thousand slaves north every year. Southward the chief Arab trade was in salt, needed in those parts so the Arabs explained to Cadamosto, "to keep men's lips from putrifying on account of the great heat." Caravans continued down to Melli (the modern Mali) in the Negro country through lands so hot and arid that three quarters of the animals and many men would perish on the way. South of Melli the blocks of salt were carried on the heads of Negroes till they reached a great water where the salt was left in piles on the shore.

The traders would then retire a half a day's journey. From across the water mysterious tribesmen who never allowed themselves to be seen would come in boats, as if from some island, and match each pile of salt with a pile of gold dust. The Arab traders would come back after they had left. If they felt the exchange was right they would take the gold dust and retire, leaving the salt on the shore. If they felt they had been skimped they would make themselves scarce again and wait for the unseen barterers to come back with a little more gold.

From Arguim Cadamosto's caravel sailed south to the mouth of the Senegal. There he found that the Portuguese had already made treaties with the native rulers so that the people were accustomed to seeing European ships. He found the Senegal to be the boundary between the tall black peoples to the south, who were merely nominal Mohammedans, and the lean and tawny Azenegues, who like the modern Tuaregs, went around with their mouths always covered and were fanatical followers of the Prophet.

The people on the south bank of the Senegal lived in miserable villages of reed huts and were ruled by a black king. Cadamosto was still laboring under the delusion that the river of Senegal was one of the mouths of the Nile which he imagined should be called the Niger. He attributed to "learned men" the theory "held by the ancients" that these rivers all flowed from out of the Earthly Paradise, situated somewhere in the middle of the continent.

Cadamosto had some Spanish horses aboard the caravel. Having been told he could get the best price for them from a monarch known as Budomel, who ruled a kingdom many leagues to the southward, he determined to push on. At a place known to the Portuguese as Palma de Budomel he sent his Negro interpreter ashore to take word to the king of the horses and the linen cloth and the Moorish silks for sale.

King Budomel promptly appeared on the shore with fifteen horsemen and a hundred and fifty footmen in attendance, and invited Cadamosto to stay at his house which was some leagues inland. Cadamosto led out his seven horses and harness and saddles to the value of three hundred ducats and the king promised to pay him in slaves. As down payment he produced a handsome young girl "to serve in Cadamosto's chamber."

Cadamosto spent twenty-eight days with King Budomel who treated him as an equal potentate. The king's subjects were only permitted to approach him crawling on their knees and throwing dirt on their heads as a sign of humility. The basis of his authority was the fear that if they displeased him, he would sell their wives and children for slaves.

Through the interpreter Cadamosto had talks with Budomel about religion. The Moors and Azenegues were instructing him in the Koran. He asked Cadamosto to recite the articles of the Christian faith. Cadamosto told him that Christianity was the only true religion. Budomel laughed and said the religion must be good, because God who had bestowed wealth and knowledge on the Christians must have given them a good religion, but that Mohammedanism was a good faith too. Since God was just, he insisted, the Negroes who were so poor and miserable in this world, must have a better chance of salvation in the next than the Christians whose lives were a paradise here below.

The weather became so stormy that there was no way Cadamosto could get back to his ship, anchored far offshore beyond some raging sandbars. With a promise of "two measures of tin" he induced two of the natives to swim out through the surf to the ship with a letter to the skipper telling him to sail back to the mouth of the Senegal. Only one of them made it. He returned with an answer. "Hence I conclude that the Negroes of this coast are the best swimmers in the world."

Budomel furnished Cadamosto with horses and guides. On his overland trip he visited markets on the lookout for gold. The merchandise was very poor: cotton, fish, nets and cotton cloths, vegetables, oil, millet, wooden bowls and palm mats. Occasionally there was a small amount of gold dust. There was no money. Everything had to be bartered. People crowded around him amazed by his white skin. They thought the white of his skin was paint and wet their fingers on their tongues to try to rub it off.

Everything on the caravel astonished them. They declared that the crossbows and bombards were the work of the devil. They thought the bagpipes a live animal. The eyes painted on the bow they believed to be real eyes which the ship used to find her way across the sea. They said the Europeans must be great magicians to find their way across the ocean when they, the poor Negroes, had trouble finding their way by land.

When Cadamosto was about to set sail, two caravels appeared in the river's mouth. One belonged to a Genoese named Antoniotto Usodimare and the other to some squires of Prince Henry. They joined forces and, sailing in convoy, rounded Cabo Verde and scudded down the coast with a favorable wind. They anchored in the mouth of a beautiful river hemmed in by enormous trees and landed one of their Negro interpreters to try to get the local natives to trade. The natives promptly crowded around him and killed him with their short Moorish swords so the caravels weighed anchor and made sail.

Their course was still southerly. They were eager to discover new lands. They came to a very wide river which they decided was the river of Gambia. Some leagues upstream they fought a battle with Negroes in dugout canoes and had to shoot several of them before they could beat them off. The Negroes discharged a flight of arrows but not a Christian was hit. This was fortunate because these arrows were poisoned. An interpreter managed to speak with the natives. They said they would never make peace with the Christians who were bad men who bought Negroes to take home to eat.

Since the natives were preparing to attack, Cadamosto's men made sail, as the wind had suddenly freshened, and bore down on the canoes that scattered in all directions. Cadamosto wanted to cruise thirty or so leagues further up the river to see if he could find better disposed people, but the crew had begun to grumble. They had had enough for one voyage. "To avoid discussion," wrote Cadamosto, "since they were pigheaded and obstinate men," he allowed them to shape their course "in God's name" for Cabo Verde and the Hispanic countries.

During all the days they spent in the mouth of the River Gambia they saw the North Star only once "about a third of a lance's length above the horizon." Due south by the compass they saw six stars low down over the sea, "clear, bright and large" in the shape of a cross. Though earlier Portuguese seafarers must have seen it before him, Cadamosto's is the first recorded observation of the Southern Cross.

The following year Cadamosto and Usodimare with the prince's help fitted out two new caravels for the Guinea coast. They were driven out to sea by a storm and happened on the Cape Verde Islands. There they found a great quantity of turtles "with shells as large as a shield"—their meat tasted like veal—pigeons so tame you could catch them with your hand, salt in dry lagoons, a great quantity of fish of kinds they had never seen before; but no inhabitants.

Having salted down as much fish and turtle meat as they could stow away the caravels set their course for the River Gambia. This time they managed to establish friendly relations with the natives. About twenty leagues inland they came upon the settlement of a native chief who was willing to trade with them. He bartered slaves, disappointingly small quantites of gold dust, apes of different sorts, civet, skins of civet cats and excellently woven cotton cloth, for Moorish silks and European "articles of little worth."

This was elephant country. Coming upon a small elephant that had been killed by hunters Cadamosto noted that the chief offered him any part of it he wanted. "I had a portion cut off which, roasted and broiled, I ate aboard ship . . . to be able to say I had eaten of the flesh of an animal which had never been previously eaten by any of my countrymen." He found it tough and insipid. All the same he salted down part of the trunk and one of the feet to take back to Prince Henry "who received them as a handsome gift, being the first he had had from the country discovered through his energy."

Cadamosto and his men were amazed by the size of the boabab trees, by the hippopotamus that seemed to thrive equally on land and in the water, by the enormous bats. An outbreak of fever forced them down to the sea again. They journeyed south until they found another great river with beautiful islands inhabited by Negroes off the mouth of it. They could find no way of communicating with the inhabitants. Their interpreters couldn't understand the language.

The violent tide puzzled them. The flood flowed four hours and the ebb eight but with such violence that three anchors in the bow would scarcely hold, even with sails set to give the ship steerage way. Not without danger they made the open sea and set their courses home to the port from which they had sailed.

In the year 1458 Prince Henry was so preoccupied with a new expedition to Morocco that "no one went to Guinea." Two years before, young Afonso V had met the call of Pope Calixtus III for a general crusade against the Turks by preparing, in the face of complaints from the Cortes, to raise an army of twelve thousand men. The other Christian kings dragged their feet. The pope died. The crusade never got started. Afonso decided to perform a feat of arms on his own against the infidel.

At first Prince Henry argued that the time had come to wipe out his disgrace at Tangier, but it was finally decided that the smaller fortress of Alcacer Seguir to the west would be equally strategic and easier to storm. The king embarked at Setúbal in September and on October 3 met the prince at Sagres. Henry was sixty-four but full of youthful vigor.

Together they sailed to Lagos where a fleet of two hundred and eighty sail, carrying twenty-two thousand men, was assembling. After a demonstration in front of Tangier they invested Alcácer Seguir and carried the place by storm in a single day.

It was Ceuta all over again. The Moors capitulated and were

allowed to leave with their wives and children and chattels but they had to free all Christian slaves in their possession. As the Moors left the castle King Afonso, Prince Henry, the king's brother Fernando who was the prince's heir, and Pedro the very accomplished son of the ill-fated regent, entered the town on foot and proceeded to the mosque which the priests had just consecrated as the Church of Our Lady of Mercy. After giving thanks to God the king appointed Duarte de Meneses, who with his father had defended Ceuta against incessant harassments for forty years, captain of the place.

Alcácer Seguir was the beginning of a series of victories for King Afonso. Over a period of ten years he took a number of the Moorish strong points on the Atlantic shore. He stormed Arzila and forced the Moors to evacuate Tangier. His campaigns won him the cognomen of "Africano" from the court poets. For his uncle the taking of this first minor fortress was the justification of a lifetime's strategy.

A second triumph enlivened Prince Henry's last years. In 1459 he won Afonso's consent for the entombment of his brother Pedro's body in the royal mortuary. As Grand Master of the Order of Christ the prince conducted the ceremonies. King Afonso was present. The breach in the House of Avis was healed.

During the last two years of Henry's life trade with the Guinea coast redoubled. His policy of conciliation of the Negroes bore fruit. The record of the trading journeys of these years is to be found in the narrative of Diogo Gomes, who was raised as a page in the prince's household. A German geographer named Martin Behaim copied the story down from his own lips somewhere in the fourteen eighties when Diogo Gomes was enjoying the fruits of his explorations as seneschal in the palace at Sintra.

Gomes sailed south in command of three caravels under the usual orders to proceed as far as he could. He visited the same Negro potentate some twenty leagues up the Gambia River who had entertained Cadamosto. There he picked up more definite information than Cadamosto or Fernandes had been able to procure about the caravan routes that crossed into West Africa from Cairo and Fez bringing merchandise to exchange for gold. The gold came from south of the mountains to which the Portuguese were soon to be giving the name of Serra Leão. The fevers drove Gomes back to the mouth of the river. He found another local potentate on the south bank of the river who had become so taken with the Christian religion that he dismissed the Moslem missionaries who were with him and asked to be baptized forthwith. Gomes said he didn't dare perform a baptism because he was not ordained but that when he returned to Sagres he would ask the prince to send down a priest.

"On the next day, however," Diogo Gomes told Behaim, "I begged the king with his twelve principle chiefs and eight of his wives to come to dine with me aboard the caravel, which they did all unarmed, and I gave them fowls and meat cooked after our own fashion, and wine both white and red, as much as they pleased to drink: and they said to each other that no nation was better than the Christian."

The most significant thing about Gomes' recollections of that journey is that he had aboard a native of India named Jacob whom the prince had sent as an interpreter in case Gomes should reach the land of St. Thomas's Christians. Pope Calixtus III had already conceded to the Order of Christ exclusive jurisdiction over all the lands acquired by Portuguese explorers beyond Cabo Não "as far as the Indies."

The farthest point south in Prince Henry's lifetime was reached by another of his captains, Pedro de Sintra, who after sighting the mountains of Serra Leão, followed the coast beyond in the southeasterly direction as far as a forest of green trees which he named Bosco de Santa Maria.

He described the people he found there to Cadamosto: "To the caravels which were anchored beyond this there came three small canoes, two or three blacks in each, quite naked, and carrying pointed sticks, which we would call darts. Some had small knives and two, leathern shields. There were three bows among them. They came alongside. Each had his ears pierced right around and the lower part of the nose. Some of them also wore teeth around their necks; these appeared to be human teeth. Several Negroes who were on the ships spoke to them but without understanding a single word, nor making themselves understood. Three of the blacks boarded one of the caravels; of these three the Portuguese detained one, allowing the others to go. This they did in obedience to His Majesty the King (Afonso V) who had enjoined them that, from the farthest land they reached, if it chanced that the people were unable to understand their interpreters, they were to contrive to bring away a Negro, by force or persuasion, so that he might be interrogated through the many Negro interpreters to be found in Portugal, or in the course of time might learn to speak, so that he might give an account of his country. For this reason they detained one of the three Negroes. Deciding to advance no further they carried him back to Portugal and presented him to His Majesty the King, who caused divers Negroes to speak with him. Finally a female slave of a citizen of Lisbon who had also come from a far-off country, understood him, not through his own language but through one known to both. What this Negro told the king through this woman I do not know, save that he said among other things found in his country were live unicorns. The said lord, having kept him several months, shown him many things of the kingdom and given him clothes, very charitably had him carried by a caravel back to his own country."

On a second journey a couple of years later Diogo Gomes and a Genoese named Antonio da Noli explored the Cape Verde Islands. According to Gomes' story, sailing home, his caravel was driven by a storm up into the Azores so that da Noli reached Lisbon first and, claiming to be their discoverer, was rewarded by King Afonso with the captaincy of the island of Saõ Tiago. Gomes ended the tale he told Behaim by the description of the death of an interloper who had been captured and brought home in irons by another of the prince's squires, Gonçalo Ferreira. This man by name De Prado, a Spaniard possibly, was accused of selling arms to the Moors. King Afonso judged his case when he arrived in Oporto on a circuit of his kingdom. He ordered that the man be tortured on a cart and then thrown into a furnace of fire with his sword and the gold he had earned by his traffic with the infidel. The Portuguese were losing no time in implementing the papal grant.

Prince Henry, meanwhile, feeling that his last illness was upon him, gave his last orders from his sickbed at Sagres. At Gomes' request he sent an abbot down to the Rio Gambia to baptize the friendly natives. He deeded his rights in Madeira and the Azores

and such of the Cape Verde Islands as had already been discovered to his nephew and heir young Fernando, reserving the
ecclesiastical jurisdiction to the Order of Christ. He died very
much in debt, particularly to the Duke of Bragança, who at eighty
had accumulated immense wealth and was enjoying a green old
age. One document quotes the amount of Henry's indebtedness
as thirty thousand gold dobras.

The only account of his death is by this same Diogo Gomes:
"In the year 1460 Prince Henry fell ill at his town on Cabo São
Vicente and died of the illness on November 13 of the same year:
and on the night of his death he was taken to the church of Santa
Maria in Lagos and there honorably buried. King Afonso was
then in the city of Evora and was very much saddened, he and
his courtiers, by the death of so great a lord, because he spent all
his revenues and all he got from Guinea in war and in continual
fleets at sea against the Saracens for the Faith of Christ. At the
end of the year King Afonso sent for me, because by his command I had stayed in Lagos near the prince's body, supplying the
needs of the priests who were employed in constant vigils and
divine offices. He commanded me to see if the prince's body was
corrupt because he wanted to translate his bones to the beautiful
monastery called Santa Maria da Batalha which his father King
John I built for the friars of the Order of Preachers. When I
approached the corpse and uncovered it, I found it dry and in-
tact, except at the tip of the nose, and it was encircled by a rough
shirt of horsehair: well sings the Church, 'Thou shalt not permit
the holy one to see corruption.' "

PART THREE

The Enterprise
of the Indies

I

TWO ROUTES EAST

When Prince Henry died, the population of all Portugal could hardly have amounted to much more than a million and a half souls. Enough settlers had been found to make Madeira a going concern, but to people the distant Azores he had to engage Flemings. With the help of his sister Isabel and her husband the Duke of Burgundy, several groups of farmers from the Low Countries were sent to colonize the farther islands. During the hundred years that followed the prince's death the tiny Portuguese population, pushing southward along the courses traced out by his caravels, took on one of the greatest colonizing enterprises in history.

The late fourteen hundreds was a time of effervescence in the arts and sciences throughout the kingdom. Printing presses with movable type first operated by Gutenberg in Alsace about 1436 spread fast to Italy, where the Venetian republic became an early publishing center, and to the Low Countries and France and then to the Hispanic peninsula. By the final quarter of the century presses in Lisbon were turning out printed books in Latin, Hebrew and the Portuguese vernacular. At the same time the art of illuminating manuscripts flourished to an extraordinary degree. The handwritten books produced for the princes and prelates of the time show great originality and inventiveness in the use of flam-

boyant gothic and early renaissance designs. Without the manuscripts it would be hard to understand how really first-rate painting
could suddenly appear in a country where that art had up to that
time been highly provincial. But neither the illuminations nor the
constant intercourse with Flanders, where the technique of oil
painting was developing fast, can really explain the sudden production of two masterpieces: the panels known as "The Veneration
of São Vincente" now in the Lisbon museum, and the tapestries
depicting Afonso V's victories in Morocco which hang on the
walls of the chapter house of the collegiate church of Pastrana in
Castile. So far as the scanty evidence goes it seems likely that
both the panels and the cartoons for the tapestries were the work
of Afonso V's court painter, Nuno Gonçalves.

The tapestries are crowded with portrait heads. The São Vicente
panels have furnished the only certain portrait of Prince Henry.
The identification was nailed down by the discovery of a mirror
copy of the same portrait in an illuminated manuscript preserved
in Paris.

At the moment of his uncle's death Afonso V was too busy
with his campaigns in Morocco to give much time to the exploration of the African coast. In 1469 he farmed out the Guinea trade
to a Lisbon entrepreneur and shipowner named Fernão Gomes.
Fernão Gomes was to take over the monopoly which was considered to have reverted to the crown on the prince's demise. He
was to pay two hundred thousand reis annually for five years to
the king and a hundred thousand to young Fernando as Prince
Henry's heir. The most important condition was that Gomes'
skippers, starting from Serra Leão, must explore a hundred leagues
of new coast each year.

Fernão Gomes' ships sailed east by south until they crossed the
equator. On the way they discovered the island of Fernando
Pó and, at about five degrees north latitude, what was to be the
great gold-trading post of São Jorge da Mina. To everybody's disappointment they found that the coast turned south again instead
of continuing to the east as the world maps had led them to expect.
When the contract with Gomes expired Afonso turned over the
management of African affairs to his son John, who in his early

twenties was showing every sign of being made of the same stuff as his great grandfather, the first John of Avis.

Father and son were both aware of the extent of Prince Henry's researches and anxious to carry them further. On the other hand they were tantalized by the possibilities of proceeding westward to India. Afonso kept giving shipmasters charters to discover and claim as their own, under the suzerainty of the king, the mythical islands that appeared in the Atlantic on the world maps of the period. Since the marriage of a Lancastrian princess into the Scandinavian royal family there had been intermittent relations between the Danish and the Portuguese courts. Rumors filtered back of lands to the westward beyond Iceland. Afonso made inquiries through his ambassador about the possibility of a northwest passage to India. There was a story going around that two Portuguese seamen, sailing under Danish auspices, had reached a "land of the codfish" beyond Greenland.

In 1474, anxious to find a basis for these rumors, Afonso instructed his close councillor Fernão Martins, a canon of Lisbon cathedral, to consult the famous Florentine geographer Paulo Toscanelli about the best sailing route to India. Already two schools of thought were developing among Lisbon shipmasters and mapmakers. Some thought it more practical to continue Prince Henry's efforts to round the African continent, but others thought a faster and cheaper route could be found across the Western Ocean.

Toscanelli replied in a much discussed letter, of which the only copy to survive was found tucked into a heavily annotated book out of Christopher Columbus's library. Along with the letter Toscanelli sent a map of his own making to Lisbon. "In another case," he wrote Martins, with whom he had talked at a church council in Florence some years before, "I told you about a shorter route to the lands of spices than that which you take through Guinea." He explained the route laid out in his chart which was based on Marco Polo's account of the realms of the Great Khan. He expatiated on the immense traffic in pepper of a port named Zaiton and on the wealth of Japan (which, like Marco Polo, he called Cippangu) where the temples and royal palaces were roofed with solid gold. According to Toscanelli's map, which has unfortunately disappeared, India was just beyond the western horizon.

"There is," he put it, in the words Seneca had used centuries before, "no great space to be traversed over unknown waters."

Toscanelli's communication had hardly been received and digested by the king and his councillors when both the lucrative African trade and exploration of routes to the Indies were interrupted by war with Castile. The impetuous Afonso V had become involved in one of the dynastic quarrels that wrought such havoc among the Hispanic kingdoms.

Afonso's sister Joana was married to the ineffectual Henry IV of Castile. When Henry died a Castilian faction, supported by the Aragonese, claimed that her daughter, also named Joana, was illegitimate and that the rightful heir to the throne was Henry's sister Isabella. Afonso, who claimed he had been named Defender of the Castilian Realm by Henry on his deathbed, raised an army to support his niece's rights, and to clinch the matter had himself married to her at Palencia in Old Castile. The couple announced that they would wait for a dispensation from the pope before consummating the marriage but they assumed the style of King and Queen of Castile.

Meanwhile Henry's half sister, Isabela, had married the astute Fernando of Aragon. It was her supporters in Castile who had invented the slur against Joana in the first place. The gallant and impulsive Afonso was no match for that pair, who were known to history as Ferdinand and Isabella. They were already embarked on the relentless policies that were to subordinate the Castilian and Catalan factions and to unite the thrones of Castile and Aragon. Afonso's troops were defeated at Castel Queimado near Toro in the valley of the Douro. Isabella's forces captured the royal tent and with it, according to one story, the magnificent tapestries depicting Afonso "Africano's" capture of Tangier and Arzila, which he had had executed at Tournai in Flanders.

Afonso took the feckless course of sailing off to France with a small army to try to induce his Burgundian relatives and Louis XI to join in a fresh war to establish him on the throne of Castile. He should have known that the Burgundians and the French were bitter enemies. That sly old intriguer, Louis XI, gave him soft words, but Afonso's cousin Charles of Burgundy told him flatly he didn't trust Louis enough to enter into any alliance with him.

The truth of Charles' suspicions was proved when Louis—whose Swiss mercenaries were formidable pikemen—suddenly caught the Burgundian army off its guard in the winter of 1477 and inflicted such a defeat on it that Charles, nicknamed "the Bold," was killed and the power of the Dukes of Burgundy destroyed forever. All Afonso's hopes were dashed. There was no help forthcoming, either, from his cousin Edward IV of England, whose realm was in an uproar and whom the death of Charles of Burgundy left without an ally in Europe.

One of the unforeseen results of Afonso's ill-timed alliance with the French was that in August 1476 a combined French and Portuguese fleet under the famous freebooter Guillaume de Villenove swooped down on a convoy of Genoese merchant vessels preparing to double Cape St. Vincent. The pretext was that the Genoese were allied to the Burgundians. The seabattle lasted all day, and broke off after heavy losses on both sides. When one Genoese cargo ship went down a lanky young red-headed seaman saved himself by grabbing one of the great sweeps and swimming for the shore.

Cristoforo Colombo was then a barely literate deckhand of about twenty-two of a family of Genoese wool carders and weavers. He had seen service on cruises to Tunis and Chios in the Greek islands and as a Genoese was a natural seadog. With the other survivors he was cared for by the people of Lagos. Somehow he reached Lisbon where he was taken in by the Genoese colony. His younger brother Bartolomeo may well have been already established as a chartmaker there.

By his own account, the following year Columbus, as he is usually known, shipped for Iceland and sailed "a hundred leagues beyond." A lively trade went on at that time between Lisbon, Bristol, Galway and "the land of the codfish." European goods were exchanged for dried and salted fish. As quoted by his son Fernando, who wrote his life, the future Admiral of the Ocean Sea noted that the seas in those parts were not frozen and quite navigable but that the tides were phenomenally high. Since the tides in Iceland have only a range of thirteen feet, could he have picked up some inkling of the Bay of Fundy? In a note jotted in the margin of one of his books he speaks of seeing "men of Cathay" in Galway, a man and a woman of extraordinary appearance found in two boats adrift. Could they have been Eskimos?

Back in Lisbon Columbus set himself to learn to read and write. His first written language seems to have been Portuguese. His native Genoese was further from the classical Italian used by the humanists and geographers of Florence than it was from the language of the docks of Restelo. He learned Castilian which was coming into fashion with the upper classes in Lisbon. He is said to have supported himself by hawking printed books and later by drafting maps in association with Bartolomeo. The Columbus brothers were hard-working energetic young men. Lisbon, the boom town of the century, stuffed with their compatriots as with every other Mediterranean tribe, offered them a far better chance to rise in the world than *Genova la Superba*, which was in the sere and yellow of its splendor. Soon Columbus was adding Latin to his accomplishments.

Portugal was riding out the war under the vigorous management of young Prince John. In France Afonso seems to have been suddenly struck by the realization of his folly. He tried to renounce the kingship and to slip away from his retainers for a solitary pilgrimage to Jerusalem. He was found hiding in disguise by the officers of his court and induced to sail home to Lisbon. The royal party arrived in the Tagus in November 1477. John had assumed the crown but immediately renounced it in favor of his father.

Meanwhile the shipmasters of Palos and Cádiz were taking advantage of the war to intrude into the Guinea trade. Caravels out of Palos anchored off the African trading posts and pretending to be Portuguese, carried off slaves and gold. In a seabattle off Morocco a Portuguese squadron protecting their Guinea ships got the worst of it and lost two galleys burned and six hundred Milanese cuirasses captured which were to be used in the war against Castile. Afonso promulgated a savage edict ordering that the crews of any foreign vessels found trespassing on the Guinea coast, granted him by papal bull, were to be thrown into the sea.

Young Columbus meanwhile was rising fast in the busy world of waterfront Lisbon. In the summer of 1478 he was employed by the Centurione family of Genoa to purchase a shipload of Madeira sugar in Funchal and to transport it to Genoa. A few months later he was married to the daughter of the Bartolomeu Perestrello whom Prince Henry had made Captain General of Pôrto Santo. His wife Felipa belonged to her mother's side to the powerful family of the Moniz. Not a bad match for an uneducated young man who had been washed up naked and penniless on the beach only five years before.

Dona Felipa's mother, who had spent her married life in Pôrto Santo and Madeira, gave him old Perestrello's logs and sea charts which filled his mind with wild surmise about the possibility of finding land across the Western Ocean. A plan was dawning on him to promote an expedition of his own to the Indies. According to what he heard from the court geographers Toscanelli placed Japan some three thousand seamiles west of the Canaries. For confirmation he himself wrote Toscanelli and received in answer a copy of the letter to Canon Martins to which the Florentine added an encouraging postscript: "The said voyage is not only possible but it is sure and certain and will bring honor and the widest renown among all Christians." He added that he was convinced that the greater part of the people of those far-eastern countries were Christians, "I am not surprised that you, a man of great courage, and all the nation of the Portuguese, who have always been men of courage in all great enterprises, should be seen with hearts aflame to carry out the said voyage."

Columbus and his brother were ambitious. Christopher had all the instincts of a promoter. He felt the peculiar respect of self-educated men toward authority and academic standing. Toscanelli's letter certainly "set his heart aflame." Toscanelli, and Marco Polo behind him, constituted the authorities on which Columbus based a plan to equip an expedition to cross the Atlantic to the land where the roofs were of gold. So long as the war with Castile dragged on there was nothing to do but draw his maps and sell his books and wait.

The war continued to go badly for King Afonso. In February of 1479 another Portuguese force was defeated by the Castilians at Albuera but Ferdinand and Isabella shrewdly refrained from pushing their advantage too far. Both sides were tired of fighting. That same year they signed a peace treaty at the Portuguese royal palace of Alcáçovas by which Afonso and Joana renounced their pretensions to the throne of Castile. Afonso further gave up his claims to the Canary Islands; but in return the Castilians confirmed the monopoly which the pope had bestowed on the Portuguese for exploration and trade down the African coast to the Indies. Peace between the two countries was to be preserved indefinitely by the marriage between Prince John's son and a daughter of Ferdinand and Isabella. On the point of renouncing his throne and retiring to a monastery Afonso V died a disappointed and remorseful man.

John II was crowned in 1481. His first business was to restore Portuguese sovereignty on the Guinea coast. He dispatched a fleet under Fernão Gomes. They pounced on thirty-five merchantmen out of Palos and Cádiz anchored off the trading post of Mina. A special embassy was dispatched to Edward IV of England to beg him to keep his shipmen from poaching on Portuguese territory. About that time the Lisbon merchants, who had been complaining in the Cortes of foreign interlopers, learned with some satisfaction that the entire crew of a Flemish tradingship had been eaten by cannibals.

At home John II's prime task was to assert his authority over the great nobles who had been running wild under his father's lax rule. With the help of the commons in the Cortes he revived his great grandfather's "lei mental" promulgated under Dom Duarte by which grants to royal vassals were to be renewed under each new reign. Each one had to do special homage for his lands. The Duke of Bragança, who had become the most powerful man in Portugal, made an uproar in the Cortes, but he committed the indiscretion of allowing a royal official to go to his palace at Vila Viçosa to fetch back the deeds that gave him title to his estates. The official, rummaging among the documents, found proofs of a treasonable correspondence with Castile and Aragon which implicated the duke and his brother the Marquis of Montemór. He laid them before the king. John bided his time.

The merchants and shipmasters who formed the bulk of the commoners in the Cortes were already on his side. They were constantly complaining of the impositions of the landed nobles; but the king needed time to consolidate their support. Two years later he struck. The Duke of Bragança was arrested on a charge of treason, tried and executed at Evora. His estates were forfeited to the crown. The Marquis of Montemór fled out of the realm. When the Duke of Viseu, King John's wife's brother, the son of his uncle Fernando, who had been pardoned in the earlier trial on account of his youth, was implicated in a plot to assassinate him, John killed him with his own hands. Up to then no Portuguese king had felt he needed a bodyguard. John II instituted the royal guard.

Afonso V had left the finances of the kingdom in disarray. He had been so hard pressed that he levied a forced loan on the churches and monasteries. He was deeply in debt to the Florentine bankers. As heir apparent John had seen enough of the Guinea trade to understand that there lay the cure for the financial ills of the kingdom. One of the aims of Prince Henry's explorations had been to find the country the gold dust came from which the Arab caravans carried across the Sahara to Morocco and Tunis and Cairo. The trading post Fernão Gomes' captains established, which the Portuguese called São Jorge da Mina, was the nearest point yet discovered to the gold-producing region. They were tapping a part of Africa the Arabs had never penetrated. It was given the name of Mina because the Portuguese still thought the bulk of the gold came from a mine, instead of from alluvial sandbeds as proved to be the case. John decided the place must be fortified.

He appointed as governor of Mina Diogo de Azambuja, an officer of his bodyguard, a man of noble birth who had been lamed in the wars of earlier reigns and who had served on a number of diplomatic missions. Dom Diogo sailed south with a fleet of nine caravels carrying five hundred soldiers and a hundred stonemasons and carpenters and accompanied by two "round ships" of 400 tons loaded with construction materials. The caravels were commanded by the best seacaptains of the realm, Bartolomeu Dias and João Afonso de Aveiro. For defense against interlopers the king, who had considerable knowledge of artillery, equipped the ships with a new type of bombard which would fire almost level with the water so that the aim was much more accurate than from the old mortars. His armorers were already experimenting with breech-loading cannons.

Dom Diogo treated the Negro chiefs as he would European dignitaries and, in a short time, at a meeting under a boabab tree, obtained their permission to erect a warehouse in the form of a castle and a church dedicated to São Jorge where masses were immediately sung for the repose of Prince Henry's soul. The place was made a municipality in 1486. According to Duarte Pacheco writing in his "Esmeralda," within a few years gold dust to the value of a hundred and seventy gold dobras was reaching Portugal each year from the factory at Mina. Trading voyages, many of them on behalf of the crown, yielded six times the money invested. Now John would buy all the silver he needed from abroad and mint gold coins to be used for foreign trade in the hands of the royal exchequer. He repaid the churches and monasteries for the forced loan his father had made on their silver and re-established his country's credit with the Florentine bankers. Soon little Portugal had the soundest currency in Europe.

It must have been on some caravel bound for Mina during the period of the building of the castle that Columbus made the trip down the Guinea coast to the equator which he referred to in notes on methods of taking sights on the sun he left in the margins of some of the books he owned. He further added that he had learned from his own experience that the opinion of the old geographers that human beings could not live under the equator was completely erroneous. On the contrary the equatorial shores were extremely populous.

Though in some documents Columbus speaks of himself as a citizen of Genoa, it is likely that during this period of his life he was considered Portuguese. Toscanelli addressed him as Portuguese. The war with Spain had resulted in considerable xenophobia among the merchants and mariners of Lisbon. Soon after his coronation a Cortes petitioned King John to rid the country of the swarming Genoese who served no function except to spy on the Guinea trade and on the discoveries being made among the western islands. This Cortes further petitioned the king to put an end to the extortions of the Jewish tax-gatherers to whom the taxes had been farmed out under King Afonso.

John II assented to neither. His feeling seems to have been that Portugal stood to gain from the immigration of Italians and Germans who brought in such valuable crafts as mapmaking and printing and from the Jews learned in medicine and astronomy who were coming into the realm in increasing numbers as riots and persecutions drove them out of Castile and Aragon—now united into a single kingdom under the iron rule of "the Catholic Kings."

In fact Jewish scientists were high in the king's councils. Mestre Rodrigo, the king's personal physician and José Vizinho, who was the pupil of a famous rabbi Abraham Zacuto, who taught mathematics at the University of Salamanca, were members of the junta of learned men—in the style of his great uncle's school at Sagres—which John collected about him to work out tables for navigation and particularly to devise methods for ascertaining the latitude south of the equator.

John was a close-mouthed ruler. He instituted a policy not only of secrecy about the African trade and the westward voyages, but actually sent out false reports to discourage interlopers, such as the story he circulated, over the protests of one of his skippers, that it was impossible for a "round" or square-rigged ship to beat back to Portugal from the Gold Coast. In his chronicle of the reign Garcia de Resende wrote that the king kept a list of those of his subjects who might be useful in exploration or administration. His aim was to pick men for their merit instead of for their influence at court. No wonder he was known as "the perfect prince" according to Machiavelli's prescription.

In order to have the Guinea trade under his eye he moved from Lagos to Lisbon the chief counting house and the mart where slaves and ivory and African pepper were sold. There he could keep track of each incoming cargo from the windows of his palace on the Praça do Comércio. So thoroughly did he examine every document that passed through the royal offices that he had to invent a stamp to use in lieu of his signature.

Diogo de Azambuja was more of an administrator than an explorer. For his next expedition the king picked an eager young man who had made a name for himself by capturing three Spanish vessels poaching along the Guinea coast. He was a young commoner named Diogo Cão. "Dog" must have been his nickname. Cão carried with him an assortment of heavy stone pillars surmounted with the crosses of the Order of Christ and carved with the royal arms to mark the capes and promontories he should discover as within the trading area of the Portuguese crown. He revictualed at Mina and sailed south to the mouth of the Congo where he set up one of his monuments.

He got along well with the Bantu tribes to the south of the great river. He sent four messengers upriver in native canoes to search out a great king the river Negroes told tales about and carried four local dignitaries back to Portugal with him as pledges for their safety. One of these men learned Portuguese, was converted to Christianity and became quite a figure at court. He was sent back with a religious mission under the name of Dom João da Silva a few years later.

When Diogo Cão reached Lisbon, King John promptly dubbed him knight, furnished him with a coat of arms, and sent him back to reclaim his messengers. Cão found them at the mouth of the Congo and was so encouraged by the willingness of the Congolese to accept Christianity and to enter into close relations with the Portuguese kingdom that he sailed his caravels up the river as far as the falls of Yelala. There he left inscriptions on the rocks which exist to this day. After that he proceeded southward along the coast setting up pillars as he went, until he reached Cape Cross in what is now the Republic of South Africa. There by some unrecorded mischance, plague or fever probably, he met his death.

Meanwhile the interest of King John and his junta in voyages across the Western Ocean never slackened. Columbus, perhaps emboldened by the success of Diogo Cão, a poor commoner like himself, wangled an introduction at court and presented to John II a plan for crossing the Western Ocean based on the reports of Marco Polo and on Toscanelli's letter. The result was reported by Barros. "The king, as he observed this Christovão Colom to be a big talker and boastful in setting forth his accomplishments, and more puffed up with fancy and imagination about his island Cypango than certain of the things he told about, gave him small credit." The king turned him over to his scientific junta. "They all considered the words of Christovão Colom as vain, simply founded on imagination or things like Marco Polo's Isle Cypango."

It is not known exactly what terms Columbus asked of the king but it is certain that the king considered the speculation too risky. He was only too glad to offer grants donatory of any lands discovered to anyone who would pay his own way. In 1485, two islanders, one from Terceira in the Azores, a Fleming whose name appeared in Portuguese as Fernão Dulmo, and the other a citizen of Funchal in Madeira, had easily obtained a license to seek the island of Antilia. They fitted out two ships at their own expense and sailed west from Terceira some months later. They seem to have been driven back by the prevailing westerlies without sighting any land at all. It is likely that other shipmasters attempting the middle Atlantic passage suffered the same fate.

These were years of frustration for the ardent Genoese. His high-born wife Dona Felipa died, leaving him one small son. Having expended a great deal of money to give her a funeral suited to her noble origin, Columbus, taking along little Diego and leaving mostly debts and rumors of wild projects behind him in Lisbon, set out to try his fortune in Castile.

King John and his junta had by this time decided to concentrate their efforts on the African route. At least these voyages brought gold to the royal exchequer and an abundance of African pepper and slaves for sale at the Casa da Guiné.

According to the records of the bakery near the Lisbon docks which turned out sea biscuit for the caravels a great many more ships must have sailed for the Guinea coast during the fourteen eighties than are mentioned in the court chronicles, but the next recorded expedition, that of Bartolomeu Dias, who was appointed to command the king's caravel *São Christovão* in October of 1486, was the decisive one.

King John still believed that if his ships continued far enough around Africa they would find themselves in the dominions of Prester John. The king was trying to establish communication with that potentate by other means, but he sent along with Bartolomeu Dias six Negroes, four of them women, who had been carefully trained to spread among the tribes news of the munificence and the friendly intentions of the Portuguese. The Negro emissaries were garbed in bright clothes and instructed to broadcast a message to Prester John asking for an exchange of ambassadors.

Sometime in the late summer of 1487 Bartolomeu Dias sailed from Lisbon with three caravels and proceeded directly to one of

Diogo Cão's last ports of call, an excellent anchorage in what is now Alexander Bay. From there they coasted south along a barren and inhospitable coast. They were lashed by strong southeast winds.

They were held up in what is now Luderitz Bay for five days by severe weather. They had reached a cool climate. On a promontory to the south they erected one of their pillars of which fragments have survived. When they put out to sea another storm blew up. The cold became intense. For thirteen days they scudded before the gale with shortened sail. When the wind suddenly moderated they steered due east hoping to sight land again. When no land appeared they set their course into the north.

Their first landfall was a harbor now known as Mossel Bay, a good two hundred miles east of the Cape of Good Hope. Dias' men called it Bahia dos Vaqueiros because of the great herds of cattle they saw grazing on the shore. When they tried to make friends with the wooly-headed natives who herded the flocks they were driven off by volleys of stones.

The coast led them in an easterly direction, but there was no sign of civilization, or of anything that might indicate an approach to India. The ships breasted a stiff current. The men were worn out after weeks of buffeting seas. They clamored to start for home.

Dias called a meeting. First he made each man swear that he would cast his vote in the best interests of his king and his country. When the vote was solid for returning home he drew up a document which he had every man sign, so that the blame for failing to press forward to India would not be his.

Then, after some more prospecting along South Africa's east coast, the crews of the caravels erected a farthest pillar in honor of St. Gregory and set their sails for home. What is now called Cape Agulhas they named for St. Brennan, the seagoing Irish saint who was supposed to have discovered so many islands that appeared on the maps of the North Atlantic, but were never sighted by seamen. This fixed the date as May 16, 1488.

A favorable breeze carried them westward to the Cape of Good Hope. According to Barros it was Dias who gave it that name. There they spent some time reconnoitering the magnificent harbor before sailing back up the west coast to the point where they had left the storeship under Bartolomeu's brother Diogo.

The storeship had been overrun by natives. Everything had been gutted and most of the crew killed. Of the three surviving Portuguese one dropped dead of a heart attack on seeing relief arrive. Abandoning the caravel which had become hopelessly foul Dias took aboard his brother and the other survivor.

Dias was heading for home empty handed. It was only through the experience of subsequent voyages that the importance of the Cape of Good Hope dawned on the Portuguese. To meet the expenses of the expedition he managed to take on a cargo of slaves along the Guinea coast and a shipment of gold at Mina. On the nearby island of Príncipe he rescued the notable explorer Duarte Pacheco stranded there by the loss of his ship.

It was late December of 1488 before Dias crossed the bar of the Tagus and triumphantly anchored his two battered caravels off the beach at Restelo. According to Columbus's own notes he was at court the day Dias showed his charts and sailing records to the king.

Columbus had come back to Lisbon after two years of hope deferred while he danced attendance on the court of the Catholic Kings. He had interested two noble patrons in his enterprise, and had found himself a charming but lowly mistress in Córdoba, who became the mother of his son Fernando, but he had failed to obtain the support of the royal pair. His brother Bartolomeu failed in a similar effort with Henry VII of England. In despair he had decided to try again with John II of Portugal, but his creditors had been so threatening when he left that he did not dare return to Lisbon without a safe-conduct. King John, whose own hopes of a passage to India had been somewhat dashed by the prolonged absence of Bartolomeu Dias, graciously assured Columbus that he need have no fear of being imprisoned by his creditors: "We promise you that neither on your way hither or during your stay with us, nor on your return, will you be arrested, detained, accused, cited or prosecuted in any suit, civil or criminal of any kind whatsoever."

It was Columbus's bad luck that hardly had he been received at the Portuguese court when the two lost caravels appeared off Restelo. Bartolomeu Dias immediately brought in his charts to prove to the king that he had circumnavigated Africa and discovered the famous Cape which was to be the pivot on which all future voyages to the Indies would turn.

John was convinced that the route to India lay open. He had no further use for Columbus.

2

OVERLAND TO PRESTER JOHN

John II was making a two-pronged attack on the problem of discovering the best route to India. First he wanted to establish relations with the Abyssinian Christians either directly through Egypt or overland through friendly Negro kingdoms up the Niger River. Second he was pursuing with ever-increasing zeal his great uncle Prince Henry's project of circumnavigating Africa.

He sent off emissaries to Abyssinia in 1482 but they were stalled in Jerusalem by their ignorance of Arabic. They did bring back fresh news of the court of the Christian Negus which added to the body of information building up in Europe through the years as a result of the visits of Abyssinian envoys.

The king's plan to penetrate the interior of Africa from the west was frustrated when a native ruler named Bemoim, whom he'd baptized and made much of in Lisbon in preparation for his acting as guide and interpreter for an expedition up the Niger, was killed in a brawl on the Portuguese flagship. Bemoim's project was to find the great king who was supposed to confirm all the lesser kings in Africa in their rule by sending them wooden crosses. Could this be some relic of early Christian penetration? The question was never answered. According to Rui de Pina, Bemoim's death was deeply mourned at the Portuguese court. His oratory was particularly appreciated there. "When he spoke," wrote the royal chronicler, "his words and sentences seemed to come, not from a barbarous Negro, but from a Greek prince educated at Athens."

The following year King John resolved to try again. A secret meeting of the *junta dos Matemáticos* was called at the mansion of Pedro de Alcaçovas, the king's treasurer and most intimate councillor. The only member of the royal family to be let in on the project was eighteen-year-old Dom Manoel, Duke of Beja, the son of Prince Henry's heir Fernando. Afonso, the heir apparent to whom the king was passionately devoted, was not old enough to take part in these deliberations. In spite of King John's having had to kill Manoel's elder brother, Manoel was becoming his favorite.

Before this gathering there appeared a royal retainer named Covilhã.

Pedro de Covilhã, though of Portuguese birth, had first appeared at the court of Afonso V as a groom in the train of the powerful Andalusian Duke of Medina Sidonia. Afonso took a fancy to him and made him his squire. He accompanied the royal party on Afonso's ill-fated journey to France. When John assumed the crown Covilhã became an officer in the royal guard. Since he spoke Castilian like a native he was detailed to watch the doings of the emigré Portuguese nobles at the Spanish court. Later he perfected his Arabic on confidential missions to Tlemcen and Fez. With his help a plan was worked out in the junta. Accompanied by another of the king's retainers, also fluent in Arabic, Antonio de Paiva, Covilhã was to disguise himself as a merchant and make his way to Cairo. Secrecy was essential because the Castilians, the Venetians and the Barcelona shipowners all had agents out in search of the sources of the spice trade. The trading nations of Europe were trying to take advantage of a lull in the war against the Turks to establish direct relations with India.

Carrying a draft on the Marchioni bankers in Lisbon cashable in Valencia and a special chart of the Indian regions drawn for them by the geographers of the junta, the travelers rode across the peninsula. In Barcelona they obtained a fresh draft on the Florentine bank run by the Medici in Naples. In Naples they learned that the Levant was safer for Christians than it had been in the memory of man.

The Knights Hospitalers of St. John of Jerusalem who garrisoned the great castles on Rhodes were under the leadership of an exceptionally able Grand Master. He had in his hands as a hostage the legitimate heir to the Sultan Mahomet who had captured Constantinople. He was using his hostage with diplomatic skill.

The travelers immediately set sail for Rhodes, where they were welcomed by one of the Portuguese knights who was the son of the king's biographer Rui de Pina. With his help they invested in a stock of honey, a commodity for which the island was famous, and sailed for Alexandria on a ship skippered by an experienced Catalan.

The first difficulty they encountered in Alexandria was that the Egyptian traders wanted wood for shipbuilding and the forbidden items: iron, sulphur and gunpowder more than they wanted honey. After weeks of haggling the two Portuguese fell ill from the malarial fevers of the place and were so near death that the local Naïb tried to seize their stock of honey. They recovered in time to get it out of his clutches. By the spring of 1488 they were well enough to proceed by caravan and ship to Aden.

Aden was then the terminus of the seaborn traffic from the Orient. Its storehouses were filled with pepper, camphor, aloes, cloves, cinnamon, cardamon, nutmeg, musk and of the velvets, silks, brocades and porcelain that came from India and China. Tin, always in short supply, was obtainable there. These goods were moved to Alexandria and thence into Europe on Italian and Catalan bottoms to the enormous profit of all the middlemen. John II's plan, for which Covilhã and Paiva were spying out the routes, was to switch that trade round the African continent to Lisbon.

In Aden the travelers separated. Paiva set out for Abyssinia and was seen no more. Covilhã sailed in a large ship which transported pilgrims to and from Cananor of the Malabar Coast. He was the first Portuguese to set foot in India. He visited Goa and Calicut and crossed over to the great Arab port of Ormuz in the entrance to the Persian Gulf. In the company of Arab traders he cruised up and down the East African coast. Three years after leaving Lisbon he was back in Cairo. There he learned of Paiva's death, and found messengers waiting for him with letters from King John. The messengers were Portuguese Jews, the Rabbi Abraham of Beja and a cobbler from Lamego named Josef. Josef had already been to Ormuz and had filled the king's ears with tales of the immense wealth of its trade. Rabbi Abraham had sworn to the king that he would not return without seeing Ormuz with his own eyes.

The only record of these journeyings to survive was the account of a Portuguese priest named Francisco Alvares who served as chronicler and chaplain to a Portuguese embassy sent up into Abyssinia thirty years later by the Captain General of the Indies. Padre Alvares tracked Covilhã down. He was alive and well. He had married a native and raised a family and been endowed with lands and feudal holdings, living at the court of the ruler whom Alvares always called Prester John. He had found it hard enough to reach the Abyssinian highlands. Once he got there he was not allowed to leave. The policy of the Abyssinian rulers was that foreigners who managed to reach their remote valleys should be well treated but should never be allowed to go home.

Covilhã made himself useful to the Portuguese embassy. To Alvares he told the story of the orders he received from John II in Cairo: "When the letters were delivered and read, their import was, that if all the things they came for were seen, discovered and learned, that they (Paiva and Covilhã) should return, and welcome; and they would receive great favors: but if all were not found and discovered, they were to send word of what they had found, and to labor to learn the rest; and chiefly they were to go and see and learn about the great king Prester John, and show the city of Ormuz to the Rabbi Abraham. . . . Here he (Covilhã) at once wrote by the shoemaker of Lamego, how he had discovered cinnamon and pepper in the city of Calicut (on the Malabar Coast) and that cloves came from beyond, but that all could be had there; and that he had been in the cities of Cananor, Calicut, and Goa, all on that coast, and to this they [the Portuguese] could sail by sea from their coast and the seas of Guinea, coasting the (East African) shore of Sofala—which he had also visited—or a great island [Madagascar], which the Moors called the Island of the Moon; they say it has three hundred leagues of coast, and that from each of these lands one can lay a fair course to Calicut."

Pedro de Covilhã was a stout fellow. As soon as he had dispatched his report back to the king, by the cobbler of Lamego, he and the rabbi took ship for Aden and Ormuz. There Covilhã left Rabbi Abraham.

Covilhã was by this time so adept at passing as a Moor that he sailed to Jeddah and visited the holy cities of Mecca and Medina. Thence, according to one account, he made a pilgrimage to the famous monastery of St. Catherine in the Sinai peninsula to beg forgiveness for having disguised himself off as a Moslem. From there he made his way to Tor on the Red Sea and to Zeila, then the chief port of the Abyssinian kingdom.

Undoubtedly Covilhã had the same sort of adventures that Padre Alvares so vividly described: the difficulty of finding baggage animals, the heat, the thievery of villagers and the threat of bandits, the treachery and ignorance of guides, flash floods in dry watercourses; the importunities of the monks in the numerous monasteries; mountains crowded with baboons; the fevers, the delays, the wild beasts that beset the camping places at night; the paths over mountain passes so steep men had to crawl on their hands and knees . . . until they came out on a land of stone churches carved out of the solid rock, and great green valleys where Prester John and his retainers lived in red and white tents that they were continually moving from place to place. Then came the difficulties and frustrations of trying to communicate with Prester John, who only spoke through messengers or on state occasions from behind a veil, and was always guarded by four chained lions.

The Prester John when Covilhã arrived was named Eskander. He received the letters of King John of Portugual "with much pleasure and joy and said that he would send him home to his country with much honor." Unfortunately he died. When his brother Nahum assumed the throne he refused to give Covilhã permission to leave. Nahum's son David succeeded him. He too refused to let Covilhã go, claiming that it was enough that he had received lands and lordships to enjoy. And so the matter stood.

"This Pedro de Covilhã," wrote Padre Alvares, "is a man that knows all the languages that can be spoken, both of Christians, Moors and Gentiles, and who knows all the things for which he was sent: moreover he gives an account of them as if they were present before him."

3

THE MALABAR COAST

The last years of John II's life were beset with tribulations. Though he was still in his thirties a kidney ailment was ruining his health. The enterprise of the Indies was stalled. For reasons which have not been completely unraveled Bartolomeu Dias' great discoveries were not immediately followed up. He seems never to have received a commensurate reward. It may be that the king was hoping that one of the voyages to the westward he was still quietly encouraging out of Madeira and the Azores might open up a shorter passage to India. Whether or not they sighted Greenland or Newfoundland or the easternmost bulge of Brazil after battling the prevailing westerlies the seafarers came home with no gold or spices to report. Among knowledgeable seamen the conviction already prevailed that there were large stretches of land within sailing distance to the west. Still Africa was where the profits were in gold and slaves. The African route had priority.

Great efforts were made to convert the Congolese chiefs to Christianity and through them to send messengers to Prester John, but every mission was balked by the vastness of the forests and the miasma of fever that hung over the rivers. Every failure stung. Barros described King John as being like a balked lion seeking his prey in a thicket of thorns and briars.

The final blow was the death of his only son. Riding down

from a royal residence near Sacavém to watch his father swim in
the Tagus, young Afonso was thrown from his horse and killed.
It was a July afternoon in 1491. The king never recovered from
his grief. Now all Portugal's hopes for the succession depended
on his cousin, Manoel, Dom Fernando's son. Already the young
duke of Beja was privy to the plans and secrets of the great
enterprise which had become the hereditary task of the House of
Avis.

The king's junta dos matemáticos already had before them the
charts and sailing directions for the southern tip of the East African
coast as far north as the Rio do Infante which were compiled
from the logbooks brought back by Bartolomeu Dias. When
Pedro de Covilhã's letters were delivered by the shoemaker from
Lamego, they could trace the outlines of the coast as far south as
Sofala. Only three hundred leagues of undiscovered territory lay
between.

Bartolomeu Dias had failed to put down a virtual mutiny of his
crews: perhaps that was why the king passed him over when he
planned a fresh expedition. Estevão de Gama, a nobleman of the
court who commanded the fortress of Sines on the sandy coast of
the Alentejo was put in charge of preparations. When he died his
sons Paulo and Vasco took over. It is hard to imagine that caravels
were not sent out annually to record the winds and currents of
the South Atlantic, because, when the expedition eventually sailed,
under Vasco de Gama, a far westward course was plotted out
from the Cape Verde Islands to the Cape of Good Hope, which
was hardly improved on during the four hundred years of more
sophisticated seamanship that followed.

On March 6, 1493, when the ailing king was resting near the
monastery of Santa Maria das Virtudes, amid the pinewoods of a
rich farming region some twenty miles east of Lisbon known as the
Vale do Paraíso, a courier arrived from Lisbon with the news that
Christopher Columbus, whom he had dismissed as a vain boaster
four years before, was anchored within the bar of the Tagus on the
caravel *Niña*, having discovered the island of Antilla and Cipangu
in the easternmost Indies and brought home gold and parrots and
captured Indians.

Columbus, that brilliant promoter, had managed to take advantage of the burst of confidence of the Spanish court that followed the subjugation of Granada in January of 1492 to induce Ferdinand to sign his famous contract. He had hurriedly outfitted three ships at Palos and set forth. Following the course recommended by Toscanelli, he had sailed due west from Gomera in the Canaries and landed thirty-three days later on what is now Watling Island in the Bahamas. On the return trip the two surviving ships— *Santa Maria* was lost on a reef off Hispaniola—made their first landfall on the island of Santa Maria in the Azores. The crews suffered some mistreatment by the Portuguese governor there who suspected them of poaching on the Portuguese dominions and, after nearly foundering in a terrific gale during which *Niña* became separated from *Pinta*, Columbus had been driven into the mouth of the Tagus.

The morning after he anchored off Restelo the master of one of the King of Portugal's most heavily armed vessels came abroad to request that Columbus come over to the flagship to show his papers. This master was the same Bartolomeu Dias who, when he appeared at John II's court after discovering the Cape of Good Hope, had caused Columbus such discomfiture a few years before. Columbus promptly told him that he was the admiral of the kings of Spain and not accustomed to leave his ship for anyone. Bartolomeu Dias then asked civilly to see his credentials. After reading them he went back to report to his captain, one Alvaro Damão "who," so Columbus noted in his log, promptly "in great state, with noise of drums, trumpets and pipes, came aboard the caravel, spoke with the admiral, and offered to do all he commanded."

The king made a show of being a good sport. He sent a fidalgo of his court with orders that *Niña* be refitted at the royal expense. Columbus was to be escorted into the royal presence. The admiral, whose ship had been crowded to the gunwale with astonished visitors ever since he dropped his anchor, "although he didn't wish to go" set out in the rain. Tradition has it that he took along some Indians and a few gold ornaments as exhibits. According to Rui de Pina, who may have been present, "the king showed that he suffered irritation and distress because he believed that this discovery was made within the seas and boundaries of his Lordship of Guinea, which was prohibited; and because the said admiral was somewhat elevated above his condition and in telling the tale always exceeded the bounds of truth and made the story of gold, silver and riches much greater than it was. Especially the king blamed himself for negligence in dismissing him for want of credit and authority in regard to this discovery for which he first presented his propositions."

For Columbus it was a ticklish time. Though King John was outwardly cordial the admiral feared foul play. He had already sent off a letter describing his discovery to Ferdinand and Isabella by a reliable messenger, but since *Pinta* had not yet been heard from he couldn't help wondering whether King John might not try to wipe out all memory of his discoveries by having his throat cut. Rui de Pina, who was privy to all the gossip of the court, wrote that the king was urged by some of his courtiers to have Columbus killed, "since the prosecution of this enterprise by the kings of Castile would cease with the death of the discoverer; and that this could be done discreetly if he consented and ordered it; insomuch as the admiral was discourteous and puffed up with pride they could fix it so that any one of his shortcomings would seem to be the true cause of his death. But the king, like the god-fearing prince he was, not only forbade this but on the contrary showed him honor and much kindness and therewith sent him away."

Before he could return to Lisbon the admiral had to pay his respects to the queen and to the Duke of Beja who were staying at a charming gothic convent near Vila Franca de Xira. He was received with every courtesy and, as soon as he decently could, kissed the hands of Queen Leonor and hurried down to a village on the Tagus shore where he hired a boat to take him back to his ship. Before he could push off next morning a squire of King John arrived with two mules as presents and offered to arrange the admiral's journey overland to Castile. Furthermore the squire brought a very large gratuity for the admiral's pilot.

Columbus was a seafaring man. He'd had enough of scrambling through bad roads in the muck and the rain. Besides he was more than a little suspicious of the king's offer. It would be too easy to get him murdered by the bandits that infested the border region. He thanked the king's squire for his trouble and embarked for Lisbon. Next day without setting foot again on Portuguese soil, he

upped his anchors and trimmed the new sails *Niña* had been outfitted with. A northerly wind and a strong ebb tide carried him
across the bar. He rounded Cape St. Vincent and set his course for
the mouth of the Spanish Guadiana, whence he had sailed seven
months before.

Columbus's return set off a great scurrying to Rome of Portuguese and Spanish diplomats. As soon as the admiral told his story
to Ferdinand and Isabella, who were holding court in Barcelona,
the representatives of the Catholic Kings obtained a papal bull
confirming them in their possession of Columbus's discoveries. Immediately King John began to equip a fleet to uphold his rights to
the navigation and trade of the Guinea coast, the islands to the west
of it and the Indies beyond. Pope Alexander VI who was a
Spaniard, Rodrigo Borja by name, and much indebted to the
Catholic Kings for his elevation to the Holy See, promptly promulgated three more bulls each setting narrower westward limits
to the future Portuguese empire.

Ferdinand and Isabella started outfitting fresh ships in Seville
to secure Columbus's discoveries. At the same time they let John II
know that they were willing to settle by negotiation the boundaries
between the unknown lands open to discovery by the Spaniards
and the Portuguese. While the Admiral of the Ocean Sea was leading out a flotilla of seventeen sail to explore the West Indies and
to establish settlements on Hispaniola, the emissaries of John and
the Catholic Kings were haggling over the position of the various
lands sighted or surmised beyond the Western Ocean. Throughout
the negotiations John II insisted that there were lands to the southward of Columbus's discoveries and that they lay in the Portuguese
sphere.

The result was the treaty of Tordesillas, signed in June of
1494, by which, measuring from some vaguely specified point in
the Cape Verde Islands, the north-south division line was pushed
some two hundred and seventy leagues further west than in Pope
Alexander's bulls. It was agreed that a commission of "pilots,
astrologers, seamen and others" should meet in the Canaries the
following year, from there proceed to the Cape Verde Islands, and
thence sail west in two caravels until they found land or reached
the agreed-upon meridian. Both parties soon came to realize that

they did not have the technical equipment to trace such a line with accuracy. No reliable method had yet been invented for establishing longitude. In an exchange of notes the Spanish and Portuguese courts agreed to let the matter ride; it would be sufficient if they let each other know of their latest discoveries. Indeed the new worlds discovered to the east and the west proved so enormous that it was many years before the Spanish and Portuguese found themselves impinging on each others' spheres of influence.

King John died in 1495 and Manoel, soon to be known as the Fortunate, ruled in his stead. Manoel I was twenty-six. For years he had been associated by his cousin with every plan connected with the enterprise of the Indies. He never forgot that his father had been Prince Henry's adopted son. In fact as a very young man he paid off out of his own revenues such of his great uncle's debts as were still outstanding.

His device was the armillary sphere, the hollow sphere used in measuring the heavens. It was symbol of a plan to circumnavigate the globe. For these enterprises he had to have peace at home. His first act was to recall the members of the vast Bragança clan from exile and to restore them to their lands. As soon as he had concluded the formalities of appearing before a Cortes in Lisbon and calling in the royal council for consultation, he set to work to hasten the preparations, which had lagged in the last years of King John's life, for an expedition to India. After Estevão da Gama's death some discussion arose as to which of his sons should be in command. The elder, Paulo, insisted on stepping aside, saying that his younger brother Vasco was better qualified. Paulo would sail as captain of one of the ships. Vasco had already proved himself a man of ruthless energy by the speed with which, when he had naval command of the Algarve, he seized all the French ships in his ports in reprisal for the plundering by French pirates of a Portuguese merchantman.

Four ships were under construction in the shipyards of Restelo. A new type of square-rigged "nao" with a larger cargo capacity was being built to replace the agile caravels. It was felt that enough had been learned about taking advantage of the trade winds in the South Atlantic to make the caravels' peculiar capabilities in beating to windward unnecessary. In order to breast the great seas Bartolomeu Dias reported off the Cape of Good Hope the ships were to be of unusually heavy construction. Although the director of the Casa da Guiné was in charge of the shipyards, Dias himself was called in to pick the timbers to be used. For armament they carried mortars and some recently perfected breech-loading guns that fired straight across the water.

The fleet sailed from Restelo in July 8, 1497. The night before the captains and crews spent in prayer in the little chapel of Nossa Senhora de Belém which Prince Henry had built for the use of seamen fifty or sixty years before. There two naos of about a hundred and twenty tons, *São Rafael* and *São Gabriel*, a weatherwise caravel of fifty tons named *Berrio* for scouting and, in addition, a heavy storeship of two hundred tons. Bartolomeu Dias, who had been appointed to the captaincy of the castle of São Jorge da Mina, kept them company in another ship.

They reached São Tiago in the Cape Verde Islands in about three weeks. There they took on meat and wood and overhauled their spars and yards.

Though there are numerous accounts by historians and chroniclers, the only actual log of the journey that has come down to us was kept by a soldier or sailor of middling rank on Paulo da Gama's ship. He has come to be known as Old Alvaro.

He tells of their sailing east from São Tiago; then south; and then south by west. From some point far south on the great semicircle to the west they must have run east before the westerly winds but Alvaro doesn't mention it. He notes that on November 4 after having been almost exactly three months at sea and having covered eight hundred leagues, they saw land ahead. The ships drew near each other, the seamen put on their gala clothes and saluted the captain-major's flagship by firing bombards and dressing the halyards with flags and standards.

This landfall was a great disappointment to the captains and pilots. They had hoped that their course would have brought them clean around the Cape of Good Hope. Finding, after another loop to the westward, that the coast was still running in the same direction, they reconnoitered a large bay which opened up before them and at last came to anchor in a smooth harbor which they named the Bay of St. Helena. There they spent eight days cleaning the ships and taking on wood.

At first they could find no trace of the wooly headed natives described by Bartolomeu Dias. The captain major—as Alvaro calls da Gama—took his great wooden astrolabe ashore to try to get an accurate observation of the sun.

"The inhabitants of this country are brown," wrote Alvaro. "All they eat is the flesh of seals, whales and gazelles and the roots of herbs. They are dressed in skins and wear sheaths over their private parts."

Alvaro bought one of these sheaths for a small copper coin and made the deduction that the Hottentots valued copper more than tradegoods. They showed no interest in the seed pearls, gold and spices that the Portuguese showed them. They preferred small bells and tin rings. Alvaro found the climate healthy and temperate, producing good pasture. He saw cormorants, gulls, doves and crested larks that reminded him of Portugal. The packs of dogs looked like Portuguese dogs and barked like them.

At first the Hottentots were agreeable and gave the impression of relishing the food the Portuguese gave them. They seemed so unwar-like that the Portuguese took to leaving their arms aboard ship, but when one of the crew tried to visit a native village they turned nasty. He was rescued in the nick of time by the crew of a boat that was fishing for whales along the shore. The captain major went ashore to see what the scrimmage was about and was wounded by an assagai in the leg.

November 16 they put to sea. Pero d'Alenquer, the chief pilot, who had piloted Bartolomeu Dias' ship eight years before, declared that he knew the coast and that the Cape could not be more than thirty leagues to the southward. According to Alvaro it took them six days and three great tacks out to sea to buck the adverse winds before they succeeded in rounding the Cape of Good Hope. He says nothing of the tremendous storms and attempted mutiny described by later historians.

Late on Saturday November 25, St. Catherine's Day, they entered the bay which Dias had previously visited and called Angra dos Vaqueiros. There they took on water and broke up the big supply ship, dividing her stores and crew among the other three. Toward the end of the following week, the Hottentots, about ninety of them, put in an appearance. The captain major and the other captains, attended by armed men and crossbowmen, landed on an open part of the beach where there was no danger of an ambush. "He made the Negroes understand, by signs, that they were to disperse and to approach him only singly or in couples. To those he gave small bells and red skull caps, in return for which they presented him with ivory bracelets such as they wore on their arms."

They behaved in a most friendly fashion. Alvaro thought news must have come overland of the good treatment the Portuguese had given the people at Bay St. Helena, "even giving things away which were ours."

Next day about two hundred came, both old and young with a dozen steers and cows and three or four sheep. "As soon as we saw them we went ashore. Right away they began to play on four or five flutes, some producing high notes and others low, so that they made a pretty harmony for Negroes who are not expected to be musicians: and they danced in the Negro style. The captain major then ordered the trumpets to be sounded, and we in the boats danced, and the captain major with us. And, when the festivity ended, we landed where we had landed before and traded three bracelets for a black steer, off which we dined on Sunday. He was very fat and his flesh was as tasty as beef in Portugal."

They killed seals and penguins on an island in the bay and after living high off the local beef for thirteen days, prepared to depart. First they erected a *padrão*, a pillar with the arms of King Manoel, and a huge cross. They had hardly left their anchorage before a group of Hottentots rushed out to tear them down.

Sailing north up the coast they encountered alternate calms and storms and found themselves breasting a stiff current. By December 16 they had passed the last padrão erected by Bartolomeu Dias. Four days later, after much tacking back and forth, they were still abreast of an island they thought to have left sixty leagues behind. Luckily a strong stern wind came up and carried them up the coast in spite of the current. By Christmas Day they had coasted along seventy leagues of undiscovered country. After this they kept far out to sea to avoid the adverse current until the drinking water began to fail. On January 11, 1498 they ran inshore and cast anchor off the mouth of a small river.

This country was full of villages. There seemed to be more women than men. The people received them so well they called it The Land of Good People. The natives traded copper ornaments for shirts. Their daggers were set in ivory scabbards. The natives brought fresh water out to the ships in dugouts, but before they had properly filled the tanks a favorable wind came up and the captain major insisted on sailing.

Four days later *Berrio* led the way into a broad estuary. Again the natives were friendly. Two lords of the place came to speak with them. One wore a turban with a silk fringe and another a skull cap of green satin. "They were very haughty and valued nothing which we gave them." A young man in their company made the Portuguese understand by signs that he had been to a distant country where he had seen ships like theirs. The Portuguese took heart; Indian or at least Arab trading posts could not be too far away. They called this river the River of Good Omens for that reason.

They spent a whole month there careening the ships, taking in water and repairing a split mast on *São Gabriel*. Many men were ill. It was the first outbreak of scurvy. Their feet and hands swelled and their gums grew over their teeth so that they could not eat.

March 2 they reached the island of Moçambique. Alvaro describes the inhabitants as being of tawny complexion and as speaking Arabic. They dressed in fine linens or cottons, striped, of rich and elaborate workmanship. Their turbans were bordered with silk embroidered in gold.

Through a sailor who spoke Arabic the Portuguese learned that their merchants traded with the white Moors. Four Moorish vessels were then in port laden with gold, silver, cloves, pepper, ginger and silver rings as well as with quantities of pearls, jewels and rubies. Alvaro understood the people to say that except for the gold all this merchandise came from the country of the white Moors. They were told by a pilot, who turned out to be a great liar, that there would be shoals and many cities along the shore and an island occupied half by Christians and half by Moslems, continually at war with each other; and that farther up the coast precious stones, pearls and spices were so plentiful that they could be collected in baskets. No need to buy them. He further reported that Prester John's territories were not too far from this island: that Prester John owned many cities along the coast inhabited by merchants who had great ships. His residence was far in the interior, only to be reached on camel back. Two Christian captives had been brought from India to the island. "This information, and many other things which we heard, rendered us so happy we cried for joy, and prayed God to grant us health, so that we might live to see what we so ardently desired."

The captain major won the local sheikh around with presents of rich garments and comfits until he consented to allow two of his people to serve as pilots. Everything went well until the inhabitants of Moçambique, who had taken the Portuguese for Turks or white Moors, discovered that they were Christians. Learning from their native pilot that treachery was being planned, the Portuguese set sail in a hurry, taking along many fowls, goats and pigeons which they had traded for small glass beads. For eleven days they struggled with calms or baffling head winds until the current forced them back into the harbor of Moçambique.

Since most of the water in the region was brackish they tried to get their Moorish pilots to show them where they could find sweet water. When a group of men carrying assagais tried to dispute their passage to the watering place they scared them off by discharging their bombards. The next morning, which was Sunday, the Portuguese had to make a full show of their artillery, shooting at the palisade which the natives were putting up to protect their village. Several natives were killed. The rest fled in dugouts to the mainland. Now the Portuguese were able to take in all the water they needed.

To further prove their prowess da Gama's men chased several of the dugouts with their boats and captured four Negroes, as well as fine cottonstuffs, baskets made of palm fronds, a glazed jar containing butter, glass phials with scented water, books of their law, a box full of skeins of cotton, a cotton net, and many small baskets filled with millet. They were in civilized country.

At last they had a favorable wind. Guided by native pilots, whom they kept under strict guard for fear of treachery, in a little more than a week they reached Mombaça. This was a considerable town with houses like European houses. They anchored outside of the port which they could see full of native ships all dressed in flags. "And we, to keep them company, did the same on our ships, where nothing was lacking except men, because the few we had were very ill." The crews were delighted with the anchorage. They hoped to go ashore in Mombaça next day to hear mass with the Christians the native pilots assured them lived there in their own quarter.

This story turned out to be completely false. Instead of the friendly reception they had been promised, a boatload of Arabs armed with cutlasses and bucklers tried to board the captain major's ship during the night. Finding that the Portuguese were ready for them they went back to shore.

The next day was Palm Sunday. The sheikh of Mombaça sent out a sheep, oranges—Alvaro said they were better than those of Portugal—lemons and sugar cane, together with a ring, as a pledge of safety. The presents were brought by two men almost white who said they were Christians. The captain major sent a string of coral as a return present and two men to confirm his assurances of peace.

A crowd followed the two Portuguese to the gates of the palace. To reach the sheikh they had to go through four doors. At each door there was a porter with a bare cutlass in his hands. The sheikh received them well and gave orders that they should be shown around the town. On the way they were taken to the house of two merchants, whom they were told were Christians. They were shown a strange drawing, which these men worshiped and which the Portuguese imagined might represent the Holy Ghost. They were so eager for signs of Christianity they saw them everywhere. The sheikh sent samples of cloves, pepper, ginger and sorghum with which they might load their ships.

While they were weighing anchor to enter the port, two of the Portuguese ships, lacking steerage way, ran afoul of each other. The native pilots took advantage of the confusion to jump overboard, and were picked up by an Arab dhow. The captain major immediately ordered the ships to anchor. That night he put two of the Moors he had aboard to the torture with hot oil. They confessed that once the Portuguese entered the harbor the plan was to seize their ships as a reprisal for what they had done in

Moçambique. On being threatened with the torture a second time, one of the Moors even though his hands were tied, managed to jump overboard. The other escaped during the dawn watch.

Fending off a number of sneak attacks they had to lie at anchor off Mombaça for two more days. "It pleased God in his mercy that while we lay off this city all our sick people became well, for the air of this place is very healthful." Alvaro gave no credit to the oranges. "We had to stay there Wednesday and Thursday even after we knew the malice and treachery these dogs planned against us."

At last the wind turned favorable. After sailing north for some leagues they caught sight of two ships and gave chase. They wanted to capture an Arab for a pilot. One boat got away but in the other they found seventeen men, gold and silver, a great amount of maize and other provisions, and a Moorish woman who was the wife of a distinguished old Moor who traveled as a passenger.

Through the sailor who spoke Arabic the captain major elicited some valuable information from their prisoners. The rulers of Malindi, the next port ahead, were on bad terms with Mombaça. There were four ships in the harbor described as Christian. Among their crews the Portuguese could surely find a reliable Christian pilot to take them to India.

Da Gama and his captains were groping through a fog of misconceptions. Their interpreter kept hopefully translating some word which the Arabs used to describe non-Moslems as "Christian." It was not until several fleets had visited India that the Portuguese were able to sort out the differences between the true Indian Christians and the worshipers of the Hindu gods. The East African seaports at the time were outposts of a part Arab, part Persian culture every bit as developed as that of their native Portugal. Nothing in the data so carefully collected by John II and his junta dos matemáticos had prepared them for what they would find in the Indian Ocean. At every juncture their Moslem informants did their malicious best to encourage every misconception.

It was Easter Sunday when they anchored off Malindi. Old Alvaro wrote that the place reminded him of Alcochete, the little town on the Tagus where the King Manoel was born. "This town of Malindi is built along the beach in a bay. The houses are tall and very well whitewashed. Along the fringe of the backcountry behind it is a very large palm grove and all about are plantations of corn and other vegetables."

Vasco da Gama was careful to anchor a half a league off shore. No boats came out from the town because the people had heard of the capture of the eighteen Moors. Next day the captain major's first move was to set the old Moor on a sandbank in front of the town. A canoe put out to take him off.

The Moor was primed to explain to the local ruler that the Portuguese wholeheartedly wanted friendly relations. In the afternoon he came back in a dhow, accompanied by some of the chief sheikh's officers and with three sheep for a present. The gist of the message he brought was that the ruler of Malindi would do everything in his power to help the Portuguese find pilots and supplies. The captain major replied that he would enter the port on the morrow, and, not realizing how piddling his tradegoods would seem to the cultivated inhabitants of Malindi, sent back a surtout, two strings of coral, three washbasins, a hat, little bells and two pieces of the striped cotton material so popular among the Negroes of the Guinea coast.

When da Gama's flotilla cast anchor within the port, the king, showing more respect for the Portuguese artillery than for their tradegoods, riposted with six sheep, along with a great quantity of cloves, cummin, ginger, nutmeg and pepper. A message suggested that he would come out in a dhow for a conference if the captain major would meet him in one of his boats.

The ruler, who turned out to be the head sheikh's son, invited the captain major to come ashore and rest in his palace. Da Gama answered that his master the King of Portugal had forbidden him to go ashore; but to prove his good intentions, he sent for the Moors he had made prisoner and allowed them to be taken ashore in native boats. The ruler cried out that this generous deed made him as happy as if he had conquered a city.

While da Gama refused to go ashore himself, since the sheikh left his son and his sherif as hostages, he did allow two of his crew to be taken to inspect the palace. Next day the sheikh appeared on the beach in state wearing a damask cloak trimmed with green satin, and a richly embroidered turban. He sat on two cushioned bronze chairs under a round sunshade of crimson satin attached to a pole. He was attended by an old man for a page who carried a short sword with a silver scabbard. Musicians played on trumpets and on a sort of ivory oboe which, though the Portuguese didn't know it, was characteristic of the Persians of Shiraz who had settled these seaports two or three centuries before.

Next day the captain major and Nicolao Coelho, skipper of *Berrio*, rowed along shore in their longboats, saluting with their bombards in the bow, while two of the sheikh's horsemen engaged in a sham fight on the beach. These civilities, interspersed with an occasional show of force by da Gama, continued for several days, until at last, in return for one of his officers the captain major was holding as a hostage, the sheikh sent out an Indian pilot, whom Alvaro hopefully described as a Christian.

This man, a native of the Gujurat known to the Portuguese as Mallema Canaqua, turned out to be an expert pilot from a famous family of pilots who had celebrated the vagaries of the monsoons in a treatise in verse. For nine days the Portuguese took on provisions and wood and water. They were entertained by fireworks and sham fights on the beach and by continual concerts of musical instruments. When finally they set sail to a favorable wind, their pilot plotted them a course across the Indian Ocean and brought them to the Malabar Coast in twenty-five days.

In Mombaça and Malindi the Portuguese met their first Hindus. Alvaro, still hoping they were truly Christians, described them as being "tawny men, wearing little clothing, with long beards and long braided hair, who claimed to eat no beef. Seeing a *retábulo* of the Virgin Mary on Paulo da Gama's ship they prostrated themselves before it. The day when the captain major saluted the town with his bombards, they too fired off many bombards from their vessels and when his boats passed them lifted up their arms and cried gayly 'Christ! Christ!' " Maybe it was Krishna they were invoking.

Buffeted by storms of thunder and rain da Gama's flotilla anchored off a coast surmounted by lofty mountains on May 20, 1498. Boats came out from the shore to ask who they were. The captain major sent off one of his *degredados* with them to spy out the land. The degredados were mostly young men, many of them of noble birth, whose sentences for various crimes and misdemeanors had been commuted to exile on their promise to embark for the Indies and there to undertake any dangerous mission offered them. According to Alvaro's account the boatmen took this man to two Tunisian Moors who spoke Castilian and Genoese. The first thing they asked him was: "What the devil brought you here?"

The man told them they came in search of Christians and spices.

"Why," asked the Tunisians, "doesn't the King of Castile or the King of France or the Signoria of Venice send ships here?"

The exiles answered that the King of Portugal wouldn't let them.

When these Moors were taken out to the ships one of them kept exclaiming in something that sounded remarkably like Portuguese: "What luck, what luck; many rubies, many emeralds. You should give many thanks to God for having brought you to a land so full of riches."

Alvaro was convinced that Calicut was a Christian city. He described the natives as being mild and well-disposed but ignorant and covetous.

Messengers were immediately dispatched to the ruler of the country telling him da Gama had a letter from the King of Portugal to present. The ruler sent a pilot out to show them a safe anchorage. Da Gama was suspicious of the pilot and anchored considerably further out than the pilot wanted him to. Even so, next day he went ashore accompanied by thirteen men, of whom Old Alvaro, who was keeping the journal, was one.

"We were all dressed in our best, and we carried bombards in the boats and trumpets and many banners. As soon as the captain major stepped ashore he was greeted by the *alcaïde* with whom were many armed men and some without arms." Vasco da Gama was placed in a palanquin borne by six men who took turns. First they were taken to the house of a chief man where da Gama's retinue were given rice with a great deal of butter and excellent boiled fish, but the captain major wouldn't eat any of it. "We crossed a river on two boats lashed together for a ferry. We were surrounded by boats full of people and the number on shore," wrote Alvaro, "was infinite . . . all come out to see us."

173

At the edge of Calicut they were taken to see what Alvaro describes as a church. "The body of the church is as large as a monastery, built of cut stone and roofed with tiles. At the principal gate there was a bronze pillar as high as a mast and on top of the pillar a bird that looked like a rooster." The Portuguese were led into a chapel where they saw a picture which they thought represented the Virgin Mary. All knelt in prayer. The ship's purser, kneeling beside the captain major, whispered in his ear, "If these be devils I worship the true God."

Even Old Alvaro was somewhat astonished at the curious aspect of the "saints" painted on the temple walls. They wore diadems, to be sure, but "their teeth were so large" they protruded an inch from their mouths "and some of them had four or five arms."

When they reached the royal palace the gates were so packed that it was with great difficulty that the visitors got in. Several townspeople were wounded in the scuffle. They found the ruler, whose title sounded to them like Zamorim, reclining on a couch in a small court. He was chewing betel nut and held a large golden spittoon in his hand. At his right was a huge golden basin, full of the herb. He beckoned the captain major to approach him. At the same time he ordered da Gama's retinue to be seated on a stone bench, where he could look at them. He had water brought for their hands and a fruit that looked like a melon except that it was rough outside and sweet inside. Then he sent for another fruit rather like a fig and very tasty. The Zamorim watched them smiling while they ate.

Then he told the captain major to explain to his courtiers what he wanted and that they would repeat it to him. In those countries it was unthinkable to address the ruler directly. The captain major answered that he was the ambassador of the King of Portugal and bearer of a message he could only deliver to the ruler of Calicut in person.

The Zamorim took da Gama into his private chamber where they had a long conference. The captain major explained the reasons for his voyage of discovery. The letters from King Manoel he promised to deliver next day. The Zamorim, according to Alvaro, declared he would send an embassy to Portugal when da Gama returned. When he asked him whether he would rather

lodge with Christians or with Moors, Vasco da Gama answered
cagily that he'd rather put up in a lodging by himself.

By this time it was the fourth hour of the night. It was raining
hard. The streets ran with water. In spite of the rain everywhere
they went the streets were clogged with crowds.

When they finally reached the lodgings appointed for them they
found some of the crew waiting with the captain major's bed and
a number of things that had been brought as presents for the king
of Calicut. These presents proved to be the undoing of da Gama's
mission. Accustomed to the primitive tastes of the Guinea coast
da Gama had prepared a gift of striped cotton cloth, washbasins,
fancy hats, scarlet hoods, coral beads along with a box of sugar
and two barrels each of oil and honey. The Zamorim's factor who
was a Moslem and the wali of the city burst out laughing. Where
was the gold? they asked. The Zamorim of Calicut would not
accept such rubbish.

Vasco da Gama was nonplussed. He hastily explained that he
was no merchant but an ambassador and that these poor presents
were his own, not King Manoel's. When he returned to establish
a trading post he would bring suitable presents. The royal officers
remained unconvinced. They refused to transmit the presents to
the palace. Da Gama insisted that he be taken back to the Zamorim.
To this the officials seemed to consent. If he would wait a little
while, they said, they would take him back to the palace.

They departed. The captain major waited all day but they never
came back. Vasco da Gama was a man of violent temper. He was
in a fury at finding himself in the hands of such "dilatory and
unreliable people." He almost made up his mind to force his way
into the palace alone but better council prevailed and he decided
to wait till the next day. "We others didn't let it worry us,"
wrote Alvaro. "We never ceased to make merry, singing and
dancing to the sound of trumpets, and enjoying ourselves immensely."

When the officials finally appeared to conduct him to the palace,
da Gama found everything strangely changed. Armed men everywhere. He was made to wait four hours outside a closed door.
This time he was only allowed to take his secretary and his interpreter in with him to see the Zamorim. His retinue had to wait

outside. "It seemed to him, as to us, that this separation augured ill."

After some discussion of what merchandise da Gama had brought with him, the letters from King Manoel were opened, one in Portuguese and one in Arabic. The first was translated by da Gama's interpreter and the second by four learned Moors specially summoned for the purpose. The Zamorim declared himself satisfied and told the captain major to go back to his ships and land his merchandise and sell it.

By the time the captain major left the Zamorim it was too late to start back to the shore. The rain never stopped. Next morning da Gama, having refused to ride a horse without a saddle as was the custom of the country, set off in a palanquin. Alvaro and the rest of the men followed after him but got lost in the crowds and the rain.

When they finally found the captain major in a resthouse by the shore the wali and a number of officials were with him but everything had become very difficult. No way of procuring a canoe to take them out to the ships. After a considerable altercation the Portuguese found themselves shut up in the resthouse under armed guard.

Meanwhile one of the sailors turned up who had been lost the night before and reported that Nicolao Coelho was waiting with boats on the beach. Da Gama sent him orders to push off at once and to place the ships in a position of defense.

"All that day," wrote Alvaro, "we underwent this agony as you have seen. When night came the armed men wouldn't let us walk in the patio as we had been doing but confined us in a small tiled court. We expected to be separated next day and that we would come to no good because they all seemed vexed with us. Still, in spite of everything, we managed to make a very good supper off things found in the village."

Next day the wali reappeared. For some reason he wore a better face. The sailors began to land the bales of samples of the textiles and the wheat, iron and bronzework they had brought along. The captain major was allowed to go back aboard ship. Two men were left ashore to attend to the merchandise.

Nobody came to buy. It turned out that the Moslem merchants, who had immediately scented competition, were doing everything possible to depreciate the Portuguese goods. After a few days permission was obtained to move the merchandise into the city of Calicut where it was hoped trade might be brisker.

Meanwhile da Gama was allowing his crew to visit the town by turns, so that the men could make such purchases as they desired on their own. The sailors were very well received by the "Christians" along the road. They were invited to sleep and eat at every house. At the same time the Portuguese welcomed the people who came to the ships to barter fish for bread. They brought their sons and little children and the captain major ordered that they all be fed. "All this was done to make peace and friendship with them, so that they would speak well of us and not ill. They came in such numbers that they were a great nuisance. Often night fell and still we couldn't get them out of the ships. The reason was the great population of the country and the scarcity of food. It even happened that when some of our men went ashore to mend sails taking along hardtack to eat, the people snatched it out of their hands, leaving them nothing to eat at all."

The Portuguese spent four months at Calicut, setting up a small trading post, and trying to counter the machinations of the Moslems and "men of Mecca" who were intriguing to get their throats cut. The sailors were finding that the shirts, bracelets and such tin as they had to sell were not bringing the prices they had hoped for, but they traded for cloves and precious stones, so as to have something to show when they got home. According to Alvaro, the captain major himself failed in an effort to trade the merchandise he had brought along on the king's behalf for a hogshead each of cinnamon and cloves.

When he announced that he was leaving for Portugal, the Zamorim put on a bad face and declared he must pay a large sum in gold before he would be allowed to leave. At the same time a guard was set on the men at the trading post so that they should not remove any merchandise.

The Tunisian Moor, whose name the Portuguese caught as Monçaide, came aboard secretly and warned da Gama and the other captains not to go back ashore because the Moslem merchants were offering the Zamorim large sums to have them beheaded. At the same time, though the Zamorim had forbidden boats to go out to the ships, Moors and "Christians" kept arriving with precious stones to trade for Portuguese goods.

Da Gama took the opportunity to seize one batch, who seemed to be men of substance, and sent word ashore that he would not release them until his Portuguese and their merchandise at the trading post were turned loose. In the end he got back his men and part of the merchandise, but as the Tunisian—who had taken refuge on *São Rafael* saying that his life was in danger since he had been discovered to be of Christian birth—warned him that the men of Mecca were preparing a fleet to annihilate the Portuguese, da Gama and his captains decided the time had come to put to sea. This time they had to do without an Indian pilot.

During the last days of August 1498 they lay becalmed off the Malabar Coast. A fleet of seventy sail put out after them. The Portuguese held the enemy off with their artillery until a sudden squall swept their three ships out to sea. The Moslem fleet put back.

For more than a month da Gama's ships hovered off the Indian coast waiting for an easterly breeze to carry them toward Africa. They bought fish and traded peaceably with the inhabitants of various islands who helped them find wood and water. On one island off the coast they careened *Berrio* and *São Gabriel* to clean the barnacles off them. During these days they held off many visitors of suspicious appearance. At the same time they traded busily with countrypeople from the mainland who brought out fish and cucumbers and pumpkins and boatloads of green boughs they claimed were off the cinnamon tree.

Among the visitors there appeared a man of about forty dressed in linen, with a fine turban on his head and a sword at his belt, who spoke Venetian well. He embraced the captain major and the other captains saying that he was a Christian from the west who had been forcibly converted to Islam and now served the Moslem lord of Goa. He claimed to be bringing an invitation from the lord of Goa to the Franks to visit his country and to settle there if they wanted to.

The captain major thanked him.

The man asked for a cheese to send to a friend ashore as a sign that all was going well in his dealings with the Portuguese. The captain had him given a cheese and two soft loaves. Meanwhile the stranger roamed about the island and talked so much he began to contradict himself. Paulo da Gama had been inquiring among the natives and was told the man was a pirate spying out the ships to find out what kind of force would be needed to take them. The man was immediately seized, taken to *São Gabriel* still high and dry on the shore, and flogged until he admitted that there were forty ships waiting in creeks and harbors to attack the Portuguese. Put to the torture he admitted that he had come to spy.

He was taken along as a captive and by the time they were two hundred leagues out in the Indian Ocean confessed that he had come to capture the Portuguese for his master who, hearing that they were valiant men lost along the coast and unable to find their way home, wanted their services in fighting his neighbors. This man turned out to have been born in Alexandria of Polish Jewish parents. He became a loyal follower of Vasco da Gama's and was sponsored in baptism by him when they returned to Portugal. Under the name of Gaspar da Gama he became a favorite at King Manoel's court and served as an interpreter on several other expeditions.

After three months of fighting calms and adverse winds da Gama's ships caught sight of the African coast. Thirty men were dead of scurvy and the rest were so ill that only seven or eight men were left well enough to navigate each ship and these very feeble. They found themselves abreast of a large town later discovered to be Mogadishu, one of the earliest Arab settlements on that coast. The city had such a formidable air "with house piled on house, and in the middle a great palace and four towers round about it" that they sailed right past shooting off bombards when they came abreast of it.

A few more days and they were back at their old anchorage at Malindi. The friendly sheikh sent out a longboat with sheep and many dignitaries to greet them. The captain major immediately sent ashore for the oranges which the sick men ardently desired. They didn't recover as quickly as they had before. In fact several more died. While they rested there the captain major arranged for a pillar to be set up with the royal arms on it as a sign of friendship and parleyed the sheikh into sending King Manoel an elephant tusk for a present. "We were there five days enjoying ourselves and resting from the labor of the crossing during which each one of us had been on the verge of death," wrote Alvaro.

At a shoal south of Mombaça which they had named for *São Rafael* because that ship had gone aground there on the outward journey they had to abandon Paulo da Gama's ship. She was foul and cranky and worn in the rigging. There were barely enough men left to man the other two. Da Gama saved her figurehead to take home with him and after she had been stripped of everything useful he regretfully ordered her to be burned.

The wind turned favorable. They passed the Cape of Good Hope without seeing it. "And those of us who had come thus far were in sturdy health but at times half dead with the cold of the great breezes of this land. We figured that this was because we came from such a hot country rather than from the actual cold."

Alvaro's journal stops abruptly when they are approaching the Cape Verde Islands. Coelho's ship and Vasco da Gama's were separated in a storm. Coelho's caravel reached the mouth of the Tagus first sometime early in July 1498.

Da Gama cruised about for a day trying to find his consort and then, since his brother Paulo was desperately ill, he put into São Tiago. There he left *São Gabriel* in charge of his purser and chartered a caravel to speed his brother home. The caravel encountered storms and was driven into the Azores. Paulo da Gama died the day after he had been landed on Terceira, and was buried on the island in the monastery church of São Francisco. When Vasco arrived in Restelo bowed down with grief in late August or early September he spent nine days in retirement before making his triumphant entry into the city of Lisbon.

As soon as King Manoel had talked to the captains and men aboard *São Gabriel* and *Berrio* he wrote the Catholic Kings, whose daughter Isabella he was on the point of marrying:

"Most high and excellent Prince and Princess, most potent Lord and Lady:

"Your Highnesses already know that we ordered Vasco da Gama, a nobleman of our household and Paulo da Gama, his brother, to make discoveries by sea, and that two years have now gone by since their departure. And as the principle motive of this voyage has been, as with our predecessors, the service of God our

1. Prince Henry, known as "the Navigator" (painter: Nuno Gonçalves)

2. St. Vincent's body guarded by ravens

3. The Master of Avis (painter unknown)

DOM · VASCO · DAGAMA

4. Gaspar Correa's sketch of Vasco da Gama

5a. A fifteenth-century Nao

5b. A square-rigged caravel

(credit: *Historia da Expansão Portuguesa no Mundo*)

(credit: *Lendas da India* by Gaspar Correa)

CANANOR.

cafa dermatos   o fpitall.   no/a fia da especiaca

6. Cananor after the Portuguese built their defenses

(credit: *Lendas da India* by Gaspar Correa)

⁓⊱⊹⸱A̅FOSO·DAḺBOQVERQVE ⊱⊹⸱⁓

7. The great Albuquerque

8. Aden in the mid-sixteenth century

Lord, and our own advantage, it pleased him in his Mercy to speed them on their way. From a message which has now been brought to this city by one of the captains, we learn that they did reach and discover India and other kingdoms and lordships bordering on it: that they entered and navigated its sea, finding large cities, large edifices and rivers, and great populations, among whom is carried on all the trade in spices and precious stones (which these explorers saw and met with in good numbers and of great size) which are forwarded to Mecca and thence to Cairo, whence they are dispersed throughout the world. Of these they have brought a quantity, including cinnamon, cloves, ginger, nutmeg, pepper, as well as other kinds, including the boughs and leaves of the same: also many fine stones of all sorts, such as rubies and others. And they also came to a country in which are mines of gold, of which, as well as of spices and precious stones they did not bring as much as they could of, for they took no merchandise with them that suited the market."

King Manoel, like his exploring captains, was mistaking Hindus for Christians. He was convinced that the Catholic Kings would rejoice as he did in the possibility of "fully fortifying" these people in the Holy Faith. Once they were properly converted, the Indians would serve as allies against the Moslems. "Moreover we hope, with God's help, that the great trade which now enriches the Moors of those parts, through whose hands it now passes without the intervention of other persons or peoples, shall, in consequence of our regulations, be diverted to the natives and ships of our own kingdom, so that henceforth all Christendom shall be able to provide itself with these spices and precious stones."

Manoel ended by reminding the Catholic Kings that Spain and Portugal were equally bent on driving the Moors out of Morocco. He called upon them to join with him in praising God "for this great favor."

The letter tingles with excitement. The prospects opened up by Vasco da Gama's voyage were indeed giddy. The story went that, in spite of the loss of *São Rafael* and the abandonment of the supply ship, King Manoel realized a sixtyfold profit on his personal investment in the expedition.

4

THE MARRIAGES
OF KING MANOEL

King Manoel was described by his chronicler Damião de Góis as being lean and sinewy with such extraordinarily long arms that when he let them dangle by his side his fingers hung to his knees. A portrait, supposed to be of the period, shows him as having a fairish complexion, a long sober face, green eyes, dark brown hair and a pointed chin. Like most of his predecessors of the House of Avis he took the responsibilities of a ruler very seriously. He was so wrapped up in the business of importing and selling spices that his contemporary Francis I of France called him *"le roi épicier,"* the grocer king. He was diligent with the paper work of the Crown, ate soberly, drank water instead of wine, and was continent in his relations with women. His chronicler admitted that he was vain and capricious, giddily ambitious, and mad for all the pomp and ostentation of renaissance monarchy.

King Manoel inherited his family's enthusiasm for architecture. The tradition goes that he had vowed, if da Gama's expedition succeeded, to dedicate a monastery to Our Lady of the Sea on the site of Prince Henry's little chapel at Restelo where all the navigators offered their last prayers before sailing. After da Gama's safe return not many months went by before strings of oxcarts were bringing white limestone from Alcántara for the building of a great new church and cloisters in a style never seen before. This uniquely Portuguese style of architecture emerged out of an amalgam of the flamboyant gothic of Batalha and the renaissance decoration known in Spain as plateresque, which Italian sculptors were introducing into the peninsula. This new style, organized by first-rate architects who showed great skill in their balancing of ornate decoration against plain surfaces, owed its peculiar quality to the work of a swarm of nameless stone carvers brought up in the intricate mozarab tradition. It is hard to believe that some of them had not sailed with Diogo Cão or Dias or da Gama, so immediate is their evocation of the forms of seaweeds and corals and parrots and seabirds, tropical animals and jungle lianas. Things the sailors saw are chiseled out with an accuracy that could only come from first hand experience. It is an art saturated with the enthusiasm of the first moment of the discoveries. Somehow presiding, directing, hiring and firing, criticizing the architects' plans and the execution of the sculptors, King Manoel managed to impress on the architecture of his reign his bombastic ambition, his keen realism, his almost unbalanced mania for magnificence. The style was early named and well named, the manueline.

Intermarrying with the royal families of Castile and Aragon had become a vice with the princes of the House of Avis. The ruling families of the peninsula were intricately interrelated. Isabella of Castile, Ferdinand of Aragon and Manoel of Portugal were all great grandchildren of John of Avis, founder of the dynasty. John II had merely followed precedent when he arranged the espousal of his heir to Isabella the Catholic's daughter, who was also named Isabella. The girl was left a childless widow by Prince Afonso's sudden death. As soon as he came to the throne Manoel decided to take her for his wife. A suitable dispensation was obtained from Pope Alexander and they were married in 1497. That same year the only manchild produced by the Catholic Kings died untimely.

The prospect opened up to King Manoel was dazzling. The conquest of Granada had marked the consolidation of the rule of Ferdinand and Isabella over the whole peninsula outside of Portugal. Further, Ferdinand was putting forth his claims to the kingdom of Naples. While the Portuguese, with their modern naval artillery, were supreme on the ocean, the Spanish foot soldiers had the reputation of being unbeatable on land. Columbus's discoveries in the West and da Gama's in the East offered prospects of empire unmatched since Roman times.

In the spring of 1498, when it was certain that young Isabella was with child, King Manoel and his bride journeyed to Toledo where the chief officers of Castile and León swore allegiance to her as heiress to the realm. The royal pair went on to Zaragosa, the capital of Aragon. The Aragonese were harder to deal with. Their Cortes refused to consider the sovereignty of a woman. Their nobles were equally intransigent and so were the burghers of Barcelona and Valencia. This opposition began to melt away when in August young Isabella gave birth to a boy.

Whether as a result of the fatigue of travel, or, as some wrote, because she had worn herself out by the asceticism of her life since her first husband's death, Isabel failed to survive the agony of childbirth. The boy lived, was named Miguel and was acclaimed as the heir to the thrones of Portugal, Castile and Aragon. A few months later all Manoel's fine plans were thwarted by the baby's death.

Daughters of Ferdinand and Isabella were in great demand among the royal houses of Europe. Catarina was married to the violent Tudor king of England, Henry VIII. Joana, later known as the Mad, was married to the Philip who headed the rising Hapsburg kingdom of Austria. The only daughter left was Maria. Manoel eagerly sought her hand. They were married in 1500.

Manoel paid a heavy price for these alliances. Before either Isabella or her daughter could consent to a Portuguese marriage Manoel had to promise to rid his kingdom of the Jews.

From the time of her girlhood in Segovia the elder Isabella had been under the influence of the Prior of the Dominican convent of Santa Cruz there. Tomás de Torquemada was an austere, shrewd, single-minded man who was convinced that all the turbulence that disorganized the Hispanic kingdoms came from the toleration of Judaism, Mohammedanism and heresy. He was truly "a hound of the Lord" dedicated to hounding to the death anyone who was even suspected of deviating from the True Faith.

After the union of Castile and León Isabella brought him to court and so well did his passion for religious integration jibe with Ferdinand's passion for political integration that the Aragonese king took Torquemada for his confessor too. From that moment Torquemada was all powerful. As early as 1479 he had induced them to re-establish the Inquisition, which had been in abeyance during the tolerant centuries when the Moorish peril was waning.

Since many prelates around the Roman court, more interested in painting and architecture and high living than in the burning of heretics, had doubts as to the usefulness of such an institution, the bull authorizing the Holy Office was obtained with some difficulty from Sixtus IV.

It is a curious fact that it was after the extinction of the Moslem threat with the fall of Granada that Christian intolerance rose to its greatest fury. Four months after he had accompanied the Catholic Kings in their triumphant entry into Granada, Torquemada induced them to sign a decree expelling the Jews from their kingdoms. This amounted to a population of at least eight hundred thousand families, among which were the ablest physicians and mathematicians, many fiscal agents of the Crown, and a host of skilled craftsmen. It was the most literate, energetic and productive segment of the population.

The flames of persecution fed on themselves. A few years later the pledge of toleration of the Moslems, which had been one of the articles of the capitulation of Granada, was repudiated and another useful, industrious and cultivated class was driven into exile or into the jail cells of the Holy Office. The Holy Office amassed an enormous treasure in the process from the confiscated goods of its victims. After having imprisoned, questioned under torture, and turned over to the civil authorities for public burning some two thousand men and women accused of apostasy, heresy or unbelief, Torquemada died like a saint in a bare cell in the convent he had built for his order in Avila.

His dogmas ruled the minds of Isabella and her daughters. Even hardheaded Ferdinand of Aragon bowed to his will, particularly when he became convinced that religious persecution was working to bring the unruly Spaniards into subjection to his throne.

King Manoel seems, from the first, to have had some misgivings about the persecution of the Jews, but the prospect of ruling the united kingdoms of the peninsula was too alluring. He too was bent on turning the limited monarchy of the earlier kings into an autocracy according to the fashion of the time. In 1496, four days after signing the marriage contract for the Princess Isabella he published a decree ordering all Jews who refused to be converted to Christianity to leave the country within the year.

Though many Portuguese Jews had made themselves unpopular as royal tax-gatherers and antisemitic feeling in the concelhos and the Cortes had grown during the past century, the measure was hardly popular at court or with the higher clergy. The Jews had played an essential part in the development of the country. A few were bankers and moneylenders but the majority were artisans or skilled tradesmen. Their value to the community had long been recognized by the Portuguese kings. Manoel himself had been brought up in this tolerant tradition.

Particularly since the establishment of the House of Avis the Jewish community had formed a state within a state. Though the Portuguese Jews were supposed to live in juderías and to wear the star of David in red on their outer garments, in practice the regulations were leniently enforced. They were forbidden to deal in precious metals and to employ Christian servants in their houses and had to pay a poll tax and sales taxes on articles of consumption to the king, but they were allowed their own courts and a system of government under their Chief Rabbi separate from the Christian administration. Converts were absorbed into the Christian community. The marriage of wealthy Jewesses into noble families was quite common. From the time of King Dinis on many of the important financial offices of the court had been held by Jews. From the time of Prince Henry Jewish mathematicians and mapmakers had been eagerly sought for in the development of the charts and tables in which the discovers based their navigation. Abraham Zacuto, who was King Manoel's personal physician, had been an important member of John II's junta dos matemáticos. Jewish printers were leaders in the new art of printing with movable type. Several of the first books published in Portugal were in Hebrew. The Portuguese kings had modeled their policy toward the Jews on the liberal provisions of the papal bulls of 1347 and 1389, which counseled toleration and forbade forcible conversions.

As the fifteenth century advanced antisemitism increased in the kingdoms subject to Castile. With each new outburst, refugees, many of them bringing great fortunes and valuable skills, crossed the border into Portugal. Their wealth and what was described as their arrogant separateness aroused the envy of the minor clergy and of the new class of office holders in the administration of the monarchy. To the common people the Jews were the descendants of Judas who had betrayed the Savior for thirty pieces of silver. They saw them as usurers and tax collectors. In 1449 the rising antisemitism of the people of the peninsula found its echo in Portugal. A Lisbon mob took advantage of the disorders which culminated in the battle of Alfarrobeira to storm the judería. Houses were sacked and several Jews killed. Young Afonso V, who was in the process of consolidating his rule, severely repressed the disorders and personally lightened some of the restrictions imposed on the Jews in the code of laws, drawn up many years before under the supervision of his father and his uncle Pedro, which he was putting into effect under the name of the *Ordenações Afonsinas*.

Toward the end of John II's reign the press of refugees from Castile became so great that that practical minded monarch determined to make money out of them. He forced the refugees to pay a large head tax on being admitted to the kingdom. They had to promise to leave within eight months. They were assured that the king would furnish them with ships. When no ships were forthcoming these Jews, to the number of tens of thousands, were herded together in Lisbon and informed that they were now slaves of the king. They were despoiled of their possessions and their children were shipped off to take their chances with fever and starvation on the island of São Tomé in the gulf of Guinea.

When Manoel inherited the throne his first impulses seem to have been humane. He liberated the Jews enslaved in the previous reign and refused a large indemnity which the Jewish community offered to pay as an expression of gratitude. His execution, however, of the edict of banishment was as brutal as any act of his predecessors. In April, 1497 he issued a decree from Evora that the children of all Jews or Moslems who refused baptism should be taken from them and educated at the king's expense. No effort was made to carry out these provisions against the Moslems for fear of reprisals against the Christians in Morocco. Twenty thousand Jews were herded into a set of vast buildings in Lisbon. Every effort was made to convert them by threats and cajolement. When these failed men, women and children, screaming and protesting, were hauled to the churches and forcibly baptized. Whole families preferred suicide to conversion.

A few prominent Jewish families like that of Abraham Zacuto were allowed to leave the country. Those who had consented to baptism were promised that they should live in peace and that for twenty years no inquiry would be made into their beliefs. After what they had suffered few families of Jewish origin wanted to remain in Portugal.

So great was the exodus of Jews from the country, mostly to France and to the Netherlands, where general religious toleration prevailed, that in April 1499 an effort was made to stop it. All exchange operations with Jews or New Christians were prohibited. Converted Jews were forbidden to leave the country except with a special permit and then only for commercial purposes and if they left their wives and children behind as hostages.

King Manoel and his advisers were in a quandary. They needed to give the impression that they were bowing to the waves of hysterical intolerance that were sweeping across the peninsula. The king had given his word to Ferdinand and Isabella. At the same time they seem to have been quite conscious of the damage done to the kingdom by depriving it of such a large proportion of its skilled manpower. The king tried to stall.

Meanwhile the populace was getting out of hand. Fifteen hundred and three was a year of crop failure. The high prices of foodstuffs were blamed on the Jews. Jews were stoned on the streets of Lisbon. A synagogue was pulled down in Evora. In 1506 there was a severe outbreak of the plague. The Jews were blamed for it. Led by two Dominican friars a mob ran wild in Lisbon for three days, looting and burning the judería and slaughtering men, women and children supposed to be Jews or New Christians. Two or three thousand people lost their lives.

The king had fled to Avis from the plague. He responded with all the force he could muster. Fifty persons implicated in the riot, including the Dominicans, were put to death. The monastery of São Domingos was closed. Looters were flogged and fined. The Casa dos Vinte e Quatro, the Lisbon guild hall which was supposed to be a center of antisemitism, was suppressed. The words "nobre e leal" were struck off the titles of the city of Lisbon.

The following year restrictions were lifted against Jewish emigration. So long as King Manoel lived no Portuguese dared lift his hand against a Jew.

5

BY ACCIDENT OR DESIGN: BRAZIL

The expulsion of the Jews and the resultant uproar was never for a moment allowed to interfere with the enterprise of the Indies. As soon as Vasco da Gama and his men, and especially the indispensable Gaspar da Gama who knew the Indian trade routes from his own experience, had told their tales, King Manoel set his shipyards to work to build and equip the greatest Portuguese fleet ever to sail the South Atlantic. Provisions were prepared for fifteen hundred men. The command was given to a young nobleman of the court circle named Pedro Alvares Cabral.

Cabral's family came from the mountainous region of the Serra da Estrêla. His father, known as the giant of Beira, was a member of the council of John II. They traced their descent from Gonçalo Velho, the first Portuguese to sight the Azores. Reputed to be as tall as his father Pedro Alvares Cabral was thirty-two when he was appointed to his command.

On March 8, 1500, a fleet of thirteen sail assembled off Restelo. There were lumbering round naos with high poops and forecastles and a number of swift caravels. The firepower of their artillery was greater than ever. The Florentine bankers, the Marchioni, who for three generations had been financial agents of the House of Avis, were allowed to outfit a ship of their own. Another was the private venture of a group of fidalgos. Aboard were all the most experienced captains in the realm, Bartolomeu Dias and Nicolao Coelho and da Gama's pilot, Pero Escolar. João de Sá who had been da Gama's secretary and Aires Correa who had set up the short-lived trading post in Calicut were to handle the commercial transactions. As interpreters there were the Tunisian Monçaide and several "Moors" whom da Gama had brought home as hostages. The crews were carefully picked. Every seaman had to have a special skill: there were carpenters, blacksmiths, woodworkers and a host of other craftsmen.

All Lisbon turned out with drums and trumpets to see them off. A pontifical mass was performed in the presence of King Manoel and the entire court garbed in their richest finery. King Manoel himself placed the royal standard in Cabral's hands.

Next morning the sails, ornamented with the red cross of the Order of Christ, were set and, speeded by a northerly wind, the fleet slipped out of the Tagus and set a course for the Cape Verde Islands. Off São Nicolao it was found that one ship had disappeared. After cruising about for two days in search of her, to no avail, the fleet continued on a southwesterly course into the South Atlantic.

As a result of da Gama's difficulties with calms and head winds, he had suggested a course further to the West than he had steered on his expedition of discovery so as to bypass the doldrums and the southeasterly trades and to take advantage of the westerlies prevailing in the extreme South Atlantic. After a month's sailing they found themselves, to nobody's great surprise, off a mountainous coast. Most of the pilots imagined it was an island, possibly Brazil, which occasionally had appeared on the maps of the past century. An account of this landfall was sent home as a letter to King Manoel by a man of some wealth who was traveling as a supercargo to assist Aires Correa in setting up the trading post at Calicut.

Vaz de Caminha wrote of seeing long weeds called "asses tails" which the sailors claimed were signs of land. Next they saw heron-like birds. That same day about the time of vespers they sighted land for sure. "First a very large mountain very high and round; then lower lands to the south of it and a flat land, with great groves of trees . . ." They took cautious soundings as they advanced and at last cast anchor about half a league from the shore near the mouth of a river. While the captains assembled on the flagship, Nicolao Coelho was sent ashore in a boat to reconnoiter the river.

"When the boat reached the mouth of the river eighteen or twenty natives appeared on the beach. They were dark and entirely naked without anything to cover their shame. They carried bows and arrows. All came boldly towards the boat. Nicolao Coelho made a sign to them that they should lay down their bows and they laid them down. There was no way of having any worthwhile understanding with them on account of the noise of the surf on the beach."

He made them presents of two hats, one red and one black, and a sailor's stocking cap which he pulled off his own head. In return one of them gave him a headdress of long bird feathers set in a little tuft of red and gray feathers like those of a parrot. Another gave him a string of tiny white beads that looked like seed pearls. "I believe the captain is sending these items to Your Highness," wrote Vaz de Caminha. As it was already dusk Coelho pushed off and was rowed back to the fleet.

That night the wind blew hard out of the southwest with squalls of rain so that the flagship dragged her anchor. At daybreak the captain ordered the fleet to move cautiously along the shore with their skiffs and jolly boats towed astern in search of a safe harbor. Some ten leagues to the north the smaller ships that were furthest inshore caught sight, behind a reef, of a safe and landlocked harbor. They anchored outside of the reef and with one accord named the place Pôrto Seguro. Cabral named the mountain Monte Pascual and the supposed island Terra de Vera Cruz: The Land of the True Cross.

The captain major's pilot, sent out to take soundings of the harbor, came back with two of the natives whom his men had snatched out of a canoe. Since it was already dark he took them to the flagship where they were very cordially received.

"In appearance they were dark, somewhat reddish, with clear features and good noses, well proportioned. They go naked without any covering. They think no more of covering or showing their private parts than they do their faces. They are as innocent about this as they are about their faces. Both men had their lower lips pierced and through them were drawn pieces of white bone, as long as the width of your hand." Caminha was amazed that these ornaments didn't seem to interfere with their speaking or eating or drinking. Their hair was smooth. They were shaved above the ears. One of them wore a sort of wig of yellow birds' feathers glued to his hair with something soft like wax but that was not wax."

When they came on board "the captain, welldressed with a large gold necklace round his neck, was seated in a chair with a carpet instead of a platform under his feet. And Sancho de Tovar and Simão de Miranda and Nicolao Coelho and Aires Correa and the rest of us who were sailing on the ship with him sat on the deck on this carpet. Torches were lighted. They came toward us, but made no sign of courtesy in speaking to the captain or anyone else. One of them caught sight of the captain's collar and began to make signs with his hand toward the land as if to say that there was gold on that shore. Then he saw a silver sconce and made signs toward the sconce as if to say that there was silver too in that land."

When they were shown a gray African parrot the captain had brought along, they pointed to the land as if to say that there were parrots there too. The sailors brought out a sheep but they paid no attention to it. A hen scared them to death. The cook produced bread and boiled fish and pastries, honeycakes and fried figs. They would eat hardly any of it and if they tasted something they promptly threw it away. Wine was brought them in a cup. They took a little in their mouths and didn't like it a bit. When they were given a jar of water they just washed their mouths out with it and wouldn't drink it.

"One of them caught sight of some white rosary beads. He made a sign for us to give them to him and seemed to enjoy playing with them. He put them around his neck and wrapped them around his arm and pointed to the beads and then to the captain's collar as if he meant that they would trade gold for beads like that. We understood his gesture that way because that was how we wanted it to be.

"The native gave back the beads. Then the two of them stretched themselves out on their backs on the carpet to sleep without taking the slightest care to cover their private parts, which were not circumcised; the hair around was neatly shaved. The captain ordered pillows to be put under the head of each one. The one with the headdress took considerable pains not to disarrange it. A blanket was thrown over them and they made no objection and lay at rest and slept."

Next morning the whole fleet entered the bay. The two natives were each given red hats and white bone beads and rattles and bells. Their bows and arrows were returned to them and they were set ashore. The captain detailed Nicolao Coelho and Bartolomeu Dias to reconnoiter and a young degredado was instructed to try to live with these people and to learn their language and customs. These reprieved convicts were becoming an important part of every expedition. Many of them were to make themselves careers in the colonies.

Vaz de Caminha went along with Captain Coelho to write up what went on. As soon as the boat touched the sand the two natives were turned loose. Their bows and arrows were returned to them and immediately they ran off among the palms.

Meanwhile a couple of hundred natives were crowding around the boat helping the sailors scoop water out of a river of abundant fresh water that poured into the bay. They helped carry the casks and tossed their own gourds full of water into the boat.

The natives sent back the degredado after making him understand they did not want him to stay with them. He seemed to be befriended by an elderly man, "all covered with feathers glued to his body like a São Sebastião. Others wore headdresses of yellow feathers, other of red or green. And one of the girls was painted from head to foot with that paint and for sure she was so well made and so prettily plump and her privates (in which she felt no shame) so charming, that many women of our land, seeing such attractions, would be ashamed that theirs were not like hers."

In the afternoon the captain major with his retinue set out in his boat and all the other captains in their boats to amuse themselves along the shore. He gave strict orders that no one was to land until they found an island that could not be reached without a boat or by swimming. "There he and the rest of us disported ourselves for a good hour and a half." The sailors hauled a seine along the beach and caught a few small fish. Since it was getting dark the Portuguese went back to their ships.

Sunday, which was the Sunday after Easter, the captain major decided to hear mass on the island. All the other captains were invited to attend. A tent was set up with a well-furnished altar and Frei Henrique intoned the mass accompanied by all the clergy who were attached to the expedition. The captain major had brought with him the banner of the Order of Christ which was kept raised on the Gospel side. "After the mass was finished Frei Henrique removed his vestments, stepped up on a high chair and preached to us all stretched out in the sand a solemn and profitable sermon on the history of the Gospel and in the end he dealt with our coming and the discovery of this land in accordance with the sign of the cross, in obedience to which we had come, which was much to the point and inspired great devotion."

The local people watched from the shore. When the mass was finished many of them blew horns or a sort of trumpet and started leaping and dancing. Others pushed out from the shore on small rafts made of logs tied together. None attempted to approach the island. The Portuguese climbed into their boats and, with the banner displayed from the captain major's boat, rowed in procession along the shore. A man who landed from Captain Coelho's boat to return a log from one of their rafts he had found floating was kindly treated. Many of the natives beckoned to the Portuguese to land. Instead they returned to their ships to eat, playing drums and trumpets and paying no attention to the natives.

The only shellfish the sailors had found round the island were some fine fat shrimp. After dinner the captains gathered on the flagship for a council. There it was decided to send home the supply ship to Lisbon with the news of the discovery of a populated island and to continue the journey to India. No natives were to be carried off, but instead two degredados were to be left behind to learn the language and supply information to the next expedition that should arrive from Portugal. Since Vaz de Caminha was a member of the council he was in a position to report its decisions exactly.

In the afternoon the Portuguese explored the river in their boats. They went well armed but the natives received them peaceably. One old man shoved his lip ornament into the captain's mouth. "We started laughing but the captain major was annoyed and turned away. One of our men gave the man an old hat for the stone, not because it was worth anything, but to show."

Up the river they gathered palm sprouts which they ate in abundance. On the way back down river they found a great crowd of natives dancing and disporting themselves. They danced without taking each other by the hand. They danced well. Bartolomeu Dias' brother Diogo, who used to be revenue officer of Sacavém, an affable and lighthearted sort of man, joined them. He took the ship's piper along with his bagpipes and danced with them, taking them by the hand and trying to make them dance in the Portuguese style; and they were amused and laughed and kept time very well to the sound of the bagpipes. After they had danced together Diogo Dias went skipping along the level ground, making many agile turns and a great leap that astonished them so that they laughed and made merry.

Later Bartolomeu Dias speared a shark and threw it up on the shore. The natives carried it off. "It suffices to tell you," added Caminha, "that up to now, in a way they are somewhat tamed; but in a flash they are off, like sparrows from a feedingplace. Nobody dares speak harshly to them for fear of their getting more frightened. Everything was done to their liking, to tame them more. . . . My impression is that they are animal-like people with little knowledge and that that is why they are so timid. Still they look well cared for and very clean. From this it seems to me that they are like birds or wild cattle, to which the fresh air gives better feathers and better pelts than to tame ones. Since their bodies are clean and plump and as handsome as can be I suspect that they have no houses or dwellings to which to shelter and that being raised in the open air makes them so."

It turned out when the Portuguese penetrated further inland that the natives did live in houses, long houses of wood and boards covered with straw. The degredados and Diogo Dias, who got along so well with them, reported that they slept in nets in their houses. They had fires to keep them warm. They seemed to live off a sort of yam and other roots.

For bells and a variety of trifles they were willing to trade very large red parrots and tiny green ones and headdresses of green feathers and a beautiful mantle woven out of the plumage of birds. "Your Highness will see all these things, because the captain will send them, so he says."

Before the Portuguese put out to sea one of their carpenters built a cross. The natives who had only stone axes crowded around them amazed at his iron tools. The natives helped them take on wood and water, and became daily more friendly. On Friday the first of May the ships' companies went ashore to plant their cross. The priests and friars walked ahead following the banner. The crews followed in procession. Some of the natives came forward to help carry the cross. This enhanced Vaz de Caminha's conviction that such simple and innocent people could easily be converted to Christianity. When the priests said mass at the dedication of the cross the natives knelt and rose when the Portuguese did. After the service Frei Henrique distributed forty or fifty tin crosses which the natives duly kissed respectfully and hung around their necks with pieces of string. When the ceremony was over the Portuguese walked up and kissed the cross in turn.

The degredados, after they had duly taken Communion, were left behind to teach the natives the rudiments of the Christian faith. Vaz de Caminha even rejoiced in the fact that a couple of seamen had deserted in a skiff. They too would spread the word. The people were innocent as Adam. Their conversion would be easy.

He described the land as being very beautiful. From the promontory to the south of their bay they could barely discern another promontory to the north and some twenty or twenty-five leagues of coast between. Toward the interior all they could see was forests. They could report no gold or silver or any other metal but the land was rich and well watered and the climate, at this season, like that of Douro é Minho. All crops would flourish there. "If it were nothing more than to have here a stopping place on the journey to Calicut it would be worth while, to say nothing of an opportunity to accomplish that which Your Highness so desires, the increase of our Holy Faith."

Vaz de Caminha ended his letter by begging the king, in return for the devoted services he would perform in Calicut, to revoke the sentence of banishment to the island of São Tiago of his son-in-law Jorge do Souro, said to have been convicted with a rowdy crew of stealing chickens, wine and bread and of having wounded a priest in a church where the gang sought sanctuary. "I kiss your Highness' hands."

"From this Porto Seguro of your island of Vera Cruz today, Friday, the first day of May of 1500."

Along with Caminha's letter went another letter from a certain Mestre João, an astrologer and geographer who was probably a pupil of the great Abraham Zacuto, author of the tables so essential to navigation in southern waters. Since Mestre João wrote in Spanish he was probably another Jew who had come to Portugal at the time of the expulsion of his people from Castile. Mestre João included in his letter a diagram of the stars which make up the Southern Cross and told of his observation of the sun with his astrolabe by which he reckoned that the situation of Pôrto Seguro was at 17° south latitude. He admits that Pero Escolar and other pilots had made calculations with different results. "As regard the situation of this land, my Lord, Your Highness should order a *mappa mundi* to be brought which Pero Vaz Bisagudo has, and on it Your Highness will be able to see the location of this land. This mappa mundi, however, does not show whether this land is inhabited or not. It is an old mappa mundi, and there Your Highness will also find la Mina marked. Yesterday we almost understood by signs that this was an island, and that there were four, and that from another island canoes come here to fight with them and they take them captive."

Mestre João apologized for not being able to give a better account of the position of the antarctic pole. The ship he traveled in was very small and so heavily laden that there was no room to make observations even if the tossing of the seas had permitted. He had been unable to check the instruments the Arab pilots used to observe the stars which Vasco da Gama had brought back with him. He was suffering from an infected leg. A sore larger than the palm of his hand had developed from a mere scratch. "At sea," he concluded, "it is better to direct oneself by the height of the sun than by any star."

From their letters it is pretty evident that both Mestre João and Vaz de Caminha believed that Cabral's fleet had landed on an island. If they had known of previous discoveries of the mainland it is likely that they would have mentioned them. Perhaps King Manoel, who had access to all the records of the voyages of the last few years, knew better.

May 2 the fleet set sail for the Cape of Good Hope. The weeping degredados left ashore were comforted, according to one account, by the natives. About ten days out a comet appeared in the sky which caused great dismay. Twenty-two days out the fleet was sailing before a favorable wind when there came "a head wind so strong and so sudden that we knew nothing of it until the sails were across the masts," wrote one of the secretaries in a narrative which has survived only in an Italian translation. "At that moment four ships were lost with all on board without our being able to give them aid in any way." Among the captains that perished was Bartolomeu Dias, the first discoverer of the Cape toward which they were bound. "The other seven ships barely escaped capsizing. And thus we took the wind astern with masts and sails broken. And we were at the mercy of God and thus we went all that day. The sea was so swollen it seemed as if we were mounting up to the heavens."

The fleet was scattered. Cabral's flagship rounded the Cape alone and was not rejoined by the others until they reached the vicinity of Moçambique. Even then Diogo Dias' ship was missing. They sailed into Kilwa and made the reigning sheikh sign a truce after almost frightening him to death with an artillery salute. They had to leave without trading. In Malindi Cabral renewed da Gama's cordial relations with the local rulers. The abundant oranges were a help to those of his men who were down with the scurvy. The sheikh furnished a Gujurat pilot. After leaving a couple more degredados with instructions to proceed if possible overland to Prester John, Cabral set sail for the East.

The ships reached Calicut on September 13. As soon as he had cast anchor in front of the city Cabral treated the inhabitants to a resounding salute to show the power of his new artillery. He demanded that men of substance be sent aboard as hostages before he would allow Aires Correa to land to set up his trading post. After the Zamorim's consent had been gained and his hostages greeted with due pomp on the ships Cabral consented to go ashore. The Zamorim received him in a house near the harbor.

The Hindu ruler was in a spacious dwelling reclining under a purple canopy on twenty cushions of silk tapestry. The covering of the canopy was of a silken material that looked like purple. He was naked above and naked below the waist. He had a cloth of very fine white cotton embroidered in gold round his middle. He wore a brocaded cap on his head that looked like a helmet. He wore earrings with huge rubies and diamonds and pearls, one of them pear-shaped and larger than a filbert nut. He had gold bracelets full of rich stones on his arms from the elbow down, a carbuncle ruby in a ring on one of his toes, and rings full of emeralds, rubies and diamonds on all his fingers and two gold belts encrusted with rubies round his waist. About him stood members of his family and officials of his court all similarly bedecked.

Cabral, who was dressed in his best, had his interpreter read an Arabic translation of a letter of King Manoel to the Zamorim which set forth the history of the explorations from the time of Prince Henry of Sagres and his desire to enter into friendly relations with all Christian peoples and to send missionaries to instruct in the True Faith those who had backslid.

This time every care had been taken to bring proper presents for the Zamorim. There were silver washbasins embossed in gold and maces with silver chains and rich carpets and tapestries. The Zamorim expressed pleasure.

Cabral returned to his ship leaving six or seven men in the house set aside for the Portuguese ashore. As soon as news reached them that he was on his way the worthies held as hostages threw themselves into the sea. The Portuguese sailors promptly fished them out. Ashore the Zamorim's armed men put a guard over the Portuguese left in the factory.

Several days were spent in bargaining. Cabral made a pretense of sailing away. At last arrangements were patched up. Aires Correa was set ashore to supervise the trading.

At this point a ship arrived from Ceylon carrying five elephants, one of which was highly regarded because it was trained for war. The Zamorim asked Cabral to capture the Sinhalese ship for him. Cabral sent out a single caravel with a bombard. Its crew overpowered the Sinhalese, who were armed only with bows and arrows, and delivered the ship and its cargo into the hands of the Zamorim's agents.

Presumably this feat disposed the Zamorim to favor the Portuguese, but the Moorish merchants, who had so hampered da Gama, kept putting obstructions in their way. It took three months to load two ships with spices. The Moors would divert the merchandise which the Zamorim ordered placed at the disposal of the Portuguese to Moorish ships which left secretly for the region still vaguely described as Mecca.

Out of patience, Cabral finally seized one of the Moorish ships. The Moors ashore raised a great tumult and assaulted the Portuguese in the factory. The trading party tried to fight their way to the shore where the ships' boats might pick them up but not many made it. Aires Correa and Vaz de Caminha were killed as well as three friars who had come as missionaries. In all the Portuguese lost fifty men, and more than a few captured, and all the merchandise stored in the factory. Every man was wounded of the thirty who escaped by swimming.

Cabral retaliated by capturing all the Moorish ships in the harbor and slaughtering those of their crews he could lay hands on. His men appropriated all the merchandise they found on the ships and then burned them. Three elephants aboard one they killed and ate. The following day Cabral's ships cruised inshore with a favorable wind and shelled the city. After destroying many houses and killing many hundreds of the inhabitants they sailed away to Cochin.

The ruler of Cochin, like that of Cananor, was at war with the Zamorim. With their help Cabral's men quickly loaded their ships and, evading a large fleet sent against them from Calicut, reached the vicinity of Cananor. A messenger came out from that city with friendly messages and a promise of as much cinnamon as was needed to complete the cargoes. So much cinnamon was brought aboard that there was no place to put it.

Then, carrying off some emissaries from Cochin and Cananor to the Portuguese court, Cabral set sail for Malindi. On the way a ship of two hundred tons was lost on a reef. The crew was saved "in their shirts." An effort was made to burn the ship to keep its cargo from falling into the hands of the Moors but the Moors came back with divers and fished up the ship's cannons which they later used against the Portuguese in the forts of Mombaça. By Palm

Sunday the surviving ships were rounding the Cape of Good Hope in calm weather.

In a harbor which Cabral's secretary called Beseguiche on the African coast abreast of the Cape Verde Islands they found the jovial Diogo Dias. He had lost his way rounding the Cape and had discovered the great island of Madagascar. He had cruised up the east coast of Africa as far as the mouth of the Red Sea and had visited Sofala which he supposed to be the Ophir of King Solomon's day. He had lost most of his crew from disease but had brought out some hair-raising tales to pour into King Manoel's private ear.

Along with Diogo Dias' nao, Cabral found two Portuguese caravels anchored in the port. These were in charge of a Florentine merchant named Amerigo Vespucci and were bound west by King Manoel's orders, to explore the shores of the dimly imagined continent that was soon to be known as America.

The expulsion of the Jews who had handled most of the commerce of the Hispanic kingdoms had opened up extensive opportunities for enterprising Italians. While the Genoese still held primacy in navigation, the Florentines, under the rule of the great banking family of the Medici, led all Europe in banking and in the import and export business. Vespucci came from a prominent Florentine family allied to the junior branch of the Medici. As a very young man he became manager of Pier Francesco de' Medici's mercantile business. After the assassination of Giuliano, Lorenzo the Magnificent's elder brother, and the suppression of the Pazzi conspiracy, life in Florence became hazardous for adherents of the younger branch who were suspected of being involved in these doings. The year that Columbus discovered Hispaniola found Vespucci in Barcelona as an agent of Pier Francesco de' Medici's son Lorenzo. From there he went to Cádiz to buy salt. In the summer of 1493 he seems to have been in Seville. So were Christopher Columbus and an enterprising Genoese shipmaster, raised in Venice, who was there known as Zuan Caboto. Vespucci with an Italian partner set up as a ship chandler in Seville. To his firm fell the bulk of business of furnishing supplies for Christopher Columbus's third expedition, which had the expressed aim of discovering the continent which the Portuguese claimed existed to the south of the Antilles.

Though a merchant by profession Amerigo Vespucci's hobbies were maps and navigation. He had been brought up in an atmosphere of cosmographical inquiry. His uncle was a scholarly monk of San Marco where Toscanelli, Columbus's correspondent, famous all over Italy for his calculation of the circumference of the earth, was librarian. Vespucci collected maps and became enthralled with the problem of the computation of longitude.

In 1499, through important contacts at the court of the Catholic Kings, Vespucci, now aged forty-five, managed to get himself aboard one of the ships he helped outfit for Alonso de Hojeda. This Hojeda was a young man whose detractors claimed first caught Queen Isabella's eye by dancing the jota on the end of a plank thrust out from an upper window of the Alcazar in Seville. Hojeda was being sent out, to Columbus's great chagrin, to supplement the admiral's discoveries. Juan de la Cosa, the enterprising Basque, was his pilot.

They had made a landfall on the continent in the vicinity of what is now Dutch Guiana and had sailed along the coast in a southeastern direction in the hope of rounding the Cape Catigara marked on the Ptolemaic maps as the entrance to the Indian Ocean. Instead they discovered the vast outpouring of fresh water of the mouths of the Amazon. Wherever they tried to land they found mangrove swamps impossible to penetrate. Somewhere in the vicinity of Cabo de São Roque the strength of the equatorial current forced them to turn back.

On the coast of what is now Venezuela they fought a battle with some warlike Indians. So many of the crew were wounded that they had to lie in harbor for twenty days. According to a letter Vespucci wrote from Seville in 1500 to Lorenzo de Pier Francesco de' Medici, he spent all these nights trying to compute the longitude of his position from his observation of the comparative movements of the moon and the fixed stars.

Hojeda and Vespucci brought home 200 slaves (thirty-two died at sea) and pearls and virgin gold and two stones that might be amethyst and emerald and a large piece of crystal that might be beryl. Some flesh-colored pearls, Vespucci wrote his Florentine patron, greatly pleased the Catholic Queen.

King Manoel soon heard of Vespucci's discoveries, probably through his bankers, the Marchioni, who were on intimate terms with the Medici. He sent for him to come to Lisbon. Vespucci was making a reputation as a cosmographer. His own computation of the circumference of the earth at the equator, roughly the equivalent of 24,852 English miles, is only sixty miles off the modern estimate.

King Manoel entrusted him with three caravels and sent him off from Lisbon in May of 1501. Juan de la Cosa sailed as chief pilot. They were off Cape Verde in time to meet a scattering of Cabral's fleet returning from India. One of the ships belonged to the Marchioni. Vespucci undoubtedly found friends aboard.

By one of the Florentines he sent off a letter to his friend Lorenzo in which he complained that the Portuguese account of India was "much distorted." It did not jibe with Ptolemy who was still his authority. He speaks of Cabral's landing "in the same land I discovered for the king of Castile." He described several conversations with Gaspar da Gama. He was much impressed by Gaspar's first hand knowledge. He carefully itemized the cargoes of the Portuguese ships: cinnamon, fresh and dried ginger, much pepper, nutmegs, mace and cloves, porcelains, cassia, mastic, incense, myrrh, red and white sandalwood, wood aloes, camphor, amber, canes, lacquer, mummy wax, indigo, opium, hepatic aloes, India paper and a great variety of drugs. Among precious stones there were diamonds, rubies and pearls. One round ruby weighed seven and a half carats. "The King of Portugal," he wrote with a touch of envy, "holds in his hand an immense trade and great riches."

Vespucci set sail for the west and Cabral's ships continued home to Portugal. Cabral was well received at court, but the fact that the next expedition was under da Gama's command, leaves the impression that King Manoel felt that the loss of four ships off the Cape of Good Hope was the result of some sort of negligence.

A few days after Cabral's safe arrival in Lisbon, King Manoel wrote the Catholic Kings telling of his discovery of the Land of the Holy Cross, as he renamed it. He described the natives in the words of Vaz de Caminha's letter. This finding of a safe harbor on the way to the Cape of Good Hope seemed to him a sure proof of divine intervention. He had changed his mind about the

Ormuz.

fortaleza

(credit: *Lendas da India* by Gaspar Correa)

9. The fort they built at Ormuz

(credit: *Lendas da India* by Gaspar Correa)

 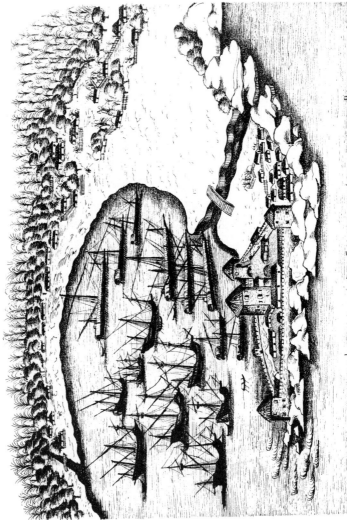

10. A strong point in Ceylon

(credit: *Lendas da India* by Gaspar Correa)

11. The Governor Lopo Vaz de Sapaio

(credit: *Lendas da India* by Gaspar Correa)

12. The oft-bloodied fortress of Diu

(credit: *Lendas da India* by Gaspar Correa)

DO JOÃ DE CRASTO

13. João de Castro, viceroy for a day

(credit: *Historia da Expansão Portuguesa no Mundo*)

14. Magellan (portrait by an unknown painter)

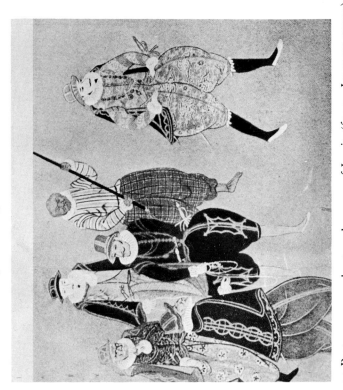

15. Portuguese merchants and a group of Jesuits (from a Japanese screen)

16. The coat-of-arms (Lisbon style) of a Congolese chief

(credit: *Historia da Expansão Portuguesa no Mundo*)

people of India being all Christians. He wrote of Calicut as being a city "of Gentiles who worship many things and believe that there is only one God." He described Calicut as a sort of Indian Bruges and included a passage in praise of the coconut palm "which produced sugar, honey, oil, wine, water, vinegar, charcoal and cordage for ships, and everything else, and a matting from which they make some sails of ships. And the aforesaid fruit, in addition to what is thus made of it, is their chief food when they go to sea."

He described the massacre at Calicut and assured the Catholic Kings that possibly Our Lord had permitted it so that the Portuguese should find better trading conditions at Cochin and Cananor.

He told of the Chinese trade with India. "They are white men with fair hair and are considered strong. The land is called Marchima and from it come porcelain and musk and aloe wood which they bring from the River Ganges which is on this side of them. And there are such fine vases of porcelain there that a single one of them is worth a hundred cruzados."

He wrote enthusiastically of having made contact with the ruler of Kilwa on the east coast of Africa and laid foundation for trade with the gold mines at Sofala.

Diogo Dias had brought strange news: The men who carried gold to the coast were cannibals and had four eyes, two in front and two behind. The cows their king owned wore heavy gold collars round their necks. "This captain reached Lisbon exactly sixteen months from the day he left Sofala."

King Manoel thanked the Lord, rather redundantly, for these numerous blessings.

King Manoel had reason to thank the Lord. Within three years the European spice trade, instead of enriching the Moslems of Alexandria, was enriching the Christian merchants of Lisbon, among whom the Portuguese king was the chief monopolist.

Vespucci, all this while, was bucking doldrums and contrary winds. It took him sixty-four days to reach the coast of what is now Brazil. "We arrived at a new land which, for many reasons which are enumerated, we observed to be a continent," he wrote to his friend in Florence. This time he kept south of Cabo de São Roque. Juan de la Cosa knew full well that a ship that sailed north of it could never beat her way back against the current. By November of 1501 they were reconnoitering the Bahia de Todos os Santos. Vespucci still hoped that each cape he doubled was Ptolemy's Cape Catigara. He continued down the coast in a southwesterly direction as far as the line of demarcation between the Spanish and Portuguese dominions which he placed at a spot he named Cananor somewhere around the present Montevideo in Uruguay. He may well have penetrated as far as the Rio de la Plata.

Back in Lisbon in the summer of 1502 he immediately sent off a letter to his friend and patron in Florence. He described the southern continent as "pleasing, full of an infinite variety of tall trees which never lose their leaves." He spoke of the abundance of beautiful birds, of the fragrance of the flowers. He enumerated the animals: wild hogs, wild goats, hares, rabbits, panthers, wolves, red deer, monkeys, wildcats, marmosets and snakes. There were no domestic animals. He had spent twenty-seven days eating and sleeping with the natives. The people went naked, ate human flesh, lived in long houses and slept in nets woven of cotton, "going to bed in mid-air without any covering."

For trade goods he wrote that there was an abundance of cassia and dyewood. "The natives told us of gold and other metals and many miracle-working drugs but I am one of those followers of St. Thomas, slow to believe."

Probably leaving their maps and charts behind in the hands of King Manoel's geographers, since exportation of such documents from Portugal was forbidden, Vespucci and Juan de la Cosa returned to Seville. They may have been a little disappointed by the rewards furnished by King Manoel.

In Seville Vespucci married a Spanish woman and became, as an expert shipchandler, a member of the Casa de Contratación which saw to the equipment of the ships plying the already well-known routes to the New World. He may have made a couple more voyages in search of gold for the treasury. Vespucci's career in Spain was so successful he gave up any idea of returning to Florence. In 1505, after Queen Isabella's death, he was made a citizen of Castile by her successor the mad Juana.

Columbus, after meeting all imaginable reverses, had died penniless in Valladolid the year before.

In 1507 Ferdinand, now ruling as sole king—since Juana had

been declared insane and put away in a monastery, and her consort, Philip of Austria (while Ferdinand was conveniently far away fighting in Naples), had been quietly poisoned by a gentleman of his bedchamber—called all the chief navigators of the land under the leadership of Vespucci to a meeting in Burgos. It was decided to send an expedition to the far south to find a passage to India around the American continent. King Manoel immediately protested and the plan was abandoned. The following year Amerigo Vespucci was appointed pilot major of Spain at a salary of fifty thousand maravedis. His last years were embittered by the fact that, for all his pleading, he couldn't get skippers and shipmasters interested in the problem of finding the exact longitude.

When the first news of his discoveries reached Florence, the Signoria ordered the ancestral home of the Vespucci to be illuminated for three nights. Lorenzo de Pier Francesco de' Medici had died and his papers had fallen into all sorts of hands. A set of forgeries under the name of *Mundus Novus* was printed in Vienna in 1504. The letters attributed to Vespucci in this volume had little resemblance to the actual letters he wrote his friend Lorenzo. Edition followed edition. The descriptions of the naked natives were a big selling point. The discoveries had stimulated the European appetite for travels real or imaginary. *The Travels of Marco Polo* and *The Travels of Sir John Mandeville* and the bogus *Book of Dom Pedro of Portugal* were making small fortunes for the booksellers.

The name America was first invented by an ingenious printer of St. Die, who twisted the forged letters attributed to Vespucci around to make it seem that they were addressed to his patron the Duke of Lorraine, a gentleman whom Vespucci probably never heard of. In a world map included in the volume the new southern continent was named America for Americus Vespucius. The book sold widely all over Europe until the name America was indissolubly linked in the popular mind with the new continent. Vespucci got a bad name with the historians who figured he must have had a hand in these forgeries.

6

THE NORTHWEST PASSAGE

Ever since the days of Prince Henry, Bristol and Galway had been ports of call for Portuguese ships carrying salt and manufactured goods to Iceland to exchange for salt codfish. By the latter years of the fifteenth century Bristol merchants were sailing to Madeira and the Azores. Enterprising Bristol seacaptains were stirred by the news of Portuguese discoveries, and particularly by their probes into the North Atlantic, to attempt some discoveries on their own. In 1481 there's the record of two Bristol ships sailing out in search of the island of Brazil, which on some medieval maps was situated about a hundred miles west of Galway. Azorean Portuguese and the Scandinavians of Iceland undoubtedly figured it to be many miles further west. Each ship carried forty bushels of salt, so they must have hoped to find fishing there. Like so many Portuguese who tried the middle Atlantic passage they were beaten back by stormy winds out of the west.

Columbus's triumphant return from the Antilles immensely stimulated the curiosity of every enterprising Bristol shipowner. Contact with the Icelanders and the Portuguese caused the opinion to prevail that, although the Admiral of the Ocean Sea stoutly contended that it was India he had discovered, what he had really stumbled on was a fringe of islands lying between Europe and Asia. About the time of Columbus's second voyage a much-traveled Venetian merchant turned up in Bristol with a plan for searching out a passage through these islands to India.

This Zuan Caboto was Genoese by birth. He made a trading voyage to the Red Sea ports, spent the early part of his life in Venice and in the fourteen eighties went to Spain in search of the opportunities for easy money thrown open to Italian entrepreneurs by the elimination of the Jews. In Seville he had connections with the Casa de Contratación and Vespucci's firm of shipchandlers. Possibly through the conversation of Vespucci and Columbus in Seville Caboto became filled with the notion of the glory and riches to be earned by discoveries beyond the Atlantic. He was formulating a plan to follow the mainland, vaguely reported by Icelanders and Bristol shipmasters, south till he found a passage into the Greater Sea which Marco Polo had navigated on his way home from China in the days of the Great Khan.

Failing to find backing for an Atlantic voyage at either the Spanish or the Portuguese courts he made his way to Bristol. Henry VII of the new Tudor dynasty was known to be an enterprising monarch interested in mercantile ventures. Early in 1496, John Cabot, as he was known in England, obtained a royal grant authorizing him to equip five ships for the discovery of any lands across the seas hitherto unknown to Christians. Almost immediately he set out to the westward with a single ship but met with such adverse winds that the crew insisted on turning back.

In 1497 accompanied, some said, by Bristol merchants who had already made the trip, he tried again with better success. He sailed west on the ship *Matthew* in May and made a landfall some six weeks later on what must have been the coast of Maine or Nova Scotia. The weather was hot. The land was evidently inhabited but he saw no one. He filled his watercasks, took possession in the name of the English crown and the Venetian Republic and departed. On the way home he coasted what seemed to be islands without going ashore. He was back in England in time to make a personal report to the king on August 10 and to receive for his pains a handsome pension payable out of Bristol customs. He called the land he had discovered Terra Prima Vista.

The following spring John Cabot set forth once more, this time with a fleet consisting of one ship furnished by the king and four by Bristol merchants. Several of the ships carried tradegoods for use when they reached the island of Cipangu. They sailed due west. Reports came back of one of the ships being driven into Galway. John Cabot was never heard of again. As his intention was to sail southward there is a possibility that he may have reached the Gulf of Mexico before he was swallowed up by the unknown. It is fairly certain that the skippers of some of the ships straggling back into Bristol to report the expedition a failure reported that a formidable continent blocked off a quick passage to India.

In Lisbon news of these ventures threw the court of King Manoel into a flurry. It was suspected that the English were trespassing on territories within the Portuguese sphere. In the late summer of 1499 a Portuguese embassy was dispatched to England, and in October of the same year a patent was issued to João Fernandes of the island of Terceira by which he was granted the captaincy of any islands he should discover on a voyage he was planning into the Northwest at his own expense.

This Fernandes, nicknamed the farmer (*o lavrador*), was already a familiar figure in Bristol. His name appears in the customs records as shipping goods in from Madeira as early as 1486. It is not known for certain when he sailed westward or whether he sailed at all, but the probability is that he was the first Portuguese to catch sight of the snowy mountains of Greenland. Certainly his name became associated with this high icebound land which the mapmakers imagined to be the easternmost tip of Asia. For twenty years Greenland was marked Terra do Labrador until the mapmakers finally discovered that this was the enormous island long familiar to Icelandic sagas and shipmen. Then the name was transferred to the coast of the mainland north of the St. Lawrence estuary which is still known as The Labrador.

The following May King Manoel made a far more detailed grant to Gaspar Côrte Real, a nobleman of the court who was the son of a powerful magnate who held captaincies in Terceira and São Jorge in the Azores. Gaspar Côrte Real had been Manoel's squire since the king was Duke of Beja. The wording of the grant: "Foreasmuch as Gaspar Côrte Real . . . has made efforts in the past, on his own account and at his own expense, with ships and men, to search out, discover and find by dint of much labor and expenditure of his wealth, and at the risk of his life, some islands and a mainland and in consequence is now desirous of continuing his search . . ." makes it obvious that members of the Côrte Real family had been sending out expeditions for some time. No record exists of previous voyages but Damião de Góis, King Manoel's chronicler, wrote of Gaspar's leaving the port of Lisbon early in the spring of 1500 "on this voyage he discovered on that north side a land that was very cool and with big trees." Instead of sailing south like John Cabot, Gaspar seems to have been seeking a passage to the northward.

He called the country Terra Verde. He found the Indians to be white, but that their skin was tanned brown by the extreme cold. This land was almost certainly Newfoundland of which Côrte Real was the first discoverer. His ships returned safely to Lisbon that fall.

Meanwhile João Fernandes, deeming it useless to compete with the powerful Côrte Reals for royal support, sought associates among the Bristol merchants to carry out his projected exploration. In March 1501 Fernandes and two other Azorean merchants joined three Bristol merchants in applying to Henry VII for the charter of what has been described as the pioneer corporation of the British empire. The purpose of the syndicate was to explore and exploit the new-found lands. It is fairly certain that an associate named Pedro Barcelos made two voyages to the southwest of Greenland in those years, but after the date of the charter the lavrador himself fades out of sight.

Gaspar de Côrte Real sailed out of the Tagus with three ships in the spring of 1501. His flotilla proceeded directly to the west coast of Greenland. When ice floes blocked their path they crossed the Davis Strait to the mainland and visited the coasts of Newfoundland and Nova Scotia. Somewhere along the way Indians they trafficked with produced a broken gilt sword and earrings of Venetian manufacture they supposed to have belonged to John Cabot and his lost crew. In September Gaspar Côrte Real sent two of his ships home. They reached Lisbon in safety. With the third he continued to explore the coast and was never heard of again.

A year later his elder brother Miguel set out to find him with another three ships. These were to search the coasts in different directions and to rendezvous at a point on the south coast of Newfoundland on August 20. Two ships joined company but

Miguel Côrte Real's ship never appeared. The following summer King Manoel sent out a third expedition to find the two brothers. The ships returned without finding a trace.

After the disappearance of the Côrte Real brothers the court of Lisbon became too absorbed in the profitable spice trade around the Cape of Good Hope to devote further efforts to discovering a northwest passage. A few years later John Cabot's son Sebastian, in the service of the English, made one more effort to sail to the north and west up to Davis Strait. He continued north until ice forced him to turn back. Soon after he gave up the English service and went to Seville where he succeeded Amerigo Vespucci as pilot major of Spain. The dream of a northwest passage persisted in England but was forgotten in Portugal. What the Portuguese did gain from their establishments in Newfoundland was the discovery of the bountiful fisheries of the Grand Banks. By 1506 the quantity of fish entering the Tagus from Newfoundland waters was sufficient to appear on the tax books.

Newfoundland was long considered a Portuguese possession but the Côrte Real brothers were forgotten by historians until an archaeologist discovered an inscription amid the mass of scratchings and pictographs on a limestone boulder on the shore of the Taunton River down in the roots of Cape Cod. The Roman letters would seem to read Miguel Côrte Real. It has even been possible to imagine the date: 1511, which would indicate that the valiant Portuguese and some of his crew must have survived for at least ten years among the Indians.

7

THE WARS AGAINST CALICUT

Even before Cabral returned to Lisbon four ships were dispatched to the Malabar Coast under João da Nova to take on cargoes at the trading post in Cananor. They steered a course somewhat to the east of Cabral's so they made no landfall in America. Instead they happened on Ascension Island on the way down and on St. Helena on the way back. Meanwhile, a much larger fleet was being carefully outfitted. These ships were heavily armed with what Gaspar Correa in his *Lendas da India* described as "beautiful artillery" with the express purpose of teaching the Zamorim of Calicut a lesson and of wresting control of the commerce of the Indian Ocean from the Moslems.

Though Cabral seems originally to have been slated to lead this expedition, some time before the date appointed for sailing King Manoel appointed Vasco da Gama in his stead. Ten great naos of heavy burden had been equipped with all the guns they could carry. Da Gama suggested adding five swift lateen-rigged caravels as cruisers. These were not ready to sail with the mail fleet but followed after under the command of a relative of his.

The day before da Gama sailed the king, after they had heard mass together in the Lisbon cathedral, presented him with a royal standard and appointed him Admiral of the Indian, Arabian and Persian Seas. The title well expressed the scope of Portuguese ambitions in the Orient. For himself King Manoel had assumed the style, in words that had all the pompous intricacy of the stone carvings of the great portal he was having planned for the abbey at Belém, of "King, by the Grace of God, of Portugal and the Algarves, both of this Side of the Sea and beyond it in Africa, Lord of Guinea and of the Conquest, Navigation and Commerce of Ethiopia, Arabia, Persia and India."

The ships encountered the usual calms along the African coast but had smooth sailing until they sighted the mountains of Brazil. From a promontory known to them as Santo Agostinho they followed Cabral's course to the Cape of Good Hope. Two successive gales scattered them. They rendezvoused at Moçambique which had become a friendly source of supplies for the Portuguese. One ship was lost on the banks off Sofala but the crew and equipment were saved. At Moçambique da Gama's men put together a fresh caravel out of timbers and fittings prefabricated in Portugal. Certain ships were detailed to run into Sofala to trade for gold.

The entire fleet sailed into the harbor of Kilwa terrifying the inhabitants with salvos of artillery. Correa who knew the place from his own experience described Kilwa as a city of twelve thousand people. There were tall, crowded buildings of stone and mortar with terraces and wooden balconies. The town was tightly girdled by walls and towers down to the water's edge and surrounded by exuberant groves of great trees, plots of vegetables, gardens of citrons and lemons, "the best sweet oranges you ever ate," sugar cane, figs and pomegranates, and a great abundance of cattle, especially of a breed of sheep with tails almost as large as their bodies and very tasty to eat.

The local Emir had rebuffed Cabral but da Gama brought him to heel by threats and blandishments. In the end the Emir promised to pay tribute to King Manoel. While negotiations were going on the Portuguese crews roamed the city, plundering where they would, "because nobody dared make a complaint," and managed to tamper with the women of the Moslem harems. Some two hundred of these ladies, described by Correa as being very beautiful, escaped from their husbands and took refuge on the ships begging to be made Christians. Da Gama saw at once that, Christian or not, their presence aboard ship would completely disrupt his expedition, so amid wailing and lamentation he ordered them taken back ashore and placed in the custody of the Emir. At the same time he proclaimed that if any inhabitant of Kilwa harmed them or punished them for their flight, he would take summary vengeance on his return trip. The husbands came for all except about forty of the women, including some young girls. These da Gama took aboard his flagship. He had them kept in locked cabins until he could find some way of getting them instructed in the True Faith. These women found husbands in the Portuguese trading posts at Cananor and Cochin; and, said Correa, the younger of them were among the first Indian women to be brought back to Portugal.

At Malindi, da Gama's ships were greeted with bursts of music and festive displays and great boatloads of food. The ruling sheikhs declared themselves firm allies of the Portuguese. The ships remained in that friendly port for a number of days while the crews fitted them with sealed wooden tanks for water such as were carried by the Arab dhows. These held more water and took up much less space than barrels or hogsheads. They found plenty of pitch for caulking the seams. The ropemakers set up their machinery on the beach to wind hawsers of coconut fiber which they found stronger than linen. The crews were not allowed in the town for fear they would molest the friendly inhabitants.

At dawn, the day they sailed out of the harbor, they sighted the five caravels which had left Lisbon late. Gunfire and a great breaking out of standards and pennants were answered with shouts of greeting and kettledrums and trumpets. The ships sailed in convoy across the Indian Ocean. The month was August. To avoid being swamped in a following gale the caravels had to run ahead of the lumbering naos. Their disappearance caused the captain major great anxiety, but they turned up safe and sound anchored off shore near the island of Anjadiva.

Along the Malabar Coast they engaged in a certain amount of skirmishing with the ships of a Hindu named Timoja, who was described as a pirate. They burned a couple of hostile villages and did away with a number of ships thought to be Moslem.

Wherever his men had speech with the inhabitants da Gama let it be known that henceforth trading in the Indian Ocean would only be by license of King Manoel of Portugal and that any ship caught trafficking with the Moors or with the people of Calicut would be burned and its crew with it.

While the Portuguese fleet was engaged in repairs and in installing a new mast on one of the naos off a mountain known to them as Mt. Dely, a large ship crowded with passengers fell into their hands. These were wealthy Moslems returning with their families from a pilgrimage to Mecca. The ship was thought to be owned by the chief among the Moslem merchants of Calicut whom the Portuguese held responsible for the attack on the trading post which resulted in the death of so many of Cabral's men. The Moor offered an enormous ransom for his life, but after his crews had stripped her of everything valuable da Gama ordered the ship burned and every man, woman and child aboard with it. His captains remonstrated with the captain major pointing out that if he accepted the ransom they could load their whole fleet with spices without cost to themselves but da Gama cried out that to accept a bribe in lieu of vengeance would be tarnishing his honor and his king's honor forever.

The ship was set on fire with gunpowder. The Moorish crew put up a desperate fight. Many were speared trying to escape by swimming. Correa cites as a notable deed that one Moor managed to raise himself in the water and to kill a sailor with his spear aboard the boat that was pursuing him. In the end da Gama consented to the sparing of about twenty of the children, who were taken back to Portugal to be raised as Christians by the Hieronymite monks of Our Lady of Belém. They saved, too, the hunchbacked pilot whom the captain major considered too valuable a captive to lose.

When he anchored off Cananor, da Gama ordered another great display of artillery. The rajah deployed all his elephants and four thousand Nair fighting men to do the captain major honor. After the usual exchange of gifts the captain major got down to business. A squadron of his fleet was to patrol the coast allowing only traders to pass who carried a license signed by his factor for the King of Portugal. Furthermore he was going to set prices for the various spices, once and for all, so that there should be no more haggling. The rajah, wrote Correa, professed to be well pleased by this arrangement.

After detailing a squadron of ships to patrol the Malabar Coast and hiring a special guard of Nairs, men of the Hindu warrior caste, to protect the trading post, da Gama set sail for Calicut. There he was thrown into a passion by finding the port clean. Every Moslem merchant had fled. Their ships and small dhows were hidden in the creeks. According to Barros the Zamorim had already sent out messengers with a plea to be allowed to negotiate indemnities for the damage done on both sides during Cabral's stay. Correa's story was that a brahmin was rowed out to the flagship dressed in the habit of one of the murdered friars, waving a white flag at the end of a pole. He was taken aboard with a promise of safe conduct.

In the name of the Zamorim the brahmin offered to give up the twelve Moslems most responsible for the riot and to pay twenty thousand cruzados for the goods seized. Da Gama, who at first thought the man really was the friar miraculously saved, was thrown into a blind fury. He replied that he had already burned one boatload of Moors that he had no intention of being bought off with money. Thereupon he sailed his fleet inshore and bombarded the city until his captains begged him to desist for fear of opening the seams of his ships.

About this time a number of sails appeared on the horizon. These belonged to two large ships and twenty-two small dhows which the patrolling caravels had captured. They were bound for Calicut with rice from Coromandel consigned to Moslem merchants. The skippers of six of the ships claimed they belonged to Cananor. These were sent off under guard to tell their story at the trading post there. The other ships were plundered of their rice and jars of butter and cotton goods and then set on fire.

Their crews da Gama ordered butchered. Some men were hoisted by their feet to the yardarms and used as targets by the crossbowmen and archers. Others had their hands and ears and noses cut off. The captain major ordered their feet to be tied together. So that they couldn't undo their bonds with their teeth he had men go about knocking their teeth in with clubs. They were thrown helter skelter into one of the open dhows. Then he had matting and straw piled on the bloody mess, the sails set for the shore and the straw lighted.

The brahmin who had come disguised as a friar was reserved for special treatment. Da Gama had his ears and nose and hands struck off and set him in a boat filled with the ears and hands and noses of the massacred men with a palm leaf hung round his neck with a message printed on it telling the Zamorim to have himself a curry made of the cargo.

Not even some men of Coromandel who claimed to be Christians were spared, though they begged in the name of St. Thomas to be baptized. Da Gama did allow them to be strangled before being hoisted to the yardarm. Correa explained piously that the arrows made no impression on their bodies but fell harmless into the sea. The captain major's heart was softened at this sight and he ordered the bodies to be taken down and given Christian burial.

After an additional bombardment of the town da Gama's fleets sailed off to complete their lading at Cananor and Cochin. There his crews built a wall to protect the trading post and stored within it a great number of pieces of artillery. Then after routing a large fleet sent after him by the Zamorim, he sailed home to Lisbon with his ships bursting with pepper and cinnamon. He left a squadron of eight naos and caravels to guard the trading posts at Cochin and Cananor and to intercept Moslem shipping in the Straits of Bab el Mandeb at the entrance to the Red Sea.

After stopping for supplies at friendly Malindi da Gama sailed into the south. His ships did not drop anchor again until they had crossed the bar of the Tagus on September 1, 1503.

No sooner were da Gama's ships hull down on the horizon than the Zamorim of Calicut began raising an army to make the Portuguese pay for their admiral's atrocities. First their ally the rajah of Cochin must be chastised. The Zamorim's army overran Cochin, killed two of the rajah's sons in battle and forced that potentate to take refuge, along with the Portuguese of the trading post, on an islet off the coast. Their situation was hardly improved by the fact that the Sodré brothers, relatives of da Gama's whom he had left in charge of the patrolling flotilla, lost their largest ships and their own lives when a storm surprised them in an unsafe anchorage off the Arabian coast. The Portuguese in Cochin were not relieved from their plight until six ships arrived from Lisbon in the following year.

Fifteen hundred and three was an unlucky year for King Manoel and his realm. The great amount of spices landed in Lisbon had temporarily glutted the market. The Venetians, still loath to send their galleys to Portugal instead of to Alexandria, were intriguing with the Turks and Egyptians against the Portuguese. The old Portuguese center of trade with the northern countries at Bruges was in the course of being displaced by Antwerp, where a flourishing traffic was building up with the North German ports. There pepper and cinnamon and the rest were traded for bronze and silver, which the Portuguese in turn shipped to India. This change in its early stages was giving rise to more dislocations than profits. At home unseasonable rains virtually destroyed the grain crop. Agriculture, never too flourishing in the kingdom, had been crippled by the drain of so many young and active men into the fleets and armies. Faced with a famine, King Manoel had to spend the money he had collected for an expeditionary force to punish the Moors in Morocco, who were always threatening the Portuguese outposts there, on purchases of wheat and barley in France and England and the Low Countries. In return for a promise to explore the American coast, King Manoel had ceded a monopoly of dyewood to a New Christian named Fernão de Moronha. Of six ships he sent to Brazil that year four were lost. Two came back loaded with brazilwood and with not so merchantable parrots and monkeys.

In spite of these difficulties two groups of three ships each were dispatched from the Tagus in the spring of that year under two members of the great Alburquerque family from the border regions of Estramadura that furnished so many powerful men to both Spain and Portugal. The first to arrive, after hardly sighting land, except some distant mountains in Africa north of the Cape, was Francisco de Albuquerque. When he reached Cananor at the end of September he found the Portuguese community engaged in barefoot processions with the cross to implore Our Lord to send them help. Learning that the more important trading post in Cochin was sore beset he set sail immediately and reached the river of Cochin in time to help the Portuguese there beat off an attack by the Zamorim's troops. They were busy consolidating their position with an additional palisade when three more large ships under his cousin Afonso de Albuquerque entered the bay.

The captain of one of his ships, was an extraordinary man named Duarte Pacheco Pereira, who seems to have been of the same Pereira family as Nun'Alvares the sainted constable of John I's day. He was brought up at court as a squire of John II, was a contemporary of King Manoel's and associated, as the prince was, with the work of the junta dos matemáticos. He was present at the taking of Arzila by Afonso V. At an early age, combining the theoretical work of a cartographer with the practical work of a pilot and shipmaster he became familiar with the West African coast. Bartolomeu Dias found him cast away on the Ilha do Príncipe when Dias was on his way home from his epochmaking voyage in 1488. In 1494, on account of his practical knowledge, he was associated with the negotiation of the treaty of Tordecillas.

What little is known for sure of Duarte Pacheco comes from a treatise called *Esmeraldo de Situ Orbis* on the cosmos in general and the navigation of the African coast in particular which he addressed in fulsomely respectful terms to King Manoel. He reviewed the Ptolemaic notions of world geography in the light of recent discoveries. In the course of his reflections as to the proportions of land to water on the spherical earth he let drop the statement, which has had all the historians by the ears, that he had explored the coast of a South American continent under King Manoel's orders in the year 1498. Since Pacheco's manuscript came down in faulty and late transcriptions, and the date may have been copied wrong, we cannot be sure that he discovered Brazil before Cabral, but it remains a real possibility that he did. His measurements of points on the map by latitude have held up well when checked by recent methods. He expressed the doubts of most thoughtful geographers of his time as to the chances of ever finding an accurate measure of longitude. He made cogent statements about estimating the progress of the tides by observations of the moon and showed an understanding of the principle of gravitation. His general attitude toward scientific investigation which, in spite of the rising tide of religious prejudice, was the attitude of most of the ardent and inquisitive spirits of his generation, is well expressed by his remark that "experience is the mother that brings forth realities and by means of experiment we get to the root of truth."

The day he landed at Cochin Duarte Pacheco had little time for geographical observations or philosophical reflections. The city was invested by the Zamorim's forces. When they caught sight of the Portuguese ships great numbers of them started fleeing in panic. From the ships crowds of armed men could be seen hurrying along a causeway by the river. Even though the rajah, who was anxious to make peace, begged the Portuguese not to attack the fleeing host the impulse to have a go at the infidel was too strong.

Duarte Pacheco had brought along a natural son of his named Lisuarte, after one of the heroes of *Amadis of Gaul,* most likely a mulatto, "a husky young man of twenty, very strong and skillful with all arms, but especially with the two-handed sword." Jumping into a skiff from his father's nao he ordered his men to row hard and was the first to reach the causeway along which troops from Calicut were skurrying. He jumped ashore with his huge sword and twenty men of his company after him, and went at the enemy so briskly, wrote Correa, that his men couldn't keep up with him. Hacking and hewing he found himself alone among throngs of the Zamorim's troops.

His father and the other captains came up and began clearing the causeway. Afonso d'Albuquerque had the triumpets sounded, "calling on São Tiago, for whom he bore great devotion since he was a knight of his habit." The Nairs—Correa said there were fifteen thousand of them—"began to think more of saving their lives than of standing and fighting."

Duarte Pacheco gave the orders to Albuquerque's trumpeters. He ordered the trumpets sounded so that the other detachments under the captain major might know where he was in the confusion, all present giving great shouts. Duarte Pacheco then charged into the press of the enemy to get a sight of his son. Lisuarte was so well armored, with greaves on his legs, that the enemy never could wound him. Behind him lay about twenty dead. When his father and the good men he had with him reached the young man to give him help they were astonished to find one of the enemy cut in two pieces without any other wound.

"The father, who didn't know he had such a son, kissed him on the face and gave him his blessing which he received kneeling.

He said that he was doing these marvels in killing and wounding the enemy just to please his father."

When those of the enemy who hadn't fled had surrendered Pacheco led his son to the captain major who took him in his arms and said, "God strengthen you in his holy service."

Lisuarte dropped on his knees and begged to be made a knight. "But we ought to be receiving this honor from your hand," cried the captain major, "you have won everything on this field"; and he knighted him forthwith.

When the rajah heard of it he told Pacheco to go back to Portugal to make more sons like that. If the rajah could keep Lisuarte with him, the Zamorim would cause him no more trouble.

From his capital the Zamorim sent messages of peace "which proved to be deceitful." At the same time the captains were hurriedly loading their ships with pepper and spices so that they could get away from the coast before the monsoon began. They left Duarte Pacheco in charge as Captain Major of the Sea with six caravels and one ship of burden. The Albuquerques saw to it that the wooden fort they had built was well stored with guns and ammunition. They warned him not to go out of his way to seek battle but to remain on the defensive, and urged him to build two shallow draft barges sturdy enough to carry large guns to navigate the rivers that protected the city.

On December 20 the Albuquerques departed. Duarte Pacheco was already on his way to Calicut to see if he could arrange for the release of any Portuguese captives there who might still be alive. Lisuarte remained in Cochin with the main body of troops, careening one of the caravels that was taking water and superintending the construction of the barges.

Pacheco developed a knack for taking advantage of the factions that struggled for supremacy in each Hindu city. Finding that there was no way of dealing with the Zamorim, he managed to arrange the escape of the small group of Cabral's men who had been held as hostages ever since they survived the slaughter of their mates. One night of storm and rain suborned boatmen managed to row them out to sea till they were picked up by the caravels. Among them, to everybody's delight, were two small sons of Cabral's factor who had been protected by a friendly Hindu family.

This exploit set the Zamorim's armies on the march again. They closely besieged Cochin. The Zamorim's agents in the city, which was riddled with treason, tried to poison the wells the Portuguese used in their fort and the food sold them in the market, but Pacheco's native informants kept him advised of every move of his enemies from Calicut. Beside his redoubtable son Pacheco had only a couple of hundred Portuguese and some doubtful Nairs to beat off an attacking force which numbered up into the tens of thousands.

His tactics were to keep continually on the move. Taking advantage of every high tide his armed barges and caravels would appear wherever they were least expected with a punishing weight of artillery in the rivers and inlets along which the besiegers were encamped.

For five months the Zamorim pressed the siege with all the forces at his command. Pacheco stubbornly defended the fords of the rivers. His advice and example stiffened the spines of the rajah's fighting men. Never risking his troops in a pitched battle, he kept making raids into enemy territory. He manned his small forts and placed his guns with the greatest skill. When one day the Zamorim had himself carried down to the riverbank in his palanquin, to view an assault on the palisade, a Portuguese gunner neatly placed a cannonball in the midst of his attendants, spattering the Zamorim with their blood. The Zamorim climbed out of his palanquin and fled precipitantly into the jungle. So great was his chagrin at this disgraceful episode that he gave up the government to a nephew and retired to a pagoda as a monk.

The Zamorim's disgrace, continual attrition by the Portuguese bowmen and gunners combined with outbreaks of smallpox, cholera and the plague caused the invading army to melt away. Correa figured that Calicut lost twenty thousand men from all causes while the Portuguese lost forty-three men, most of whom died, Correa claimed, on account of imprudences committed after they had been wounded; and a few more left cripples.

Pacheco's defense of Cochin made an immense impression in India. To the Portuguese his feats became legendary. Camões was to call him the Lusitanian Achilles. So great was his reputation that, descending on the port of Coulam after the siege of Cochin was lifted, he forced, without firing a shot, five great ships of the Moslems he caught loading cargoes of pepper there, to unload every grain of it. He had it stored in a warehouse until the next Portuguese fleet should arrive. He was still engaged in this business when news came to him that ships from Portugal had indeed made a landfall.

This was a fleet of nine great cargo ships, and a number of small vessels destined for the coastwise trade under a new captain major, Lopo Soares. The king and the Lisbon merchants all invested heavily in this venture. Largely due to Duarte Pacheco's work of preparation Lopo Soares loaded his fleet in record time. According to Correa his ships crossed the bar of the Tagus on June 20, 1505. On the same flood tide entered three caravels bringing gold from São Jorge da Mina and two merchant ships with rich cargoes from Flanders. Correa declared that this was the richest single tide that had flowed into the Tagus up to that time.

Duarte Pacheco returned home with Soares' fleet. King Manoel made much of him. He ordered a public thanksgiving for the defense of Cochin. The entire court went on foot in procession from the cathedral to the monastery of São Domingos where the Bishop of Beja preached a sermon in Pacheco's honor. Pacheco was made to walk by the king's side. When he married a lady of rank the king furnished her a dowry of a hundred and twenty milreis. Pensions were paid to his children and grandchildren.

It must have been during this period of opulent retirement that Pacheco went to work to collect his logbooks and maps and sailing charts in the *Esmeraldo*. The charts and drawings have been lost. The work breaks off suddenly, possibly when he was sent out to capture a powerful French pirate named Mondragon whose fleets were preying on Portuguese merchant ships. A few years later he was appointed governor of São Jorge de Mina. In that nest of intrigue he was set upon by evil tongues and, as a result, recalled to Lisbon in chains. He was exonerated of the charges of peculation and reappointed to his post, but, according to Camões, he died in poverty and neglect. Damião de Góis made his sad fate the occasion of a sermon on the ingratitude of princes.

8

THE TAMING OF INDIA

In 1505 the king and his council decided that the time had come to unite the various enterprises east of the Cape of Good Hope under a single authority. King Manoel picked Francisco de Almeida to sail as viceroy with the next fleet with supreme powers over all Portuguese forces on land and sea. Dom Francisco was a generous open-handed man. He came of a family long associated with the House of Avis. His grandfather had been royal treasurer under Afonso V, and his elder brother, now Bishop of Coimbra, had been one of the executors of John II's will. Almeida chose his only son, Lourenço as second in command.

The greatest fleet ever to sail out of Libson was under construction. According to Correa the king was so anxious to follow every detail of the work on the ships that he had himself a new palace built, Paços da Ribeira, near the shipyards. The ground floor was to consist of warehouses for goods arriving from Africa and India while the upper floors were arranged for the acommodations of the court.

Eight great cargo ships were constructed, six small "navetas" and six lateen-rigged caravels. In addition the fleet was to carry out the prefabricated parts for two galleys and a "brigantine." This was a small maneuverable galley with sails becoming popular at the time. These, with the ships already in India, would make up an armada of thirty sail, considered enough to sweep the seas of the infidel Moors.

Vasco da Gama, who remained King Manoel's chief consultant in these matters, supervised the outfitting of the fleet. Carpenters, caulkers, ironworkers, ropemakers were enlisted in great numbers and every sort of equipment for the needs of the sailors and fighting men and their artillery was stowed in the holds. Each ship carried a well-provided pharmacy, with a barber for bleeding, a doctor for curing the sick and two chaplains to hear their confessions.

One ship was lost in a squall in the Tagus and another in tropical waters but in each case the crew and cargo was saved. The fleet rounded the Cape of Good Hope in cold and snow on June 18, 1505. The first anchorage was in the harbor of Kilwa.

Before Almeida left Lisbon a policy had been decided on in council with the king and da Gama. The Portuguese were to attempt no conquests on land but were to control the spice trade from a series of fortified bases.

The fleet was manned by a thousand sailors and fifteen hundred soldiers enlisted for three years of service, a force thought strong enough to overawe any adversary. When the ruling sheikh of Kilwa proved refractory, the town was assaulted and sacked. The Portuguese lost no dead but many wounded fighting from rooftop to rooftop and from doorway to doorway through the narrow streets. The sheikh escaped into the hinterland but a relative was induced to rule in his stead as vassal of the Portuguese king.

All hands pitched into the building of the fortress. Directed by stonemasons brought along for the purpose soldiers and sailors chiseled stone and mixed mortar. Barros tells of captains and fidalgos cheerfully pushing wheelbarrows. The new ruling sheikh furnished construction workers. The work was speeded by pulling down the houses of the retainers of the old sheikh who had fled the city and using their squared stones. Working day and night the walls were raised to a height deemed sufficient in sixteen days. A captain was left in charge and two small ships detailed to cruise the coast.

The next port of call was Mombaça. There Almeida's fleet was greeted by cannon shots from the guns which the Arabs had fished up from a sunken Portuguese ship some years before. After offers of peace were rejected, the viceroy ordered the assault. In the bitter house to house fighting that followed half of the city was destroyed by fire. Before the Moors surrendered the Portuguese lost more than thirty men killed and many more wounded by poisoned arrows from which several men died. Correa wrote that more men would have died if a captured Moor hadn't told them to put strips of bacon on the wounds. The bacon saved many men, and the viceroy promptly gave the Moor his liberty and rich presents besides.

Almeida intended to invest Mogadishu, the northernmost city of any size on the East African coast, but his pilots assured him that the season was getting late for a fair wind to India. After a favorable crossing they anchored in the roadstead off the island of Anjediva not far from the city of Goa which, the perpetual interpreter and informant, Gaspar da Gama had recommended as the site for a Portuguese fort. When the spoils of Mombaça were finally divided among the captains and crews Francisco de Almeida took for his share only a single arrow as a memento.

Leaving a detachment to build and defend the fort, and having reached an understanding with the local potentate, Almeida proceeded to Cananor. There he found ambassadors from the Hindu empire of Vijayanagar which was the mainstay of the Hindu principalities warring against the Moslems. The pirate Timoja also sent emissaries offering his services to the viceroy. What seemed to be in the making was a loose alliance between the Portuguese and the various Hindu rulers who were intermittently struggling against the Moslem. Of these the rajah of Vijayanagar was by far the most powerful.

Consolidating the Portuguese enterprises proved a desperate task. Communications were slow. Captains and men were unruly. As victory went to their heads discipline became harder to maintain. The climate was a constant drain. Almeida had barely established his bases on the Malabar Coast before news came that the captain he had sent to Sofala to construct a fort which would command the export of gold dust was dead of the fevers, and that the ailing garrison there was having a hard time keeping the Moors at arms length.

Moslem resistance stiffened. Arab merchant ships were trying out a new route from the Spice Islands in the distant Orient to

Ceylon and thence through the Maldives Islands to the Red Sea, by which they hoped to bypass the Portuguese strong points. At the same time rumors multiplied of the great fleets the Sultans of Egypt and Turkey, egged on and assisted by the Venetians, were assembling at Suez. These ships were said to be armed with artillery even superior to the Portuguese.

Almeida sent off his son Lourenço to occupy the Maldives. Something went wrong with the calculations of his pilots. After eighteen days sailing they found themselves entering an unknown harbor on the much more important island of Ceylon. Lourenço de Almeida sailed boldly into what turned out to be the port of Colombo. The roadstead was stuffed with shipping. He dispatched his brigantine to find out what cargoes the ships carried.

This was easy because the crews had all fled ashore at the first sight of the red crosses on his ship's sails. Fear of the Portuguese had spread from the Malabar Coast. Lourenço's men reported that the principal exports seemed to be cinnamon and baby elephants. Next in order of importance were green coconuts, copra for coconut oil and spars and ship's timbers and planking on the way to Ormuz where there was a great market for building materials. They weighed the anchors on three great ships loaded with cinnamon and elephants which they believed to be out of Calicut and towed them out to the anchorage of the Portuguese flotilla.

Lourenço immediately sent a message to the ruler of the place who was the most powerful of the princes that ruled the island. Lourenço told him that he had arrived in his realm by mistake but that he was a merchant and brought merchandise to sell and would buy what they had to sell on the island in peace and friendship. He added that he was the slave of the King of Portugal who was Lord of all the seas of the world and treated well good people who treated him well, while he gave short shrift to the ungodly.

Friendly relations were established. The prince sent a cat's eye ring of great price out to the flagship as a pledge of his sincerity. Lourenço sent back the ring with a message in high style that the prince's word was sufficient. Along with it went as fine a present of crimson velvet as he could rustle up out of his ships. After this exchange of civilities the prince offered to trade as much cinnamon as the Portuguese wanted to buy. He sent an abundance of fowls and figs and sweet oranges and lemons and other fruits and fragrant herbs out to the ships. Furthermore he promised to furnish the King of Portugal with two elephants and a cargo of cinnamon every year.

The Portuguese could hardly believe their good fortune. Correa wrote enthusiastically of their new island's healthfulness and fertility and its magnificent springs and rivers of sweet water, and of the honey the wild bees made in the forests and the fine hunting: "birds of every description and beasts of every kind there were in the world." It was the only place where the cinnamon tree grew. In the forests there were many elephants and men trained to tame them. The prince had great stables for elephants "the way we do for horses," and raised them to fight.

In the midst of the island there was a mountain so high that its stone peak was always lost in cloud and on the summit was the print of a human foot a yard long and half as wide made by Adam our first father. This peak was venerated by a class of monks or hermits that swarmed on the island. They let their hair go uncombed and daubed their bodies with the ashes of their dead predecessors. They went naked except for a G-string to cover their shame. Not even bandits or pirates did them harm, nor fighting men in war or peace. Someone told Correa that young men often became monks for a while just to see the world without expense or danger.

Correa added a tall story of a monster that lived in a cave in a cliff not far from Colombo. Popular legend had it that it was black with great scales. It had two feet, a long tail, a short neck, a long head and a huge mouth and teeth. It had lived in the cave for some two hundred years and ravaged the countryside in search of food so that the people took it fish every day to the mouth of the cave. Lourenço offered to go in and kill the beast with his halberd, but the prince said on no account should he risk his life, so Lourenço ordered a mine to be dug at the place where the creature came to eat the fish and set up two falconets on stands trained on the mouth of the cave. When the thing came out it was blown up but the smell was so horrible nobody could go near it. "I saw with my own eyes some of the bones of this creature," wrote Correa, "the year the Turks besieged the fortress of Diu."

After slaying his dragon like Saint George, Lourenço set up a pillar with a cross at the top and the arms of King Manoel. He told the prince that the peace they had signed would last as long as the pillar was left standing. He reached Cochin in time to load his cinnamon on the ships about to depart for Portugal. His father, wrote Correa, was delighted with him for having acquired such a great domain for their lord the king without any expenditure of money or labor. As if by accident the source of all the cinnamon had fallen into Portuguese hands.

From Lisbon King Manoel was anxiously assessing what news he could get of the plans of the Turks and the Egyptians. He was intent on blockading the Red Sea. Two more fleets were equipped, one under the court favorite Tristão da Cunha and another under Afonso de Albuquerque whom King Manoel felt had conducted himself well on his previous expedition. In his pocket Albuquerque carried a commission to succeed Almeida as governor of India when Almeida's three year term should expire.

These forces met with many delays. Da Cunha, who had more taste for exploration than for empire building, wasted many months investigating the coast of Madagascar. He finally landed on the barren but unhealthy island of Socotra at the mouth of the Red Sea and built a church and a fortress there. Marco Polo spoke of Socotra as the seat of a Nestorian Christian bishopric, but the Christians had so degenerated it was hard to tell them from the heathen.

Albuquerque believed in action. He sailed off on his own with six ships and began plundering the Arab cities of the Oman shore. On September 25, 1507 he appeared off Ormuz. Ormuz had been high on the list of Portuguese projects for conquest ever since John II sent a Jewish rabbi to spy out its trade. There were between a hundred and fifty and two hundred cargo ships and war galleys in the harbor. Overruling his captains, who were for holding off, Albuquerque sailed close inshore and bombarded the city. His guns caused such destruction that the sheikh in charge offered to pay a tribute to King Manoel and to allow the Portuguese to build a castle there.

The heat was too much for Albuquerque's crews and their captains. The men protested against acting as stonemasons under such a sun. Three ships took French leave and Albuquerque, who was not yet in position to display his credentials as governor, was forced to retire to Socotra. As a result Almeida went a whole year without reinforcements on the Malabar Coast.

In the spring of that year the viceroy lost his son. Lourenço, sent north with a flotilla of small ships to scout out the position of an Egyptian armada rumored to be occupying the seaport of Diu, allowed himself to be caught napping and bottled up behind the bar in the river at Chaul. He put up a brave defense in spite of a shortage of gunpowder, but his flagship ran afoul of some trap-net poles in the river. Unable to maneuver, the ship was sunk in shallow water by the Turkish artillery. Lourenço refused to take to the boats with the bulk of the crew and was killed by a cannon-ball that shattered both legs. The ship and some of the crew were captured. So proud were the Moslems of their victory that, according to Correa, they had Lourenço's skin stuffed with straw and sent as a trophy to the Grand Turk.

At Cochin none of the captains, knowing Dom Francisco's near adoration of his son, dared break the news. "He was only one man," the viceroy cried out. He scolded them for their weakness and begged them to leave him in peace. Words of comfort were for women.

Two years later he had his revenge. When news came that a reinforced Egyptian fleet had assembled at Diu, which was held for the Sultan of Cambaya by a Russian slave-commander known as Malik Ayaz, he set sail with a force of nineteen ships and thirteen hundred men. Duarte Pacheco's prodigious bastard Lisuarte, who had lived through the defeat at Chaul, commanded a caravel. February 2 the Portuguese sighted the great fleet anchored off the island city. Toward noon the following day a favorable breeze came up off the sea. They weighed anchor, put on a press of sail and bore down on the infidel.

The battle lasted all afternoon. At first artillery fire. Then grappling irons and cold steel. By nightfall the Turkish flagship was sunk and the Moslem fleet scattered in confusion. Both sides suffered heavy losses. Lisuarte Pacheco though severely wounded survived the fray.

The defeat was decisive for Ottoman power east of Suez. Malik Ayaz capitulated. Though the Portuguese that had been captured at Chaul had been kindly treated, the viceroy took bloody vengeance on every unfortunate Turk who surrendered, the old story of chopping off hands and feet and burning up what was left.

In the name of King Manoel he accepted the suzerainty of Diu. Laden with booty the fleet set sail for Cochin. Passing Chaul, Almeida butchered a few more Turks in the mouth of the river to make sure that his son was properly avenged.

When he reached Cochin he found Albuquerque ready to replace him in the government. João da Nova and other captains who had rebelled against Albuquerque's authority at Ormuz implored Almeida not to give up the post. A long wrangle ensued. At one point Almeida had Albuquerque shut up in the tower of the new stone castle which had replaced the old wooden fort at Cananor. The problem was not resolved until the Grand Marshal of the Realm Fernando Coutinho arrived from Lisbon with express orders from the king to install Albuquerque as governor. As a later historian put it: "Portuguese officials and their places were like soul and body, not to be parted without agony."

Francisco de Almeida set sail for home with three ships. Favorably winds gave them pleasant sailing. Table Bay seemed the sweetest place in the world for a little repose ashore after the hacking and hewing on the Malabar Coast. There the first viceroy met his end as the result of a brawl between his sailors and the local Hottentots over the price of a cow.

The watering place proved to be fairly far from the shore. Thinking that the Hottentots were so poorly armed as to be harmless, Almeida and his staff formed the habit of eating their meals and taking their afternoon naps ashore under some great trees near the river, while the sailors carried water down in kegs to fill the hogsheads in the boats. When the dispute started, caused, so Correa philosophically put it, "by the nature of the Portuguese, always ready to take what wasn't theirs from the poor of the earth," Portuguese and Hottentots came to blows. The Portuguese used their lances and the Hottentots stakes with sharp points hardened in the fire. Some natives were killed. Using an old trick of theirs, the Hottentots stampeded their cattle by a series of shrill whistles. Hearing the whistles and the uproar, Almeida and his party started back toward the boats. His red cloth tunic caught the eye of the savages. One of them knocked him down with a stone.

Before his men could intervene another drove a fire-hardened stake through his neck and killed him.

The sailors were too busy defending themselves against the charging cattle to come to his aid. An attempted counterattack to recover his body proved unavailing. When the Portuguese struggled back aboard ship they found that they had lost more than thirty men killed and many wounded. The last that was seen of Francisco de Almeida the Hottentots were fighting among themselves over his red tunic.

Afonso de Albuquerque was fifty-six years old when he was installed as governor of India. In the portrait sketch by Gaspar Correa which has come down he is shown as a smallish, dour man with very large eyes, a very long nose and a beard that reached to his belt. His finger is raised in a gesture of admonition. Although he had seen service in Morocco as a page in the train of Afonso V and as an equerry of John II's his only claim to military fame was the far from successful effort to build a fortress at Ormuz. His first problem was to establish his authority.

As marshal that fat, opinionated courtier Fernando Coutinho outranked him on the Malabar Coast. Furthermore, with the disregard for the feelings of his subordinates which was becoming habitual, King Manoel had handed out two independent commissions that year. Duarte de Lemos was furnished with a fleet to cruise off the outlets of the Red Sea and the Persian Gulf and Diogo Lopes de Sequeira, son of a Lisbon merchant who had built a castle for the Crown on the Moroccan coast, was entrusted, in a fresh probe into the sources of the spice trade, with the important commission of establishing a post at Malacca, the great oriental port on the Malay Peninsula. One of Almeida's last acts as viceroy was generously to furnish Sequeira with a contingent of troops when he passed through Cochin. Among these was a most knowledgeable geographer, Fernão de Magalhães by name.

Though an old man by the standards of the age Albuquerque was bursting with ambitious plans. One was to strike at the heart of Moslem power by invading Mecca. Another was to weaken the Turks by fomenting a war between the Sunni sect represented by the Ottoman sultan and the Shiite heretics now led by an enterprising Persian Shah named Ismael. First he had to consolidate

Portuguese control over the spice trade. During this period of divided authority all he could do was bide his time.

Within the year Albuquerque had the field to himself.

Lemos found prizes scarce off the Arabian coast, and leaving most of his fleet in the governor's charge, sailed off home. Sequeira allowed himself to be forced out of Malacca, abandoning a sizeable land party as prisoners of the hostile Malays. Outside of the usual cargoes of spices all he had to show for himself when he reached Lisbon was a variety of information about trade and commerce east of the Straits.

He had established friendly relations with the opulent kingdom of Pegu which roughly approximated modern Burma, and had established contacts with the Chinese. Damião de Góis, King Manoel's official chronicler, who must have heard the story at court from some member of the expedition, reported that the skippers of four Chinese junks called on Sequeira the first day he anchored off Malacca "and that he found them so congenial, almost like people from Europe, that they visited back and forth and ate at each others' tables with the greatest familiarity." From these Chinese friends he got much information about the Spice Islands and the China Sea. They warned him against the plots of the treacherous Malays who were bound they would cut every Portuguese throat; unavailingly it turned out, because Sequeira eventually had to run for it, leaving the staff of the trading post in their power.

Coutinho met his death in a foolhardy raid on the Zamorim's palace in Calicut. The marshal was bound to have some great exploit to his credit before he sailed home with the spice ships. News that the old Zamorim, who had long since taken back the rule from his incompetent nephew, was ill at a place some leagues inland gave the plan of attack a certain plausibility.

Though a landing before daybreak on the beach in front of the city was accomplished successfully the expedition suffered from divided authority. The marshal, whose troops landed late, was indignant because the governor's forces, in the first rush, chopped down and carried off as a prize for King Manoel the gold-encrusted gates of the palace compound. He ordered his men to fling them into the sea and swore that he would get better ones, crying out that these people were just little naked niggers who ran like goats and that a man should be ashamed to go armed against such folk. He tore off his helmet and put a red silk cap on his head, took a cane in his hand and ordered Gaspar da Gama, the perennial interpreter, to lead the way to the palace.

Albuquerque stood leaning on his lance. He begged the marshal to be careful making his way through the narrow lanes. He would find that these little naked niggers were dangerous fighting men.

The marshal answered he wanted none of the governor's advice. "Stay here and mind the boats. Get aboard them if you are so satisfied with your feat."

He set out with a mounted field gun and three gunners and some sailors carrying cannonballs and powder in a barrel. Some four hundred men followed him, fingers itching for the spoils of the palace. Albuquerque muttered to his men that the result would be as God willed. There was nothing he could do. The king had given him no authority in this case. He immediately set about organizing his rearguard to protect the landing place and prepared for a careful investment of the city.

At first Coutinho's column met slight resistance. Setting fires as they went so that the city was ablaze behind them they wound their way between stone walls "steep as the walls of a well" to the Zamorin's palace. Suddenly they came out into an open square. The Nairs started shooting arrows at them from the roofs of the houses. Several men-at-arms who were clearing the way with their two-handed swords were struck down. Among them was Duarte Pacheco's son Lisuarte, who had survived so many bloody engagements. He met his end that day when an arrow struck him between the corselet and the helm.

Rushing through to the palace which seemed undefended, the marshal and his men found themselves in a great patio surrounded by richly carved doors. When they broke down the doors they were wading in such a mass of gold-threaded stuffs and caskets of gold and jewels that they could think of nothing but plunder. Each fighting man loaded his slaves and pages with all they could carry. Not one of them reached the beach alive.

By this time every rooftop swarmed with Nair bowmen. The governor's men came up in good order to protect the marshal's retreat, but he refused to budge until he had finished plundering and burning the palace. Soon the Nairs were doing such execution among his men that he had to retire. Though a young man Coutinho was fat and short of breath. In a narrow lane he was hit in the foot and fell. His attendants tried to carry him but had trouble because he was so heavy. Choking from the smoke of the burning buildings his men started running under great flights of arrows through the lanes toward the beach. The bowmen made short work of the marshal and his suite.

Albuquerque, who had been expecting the worst, had disposed his men to protect a retreat to the boats. When he heard that the marshal was down he started back into the maze of lanes. Few men followed him. Nobody dared go back into the burning city. On account of his age he was not as agile as he might have been. Soon he was wounded by an arrow that penetrated the bone and left him with a crippled arm for the rest of his life. He was carried off to the boats in great pain. As soon as he reached his ship and had his wound dressed he went on directing the orderly evacuation of the landing parties. He sent off surgeons and doctors to tend the wounded and covered the Portuguese retreat with heavy gunfire.

The attack on Calicut had proved a costly failure but at least it left Albuquerque in sole command of the enterprise of the Indies.

The last six years of the governor's life were unbelievably active. His first task was to establish a capital in a more defensible situation than Cochin or Cananor. He had long since settled on Goa, the principal city of the Moslem sultanate of Bijapur, which was situated on a triangular island between two deep rivers joined by a muddy creek infested by a particularly savage breed of man-eating crocodiles. Timoja, the pirate who had become a firm ally of the Portuguese, had agents in the city who reported that the Hindu population was ready to rebel against the Moslem rule. Chosing a moment when the sultan was engaged with his army in a war against a neighboring principality, Albuquerque sailed across the bar of the Mandavi River with a considerable fleet accompanied by a swarm of Timoja's dhows. The city authorities capitulated immediately. The men of the Turkish garrison jumped on their horses and fled to the mainland.

Albuquerque started to organize a city government and to distribute estates on the as yet unconquered mainland to Timoja and his friends. Everything went well until the sultan appeared on the mainland behind the city with fifty or sixty thousand troops.

One rainy night his advance guard crossed the treacherous ford and surprised a fort on the island side whose guns dominated the entrance to the city from the mainland. At the same time bodies of troops crossed the rivers on rafts made of many canoes lashed together. After some disorderly skirmishing the Portuguese were forced to take refuge on their ships. The Hindus proved no help at all.

It was almost three months before Albuquerque's ships found a favorable wind to sail out of the harbor. They had to lie there, while their supplies rotted in the damp corrosive heat, exchanging occasional cannonades with their own abandoned guns which the sultan's men had disposed as shore batteries.

In late November 1510 Albuquerque came back with fresh troops and a squadron of big ships newly arrived from Portugal to invest the city again. The sultan was dead, leaving his kingdom in the hands of the guardians of an infant son. The defenses of Goa were in the hands of Turkish and Persian mercenaries. On St. Catherine's day Albuquerque took the city by storm. This time he decided to clean out the "Moors" for good. The great majority had fled during the fighting. Hundreds were drowned trying to escape in boats and became food for the crocodiles. Saving alive a few of the best-looking women to serve as wives for his troops and some children to bring up as Christians, he ordered the rest, men, women and children, put to the sword.

At the same time he sent Timoja's men all over the island to reassure the Hindus who were hiding in palm groves or in the thatched huts of villages that their lives and property were safe and that the city government would continue according to their customs and traditions. Correa noted that little booty was found in the city because it had been thoroughly sacked by the Moslem troops five months before.

Albuquerque put his men to work immediately to rebuild the citadel and the city walls. He established a mint to coin money. He started a shipbuilding industry and found armorers to make muskets. He found native wives and pieces of land for such of the degredados as had shown zeal in his service. Other poor men he set up as bakers and tavernkeepers. Whenever he found a shoemaker or a stonemason or carpenter or tailor or any other useful craftsman he tried to induce him to marry his slavegirl if he had one and to bring her up as an honest woman in the Christian religion. He urged all of his people who were to remain in Goa to marry and proselyte. Goa he assured them would remain Christian and Portuguese till the end of time.

He had hardly settled the affairs of Goa before it became obvious that something had to be done to succor the Portuguese in Malacca who were under constant pressure from the Malays to turn Mohammedan. He had impressed a squadron of ships bound for Malacca for service in Goa and their commander Diogo Mendes was threatening to sail home to Lisbon to complain to King Manoel of Albuquerque's high-handed behavior.

Diogo Mendes did indeed set sail but Albuquerque's ships overtook him. He was sent back to Lisbon under arrest and his staff put in irons. Two of his pilots were hanged from the yardarm for desertion. According to Correa, who saw all the documents as the governor's secretary, Albuquerque soon repented of his violence in this case and wrote King Manoel apologizing and explaining that he had to preserve his authority by whatever means he could.

In April 1511 having reduced the Portuguese captains in Cochin and Cananor to obedience as well as the people of Goa, he departed for Malacca with a large fleet. Off Ceylon on the way he made prizes of some Moorish merchant ships out of the port of Mecca which were laden with copper, vermilion, coral, dyed cloths, rosewater and much currency in xarafims minted at Aden. At Pedir on the Island of Sumatra the governor got word from natives who brought out foodstuffs from the shore that the local headman had nine Portuguese in his power who had escaped from Malacca. Albuquerque sent him a message that if he didn't send him the men Albuquerque would carry off the pillar Sequeira had set up there as a sign of peace and amity with the Portuguese realm. The headman promptly gave up the nine men and sent a great store of foodstuffs with them aboard the ships.

It was early July before the Portuguese fleet anchored off Malacca. The port was full of a diversity of rigs, Hindu ships from Cambaia, Malay prams, Chinese junks, Arab dhows of every size, Sinhalese cinnamon boats, vessels from Pegu and Java and from the Riukiu Islands off Japan. Each of these nationalities had separate quarters in the city, ruled by their own headman under the general dominion of the Malay sultan.

Albuquerque's first act was to demand the release of the Portuguese captives. Through friendly Hindus he was already in communication with their chief, Rui de Araújo, who wrote him to do what he thought best without regard for their fate. Araújo was kept informed of all the plans of the Malay sultan by the Malaccan women who had taken up with the captives and who proved faithful and loyal. He sent the governor word that the Malay plan was to engage in parleys and delay until the monsoon winds came up when they expected to have the Portuguese at their mercy. Sure enough the sultan's reply was that he wanted to negotiate terms of peace before releasing the prisoners.

While the governor was debating with his captains what action they should take six friendly Chinese, skippers on junks detained by the Malays, came aboard the flagship with full reports on the strength of the sultan's armament: guns, poisoned arrows, hidden entrenchments, elephants trained for war. They told Albuquerque they would much rather have the Portuguese take charge of Malacca than the Malay rulers whom they found arbitrary and treacherous. The governor was delighted and told them that if they would wait a couple of weeks they would see with their own eyes how the Portuguese destroyed their enemies. The Portuguese weren't afraid of anything, he boasted, and were used to dealing with war elephants. Albuquerque had about six hundred fighting men. The Chinese estimated the sultan's strength at thirty thousand.

That same night he sent his galleys and brigantines inshore to bombard the city while landing parties in small boats fired the palm-thatched houses set on piles along the waterfront. By morning the beach was burned clear of houses. The sultan sent a message begging him to lay off, and to give him time to decide how best to make peace. Albuquerque's answer was to set his guns to firing again. All the same he was anxious to take the city, where many of the inhabitants were turning out to be friendly, with as little damage as possible.

Suddenly the Portuguese captives, whom the sultan had turned loose without warning, appeared in the midst of a landing party crying out "Peace, Peace." The troops signaled the ships to stop the bombardment. The liberated captives were taken out to the flagship where they were greeted with tears of joy and hearty embraces. Hearing of the tortures they had suffered at the hands of the Moslems who tried to force them to embrace Islam, Albuquerque swore by his long beard, "all white by this time," wrote Correa, that they would be avenged.

Immediately he called a council to decide whether to negotiate or fight. Araújo's advice was fight first and negotiate afterwards. These people, he told the governor, "thought more of a subtle treason than of all the chivalry in the world." Albuquerque made up his mind to demand a grant of land on which to build a Portuguese trading post. Negotiations dragged on as Araújo said they would. Finally it was decided to take the place by storm.

Malacca consisted of a series of compounds filled with palm-thatched houses. Between them stretched wide grassy avenues shaded by palms, where goats and cattle grazed. The compounds were piled with merchandise from every quarter of the eastern world. A deep river, spanned by a single bridge where it entered the bay, divided the city into two halves. Albuquerque's plan was to seize the bridge.

He ordered a general assault for the day of Our Lady of August. Around midnight, at a signal from his saluting cannon, he had the entire fleet bombard the sleeping city. "It was a frightening thing," wrote Correa, reporting some eye witness account, "to hear in the darkness the whole city thrown into uproar, the cries and shouts, people fleeing with their children and household goods on their shoulders without knowing which way to go." The bombardment lasted till dawn.

Then the ships were hauled inshore on their cables with the guns at an angle so that the projectiles would fall in the city and not on the shore where the troops were about to land. The landing parties promptly occupied the bridge which they protected from poisoned arrows by sails spread on spars set up in barrels of earth. At the top of each spar was a banner and the royal standard in the center. There the governor directed operations. In spite of some complaint from his captains he was determined to go no further that day.

Next morning they began their advance into the city. The men-at-arms were provided with large canvas shields against poisoned arrows and were followed by slaves carrying planks which they used to cross the pitfalls and mines of gunpowder which the Malays had dug in the entrances to the streets. In the mosque there was a pitched battle with many Malay chiefs. When they started to run Albuquerque sounded his trumpets to keep his men from pursuing them too far.

Two Portuguese squads that had penetrated one of the long avenues found themselves faced by the sultan and his son each in a sort of castle on a back of a war elephant. There were ten other elephants besides. At first the Portuguese were frightened by the roaring and charging of the war elephants but soon they discovered that they were easily routed by a lance thrust in the eye or the ear or the belly. The elephants trampled many of the enemy to death as they fled.

The next night the Portuguese brought some of their great guns ashore and placed them so as to shoot straight down the avenues to keep the Malays from digging fresh trenches for defense. The Portuguese had lost twenty-eight men, mostly from poisoned arrows and darts, and many wounded, who were sent back aboard ship until their wounds should heal.

All the while Albuquerque, through Araújo's connections, was dickering with the sultan and with the headmen of the foreign settlements for a peaceful capitulation. To merchants who professed friendship he distributed small pennants with the royal arms to place on their doors for protection when the Portuguese should storm the city.

After nine days he felt that his wounded soldiers were well enough to join in another assault. In one morning they cleared the avenues of the remaining Malays. The sultan and his chief men fled into the jungle. Next day the city was systematically sacked. Correa tells of the streets odorous with piles of benzoin, jars of musk and camphor and aloes, and boxes of sandalwood the plunderers didn't carry off on account of the weight. Open places were piled with Chinese porcelains nobody wanted. Some found jars of gold dust buried in the ground and wrecked many houses digging for treasure. The plunder was the richest in any of the Indian wars before or since.

At nightfall Albuquerque ordered the trumpets sounded and declared the sack at an end. Henceforward no soldier or sailor would be allowed in the city except on express orders. His troops were happy because many of them were rich. Next day they started selling their plunder to the local merchants. They sold it cheap but at that men-at-arms were left with three or four thousand gold cruzados and the captains with twenty or thirty thousand, besides the fine things they had stored away on their ships. For King Manoel they set aside a stool encrusted with precious stones to the value of sixty thousand cruzados, four golden lions full of perfumes that had supported the sultan's bed, pearls and jewelry to the value of four hundred thousand cruzados, and pretty slavegirls: the prettiest they saved for the queen.

Though his captains wanted to sail home with their booty right away, Albuquerque insisted on building a castle and setting up a Portuguese government to take the place of the Malay over-lordship. As he had done in Goa he allowed the native inhabitants, in this case the various foreign settlements; Javanese, Hindu, Chinese and Japanese to manage their own affairs. At the same time he sent an ambassador to the king of Siam aboard a Chinese junk, offering trade and the friendship of the Portuguese king. That monarch showed Albuquerque's ambassador every attention and even brought out his sacred white elephant to do him honor. News of the feats of the terrible Portuguese was spreading through all the archipelagos of the far eastern ocean. Particularly the non-Moslem peoples were ready to receive them as allies.

Albuquerque's policy was of terror on the one hand and con-ciliation on the other. Having executed a pair of Javanese chiefs who looked as if they might give trouble, he sent out embassies to establish friendly relations with the other rulers of Java and of the Malay states. When he sent out three ships under Antonio d'Abreu to discover the Moluccas, which the local shipmasters described as the most distant of the Spice Islands, where cloves came from and nutmeg and mace, he gave the skippers careful instructions. He instructed d'Abreu to have no dealings with any ship he met on the seas, only to repel attacks; and when he reached the islands to let no one ashore except the factor and secretary whose business it was to buy spices: to take nothing without paying for it, and to treat the people in a friendly fashion, even paying high customs duties if it seemed advisable. For trade-goods the ships were laden with Indian stuffs from Cambaya. A Malacca merchant on a junk stocked with merchandise by a friendly potentate went along. Albuquerque specially admonished d'Abreu to take the Malaccan people's advice on how to follow local customs.

The expedition reached the Spice Islands in the last days of 1511. D'Abreu turned back after taking on a load of cloves on Amboina. Another captain landed on Banda, where he found nutmeg and mace growing on trees that were like peach trees only larger. Francisco Serrão went on to the Moluccas. Off Ternate he lost his ship in a storm, but landed his crew safely in his boat. The Portuguese were so well received by the local headmen on the island and found life so pleasant there that most of them gave up any idea of returning home. This Serrão was a close friend of Fernão Magalhães who was soon to embark on the daring project of reaching the Moluccas from the east.

Without waiting for reports from this final chapter of the long-term project to trace the spices to their source, Albuquerque set sail for Goa. Malacca was pacified. He left two hundred men-at-arms to guard the castle and three hundred sailors to man the fleet which was to protect Portuguese traders. His final care was to see that Malacca was properly stocked with pepper to sell to the Chinese when their junks should appear in the following season.

The governor set out for India on his fine flagship *Flower of the Sea*. On a chartered Chinese junk he embarked sixty Javanese carpenters with their wives and children to settle in Goa. Two other naos sailed in convoy.

Flower of the Sea foundered in a storm off Sumatra, carrying with her to the bottom, wrote Correa, the greatest wealth ever lost in a single shipwreck. The governor and his captains saved themselves on a raft they made by cutting up the ship's masts and lashing them together. They spent the night fending off with their lances the Negro slaves who tried to clamber up in such numbers as to swamp the raft. In the morning they were picked up by another of the ships. This nao was taking water through every seam. Half dead from continual pumping they reached Cochin in January of 1512.

The junk came to grief on a reef in the Maldive Islands, but the Portuguese factors there saved passengers and crew and all the rich freight.

The governor had hardly time to get his breath ashore before news came to him that Goa was under siege by a fresh Moslem army and that the colony was in dire need of relief. The worst part of the story was that some of the Portuguese and Spaniards whom he settled and married there to populate the city had joined the enemy. He immediately set to work with the meager resources at his hand to prepare another fleet. Luckily the annual relief arrived from Lisbon in time, twelve large naos under Jorge de Mello Pereira. They brought good news, too, for the governor. The king was so pleased with his exploits in taking Goa and Malacca and exploring the Spice Islands that he was not replacing him at the end of three years as Albuquerque had feared. Quite the contrary King Manoel was promising him great rewards for his services.

This was the fleet that brought Gaspar Correa out to India for his first tour of duty. He came of the minor gentry and was inscribed as a page in the royal household about the time of the birth of Dom Manoel's third son Prince Luis. He volunteered for India, and almost immediately after his arrival in Goa, though he can hardly have turned seventeen, became one of Governor Albuquerque's secretaries. In his spare time, relying on other men's notes and the archives under his care for the earlier period, but from personal observation from 1512 on, he compiled his uncompromisingly frank history of the deeds of the conquerors. Beside developing a colored and amusingly anecdotic prose, he had a knack for drawing. He made sketches of the governors and viceroys he came in contact with, and in the style of the pilot-books drew profiles of the cities and landmarks he visited. His *Lendas da India* remains one of the vividest of the chronicles which illuminate early Portuguese history.

Leaving Pereira in charge at Cananor, Albuquerque ran along the shore to Goa. He had crowded his ships with all the troops he could muster equipped with the fine new steel arms and the many muskets the king had sent out with Pereira's fleet. As soon as he crossed the bar he found that the Moslems had greatly strengthened the defenses of the fortified village which commanded the ford that gave access to Goa from the mainland. His first business was to dislodge them from there. He deployed his troops on the island side and took personal command of the ships he moved upriver into the shallows opposite the Moslem fort. In eight days of bombardment so incessant that his gunners were left deaf, he knocked down the enemy defenses. A party in boats intercepted a train of oxcarts bringing supplies across the ford and carried off many of the oxen for their own eating. The garrison came to terms. It was in the nick of time because Albuquerque's ships were riddled with stone shot and his men were worn out.

The terms were that the Moslems were to leave all their artillery, horses and munitions and to walk out of the fortress with only the clothes on their backs. Furthermore the nineteen renegades who had helped serve the enemy guns and committed various atrocities against their fellow countrymen were to be delivered up. The Moslem leader insisted that their lives be spared. Albuquerque agreed.

Albuquerque's captains complained that he was letting the foe off too easily; but, so Albuquerque wrote the king, he felt that in this case peace would do his highness more service than war. He hadn't killed the renegades, he added, but he had them tied up to the pillory and thoroughly maimed and mutilated "to spread terror of the treason and evil they wrought."

"My present situation is the following," he added, allowing himself a certain unction, "my fleet has crossed the bar and I am on my way to Cambaia to secure the peace there. The cargo ships I sent off to take on their freight: the others, with the help of our Lord in the coming year will go to Cambaia. I hope to take on supplies and with the help of the Passion of our Lord, He helping us as He has always done, if He please in His Mercy, to terminate this business as Your Highness desires with the growth of your estate and fame beyond that of all the princes of the world: India remains tamed and terrorstruck, placed in due subjection and obedience to Your Highness . . . written in Goa the 23rd of November 1512."

Along the way a message reached the governor that a sheikh of Chaul had in his power a man who represented himself as an ambassador of Prester John who was asking to be sent to Goa. This turned out to be a certain Mateus, an Armenian merchant from Cairo who said he had been commissioned by Queen Helena of Abyssinia to establish friendly relations with the Portuguese court. Albuquerque sent off a galley to fetch him, and the captain of the galley—such was the terror inspired by the Portuguese, forced the sheikh to restore Mateus' goods and womenfolk and servants that he had seized. Mateus turned out to be "a white man of good presence, about fifty years old with two respectable-looking women and eight servants in his train."

Mateus reported that Pedro de Covilhã, the envoy of John II, was still living and honored in Abyssinia and that he brought letters to King Manoel from Prester John and a tiny box, which he was required to defend with his life, containing a piece of the wood of the True Cross. After talking with him Albuquerque sent him off on a swift dhow to Cananor with instructions that he be embarked on the next ship that came in to load ginger on its way to Portugal.

In Cananor, so Correa tells the tale, the Moslem merchants laughed at Mateus' story. They told the Portuguese captains that Mateus was only pretending to be a Christian, and was probably a Turkish spy. As a result he was given a rough time on his way to Portugal. When his caravel had to winter in Moçambique the captains in charge put him in irons there and mussed up his beard and slept with his women making great sport of that old fool Albuquerque who had been taken in by an imposter. They changed their tune when orders arrived from King Manoel to treat Mateus with due ceremony as an ambassador bringing a holy relic from a friendly prince. As soon as they reached Lisbon they were arrested by order of the king.

Before he left Goa, Albuquerque had received a message from Calicut offering, for the first time, solid terms of peace. The old Zamorim, who had given the Portuguese so much trouble, was dead and a new one reigned in his stead. This prince offered to allow the Portuguese to build a fort wherever they would on the waterfront. In return he asked that merchant ships out of Calicut be given safe conducts like the ships of Cochin and Cananor. The governor immediately accepted his terms and dispatched galleys with stonemasons and carpenters to begin constructing a castle.

It was January of the following year before he could gather his troops and shipping for the projected investment of the great port of Aden which dominated the Red Sea trade. This turned out one of his least successful enterprises. Aden was built in a semicircle in a crater-like saucer of jagged rock. The city was heavily fortified and well defended. The Portuguese artillery did no damage to its stout stone towers. In spite of a heroic effort, in which many valuable lives were lost, to scale the walls with ladders that turned out to be too short, the assault failed. The governor had to content himself with plundering and burning the Arab ships in the harbor.

While the many wounded were recovering the fleet cruised up into the Red Sea. All on board congratulated themselves, "praising the Lord because they were the first Portuguese to enter these straits in martial order with the royal standard aloft." One moonlight night some of the shipmen claimed to make out a new constellation of nine very bright stars in the shape of a cross which rose in the east and set toward dawn in the west behind the mountains in the land of Prester John. "The governor cried out that Our Lord was showing us the road we should take."

That day the governor and his captains and many men rowed ashore on the Abyssinian side and raised on a high promontory a rude altar of stones. One of the chaplains said mass and they set up a wooden cross on a tall pole, which, noted Correa, remained there for many years "until it rotted and fell down."

The winds proved baffling and contrary. The heat was terrible. The weather foiled every effort to establish contact with the Abyssinians. The ships were running out of water. At last they reached the island named Camarão where the pilots had been promising plenty of water. On the way they captured two dhows laden with foodstuffs. The place turned out to have palm trees and wells, but for food there were only goats. The inhabitants had fled to the mainland in skiffs at the first sight of the Portuguese sails.

At Camarão Albuquerque's fleet was windbound for three months. Not a drop of rain fell. Food was scarce. Many men died of fevers, particularly the people from Malabar who could not support privation as well as the Portuguese.

At last the wind turned favorable. Having detailed a pair of caravels to reconnoiter the Arab ports of Zeyla and Berbera on the Abyssinian side the governor headed for Aden. After chasing away with gunfire the crews of the ships beached in these ports, the crews of the caravels appropriated a great store of rice, wheat, butter, and "of very good honey in leather containers." Furthermore they collected quantities of dry salted mutton. These food-stuffs were much appreciated by the famished Portuguese when the caravels rejoined the fleet. You can almost hear Correa smacking his lips when he writes about them.

The second attack in Aden was more successful than the first. A landing party captured some of the harbor defenses, climbed up to a battery above, and turned its guns on the town. That night an Abyssinian man swam out to the flagship with the story that he was a Christian from the land of Prester John. He said a large number of the ships drawn up on the Aden shore were sailing with Portuguese safe conducts and that the shipowners begged the governor not to burn them. The local sheikh was offering for ransom eighteen Portuguese captives he kept loaded with chains in a cistern underground. These were the crew of a brigantine lost in a storm off some adjoining islands. Next day an Arab chieftain came out in a canoe with a white flag, but nothing came of the parley. The governor had as many ships as he could reach burned the following night and put to sea without rescuing the captives. The Abyssinian he treated with honor, dressed him in fine clothes and later sent him to Lisbon to give King Manoel a first hand account of the realm of Prester John.

The governor retired to his capital at Goa to prepare a final expedition against Aden. He had sent grim word to the local po-tentate that next time his scaling ladders would be longer. In Goa he established a great bakery to make seabiscuit and set his skilled armorers to work building muskets. One of his difficulties at Aden had been that many of his men had not learned how to fire the new matchlocks; now he set regular times and places for target practice. Twice a month he led his entire force out for military maneuvers. Every day, wrote Correa, he dined four hundred captains at his table.

"The governor always ate to the music of trumpets and kettle-drums. In front of the buildings where he lodged there was a great court where the *naïques*, captains of the native people, as-sembled. Every Sunday they came to be reviewed by the governor with their musical instruments and their little trumpets which are very martial. In front of the ranked soldiers stood a man who played on a great double-barreled copper instrument which was heard above all the others and made a startlingly warlike sound.

"Dancing women came to the great court with their instruments, because this is how they make their living, dancing and singing at mealtimes: this at dinner or supper, with torches of lint wicks set in copper pipes which they replenish with oil they bring in little copper kegs: and here they reviewed the twenty-four elephants that worked in the city—some were taken in Goa but others had been captured as prizes on ships from Ceylon. The elephants came to make their curtseys to the governor; but, the minute he finished dining, they all went away."

Sunday afternoons the governor rode out into the country with all his captains on foot behind him. Weekdays he rose before day, then went with his guards to hear mass. After that he rode out alone, a cane in his hand and a wide straw hat on his head, attended by his guard of halberdiers, to visit the shore or the walls, wherever work was being done he was interested in. He had to see everything with his own eyes. "He took along four secretaries of the royal household with ink and paper, making out orders and dispatches which he signed right there riding on his horse: and I Gaspar Correa, who am writing this story, worked like this as his secretary. He had a great flow of words. He wrote to the king telling him everything, even listing ruptured cannon; he wrote to the dukes and counts and everybody on the council, giving them a minute account of the whole condition of India and everything that was accomplished; and to the overseers of the treasury he wrote of what provisions there were in India and what it was necessary to provide. He wrote every year by four separate channels. The secretaries retained the minutes of what he wrote, which afterward they compared with the answers that came, so that nothing should be forgotten that they failed to provide."

It was January of 1514 before the governor's new expedition was equipped and ready. He postponed the attack on Aden because he was particularly vexed with the rulers of Ormuz who had sent an embassy overland direct to King Manoel with what he considered fraudulent offers of subjection. Aden could wait. He had dispatched a small flotilla to plunder its shipping. Now fresh orders came from King Manoel to build a castle at Ormuz.

The word from Ormuz was that the sultan who had sent an embassy to King Manoel had been poisoned by his vizier. This vizier had established one of the dead sultan's relatives as a puppet sovereign. All accounts agreed that the most powerful man there was the vizier's nephew, a Parsee named Rais Achmad. The latest exploit of this Rais Achmad had been to shut his uncle up in prison and to take over the government in his stead.

The fleet hove in sight of the dazzling white rock mountains of Ormuz one day around noon but the wind was so light it was vespers before the ships could be deployed in front of the city. As soon as the governor had finished his supper he went up to the stern castle of his flagship and ordered his trumpets to sound and his guns to fire. The rest of the fleet followed suit, "firing beautifully," wrote Correa, "so that it looked in the gathering darkness as if the ships were on fire."

At dawn the whole fleet bristled with banners and lances which glinted in the rising sun. The galleys already could be seen with their prows to the beach in front of the sultan's palace, waistcloths in place and rope ladders ready. From where young Correa stood the men with shining arms climbing up to the fighting tops seemed on a level with the crenelations along the roof of the sultan's palace.

The captains first came aboard the flagship, which was decorated with figured tapestries from Flanders. A sideboard stacked with silver dishes was set out on the quarterdeck. The dishes had been recently sent out by the king because the governor complained of the expense of continually replacing porcelain tableware. From the bulwarks above the waistcloths hung rich suits of armor, with their corselets and breastplates and helmets and aprons and thigh-pieces; and swords fastened to the belts, and bucklers "beautiful to look at"; and below between decks were many lances and pikes and halberds "very clean and polished because the armorers were always working on them." There were benches around the whole forecastle covered with carpets for the fidalgos to sit on. The governor's chair was upholstered in black velvet embroidered with silk and gold, placed on a great carpet with a sail overhead for an awning.

When the governor and his captains were all seated there came out from the shore in a skiff a noble-looking Moor squatting on a rug. The man beside him dressed in a long coat looked like a Portuguese. As the skiff approached the ship he got to his feet with his cap in his hand and called: "God save the *senhor governador* and the ship and the company." To which the sailors responded with trumpets and kettledrums and all the people raised a great shout when they heard the man speak Portuguese.

He turned out to be Miguel Ferreira whom Albuquerque had sent as ambassador to Ismael Shah, the Persian monarch. While the Moor returned to shore, Ferreira remained with the governor reading out of his travel diary an account of the situation in Ormuz and of everything that had happened since he left Chaul many months before. "This diary," added Correa, "I once had in my possession."

Miguel Ferreira's story was absorbing. Traveling with a home-bound envoy of Ismael Shah's, he landed in Ormuz where he was well received by the late sultan. From there he crossed to the mainland and proceeded by camel caravan up into the Persian highlands. They traveled in wickerwork saddles shaded by awnings from the sun. These saddles were so comfortable you could doze off when you felt like it.

The country was poor. The people lived in miserable clay huts. The chief food was dates. Then the road led them up into high cold snowy wastes where any kind of provender was hard to come by. Ferreira almost lost his life when a slave whom he'd had thrashed tried to poison him. He was ill for three months until Ismael Shah sent a litter to carry him to his capital. The Shah sent word he'd have the whole party beheaded if they allowed the Portuguese ambassador to die. Ferreira was wrapped in furs and conducted in the tightly shrouded litter to Shiraz. There the Shah's own physician cured him of the aftereffects of the poison. The Shah proved anxious for a Portuguese alliance against the Turks who were giving him a bad time in the north. He couldn't do enough for Ferreira.

He offered to set Ferreira up with a small harem, so that he would leave children behind him when he went home, but Ferreira tactfully explained that he had a wife in Portugal and as a Christian was bound to be true to her. The Shah approved of his constancy. He took him on a royal hunt, sent him on a visit to the Christian kingdom of Armenia, and then dispatched him with all honors to Ormuz, accompanied by an ambassador of his own laden with rich presents for King Manoel's governor.

Miguel Ferreira kept the governor up all night with his stories of the Persian court. Next morning a message came from the young sultan through whom Rais Achmad now ruled Ormuz inviting Albuquerque to rest ashore. The governor answered politely that he was so accustomed to sleeping aboard ship that he really preferred it.

Meanwhile he had learned by an exchange of messages that the timid young sultan feared that Rais Achmad was planning to kill him. Albuquerque offered to take the sultan and his court under his protection. For that purpose he asked leave to establish a small palisade ashore. During the series of guarded civilities that followed Albuquerque organized a working party which, in one night, without anyone in the city's catching on, set up a fort on the beach armed with culverins and falcinets and protected by breastworks made of baskets filled with sand. Since the island was waterless the first care of the Portuguese was to bring in wooden tanks filled with water. The fortification was finished and the shelters within it well under way, between dark and dawn, so that the Arabs were thoroughly astonished by what they saw in the morning light.

As soon as everything was ready Albuquerque established his court ashore. His first move was to receive the Persian ambassador in great state. He sent armed men parading through the town in his honor to give the inhabitants a good look at the armament of the Portuguese soldiers. The ambassador formally presented a letter to King Manoel and a suit of chain mail and a golden basin and ewer and two cheetahs and their trainers. For Albuquerque he brought a Chinese silk tunic so magnificent Albuquerque cried out that none but a king should wear it. As soon as the ambassador had retired the governor told his men that he would send the tunic to the shrine of Our Lady of the Mountain which he had erected in Goa. The coat of mail would go to Prince Luis; the basin and ewer to the queen, and the cheetahs to the young sultan of Ormuz.

With the cheetahs Albuquerque sent a message suggesting that the sultan might well lend him a little money to pay the expenses of the fleet until he should have an opportunity to sell some merchandise. The sultan immediately ordered his vizier to count out a hundred thousand xarafims into the hands of the governor's messenger. According to Correa, Rais Achmad the Parsee vizier paid out the money, in packages of five thousand xarafims each, with very ill grace. Word was immediately brought to the governor that the vizier was planning his murder as well as the sultan's. Albuquerque, who hadn't liked the Parsee's looks from the beginning, decided to take his own precautions.

He called a secret council of his captains and explained that the sultan was a mere figurehead. If he could get rid of Rais Achmad he would have Ormuz in his hands. He let it be known among the sultan's courtiers that he was about to depart for India and would be grateful for a new loan which he would repay in pepper and Portuguese products which he would remit as soon as he reached Goa. It was decided that the bonds should be signed to secure the loan at the governor's quarters within the palisade on the beach. At the same time the sultan's friends got wind of a plan of Rais Achmad's to invite the governor to his house for a siesta during which he would have him quietly killed. The governor was forewarned.

The day of the ceremonies, which were to take place in the presence of the ambassador of the Shah Ismael, the governor had the patio of his quarters hung with his Flanders cloths and carpets and covered by an awning. He and his captains were dressed in their best. Every man wore a dagger under his clothes. Men-at-arms lurked behind every partition. On board the ships every gun was loaded. The gunners stood ready with their matches.

The young sultan entered the room first and with his hand pointed out the places where his attendants were to stand. Rais Achmad strode in showing signs of great excitement. Without paying any attention to the sultan he walked straight up to the governor who stood in the patio with his captains about him. Though it had been agreed that no one should come armed, he wore a dirk on a bandolier, a short sword and dagger at his belt. Hanging from his shoulder was a sheaf of knives. He carried a small battle-ax in his hand. All these weapons were garnished with gold and precious stones of great price. His tunic was of rich brocade.

When he reached the patio he made a grand salaam before the governor. The governor immediately asked him through his interpreter why, since it had been agreed that no one should carry arms, had he come armed to the teeth. The Parsee turned to leave but found that the door had been barred from the outside. When the sultan and his suite advanced to make their salaams Rais Achmad followed them. The moment he came near Albuquerque grabbed Rais Achmad by the hand, pulled the man toward him and said to his captains, "Take him."

Rais Achmad jumped forward to seize the governor by the throat. His short sword was halfway out of the scabbard. The captains were too quick for him. They plunged their daggers into him, so many at once that some of them wounded each other. He fell dead.

The sultan and his suite cried out in terror that the Portuguese were going to kill them. There was a great outcry all over the city, particularly from the friends and relatives of Rais Achmad who barricaded themselves in their houses.

Since the sultan and his attendants had no way of escaping they had to listen when the governor assured them that no harm would come to them. The young sultan was a wise ruler, he said, and would have every assistance from the Portuguese. With his own hands he dressed the terrified potentate in a cuirasse trimmed with white satin and girded him with a golden sword and a gold-encrusted dagger. He hung a chain of gold around his neck and told him: "Ruler of Ormuz you are now made a knight in the name of the Portuguese king."

The sultan tried to throw himself at the governor's feet. The governor would have none of it. Instead he took him up on the roof where the people could see him togged out in his new finery.

Rais Achmad's body he ordered thrown out on the beach. But first it must be despoiled of its fine clothes. He told his followers that each one should pick out what he wanted. Some of them became rich from these spoils. "I myself," confessed Correa, "took a handkerchief off him embroidered with gold, which brought twenty xarafims."

With Rais Achmad disposed of and the young sultan thoroughly intimidated nothing stood in the way of building a proper castle. For five months every man, from the proudest fidalgos to the ship's boys, worked on the building of a great stone fortress which was armed with the heaviest guns of the fleet. Rumors, which turned out to be unfounded, reached the governor that a Turkish fleet was approaching. This lashed him to further efforts.

These were the summer months. The heat was unbearable. Many men died of fevers and dysentery.

When Albuquerque himself took to his bed with dysentery, Correa attributed his collapse to a conversation he had had with an old friend recently arrived from Portugal. This friend, who had close connections at court, told him that King Manoel was planning to recall him and to endow him with a rich county so that he could at last have a little rest from his labors. This news depressed Albuquerque immensely. Some day he might go home and "lean on the handle of a hoe," he said, but first he had to conquer Aden. "Portugal is a small country. What honor is there in Portugal equal to the government of India?"

The governor became so ill news got about that he was dying, but he still managed to drag himself to a low window in his quarters from which he could watch the work on the castle and give orders to his captains in regard to every detail. Feeling himself weakening day by day he made his confession, took Communion, and sent for all his captains and made them swear to obey the men he left in charge as they would have obeyed himself. At the beginning of November 1515, encouraged by his doctor who said the sea air might help him, he set sail for Goa.

Crossing the gulf they met a Moslem ship. The men aboard had heard that a new governor had arrived in Goa with new captains appointed to command all the fortresses. At this news Albuquerque's health took a turn for the worse. He wrote a letter to the new governor begging him not to auction off his clothes when he died so that people wouldn't see his ragged breeches. He asked to be buried in the chapel of Our Lady of the Mountain, which he'd had built in Goa. His house furnishings he asked to be sent to his sister in Portugal, the proceeds to be spent on the education of a small boy she was raising who was rumored, wrote Correa, to be his own son. In his last letter to King Manoel he asked that whatever pensions or emoluments might have been destined for him should be paid to his son Blas. Blas was half-Negro. Years later under the name of Afonso de Albuquerque he was to write a worshipful history of his father's exploits.

Albuquerque was fighting to keep alive long enough to have a last look at Goa. His ship was approaching the bar of the Mandavi. They had spoken to another dhow in the mouth of the river. The

names of the new officials that came across the water were Lopo
Soares as viceroy, Gotorro de Monroi as captain of Goa, Alvaro
Telles for Calicut—all enemies of Albuquerque's—and for Cochin,
the man he had sent home in chains, Diogo Mendes.

"Good news for me" he cried out when he heard it, "that the
men whom I sent off as prisoners, of whom I wrote disparaging
things, have come back honored . . . my sins must seem to the
king very great. So I am in wrong with him for the love of my
people and in wrong with my people for love of the king . . . it is
time to call in the Church."

He asked to be dressed in the costume of the Order of Santiago
of which he was a knight. They dressed him in brown buskins with
golden spurs and a black damask shirt under his cloak and a filet
of black and gold round his head and over it a black velvet cap and
a scarf of black velvet over his shoulders. This was the costume in
which he wanted to be buried.

It was still night. As the fleet glided up the river toward Goa
he sent a brigantine in for his friend Frei Domingos de Sousa, the
vicar general whose consolations he needed. Besides he asked for a
little Portuguese red wine. With the first light he had himself
lifted out of bed and supported to the door of his cabin where he
stood against the jamb looking out at the city and the chapel of Our
Lady on the island. He bowed his head, muttered his last prayers,
and died just as the ship came to anchor.

PART FOUR

Peak of Empire

I

THE COURT OF
THE FORTUNATE KING

"King Manoel was the first of the Christian kings of Europe to whom elephants came from India," wrote Damião de Góis in the chronicle of King Manoel's reign he compiled forty years after the monarch's death. Góis was one of the great scholars of the period. His earliest recollections were of his service, as a boy of twelve or thirteen, in King Manoel's household. He was present at the reception of the Abyssinian ambassador, when Mateus, after so many vicissitudes, finally reached the Portuguese court. Young Góis was so impressed by Mateus' account of the religion and customs of the dwellers in the high Abyssinian valleys that the study of their type of Christianity became the central interest of his life. When at fourteen he was sent on a mission to the Portuguese trading post in Antwerp, he was already exchanging letters with Abyssinians in Lisbon on points of doctrine and on details of life in their highlands.

Besides the Abyssinians, Góis remembered the king's elephants with particular affection, filling pages of his chronicle with accounts of the strength and sagacity of the mighty pachyderms. He told some tall stories: "Of elephants it is written that some have been able to read Greek. Another account I would hardly believe if it weren't on the authority of Diogo Pereira, a nobleman whose word can be trusted. When he was visiting the sultan of Narsinga"

—Narsinga was the Portuguese name for the Hindu sultanate of Vijayanagar—"in the city of Bisanaga, that ruler had brought into the courtyard of his palace an elephant who traced readable letters on the ground with the point of his trunk. Afterward when he was asked what he wanted to eat he replied in a clear voice that everybody understood, 'Rice and betel nut.'"

Góis' narrative, written when he was in his fifties at a time when the glories of empire had already begun to fade, still reflects a warm afterglow of his boyish enthusiasms. "The king had five elephants, four males and one female." They tramped through the streets before him when he rode out in Lisbon or journeyed across country. At the time when Góis first remembered these progresses the elephants were preceded, far enough ahead so that they couldn't see it, because they were scared to death of it, by a rhinoceros. This rhinoceros had fetters on its legs and was led by Indian trainers at the end of a long chain. The hostility between the two great beasts was proverbial.

Remembering the Roman circus King Manoel one day determined to see which would win in a fight. He had a young elephant placed in a corral outside of the Ribeira palace along with a rhinoceros. The rhinoceros charged with his muzzle low and his horn aimed at the elephant's belly, "breathing so hard he raised dust and straw from the ground like a whirlwind." Góis figured that the elephant, "because he was young and didn't have long enough tusks to fight with," thought discretion the better part of valor. He bolted out of the corral through a barred window, bending the bars aside in a flash with his trunk. Everyone was amazed that such a large body could pass through such a small opening. Trumpeting and roaring as he went he galloped off through the crowds along the waterfront to his stable. The rhinoceros stood his ground and gave the impression, wrote Góis, by his manner and attitude, that he surely would have won the victory if the elephant hadn't run. This all confirmed the people of Lisbon in their conviction, already supported by Holy Writ, that the rhinoceros was the most powerful of living beasts.

During these royal progresses through city or country, right after the elephants there pranced a caparisoned horse ridden by a Persian hunter. On a special saddlecloth on the horse's crupper rode the hunting leopard which was a gift of the ruler of Ormuz.

Next rode King Manoel, followed by his fidalgos in attendance. "With this pomp and to the music of trumpets and kettledrums he rode through the city."

Góis, like the earlier chroniclers, often dwells on King Manoel's fondness for music. "Often when he worked in his office and always at the time of his afternoon nap and after he had gone to bed, he had musicians play for him. For his chamber music and for his chapel he collected famous performers from all parts of Europe. These he supported honorably and did them other favors, so that he had the best choir of any of the kings and princes then alive."

He brought Castilian jesters to his court. He enjoyed their jokes and jibes "not so much for what they said as for the veiled rebukes they leveled at the members of his household, reminding them of their vices and foibles so that they sometimes took the hint and mended their ways."

Sundays and holidays after dinner he liked to go to the races. Góis was of the opinion that the king's enthusiasm accounted for the excellence of the horses and the riding in those days. "He often ordered up bullfights and tourneys with cane lances. So that his fidalgos shouldn't spend too much on these games, he kept a store of trappings and Moorish costumes in his wardrobe which he loaned out. He sometimes joined in the game of canes himself. He did well. His arms were so strong and he had such a good seat on a horse and aimed so dextrously with a lance or cane that nobody could get the better of him. . . .

". . . Holidays and even some weekdays when he was in Lisbon he used to go out in a barge on the Tagus, a small galley with an awning, all upholstered with silk, taking musicians along and any official he was doing business with. He would order up a picnic of fresh fruits and preserves and sweet confections and wine and water. The fidalgos he'd invited and the musicians, the young noblemen of his chamber and the oarsmen all had their share. . . .

". . . He loved hunting and was a good hand with the crossbow. He never went out without musicians to play and sing to him out in the field or in the houses where he ate or took his repose. He was so merry and pleasant that when he went hunting he made his grooms and beaters dance their rustic gigs in front of him. They, knowing how benign and human he was would besiege him on the road, crowding round his horse and when they had him surrounded each one would ask the favor he wanted, which often he would grant outright, or if there were some hindrance he'd tell them not to worry about it, or would send them to the officials at his office."

Every Friday he fasted on bread and water. On that day he went to the courts to hear the pleas of the prisoners and to be present when they were sentenced. In this he never failed nor let anything interfere except illness. The days when the king gave audience there was always in the room someone playing the clavichord and singers.

He had a great inclination for learning and for men of letters and had a good understanding of Latin, which he had been taught as a child. He knew the language so well he could judge between good and poor style. He was so eager for the nobility of the kingdom to be instructed in letters that he sent any of his pages or of the young noblemen of his chamber who showed signs of ability to follow a daily lesson in grammar in the scholars' quarter where the national university was in those days. "He was much given to Judaic astrology, so that when the ships sailed for India, or when they were expected home, he asked for predictions from the great Portuguese astrologer who lived in Lisbon, named Diogo Mendez Vizinho, born in Covilhã, nicknamed the Cripple; and after he died, the king made the same requests of Tomás de Tôrres, his physician, a man very learned in astrology and the other sciences. Not withstanding the fact that the king had faith in astrology, this physician never would resort to divination. He was hostile to the very idea and regretted that the king was addicted to it."

King Manoel was very clean in his person, spic and span and well-dressed. He liked to wear something new every day. As a result he had so many clothes that twice a year he divided up his silk and cloth suits among his fidalgos, knights and squires, and the young noblemen of his chamber.

This king, explained Góis, was a man of much business and very assiduous in dispatching every document that came under his hand. He was a careful eater, always drank water and never ate olive oil or any oily food. He was so temperate in his appetite that you hardly knew whether he liked one food better than another.

He slept so little that no matter how late he went to bed he was always up before sunrise.

He was very obedient to the Holy See, a very Catholic Christian, who carefully observed all the customs, feasts and fasts of the Church. The three days before Easter, when the Holy Sacrament is covered up, he slept near the altar, on the floor without undressing those three days. Easter day in the morning he went out with all the court in solemn procession with every musical instrument he had in his palaces. On Christmas Eve he ate supper in the great hall with every sort of mace carriers, kings-at-arms, trumpeters, drummers and pipers. He invited the whole court to the supper which was all of fresh fruit and confections of sugar and preserves they brought him from the island of Madeira. His evening parties to celebrate the births of his children or royal marriages were sumptuous with music and dancing and other entertainments. On these occasions the king himself sometimes danced.

"He was happy and prosperous," wrote Góis summing up all his memories, "during all the time that he reigned, so that I often saw merchants who came to India House with bags of gold and silver coins to pay for spices they had bought told to come back another day because the officials didn't have time to count all the money that had come in since morning." Albuquerque in one of his letters estimated the king's take from the India trade alone at a million gold cruzados a year.

One feature of King Manoel's evening parties which Góis neglected to mention was Gil Vicente's plays. There has been a good deal of discussion among scholars as to who Gil Vicente was. If he was the same Gil Vicente patronized by John II's widow Dona Leonor, who came of a family of goldsmiths in Guimarães, and was on record as a member of the goldsmith's guild in Lisbon and sometime Master of the Mint and whose greatest work as a jeweler was a monstrance made out of the first gold Vasco da Gama brought home from India which is still shown at the Hieronymite monastery at Belém, he was one of the most versatile artists in history. Even if the poet and the goldsmith were two different men the second Gil Vicente had plenty to show for himself.

His name first appears as the author of a short eclogue to celebrate the birth of King Manoel's first born, the prince who was to succeed him as John III. The simple, salty lyrics were recited by the poet himself disguised as a herdsman. The courtiers received Gil Vicente's recitation with such enthusiasm that the queen, Dona Maria, asked that it be repeated in her bedchamber. Since the theme could be applied to the birth of our Lord the ladies of the court asked that this "cosa nova" be performed once more for Christmas. Instead Gil Vicente produced his own version of the conventional mystery play of the time in which the angels appear to the shepherds at Bethlehem. The difference was that the shepherds were all characterized.

From that time on no court function was complete without a dramatic sketch by Gil Vicente. At first he drew on the crude mysteries current in France and Spain, but as his talent developed he filled his presentations with lifelike characters. Satirical skits began to appear, interspersed with lyrics of rare freshness. The poet poked as much fun at courtiers and ecclesiastics as at peasants and burghers. The fact that the king and his fidalgos laughed wholeheartedly at these sallies gives the measure of a certain breadth of mind among King Manoel's entourage which would have been inconceivable at the Portuguese court in the generations to come.

Men of letters hailed Gil Vicente as the Portuguese Plautus, but the light touch and the singing verses would seem to be more reminiscent of Theocritus. Sometimes he seems to be reviving the cossantes, fresh from countrypeople's singing matches, so popular at the court of King Dinis. The forty or so eclogues, religious mysteries, farces and comedies which have come down constitute—a generation before the Spanish dramatists and two generations before the Elizabethans—the earliest flowering of the Renaissance theater.

Underlying the comic episodes and the rustic foolery were profound religious convictions. Gil Vicente's drive for the reform of the Church echoed the thinking of such humanists of the school of Erasmus as Damião de Góis, and the opinions of King Manoel himself as expressed in his remonstrances to the pope against the simony and immorality of the Roman clergy.

The plays of Gil Vicente, the naturalistically decorated architecture of Belém and Tomar and of the "unfinished chapels" at Batalha reflected the enthusiasm for discovery and experiment which animated Portuguese life in the reign of the Fortunate King. Even in painting, where the Portuguese were weak, there appeared fresh flashes of originality in the paintings at Viseu associated with the name of Grão Vasco.

These were heady years. Though ruling a tiny realm King Manoel was peer to any of the great monarchs of Europe. He was twice son-in-law of the Catholic Kings of Castile and Aragon. He and Henry VIII of England had married sisters. His daughter was the wife of Charles V, the Hapsburg king of Spain who was soon to be chosen Emperor of the Holy Roman Empire.

From the vast regions dominated by Portuguese seapower every returning ship brought news of fresh successes. In Morocco his captains were completing the chain of fortresses from Tangier to Mogador which cut off the Moslems from the navigation of the Atlantic. In the far East his skippers were monopolizing the trade of the Spice Islands. In the West sugar cane carried over from Madeira was beginning to give the tiny Brazilian settlements an export crop which soon would rival dyewood. In West Africa the campaign for the conversion of the Bantu of the Lower Congo begun by John II, who built the first church there, seemed about to bear fruit.

The two early missions composed of priests and monks versed in agriculture who had worked to introduce new crops and to improve the economy of the tribes had suffered more from the fevers than from the opposition of the inhabitants. A third mission showed results. A local chieftain enthusiastically accepted baptism and was hailed as Afonso I, king of Manicongo. His son Henrique was brought to Lisbon to be educated along with a number of young men of the ruling Congolese who were distributed among monastery schools to be taught reading and writing and grammar and "the things of the Faith." The Congolese ambassador, who had been christened Pedro, and his wife, became familiar and popular figures at the Portuguese court. In 1513 after much urging from King Manoel, who promised to pay its expenses, a Congolese embassy was dispatched to Rome. The Portuguese were delighted with the progress of their Bantu pupils. Góis wrote that several of them became good Latinists. Their king's son, Henrique, took holy orders and was eventually consecrated a bishop.

The Congolese mission to Rome exhibited King Manoel's desire to disseminate the faith. The mission that followed was accompanied by a display of wealth which was the astonishment of Christendom.

Cardinal Giovanni de' Medici, who had been the right hand man of Michelangelo's patron, Julius II, had just been elected pope, largely through the intricate maneuvering of his cousin, Giulio de' Medici. As Leo X he headed, not only the Church of Christ and the Papal States, but the elder branch of the great Medici family now restored to power in Florence. He was a comparatively young man of thirty-seven. Under the warrior Pope Julius he had been so unchurchly a cardinal that it was only four days after his election as pope that he was ordained a priest. A short time later he was made a bishop. Though hardly a fervent Christian he had his father, Lorenzo the Magnificent's enthusiasm for humane learning and painting and sculpture and fine architecture. His term in the papacy has been generally considered to represent the apogee of the High Renaissance.

From the time of John I there had been a warm friendship, backed up by commercial relations lucrative to both parties, between the House of Avis and the Florentine Medicis. King Manoel determined to celebrate Pope Leo's election by an embassy which would outdo in splendor anything that had been seen in Christian Rome. The popular Tristão da Cunha was chosen to lead it. He took with him his three sons, an assemblage of dignitaries, the most accomplished orator at the Portuguese court and a sumptuous collection of presents. Knowing that Pope Leo was fond of hunting, the king sent along his hunting leopard, its Persian trainer and the famous horse. Of all the gifts he had carried to Rome Pope Leo was reported to have been most pleased by the elephant.

Damião de Góis told a quaint tale of the great beast's embarkation. "I was present at the stone docks in the city of Lisbon when they embarked the elephant the king was sending to Pope Leo X." There was no way of inducing him to enter the barge which was to take him out to the ship until the king twice sent him messages through his Indian trainer, to tell him to go on board. The king promised on his royal honor that he was sending him to an even greater lord, who would treat him even better than he had been treated before; and if this didn't turn out to be true, the king promised to bring the elephant back to the same place from which he had left. "The elephant trumpeted twice to signify his agreement and, with tears in his eyes, allowed himself to be embarked."

The ship carrying the embassy landed at the port of Hercule in the territory of Siena. Da Cunha and his family and attendants rode off directly to Rome leaving the elephant and the hunting leopard to travel by slow stages "because they were accompanied along the way by such a crowd of people on horse and afoot who had come to see the elephant that they could hardly get along the road or enter any town."

The pope appointed the first Sunday in Lent as the day of the embassy's reception. On that day the ambassador and his staff assembled before dawn at a villa in the gardens of Cardinal Adrian, the Fleming who was to succeed Pope Leo. A couple of hours after noon a vast throng of men, women and children started moving toward the city followed by trumpets and pipes and the hunting leopard and the elephant conducted by the Assistant Master of the Royal Stables on a magnificent steed with harness and saddlecloths embossed with gold and adorned with seed pearls and colored silks.

The cardinals and their families and all the ambassadors attached to the papal court rode out to meet the Portuguese embassy. While these dignitaries were exchanging Latin harangues, the governor of the city, prelates of the papal staff and His Holiness's Master of Ceremonies arrived to indicate the order of the procession in which the Portuguese should enter the city. The elephant, carrying on his back a great chest containing the king's presents and surrounded by Portuguese trumpeters and pipers marched in followed by the pope's Swiss Guards. The streets were filled with so many people, beside those who looked out from windows and rooftops "that without the authority of the alcaïdes and other officers of justice the procession would never have gotten through."

The pope viewed the scene from a window in a lower story of the Castle of Sant'Angelo. The elephant made three curtseys, and, filling his trunk with water in a trough placed there for the purpose, shot a stream so high above the window where the pope was that it landed on a number of cardinals looking out from the

upper stories. The cardinals and their attendants and many gentlemen of quality were thoroughly sprinkled. Then he shot water into
the crowd around until they were so well drenched they gave
ground. "After these and other amusing tricks which his trainer
instructed him to perform he moved along. The pope never took
his eyes off him until he passed out of sight."

The elephant and the hunting leopard and the splendor of the
pontifical robes made King Manoel's embassy famous throughout
Europe. The Emperor Maximilian's ambassador wrote his master
a Latin epistle describing the affair which, translated into Italian
and Portuguese, was widely circulated by the printing presses. He
went to some length to describe the fabric, decorated with the
royal arms woven a gilt thread, which covered not only the chest
full of gifts but the entire elephant, and the elegant trappings of
the sumpter mules and the liveries of the servants and Tristão da
Cunha's hat which was entirely covered with large pearls. He
went on to tell of the papal regalia laid out for inspection in the
Belvedere: "All these vestments were woven with gold thread and
so covered with precious stones and pearls that only in a few
places could you see the cloth of gold; but only the pearls and
precious stones, set with admirable artifice—sumptuous, magnificent—with knots in the shape of a pomegranate marvelous to see,
so that in certain places the fabric appeared as if painted in gold
and silk with the face of our Savior and of the saints and apostles
all outlined with pearl and those gems we call raw rubies, not
worked or polished, but used just as they came from the places
where they were found in their natural splendor. This is as it
should be in dealing with divine things. In a word the material was
precious but the workmanship overshadowed it."

Pope Leo received the Portuguese embassy a number of times.
In Latin acclaimed as most elegant by all present, King Manoel's
court orator Diogo Pacheco declared that he laid these gifts, the
first fruits of the Orient, at his Holiness's feet. Then he embarked
on the three requests which the Portuguese king wished to have
granted. First he begged the pope to second with all his power the
projects for reform of the church at present being considered by
the Lateran council. Second he called for vigorous prosecution of
the war against the Turks and third he asked that King Manoel be

allowed to use certain of the revenues of the Portuguese dioceses in his crusade against the Moslem in Morocco.

Pope Leo gave him fair words on the first, evaded the second by offering the command of a fleet to be assembled to fight the Turks off Sicily to da Cunha, who refused it, and bargained hard on the third. In the end the ambassador carried home to King Manoel a papal bull granting him certain ecclesiastic revenues in return for an annual subsidy to the Vatican.

All in all King Manoel was so well satisfied with the results of his embassy that in 1517 he sent the pope a fresh shipload of presents. These included his rhinoceros. The ship made port at Marseilles where the rhinoceros was inspected by none other than Frances I, the new king of France. Between Marseilles and Genoa the ship was lost in a storm with all hands. The carcass of the rhinoceros was found washed up on the beach. It was carefully stuffed with straw and forwarded to the pope. Albrecht Dürer made a sketch of it in Rome which became the basis of one of his most successful engravings.

The loss of his second embassy to Rome was somewhat made up for by the safe return to Portugal of Fernão Peres de Andrade whom King Manoel had instructed to seek friendly relations with the Chinese. Andrade entered the Pearl River with a fleet of nine ships and in spite of the remonstrances of the authorities made his way through the Tiger's Mouth and upriver to Canton. There he spent a number of months trading and patiently conciliating the xenophobe mandarins, while a Portuguese envoy journeyed to the imperial court. Portuguese caravels had reconnoitered the coast in the years before but it was Andrade who brought back to Portugal the first circumstantial account of the forbidden realm of the Ming emperors.

Finding Lisbon in the throes of one of the frequent outbreaks of bubonic plague which marred the prosperity of the reign of the Fortunate King he followed King Manoel and his third wife to their refuge in Evora. There, well received by a monarch always eager to hear of newly discovered lands and fresh opportunities for trade, he made his report.

The Chinese were more white than swarthy. Particularly in the north they were as white-skinned as Germans. They dressed like

Tatars in narrow cassocks of silk brocade or cotton trimmed with furs which abounded in the land. They had many horses and a great abundance of produce, breadstuffs, livestock and game, all very cheap. They were sturdy men-at-arms with steel weapons which were not as well tempered as those of Europe. They used lances, halberds, bows, and small iron bombards and muskets: "But as soon as they saw our arms and artillery they went to work to make everything our way which they accomplished with great perfection." They ate at high tables like Europeans with table-cloths, napkins and, "for cleanliness," forks; they were great people for banquets where they get more merry than necessary. The women are comely and well gotten up. The nobles went through the streets in carts roofed in with silk materials and gilded and very well painted. They said that their history went so far back that they couldn't remember when it began. There was much gold and silver in the land, outside of what was brought in from the Riu-kiu Islands and Japan.

The Chinese believed in one God, creator of everything. They worshiped three images of a man all exactly alike. They greatly honored the image of a woman whom they called Nanman and considered a saint. She was the advocate before God of all those who walk on land and those who cruise on the sea. They esteemed also a man whom they said was so good and such a just and perfect knight that in his life he did many miracles such as crossing a river fully armed with his feet on a naked sword to reach an army he was captain of.

Andrade brought home with him paintings of figures set in landscapes and among trees "almost like the paintings on canvas they make in Flanders." He reported that the temples were sumptuous. There were religious edifices they called pagodas and convents of friars and nuns. There were clocks in the pagodas and very good bells. The language in which they prayed and performed religious services was not understood unless you studied it "like Latin with us." They had universities and colleges where they learned philosophy, mathematics, astrology, liberal arts, laws, medicine and theology according to their beliefs. In all these could be found very learned men. In the mechanical arts they surpassed all the nations of the world. They thought so highly of themselves that they said that a man who wasn't Chinese wasn't a man.

Góis went on to tell in his chronicle of the unfortunate turn relations with the Chinese then took. At first everything went well. The Portuguese ambassador Tomé Pires, a Lisbon shopkeeper particularly versed in foreign trade who was sent with the usual friendly letter from King Manoel, was received in Peking, which he reached in four months from Canton; but suddenly he was sent back to Canton and thrown into prison. There he died, it was suspected, of poison. The same fate befell all the Portuguese in Canton. News had reached the Chinese court of the plundering of some islands along the Chinese coast by Fernão de Andrade's brother Simão, "who behaved," wrote Góis, "toward those of that land so as to destroy the peace his brother had established and to turn all the love and friendship the Chinese bore toward the Portuguese into hatred and suspicion."

Manoel died after a short illness in December 1521. "King Manoel being in the city of Lisbon, in the highest and most prosperous state that any king might desire," wrote Góis, "having discovered, conquered, and subjugated all the maritime provinces from the Strait of Gibraltar to the seas of Arabia, Persia, the islands of Ceylon, Sumatra, Java, the Moluccas, all the way to China and the Riukius. He had ambassadors at his court from most of the European kingdoms principalities and lordships and from the Supreme Pontiff; and from many kings and rulers of Africa and Asia, all his vassals, and from others allies and friends. Great richness of gold, silver and spices came in every year from his conquests. He was well liked and loved by his people and by those of other nations wherever the fame of his royal person extended. His realm was peaceful and calm. He had six sons and three living daughters from his second and third marriages, all gifted with beauty, good dispositions and virtue—a state from which nothing better could be expected or anything desired except the rule of the court of heaven for which God for His service removed him from this life. . . . He died in the Palace of the Ribeira of a fever which seemed a sort of lethargy of which many people died in Lisbon at that time. He was fifty-two years old. He had reigned twenty-six years."

2

WESTWARD TO THE ORIENT

One of the griefs of the latter years of King Manoel's reign was the defection of a minor nobleman named Fernão de Magalhães. Magellan, as his name is usually written in English, hailed from the Minho. At a tender age he served as a page to John II's widow, the accomplished Dona Leonor. Vasco da Gama's triumphant return from his first voyage to India fired all the young bloods at the Portuguese court with a fever of discovery. Along with his friend Francisco Serrão, Magellan enlisted in Almeida's expedition in 1505. He fought in East Africa under various leaders and took part in Almeida's greatest victory at Diu. He and Serrão joined Sequeira's fleet that went to establish the first trading post at Malacca. There he won a reputation for alertness and bravery in the set-to with the Malays which ended the first Portuguese attempt to dominate that chief mart of the Orient. Although he was said to have had misunderstandings with the governor he played an important role in Albuquerque's final capture of Malacca. He did not accompany Serrão on his exploration to the Moluccas to find the source of the cloves but he may have made trips into the China Sea and south toward the islands on the fringe of what is now New Guinea.

Magellan sailed home to Portugal after having accumulated a small store of cash and a vast amount of information about the sea and peoples of the extreme Orient. In his study of the ethnography and geography of these regions he was associated with a relative of his named Duarte Barbosa who belonged to a family that adhered to a branch of the Braganças that had remained disaffected even after King Manoel's amnesty. Barbosa seems to have sailed to India with Cabral's fleet in a ship outfitted and financed by a Dom Alvaro de Bragança. After years of travel throughout East Africa, India and the Straits of Malacca he returned to Lisbon and compiled what has remained a most useful pilotbook of these regions as first seen by the Portuguese. So closely was Magellan associated with the work that some scholars attribute the whole book to his pen. He married Duarte Barbosa's sister.

Magellan had not gotten along with Albuquerque. His friend Serrão disobeyed the orders of the governor of Malacca and set himself up as an independent chieftain on the comfortable island of Ternate. From there, for reasons known only to himself, he wrote Magellan a description of the Spice Islands which located them much further to the east than they really were. This gave Magellan a notion that they might lie in the seas granted to Castile by the Treaty of Tordecillas.

Associated as he was with the Barbosa family Magellan found his hopes of preferment at court thoroughly blocked. He joined an expedition to Morocco which was led by Jaime, the ruling Duke of Bragança, who was loyal to King Manoel. There he was wounded in an attack on some Moorish encampments and got into hot water in a wrangle over the sale of a herd of captured Moorish cattle. When he returned to Lisbon his plea was turned down for an increase, on account of his wound, of his allowance as noble of the court. King Manoel himself refused his request of a ship to explore the islands beyond the Moluccas.

To Magellan's impatient spirit this seemed the last straw. He left the country for Seville. Along with him he took an astrologer and cartographer named Rui Faleiro whom the Portuguese chroniclers claimed was already half cracked, and a group of disaffected pilots and seamen. Magellan had turned their heads with the reports he had from his friend Serrão of the fine life he was leading on Ternate and the wealth that would come to whomever could monopolize the trade in cloves at its source.

In Seville Magellan found his father-in-law, Diogo Barbosa,

another veteran of Portuguese India who had entered the Spanish service, captain of the castle. The Barbosas' patron Alvaro de Bragança was living there in exile. These connections made introductions easy to the court of Charles V. The young Hapsburg prince, who had been brought up in Flanders, found himself at sixteen, without knowing a word of Spanish, king of Castile and Aragon. His chief councillor on Indian affairs was his old tutor, Cardinal Adrian of Utrecht. They invited Magellan and Faleiro to Valladolid where, with the help of a swarm of French and Flemish advisers, Charles was setting up an administration for his realm. With their maps and globes they had little trouble convincing the novice king that the islands the cloves came from were in the region assigned to Spain.

In spite of the remonstrances of the Portuguese ambassador who told Magellan that his project was an offense against his God and his king; that it would result in the disgrace of his family and be a stain on his own honor forever, as well as the cause of strife and ill-feeling between two friendly monarchs, Magellan signed a contract by which he and Rui Faleiro would be awarded a handsome share of whatever profits accrued to the crown of Castile from the enterprise. King Charles made him a knight of Santiago and appointed him admiral in command of a fleet of five ships.

The fleet was fitted out by the India House in Seville. Except for Magellan the ships' captains were to be Castilians, but several of the pilots and some thirty of the crewmen were Portuguese. When it became obvious that Rui Faleiro was too unstable for such an enterprise, King Charles sent down to Seville one Juan de Cartagena to take his place as joint commander. Cartagena and Magellan never hit it off for a moment. In spite of protests from Valladolid, Magellan took along a number of friends and relatives, Duarte Barbosa among them. Of the 260-some men who manned the fleet there were besides Spaniards and Portuguese; Flemings, Germans, English and Italians. Among the Italians was a young patrician from Vicenza named Antonio Pigafetta, who obtained his appointment as special servant of the admiral and supernumerary on the flagship *Trinidad* by pulling strings at court. He seems to have joined solely for the adventure. The narrative he got up from his diary forms the only eyewitness record of this first cruise around the world.

The little fleet sailed out of the Guadalquivir on September 20, 1519. After six days at sea they took on wood, water, meat and pitch to caulk the ships with from the Spanish island of Teneriffe. From there Magellan set his course south through the Cape Verde Islands and skirted the coast of Sierra Leone. They ran into contrary winds, torrential rains and dangerous squalls. Pigafetta, who was pretty much of a greenhorn, was amazed by the phenomenon of St. Elmo's fire, which the crews regarded as a good omen. Off the African coast the first real altercation took place between Cartagena and the admiral. The Spaniard, who was skipper of *San Antonio*, drew abreast of the flagship and complained that they were too near to the coast and should be steering a more westerly course for Brazil. Magellan told him to mind his own business and to steer by his flagship *Trinidad* which—as had been agreed—would show a banner by day and a lantern by night. They had words again at the courtmartial of an officer and a crewman accused of sodomy on *Victoria*. Magellan removed Cartagena from his command and placed him under arrest.

After losing sight of the north star they reached the Brazilian coast and anchored in the bay of Guanabara. There they suffered from the heat more than they had crossing the equator. "We provisioned ourselves abundantly with fowls, sweet-potatoes"—Pigafetta found they tasted like chestnuts—"and a sort of fruit that looks like a pine cone but is extremely sweet and with a delicious aroma." He was eating his first pineapple. They had sugar cane and the meat of the tapir which he found like beef. He was amazed by the cheapness of everything. "For a fishhook or a knife they would give us five or six hens; for a comb, a brace of geese: for a mirror or a pair of scissors enough fish to feed ten men. We even traded with playing cards. For a king of diamonds they gave me six chickens and thought they were doing good business."

"These people are very credulous and good and it should be easy to convert them to Christianity. By chance they came to look upon us with veneration and respect. The country had been suffering from drouth for two months and just as we sailed in the sky opened and the rain poured down. They said we had come from the sky and brought the rain with us. When we went ashore to say mass they listened in silence with a respectful air. Seeing us launch-

275

ing our ships' boats into the sea they thought the boats were the ships' children and when they lay alongside or were towed astern they thought the ships were nursing them."

From the Brazilian port they sailed south along the coast, crossing the mouth of the Rio de la Plata where a Spaniard named Juan de Solis, also in search of a passage onto the southern ocean, had been eaten by cannibals with sixty of his crew a few years before. In some islands populated only by seals, and by penguins which they clubbed in great numbers for food, the ships were battered by a storm. They took refuge in the harbor of San Julian, which had possibly been visited by Vespucci eighteen years before.

Two months passed before they saw a human being. Then suddenly a gigantic naked man appeared on the crest of a dune, singing and dancing and throwing dust on his head. The admiral sent a sailor ashore and told him to make the same gestures. Thus the man was induced to come down to the beach. According to Pigafetta, who liked to pull a long bow for the benefit of credulous readers, the man was such a giant that the crewmen's heads only reached to his waist. The Patagonian was enticed aboard ship and given food and drink. When he was shown his own face in a mirror he jumped back in such a fright that he knocked down four of the sailors who crowded about him. He was given bells, a mirror, a comb, and some printed Pater Nosters and allowed to go back to his people.

Tolerably good relations were established with the Patagonians. Pigafetta described their culture at some length. They lived off the flesh of some animal of the Llama family which he noted as having the head and ears of a mule, the neck and body of a camel, the feet of a deer and a horse's tail. They ate its flesh raw. From its skin they made cloaks and rude shelters to keep out the cold. From its guts they made bowstrings. Their arrows were like European arrows but tipped with flint instead of steel. They painted their faces and bodies and cut their hair, which they dusted with a white powder, in a halo like monks. Their women were shorter and fatter than the men, had prodigiously long breasts and "carried everything, laden like donkeys." The Portuguese baptized one of the "giants" and tried to teach him the Pater Noster. Magellan was determined to take a couple back as exhibits to the court of Castile, but after he had inveigled two men into putting their feet in some fetters, he had trouble establishing any further contact with the rest.

The chief cause of the long delay at San Julian was a mutiny of the Castilian captains. Led by Cartagena, whose wrath had been smouldering ever since his arrest, the Spanish faction seized three ships of the fleet and took prisoner Magellan's cousin, Alvaro de Mesquita, whom Magellan had appointed captain of *San Antonio* in Cartagena's stead. In the scuffle Mesquita's mate, a Basque named Eloriaga, was so severely wounded that he soon after died. Magellan woke up next morning to find himself master of only two ships, *Trinidad* and the small *Santiago*, where the captain, though a Spaniard, remained loyal. The conspirators sent Magellan a message assuring him that the rebellion had been caused by his lack of consideration for the Spaniards. If he changed his ways they would return to obedience. They suggested a parley.

Magellan lost no time in executing a countercoup. As if to arrange a parley he sent his constable with six men, who were heavily armed under their cloaks, to take a letter to Captain Mendoza of *Victoria*. While Mendoza was reading the letter the constable drew his dagger and struck him in the throat. The crew made no move to resist. Duarte Barbosa, who was a subordinate officer, took command as soon as Mendoza was dead and ordered the ship moved to an anchorage beside *Trinidad*. Boarding parties immediately subdued the other ships. *San Antonio* tried to escape under cover of night but was stopped by a salvo of artillery.

Magellan set up a formal courtmartial with Captain Mesquita as presiding officer. Forty men were condemned to death. Since it was impractical to deplete the personnel of the expedition the sentence was only carried out on Captain Quesada who was blamed for Eloriaga's murder. Quesada's servant was given the choice of beheading his master or dying with him. The bodies of Mendoza and Quesada were cut into quarters as befitted traitors. According to one account the bloody remnants were exhibited on stakes on the beach. Cartagena and a French priest convicted as his accomplice were sentenced to be marooned. They were left on a rocky islet with some bags of biscuit and a few skins of wine and nothing was heard of them again.

A further disaster which overtook the fleet at San Julian was the loss of the little *Santiago*. On a cruise southward to reconnoiter the coast she was wrecked on a reef. The crew reached shore. They were able to salvage much of her gear and equipment. The chief difficulty was to establish communications with the rest of the fleet through these trackless regions where the only water the sailors could find was frozen.

On August 21, 1520, the four surviving ships sailed out of San Julian. They were almost lost in a furious gale but found safe anchorage in a freshwater river. Again Pigafetta attributed their salvation to the heavenly bodies who manifested themselves as lights at the mastheads. The river was full of fish. They spent two months there refitting the ships, salting fish and taking on wood and water. Before the next venture into the frozen south all hands went to confession and took Communion.

October 21, the day sacred to the Eleven Thousand Virgins who were drowned in the Rhine, they found themselves at the opening of a strait surrounded by high, snow-covered mountains. It was Pigafetta's opinion that they would never have found that strait if Magellan hadn't known of its existence from a map drawn by Martin of Bohemia which he had seen in the royal treasury in Lisbon.

Immediately the captain major ordered *San Antonio* and *Concepción* to explore the strait while his flagship and *Victoria* sought an anchorage in the bay. That night a wild gale came up. The ships dragged their anchors and drifted helplessly.

Meanwhile *San Antonio* and *Concepción*, unable to beat back round the cape to the anchorage, ran before the wind which drove them back into what they thought was the bottom of another bay. They expected every moment to be dashed to pieces on the rocks. Just when they thought they were lost the crews discovered that what they thought was a cove in the bay was actually a narrow channel. They ran on through until they found themselves in a larger bay. They sailed on through that until they reached another strait which opened into a third and much larger bay. When the wind moderated, the ships came about and started beating their way back to the captain major's anchorage to tell him what they had seen.

Pigafetta and the crew of the flagship thought the reconnoitering ships had been wrecked. They figured that some smoke signals they saw were sent up by such of the crews as had managed to reach shore; "but just at the moment when we had given them up for lost we saw them come scudding into sight with all sails set and banners flying. When they got close they set off bombards and the crews broke into joyous cheers."

The flagship hauled in her anchors and the four ships in convoy sailed through the strait. At the end they found two openings each of which seemed to lead into the West. While he sent two ships to explore one of them Magellan and his consort anchored in a river they called Sardine River on account of the great shoals of these fish they found there and sent a small sloop to see what lay beyond. In three days the sloop came back reporting a great cape and open ocean beyond it. The captain major named it Cabo Desejado, the Desired Cape. "We all wept for joy," wrote Pigafetta.

Concepción returned in due course to Sardine River but nothing was seen of *San Antonio*. It turned out later that the pilot, a Spaniard named Gomez who was particularly irked at taking orders from the Portuguese, had conspired with other Spanish members of the crew to clap Captain Mesquita in irons and to give Magellan the slip. He sailed back to Spain to report the discovery of the strait. He had hoped to show off one of the captured Patagonians they had on board but the poor giant, not being able to stand the heat, died before they crossed the equator.

"We named that strait the Strait of the Patagonians," wrote Pigafetta. "We found safe harbors in it at every half league with excellent water, cedarwood, sardines and shellfish in abundance. There were herbs, too, some of which were bitter but others edible, particularly a sort of sweet celery growing near the springs which we ate for want of better food. In fact I believe that in the whole world there doesn't exist a finer strait than this."

On Wednesday, November 28, they sailed out into an ocean so calm that Magellan named it the Pacific.

"For three months and twenty days," wrote Pigafetta, "we never tasted fresh food. The biscuit was no longer bread but a powder mixed with worms that had an insupportable reek of rats' urine. The water we had to drink was putrid and repugnant. So as not to die of hunger we reached the point of chewing on the leathers set round the yards to keep them from being chafed by the shrouds. Nineteen men died of scurvy and thirty-five were

279

ill from it. . . . As for me I can never give enough thanks to God that during all this time and in the midst of all these calamities I was never sick one day. Some days we had nothing but sawdust to eat. Even rats which are so disgusting to men came so high that sometimes a single one brought half a ducat."

Pigafetta amused himself during the crossing putting down a vocabulary he learned from their captive Patagonian. The savage in turn showed Pigafetta how they made fire by rubbing two sticks together on a piece of tinder. At first he thought his god Setebos would kill him if he made the sign of the cross but when he became ill he asked for a cross and to be baptized. They baptized him under the name of Paulo before he died.

"During those three months and twenty days we made more or less four thousand leagues across the sea which we called Pacific because in our whole crossing we did not meet the slightest storm." They saw no land except two desert islets where they found nothing but birds and trees and which they named the Unfortunate Islands. "According to the ship's log we made sixty or seventy leagues a day and if God and his Holy Mother had not given us good sailing we would have all died of hunger on so vast a sea. I believe that in future no one will ever try such a voyage again."

Magellan seems to have been steering for Ptolemy's Cape Catigara, shown on the old world maps as dividing the two parts of the Great Gulf, which had so intrigued Vespucci and Columbus. His first landfall was in the Micronesian islands now known as the Marianas. The people there proved so troublesome, stealing everything they could carry off from the ships, and even getting one of the ship's boats away from her cables, that, after burning a village of palm huts and killing a few of the inhabitants, Magellan pressed on. For centuries thereafter these islands were known as the Ladrones. Pigafetta reported that the inhabitants considered themselves to be the only people in the world.

After sailing due west for three hundred leagues the voyagers saw high land ahead. They found themselves in an archipelago. They picked an uninhabited islet to pitch two tents on so that the sick could rest ashore.

Two days later they saw a boat approaching with nine men in it. The captain gave orders that no one should move or say a word without his permission. These islanders were dark heathen people with long black hair, but they wore gold earrings and wrapped strips of cloth woven from the bark of a tree round their middles. Their manners seemed gentle. They greeted the Europeans civilly. "The captain major seeing that they were so peaceful ordered food to be set before them and gave them red caps, little mirrors, bells, buckrams, some ivory jewelry and other fripperies of this sort." Not to be outdone by the captain's courtesy the natives brought out of their boat fish, a vessel full of palm wine, bananas, some large and others smaller and tastier, and two coconuts. Pigafetta was as astonished as King Manoel by his first encounter with the coconut. Bread and wine and oil and vinegar, he wrote, to say nothing of fiber and cloth, came from the same tree.

Their first encounter with the people of the Philippines was disarming. Magellan took his visitors aboard *Trinidad*. When he showed them samples of cloves, cinnamon, pepper, ginger, nutmegs, mace and gold they assured him by sign language that all these things would be found in abundance in the islands he was headed for. He made them understand that the ships needed supplies and they replied that they would return in a few days with quantities of food. As they were leaving he threw them into a great fright by setting off a bombard. The captain major named the island the Wateringplace of Good Portents because there they had their first sight of gold. Pigafetta called the archipelago, later known as the Philippines, the Islands of St. Lazarus since they had been discovered the fourth Sunday in Lent, St. Lazarus' day.

Four days later their friends returned with two boatloads of coconuts and sweet oranges, palm wine and a single rooster, just to prove that fowls were available. Magellan purchased the lot. After this he took a bowl of palm wine to each sick man every day with his own hands "which comforted them greatly." When the symptoms of scurvy began to disappear and the men seemed strong enough to work, the ships weighed anchor and sailed to explore these lovely islands.

The captain major had a Sumatran slave who spoke Malay. To everyone's delight this slave discovered he could communicate with some fishermen they overhauled in a small boat. Through them they reached an understanding with the headman of a large town of thatched houses set high on piles. This "king," as Pigafetta called him, came aboard, and delighted with the good treatment he received, invited Magellan to visit his settlement while they arranged to trade for supplies. Magellan, in a cautious mood, chose two men to go in his stead. Pigafetta was one of them.

The visit was conducted with a great deal of ceremony. As soon as they stepped ashore the king lifted his hands toward the sky. Pigafetta and his companion did the same. Then the king led Pigafetta by the hand on board of a sort of long galley drawn up under a bamboo awning. One of his attendants did the same with Pigafetta's companion. They sat in the stern of the galley and were immediately served with a dish of pork which they washed down with palm wine out of a large jar. With every mouthful each man had to drink a cup of wine. The king and Pigafetta drank out of the same cup. Every time the king got ready to drink he raised his clasped hands toward the sky. Then raising the cup in one hand he pushed the clenched fist of the other toward Pigafetta. "The first time I thought he was going to strike me," Pigafetta noted. He copied every action of his host although he was worried about having to eat the meat because the day was Good Friday "but I couldn't help myself."

Pigafetta delivered the presents which the captain major had sent the king and busied himself jotting down a vocabulary. His hosts were astonished by seeing him write and particularly when he read off words just as they'd said them. At that point two large porcelain dishes were brought in along with others full of pork in gravy. After they'd finished eating they went to what Pigafetta described as the royal house which "looked like a hayloft. It was thatched with banana leaves and stood high off the ground on four great piles. We had to climb up by ladders." The king made them sit cross-legged like tailors on cane mats while he sent for his eldest son. Immediately another meal was produced, this time of roast fish with fresh-cut ginger. After the roast fish there was more fish in a sauce, and rice. "I ate out of the same dish as the son and heir." Pigafetta added that his companion drank recklessly and got quite drunk. After dinner they both slept on the same palm mat as the heir apparent.

Pigafetta described this king of Mazaua as being the handsomest of all the islanders. His black hair hung to his shoulders. He wore a silk scarf over his head, had gold rings in his ears and three gold dots on each tooth which made it appear that his teeth were framed in gold. The cotton cloth that covered him from waist to knees was embroidered with silk and his sleek olive skin was painted in various colors. He was perfumed with benzoin and storax. At his belt he wore a short sword with a long gold haft.

"He told us that digging in the ground on his island people found gold nuggets the size of nuts or even hen's eggs, and that all of his household vessels and even some of the ornaments of his house were of gold."

Relations seemed so cordial with the islanders that Easter Sunday, which was the last day of March that year, the captain major and fifty men, all handsomely armed and dressed, went ashore to hear mass. The king and his chiefs were sprinkled with holy water, and kissed the cross when the Christians did, and at the elevation of the host adored the Eucharist with their hands joined "just as we did." At that moment it had been arranged that the ships should fire a salvo of artillery. This left the islanders noticeably moved. After taking Communion the men-at-arms, on the captain major's orders, executed a sword dance which delighted the islanders. After that a cross was brought forward adorned with the nails and the crown of thorns. "We kneeled before it and so did the islanders."

Then the captain major, addressing them through his interpreter, told the islanders that this was the standard which his king had put in his hands to set up in whatever lands he discovered and if it were set up on a high hill it would be a sign to all European ships that they were at peace with these islands. The king consented, but when the captain major asked why he was having so much trouble obtaining supplies on this island the king explained apologetically that this was not his principal town. He would furnish the Christians with pilots to take them where supplies were plentiful. Then the captain major cried out that if the king of Mazaua had any enemies he only need say the word. The Christians would reduce them to obedience in short order. The king thanked him but replied that this was not the proper season for that sort of thing. The occasion ended with a discharge of musketry.

After numerous delays while the king of Mazaua was getting

his rice harvested he produced pilots for the ships and they set sail.
The king followed in his own vessel. In a few days they reached
the port of Cebu which turned out to be the center of a heavily
populated region. All the houses were set high on piles. When
Magellan anchored off the town he lowered his sails, hoisted all
his banners and fired a great salvo of artillery. Then he sent his
Sumatran ashore to tell the people who were in a great fright that
this was a mere salute, that his master was the greatest king in the
world and that he was bound for the Moluccas and that all he
wanted was to trade peaceably for supplies.

There were Chinese and Moslem merchants in the city, trading
for gold and slaves. When the interpreter came back aboard, he
told Magellan that he had heard one of the Moslems warn the
local potentate: "Lord take care. These are the same men who
conquered Calicut and Malacca and all the greater Indies." Magellan retorted with another message: the king he served was much
more powerful than the Portuguese king. The local potentate,
who outranked the king of Mazaua, sent his chief men aboard the
flagship. Magellan received them seated in a red velvet chair. The
parley proceeded so favorably that Magellan decided to try to
convert his hosts to Christianity then and there. His speech was so
eloquent that the king of Mazaua and the chief men of Cebu
burst into tears and asked to be instructed in the Christian faith.

Amid mutual embracings all present swore eternal peace. The
captain major ordered a handsome luncheon to be served and the
islanders produced, as a gift from the king of Cebu, some large
baskets full of rice; pigs, goats and hens. They were profuse with
their apologies that at the moment they had nothing better to give.
In return the captain major produced presents for everybody except the king of Mazaua who had already been given a rich robe
from Cambaya.

Pigafetta was sent ashore with drinking cups, a red cap, a
yellow and violet silk tunic in the Turkish style and strings of
crystal beads piled up on a silver platter as presents for the king of
Cebu. He found that potentate to be a short fat man squatting on
a palm leaf mat in the midst of a great multitude of his subjects.
He was stark naked except for a cotton cloth about his private
parts. He was tattooed all over. About his head he wore an
embroidered scarf. Pigafetta noticed particularly his heavy gold

earrings set with precious stones and the rich necklace he wore. The king was eating turtle eggs out of a porcelain dish. In front of him were four open jars of palm wine covered with fragrant herbs. He sucked up the wine through a hollow reed. He immediately invited his visitors to eat some turtle eggs and to take some wine while his emissaries reported on the captain major's invitation to accept Christianity. The king was all smiles.

Next the king's son-in-law took Pigaffeta and his companion to his own house where they found four girls playing strange music on a series of gongs and small cymbals. They played well. These girls were very pretty, almost as white as Europeans and quite naked. The king's son-in-law had three of them dance for his visitors. After some light refreshments, wrote Pigafetta, he went back to his ship.

Next day two men died on the ships. Magellan sent word to the king asking for permission to consecrate a piece of land so that they could be buried ashore. When permission was granted the burials were carried out in the public square with all the pomp the navigators could muster. At the same time they brought ashore a store of merchandise for trading. The king took the merchandise and the four men left to deal with it under his personal protection.

"The following Friday we opened our store," wrote Pigafetta. The islanders stared with amazement at the articles exposed for sale. For objects of bronze, iron and other metals, they gave gold, ten pieces (each worth a ducat and a half) for fourteen pounds of iron weighed out on their own scales. The captain major gave orders that his people shouldn't show too much greed for gold. If he hadn't, explained Pigafetta, the sailors would have sold everything they had for gold and so ruined the market.

Magellan had promised the king of Cebu to make him a Christian the following Sunday. Saturday he had a platform built in the consecrated square, which he had ornamented with palm branches and tapestries. A great cross was set up behind it. Sunday morning forty men came ashore with the royal standard. Two men armed cap-a-pie formed the guard of honor. The islanders were thrown into a fright when the artillery roared out a salute though it had been explained to the king in advance that the guns would not be loaded. The captain major and the king embraced each other and were seated on two chairs upholstered with green and blue velvet. The principal islanders were seated on cushions or mats.

The captain major, clad all in white, led the king of Cebu up to the platform where he was baptized with the name of Carlos. The king of Mazaua was baptized John and so on until five hundred had been baptized. Then mass was said. The king of Cebu cautiously refused an invitation to dine aboard ship. He and Magellan took leave of each other at the shore amid another discharge of artillery.

After dinner the chaplain was rowed ashore again to baptize the queen whom Pigafetta described as young and comely. She came dressed in black and white cloth with a large palm-leaf hat on her head which had a triple crown a little like the pope's tiara. Her mouth and fingers were painted bright red. With her came forty female attendants all naked except for a tiny covering of coconut fiber over their private parts and the scarves they wore on their heads. She seemed so touched by a little image of the Virgin and Child which Pigafetta had brought along that he gave it to her to take the place of her idols. Later when she went to hear mass the chaplain sprinkled her with musk water, "a perfume much appreciated by the women in those parts." In another ceremony Magellan had the king swear eternal allegiance to King Charles of Spain and presented him with a velvet chair to have carried before him wherever he went.

Magellan and his men went about zealously baptizing the heathen throughout the island. Many villagers were induced to burn their idols which they did to the cry of "Castilla, Castilla." When the people on an adjacent island proved recalcitrant Magellan had their village burned to teach them a lesson.

Mactan, the island which sheltered the harbor of Cebu, hung in the balance. Mactan was ruled by two chiefs. One of them accepted Castilian sovereignty but the other would have none of it.

When the loyal chief asked for help against his rival Magellan decided that the time had come to make a show of force. He set out one night with three boatloads of armed men, sixty in all. The christianized king of Cebu and his chiefs went along with a fleet of native boats but were told not to join in the fray. They were to remain in their boats and watch the Christians teach the heathen a lesson.

"When morning came," wrote Pigafetta, "we leaped out of the boats into water up to our thighs since the boats couldn't get near to the land on account of the reefs. We were forty-nine and we left eleven men to guard the boats. We had to wade quite a distance through the water before reaching land." The islanders fifteen hundred strong, were drawn up in three battalions. "They rushed at us making a horrible noise, one group attacking on each flank and the others in front. The musketeers and crossbowmen discharged their weapons uselessly for half an hour because the islanders kept leaping from side to side covering themselves with light wooden shields." Magellan shouted to his men to stop firing but his voice could not be heard above the din. He tried to distract the enemy by sending some men to fire their houses. The houses burned but, having killed two of the men, the islanders only attacked with greater fury.

The Christians were still wading painfully through the water. Magellan was shot through the leg with a poisoned arrow. He ordered his men to retire slowly but instead they all took precipitantly to flight except eight or so who stood by him. The bombards in the boats were too far away to be any help. The natives noticing that their arrows had no effect on the armor of the Christians aimed at their bare legs. Up to their knees in water, Magellan with his little group of supporters tried to make a slow retreat toward the boats. The swarms of the enemy were too much for the captain major. They knocked his helmet off. He killed a man who came at him with a bamboo lance, but the next one slashed him with a big scimitar and he fell face down in the water. "So died our guide, our light and our salvation," wrote Pigafetta solemnly.

Magellan's death changed everything. The islanders, who had thought the Christians were invincible, changed their tune when they saw how easily the captain major had been done to death. The king of Cebu forgot all about his conversion and concocted a plot with the help of the Sumatran interpreter. Magellan's slave had been faithful so long as his master lived, but as soon as he was dead he turned his coat.

The Christians had elected Duarte Barbosa and a Spaniard named Juan Serrano joint commanders. On the pretext of presenting the new commanders with certain jewels he was preparing to send to the Spanish king as a sign of allegiance the king invited the commanders to dinner. Twenty-four men went ashore. Pigafetta's life was saved because his face was all swollen up from a wound from a poisoned arrow he had received on Mactan so he decided to stay aboard. At the banquet the Christians were set upon and killed.

Hearing the shouting and lamentations, the men on the ships began to fire into the town. Juan Serrano all bloody with wounds appeared on the beach and begged for a boat to be sent for him. According to Pigafetta the Portuguese Carvalho who had taken charge of the expedition insisted on making sail immediately and left Serrano to his fate.

Carvalho turned out to be a poor commander. His first act when they were far enough away from Cebu to be safe from pursuit was to take the crew and equipment of *Concepción* and burn her to keep her from being used by the enemy. Even at that the ships were shorthanded. Instead of heading direct for the Moluccas, Carvalho roamed like a pirate through the islands, feeding his men off the booty he got from raiding villages and seizing native craft. Captured Moslems he kept aboard as slaves to help work the ships. The best-looking women he hoarded for himself in his cabin.

At last while the crews were at work careening and caulking the two ships in a harbor on the north coast of Borneo, dissatisfaction came to a head. Carvalho allowed himself to be deposed and Espinosa, who as Magellan's constable had shown such energy in ending the mutiny at San Julian, was elected captain of *Trinidad*. A dour Basque mate, Juan Sebastian Elcano took command of *Victoria*. Since he was the only one who understood navigation he was the man in charge from then on. In short order Elcano discovered the proper course for the Moluccas. On November 8, 1521, the two ships sailed into the harbor of Tidor.

There they learned of the death by poisoning on nearby Ternate of Magellan's friend Francisco Serrão. They were told that his Javanese wife, his children and some Christian servants still lived in the islands. The ruler of Tidor was on the outs with the Portuguese. It did not prove too difficult, by promising him support against his local enemies, to get him to swear allegiance to the king of Spain. Spices abounded.

While the ships were being loaded with cloves in preparation for the voyage home, a Portuguese named Pedro Afonso asked to be taken aboard with his family and possessions because he was on bad terms with the Portuguese governor of Malacca. Espinosa took him aboard *Trinidad*. When the ships were loaded to sail *Trinidad* was found to be leaking so badly that she had to jettison half her cargo. Elcano sailed off without her on *Victoria*. With his extraordinary capacity for landing on his feet, Pigafetta managed to be aboard.

Three months passed before *Trinidad* could get under way. Espinosa decided to try to join a Spanish fleet reported to be outfitting in Panama to explore the northern shores of what was still thought of as Ptolemy's Great Gulf. For four months he bucked storms and adverse winds. Food gave out, scurvy decimated his crew. He turned back and sailed into the Moluccas with nothing to show for himself but the discovery of the Caroline Islands. Immediately he fell into the hands of a Portuguese expedition under Antonio de Brito. Brito had Pedro Afonso decapitated as a traitor, and put the rest of the ship's company to work on the fortress he was building for the protection of Ternate. Most of them died of fever, but a small handful including the doughty Espinosa were taken to Lisbon and eventually allowed to go back to Spain.

Elcano's plan was to round the Cape of Good Hope while keeping out of the way of Portuguese shipping routes. Though supplies of food and water were low after crossing the Indian Ocean he turned down pleas from his crew that he put in at Moçambique. He felt that would mean certain capture. At first he tried to round the Cape in high southern latitudes but after weeks of beating into adverse winds found he was making no progress. Then he ran inshore and was forced into Saldanha Bay. There he was confronted by a Portuguese vessel bound for India. The ships spoke each other but Elcano was allowed to sail on without interference. As he worked his way north along the coast of West Africa men died daily. Pigafetta made the quaint observation that the corpses of Christians sank with their faces toward the sky, while the heathen sank head down. There were thirty-five men left alive when *Victoria* made port on São Tiago in the Cape Verde Islands. Pigafetta was astonished to discover that it was Thursday in those parts while by his careful reckoning it was only Wednesday for him.

Elcano tried to pull the wool over the eyes of the Portuguese authorities with some cock-and-bull stories as to where he had been, but the truth came out when he used East Indian spices to pay for the supplies he absolutely had to have. He set sail suddenly leaving thirteen men ashore. When *Victoria*, after fifty-four days of desperately hard work and short rations, crossed the bar of the Guadalquivir at Sanlucar on September 6, 1522, only eighteen Europeans and three East Indians were left alive.

From Seville Pigafetta rode off post haste to Valladolid to tell his story to Charles V, now emperor of the Holy Roman Empire as well as king of Spain. From Valladolid he backtracked to Lisbon to read his diaries to John III who had succeeded to his father's throne the year before. Not finding quite the right audience at the Portuguese court he journeyed to France where Francis I's mother, Maria Louise of Savoy, a lady of some learning, listened with attention. Telling the story of the circumnavigation of the globe became a career for Pigafetta. He told it at the Marquese's court of Mantua and then before the signoria in Venice. Giulio de' Medici, now Pope Clement VII, invited him to Rome. A pirated version of Pigafetta's travels came out in French, followed by accounts in other languages. Somewhere along the line he became a Knight of Rhodes. When his own Italian text left the press in 1536, dedicated to the Grand Master of that Order, Pigafetta may well have been dead.

3

VASCO DA GAMA'S
LAST COMMAND

Elcano's return from the Moluccas with a cargo of cloves brought
Portugal and Castile to the verge of war. John III had inherited
his father's throne at the age of nineteen. He had been brought up
very much in his father's shadow. Though King Manoel attracted
the best possible tutors to his court the prince never showed much
aptitude for study. The king had so little regard for his abilities
that he repeatedly delayed setting him up in an establishment of
his own. The crowning slight came when the father married the
princess intended for the son. Though she was twenty years his
junior, King Manoel was so much taken with the sprightly Dona
Leonor, the sister of Charles V who had been contracted for as
his son's bride, that he married her himself.

Outwardly John remained a dutiful son but his influence was
felt at court on the side of the party in the King's Council that
opposed some of Dom Manoel's projects, such as the extension of
Portuguese power in Morocco and the building of new castles in
East Africa and the Orient. John further showed his independence
by seducing one of Dona Leonor's ladies in waiting who, the year
his father died, produced the first royal bastard in a generation.

Though a cautious and possibly a slow witted man John III
showed more energy and astuteness than had been expected of
him. He immediately wrote Charles V claiming *Victoria*'s cargo

and demanding the punishment of those responsible for poaching on the Portuguese domain. Charles' first response was to order two new expeditions to explore the Spice Islands, one out of Panama and another out of the western ports of Galicia. Since these efforts came to nothing John went patiently to work to arbitrate the dispute.

Committees of cartographers and astrologers were assembled and argued at length without reaching a decision until Charles, who as emperor was overextended in every direction, renounced his claim to the Moluccas in return for a settlement of nine hundred thousand gold dobras. A bargain for him because the islands were clearly in the Portuguese sphere. Peace between Portugal and Castile was further sealed by a pair of royal marriages. John married Charles' sister Catherine and Charles married John's sister Isabel. The widowed Leonor, leaving King Manoel's small daughter to be raised at the Portuguese court, returned to Castile and eventually became the wife of Francis I of France.

Meanwhile bad news came in from India with every returning vessel. Duarte de Meneses, whose father and grandfather had made such a reputation in Morocco, proved a failure as governor on the Malabar Coast. Ormuz was in revolt, cutting off the profitable trade in horses which was one of the mainstays of the Portuguese administration. Moslem leaders reoccupied the rich hinterland of Goa, cutting off a fruitful source of revenue. An expedition to establish a trading post below Canton on the Pearl River was a failure. At the same time insubordination was growing among Portuguese commanders who were setting themselves up as petty satraps in the various ports in the style of the local sultans.

In the Atlantic the French privateers, mostly out of La Rochelle and Dieppe, who had preyed on Portuguese shipping only intermittently in King Manoel's day, became a real menace to navigation. Even coastwise shipping was in danger from these marauders. Ranging as far as the Brazilian coast they captured any Portuguese or Spanish ship they found insufficiently defended and sailed home to sell their cargoes in the Channel ports. When a Spanish ambassador demanded that Francis I exercise more control over his subjects he exclaimed that such incidents should not be made a cause for war. Every nation had its place in the sun. "I should very much like to see the clause in Adam's will which excluded me from the partition of the world."

John III came to the throne just as the wars which were to prove the curse of the bloody sixteenth century were beginning to tear Europe apart. Underlying all the crosscurrents of the power struggle between Francis I and the Emperor Charles V was the great schism in the Christian Church. In the agitation led by such humanists as Erasmus and Sir Thomas More the Portuguese court and clergy had consistently favored the reform of abuses. Damião de Góis, Erasmus' leading Portuguese disciple, became court chronicler under John and his brothers. The policy of the House of Avis from the beginning had been to encourage Christian unity by turning European military power against the Moslem and the Turk. But now a new intransigent voice was raised in Germany.

In 1517 Martin Luther tacked his ninety-five articles on the church door in Wittemberg. Three years later he burned the papal bull which Leo X issued in condemnation of his doctrines. At Worms before a full Diet of the Empire, presided over by Charles V himself, Luther defended his dogma of salvation by faith which made the hierarchy of priests and bishops unnecessary as intermediaries between God and man. The reformer and his theories were placed under the ban of the empire but Luther, who had been protected by a safe conduct, was spirited away into the mountains by the Elector of Saxony. From then on arms began to speak louder than words in the religious controversy. Adherents and opponents of Martin Luther formed leagues and counterleagues.

The imperial Diet met at Worms the year John III became king. The same year Francis I and Charles V, who had been rivals in the imperial election, came to blows for the first time over their claims to the sovereignty of various Italian cities. The fighting was mostly in Italy involving the possession of Milan. The war culminated with the total defeat of Francis I's forces at Pavia. The French king was captured and carried off a prisoner to Madrid. It was the demands of this war that made Charles willing to barter his claims on the Moluccas for ready cash. As these various conflicts became more intense and brutal, John III, convinced that Portugal's destiny lay overseas and that she must not become involved in European quarrels, had to steer a shrewd and cautious course.

An added problem was the resurgence of Turkish power under the Sultan Suleiman, known in the history books as the Magnificent. In the year John came to the throne his troops captured Belgrade. From there they forced their way up the Danube and across the plains of Hungary until a few years later they were besieging Vienna. In 1522 the Turkish fleet, after a year of siege, forced the Knights of St. John to give up Rhodes, thus abandoning the last bastion of European power in the eastern Mediterranean. From then on no Mediterranean port was safe from raids by Turkish corsairs.

Francis's reckless flirtation with the Turks, which eventually culminated in an alliance against the Hapsburgs and the Spanish, shattered the Christian unity which had been the cardinal aim of the foreign policy of the Portuguese kings. Aided by the Venetians and by Christian renegades and captives who brought with them the latest techniques in shipbuilding and artillery, the Turks, who had conquered Egypt a few years before, were constructing new fleets at Suez. When John III came to the throne he found every lifeline in danger of the network of trading posts that had lent such splendor to his father's reign.

It was becoming clear that Portugal lacked the manpower to carry on such far flung enterprises. Agriculture at home was ineffectual. South of the Tagus the wheat farms were worked by African slaves or not at all. Even in the fertile northern provinces the peasants had for generations been leaving the soil to crowd into Lisbon or to try their luck for fame and fortune in the East. The plague carried off thousands almost every year. It was becoming harder and harder to find the men-at-arms and experienced mariners needed to man the annual fleets that had to keep the Moslem on the run and to bring home the spices which financed the royal establishment and bought the grain needed in seasons of scarcity to feed the population.

To restore the royal authority in India John appointed Vasco da Gama as second viceroy. Though Dom Vasco had been living in retirement for a number of years his prestige as first discoverer had become legendary even before Camões celebrated his deeds in heroic stanzas. Now in his middle sixties, though he had failed to obtain the overlordship of his home port of Sines which he so coveted, he held the rank of Admiral of the Indies and enjoyed the revenues of the county of Vidigueira as well as a share of the king's take from India House which made him a wealthy man indeed. The king gave him command of a fleet of fourteen ships which sailed in April of 1524.

Dom Vasco accepted the post with grim determination. He collected the most competent administrators he could find to replace those who had been found wanting. His two oldest sons sailed with him. He put up a brave show. The pikes of a personal guard of two hundred liveried men-at-arms were gilded. His pages wore gold necklaces. His doorkeepers bore silver maces. At his table the silver services, the brocaded cloths, the great platters and salvers were exactly like the king's. He intended to be a viceroy indeed.

The winds were propitious on his voyage to Moçambique. Crossing the Indian Ocean he lost one ship off the East African coast and another by a mutiny. The crew murdered the ship's officers and sailed off to live as freebooters in the Straits. Correa noted dryly that the ship was recaptured and the crew brought back to India, "where they were all hanged."

Vasco da Gama's great flagship *Santa Catarina do Monte Sinai* anchored off the bar at Goa in early September. He descended on the city like an avenging angel. He refused to be flattered by the sumptuous procession that conducted him to the cathedral. When Captain Pereira, the military commander of whom he had heard bad reports of extortion and peculation, conducted him through the defense works, he remarked that everything seemed in order there; he hoped that Pereira's accounts were in as good condition. When it turned out that they were not he dismissed Pereira and forced him to make immediate restitution of sums demanded of him by outraged citizens.

"The viceroy was a friend of the king's interests," wrote Correa. He said men came to India poor and left it rich. The viceroy's business was to enrich the king: it was the greatest benefit to the people if the royal treasury were kept well furnished. He was suspicious of royal officials who seemed too rich and of those who came with royal appointments. Before he would let them take up their charges they had to prove themselves capable of performing their duties. If a man was supposed to be a secretary he would insist on his showing how well he could write, then and there. He didn't believe in giving men offices in return for services. Services should be recompensed by honors and thanks and not by offices men could make money on. Offices were for men competent to discharge them.

He had it proclaimed that every man who was outlawed and a fugitive on account of crimes committed before he arrived in India could get his pardon if he returned immediately to the service of God and the king. He announced under pain of death and loss of property that any man who had guns or muskets in his possession belonging to the king should turn them in to the arsenal within a month. "So," Correa noted, "he recouped a great deal of artillery belonging to the king including powder and shot which the merchants were selling with the connivance of the royal officials."

Before leaving Belém Vasco da Gama had proclaimed that any man who brought a woman aboard ship would be sent home in chains and the woman publicly flogged. In Moçambique three women stowaways were discovered. He sentenced them to be flogged through the streets of Goa. The city rose in a storm of protest. The Company of Mercy came in a body to beg them off. The fidalgos, the friars, pleaded with him. Several important men offered to ransom them with a large sum of money. The crusty old viceroy was obdurate. Correa wrote that "people were scandalized by the fate of these women, judging the viceroy to be unnecessarily cruel, but seeing such firmness of execution they were much afraid of him and became cautious in their actions and mended their ways of the many ills that there were in India, especially the fidalgos who were dissolute in wrongdoing."

When the viceroy moved down the coast to Cochin his reputation had gone before him. The Moslems left town in a body and many Portuguese took refuge in Coromandel. In Cochin, with the help of a famous mathematician named Dr. Pedro Nunes, the viceroy reorganized the finances as he had in Goa and put factors he could trust in charge of the trading post so that no more pepper should be shipped to Lisbon adulterated with sand.

He had brought along a Genoese shipbuilder specially gifted in the construction of small fast galleys. With these and by equipping each oarsman as a grenadier and offering him a good share of the booty of every ship that was captured he put an end to the depredations of the Arab pirates that were beginning to infest the coast. Like Albuquerque he left his door always open for complaints from the citizens and like Albuquerque he attended to every detail of the administration himself. He wore himself out in three months.

When Duarte de Meneses, the retiring governor arrived in Cochin from Ormuz to relinquish the office he had very much abused, Vasco da Gama refused to let him come ashore. He sent him word to report to the ship *Castello* then loading with the spice fleet and to consider himself under arrest. Meneses, who had heard of the viceroy's ill health, tried to gain time. He sent his brother Luis to talk the viceroy into letting Duarte turn over the office to him in due form. Trying to make a joke of the charges against his brother Luis declared that at least Duarte was not accused of selling any of the king's fortresses. Dom Vasco answered sourly that if he had he wouldn't have his head on his shoulders today. Luis insisted so that Dom Vasco lost his temper and told him to go join his brother aboard ship. He ordered them both to be shipped back to Lisbon on parole.

After much insistence by the viceroy and his officers the brothers reluctantly took up their lodging aboard *Castello*. The viceroy sent out his fiscal officer to try to collect great sums he claimed Duarte owed the royal treasury. Duarte replied that the king had placed these matters in his hands and that only to the king would he give an accounting. According to a story Correa heard from the vicar of a monastery on the shore outside of the walls of Cochin, Duarte de Meneses was so afraid that the viceroy would try to seize his effects that he took a great coffer full of pearls and jewels ashore one dark night in a boat manned by Malabar natives. He and the vicar, who was a faithful friend and in on all his secrets, carried the coffer slung on an iron bar between them and buried it in the sand. They tried to take cross bearings on the monastery wall and set the skull of an ox over the place as a marker, but when the time came to dig the coffer up somebody had carried off the skull. It took nights and nights of probing with crowbars and the hafts of javelins before they found it again.

These frustrating disputes with the retiring governor, the constant labor of superintending the loading of the spice ships and the equipping of a small fleet intended to scour the shores until, so the viceroy put it, there wasn't a Moslem left alive on land or sea on the Malabar Coast, exhausted the old man. He developed carbuncles on his neck. They gave him great pain and made it hard for him to move his head. What disgusted him most with his illness, wrote Correa, was that it interfered with the immense number of things he was planning to do to reform the administration of India. The pain became so great he was almost speechless. He decided he was dying.

He intrusted the government to Lopo Vaz de Sampaio whom he had made captain major of Cochin. It would be Sampaio's duty to see that the royal seal was broken on the packet which contained the letter of appointment of the next governor general in case the viceroy died in office. Then he had himself moved out of the fortress to a friend's house across from the church. There he called for a priest, made his confession and received the sacraments. In his will he ordered his sons to go back to Portugal with the spice fleet and to take all his household goods with them and his staff of servants and to see that they were properly paid for their services. His personal clothing and silk hangings were to go to the church and the hospital in Cochin. He begged to have his bones taken back to Portugal. It is characteristic of the old curmudgeon that he left a hundred thousand reis to each of the women he had had flogged, so that they could find good husbands and lead honest lives.

Vasco da Gama died on Christmas Eve. Dressed in black velvet with the cross of the Knights of Christ on his breast and wearing a gold sword and sword belt and gilded spurs he was temporarily interred in the Monastery of Santo Antonio.

When the envelope containing the appointments was opened before assembly of all the fidalgos and captains in Cochin it was found that another member of the Meneses family, Dom Henrique, whom Vasco da Gama had left as captain major at Goa, was appointed to succeed the viceroy. Immediately arrangements were made for a more comfortable voyage home for Luis and Duarte, one on *São Jorge* and the other on the viceroy's old flagship, *Santa Catarina do Monte Sinai*. With them went the entire requisition which the viceroy had gotten up against Duarte. According to Correa Luis felt that the immense store of treasure which his brother managed to smuggle aboard ship would be sufficient to pay off any claims the king might have on him.

Luis admitted he was a little afraid his brother would bolt off to Castile instead of returning home, but he assured everyone he wouldn't take his eyes off him until he was safe across the bar in Lisbon.

The winds ruled otherwise. The ships were separated in a storm off the West African coast. Neither of them reached the appointed rendezvous at St. Helena. Luis' ship was captured by a French pirate, plundered and sunk with all on board. Not a man survived. Duarte de Meneses, after riding out the storm, took on wood and water in Saldanha Bay and made a landfall near Faro on the coast of the Algarve. There resided a cousin of his, a certain Dona Branca. According to Correa, Duarte landed a quantity of treasure which he left in her care. There too he got word of how the winds blew at court. Next, in spite of the protests of the pilot and the ship's officers, he insisted on being landed with his remaining coffers and a great deal of baggage at the little fishing port of Sesimbra which was within his baronial domain. He left orders for the ship to proceed to Lisbon without him. That night while *Santa Catarina do Monte Sinai* was still at anchor a gale blew up. The great galleon drifted ashore and was lost. Correa's story was that somebody cut the cables. "The ship was lost," he wrote, "which was worth a great deal of money, and all the wealth she carried, and all the poor savings of the poor men aboard, and it was said that this was Dom Duarte's work so that people would think all his wealth was lost. Now Dom Duarte could show equal loss before the king and all mankind, with the loss of his brother and of so many of his people, with the king's loss."

The king was tremendously vexed at the loss of the ship but he forwarded a message to Duarte de Meneses couched in friendly terms. At the same time he dispatched trusted agents to watch him carefully until he reached the royal court at Almeirim. Others ransacked the beaches at Faro in search of the treasure supposed to be buried there. The king greeted Duarte affably, allowed him to kiss his hand and listened half the night to his tales of

India. As soon as he left the royal presence he was arrested. Eventually he was imprisoned at Tôrres Vedras. The royal prosecutor presented a great case against him but the king, who perhaps hoped he would disgorge some of his ill-gotten gains, refused to have him beheaded. Duarte de Meneses made no move to pay up and eventually, after various marriages between members of the house of Meneses and some of the king's councillors, he was released and restored to the governorship of Tangier.

"I write this from hearsay," wrote Gaspar Correa, "from stories told by people coming back from the kingdom, maybe it's all lies, as are all the things of this world except the love of our Lord God."

4

BEHOLD PRESTER JOHN

One of the complaints against Duarte de Meneses among the king's councillors was that he had failed to maintain contact with the Portuguese embassy which had been waiting for years to be brought home from Abyssinia. An experienced diplomat had been sent out by King Manoel with a considerable suite in 1515 to accomplish the long delayed return of Mateus to the court of Queen Helena. They sailed with the fleet of Lopo Soares de Albergaria, whom Albuquerque so despised, and who took the great governor's place after his death. According to Correa Lopo Soares had no interest in carrying out any of Albuquerque's projects. He took the embassy as far as the Red Sea but never managed to find a safe landing for it in an Abyssinian port. The diplomat sickened and died on lonely Camarão. It was not till early in 1520 that the next governor, the enterprising Diogo Lopes de Siqueira, who had made the first attempt on Malacca, took command of a small fleet which landed the survivors at Massawa.

There he appointed a well-connected fidalgo named Rodrigo de Lima as ambassador. Along with him went one of the numerous da Gamas, a secretary, an interpreter, a painter, an organist, a number of aides and bodyservants, a somewhat mysterious Gallego known as Mestre João, a Jack-of-all-trades who had come out as barber and bleeder with the fleet, and "I, the unworthy priest Francisco Alvares."

It was Padre Alvares, the parish priest from Coimbra, who was to leave the humorous and discerning narrative which is the source of almost all the information we have about Abyssinia before the destructive Moslem and Galla invasions in the middle of the century.

The padre was a modest man but he knew his worth. He quoted Siqueira as declaring "in the presence of all, 'Dom Rodrigo I don't send Padre Francisco Alvares with you, but I send you with him and be sure to do nothing without his advice.'"

Massawa was Moslem but capitulated without a struggle. The adjoining port of Arquica was Christian, under the rule of a chieftain known as the Barnagash, "lord of the sea," who was a feudatory of the Abyssinian monarch. The Barnagash sent hospitable greetings. Seven monks came down from the monastery of Bisao, in the mountains some leagues away. They made much of poor Mateus who had suffered so many hard knocks in his long travels. "They kissed him on the hand and on the shoulder as the custom of the country was."

These friars all carried crosses in their hands. The laymen too in Arquica wore round their necks little crosses of dark wood. The crewmen enthusiastically bought these crosses and wore them the way the natives did. Contact with the kingdom of Prester John had been a Portuguese aspiration for a hundred years.

After a solemn exchange of gifts with the Barnagash, who was eloquent with promises of assistance, and the celebration of High Mass in the mosque at Massawa which Siqueira had consecrated and renamed Sana Maria da Conceição, the expedition prepared to set off. The padre noted regretfully that the gifts they took along for Prester John were not as fine as they should have been because most of the merchandise was lost in the wreck of a ship which foundered in the Straits of Bab el Mandeb. They consisted of a fine sword, a dagger, tapestries, inlaid cuirasses, a helmet and two culverins, touchpans, powder and shot, a world map and some portable organs.

On Mateus' advice, instead of accompanying the Barnagash and his train, the embassy set off on its own for the monastery of Bisao. As a result the Barnagash showed signs of pique. He would only furnish them with eight horses and thirty camels for their baggage. Father Alvares felt the beasts of burden were insufficient.

As soon as they passed out of sight of the sea they knew that the governor would order his ships to set sail. Resolutely, they plodded inland through a dry and desert country. The heat was intense. At the first wateringplace they met a most agreeable man who said his name was Frei Mazqual and that he was the Barnagash's brother-in-law. He was mounted on a fine horse and accompanied by a handsome mule and four men on foot. Mateus claimed he was a robber and would have nothing to do with him.

The Abyssinian ambassador was becoming a problem. He tried to lead their camel train off the main road across country declaring that he knew the best paths. They struggled through trackless wilderness. Then suddenly Mateus fainted. For an hour they thought he was dead. When he came to, they set him on a mule with a man on each side of him to hold his hand. With the help of Frei Mazqual they found the main road again where caravans continually came and went. The road led up through dry watercourses that flooded in the rains but the ground was so dry and porous that the rivers never reached the sea.

The mountains were full of wild beasts of every conceivable sort: lions, elephants, tigers, panthers, wolves, wild pigs, various varieties of deer, everything except bears and rabbits. They saw every imaginable kind of bird except for magpies and cuckoos, some known to the Portuguese but most unknown, and besides the native herbs they found beds of basil which were very sweet-smelling.

Mateus had become a burden. He insisted on going to the monastery of Bisao though everyone they met told them the road was execrable and it would be much better to stick to the caravan route where they would be safe.

Travel had become slower and slower. They had reached a region of cultivated fields. The cattle were fine: cows and goats. The people were Christians but very dark and went almost naked. The camels groaned and complained at the heavy going. They toiled up defiles crowded with apes. Mazqual left them.

At a small monastery named for St. Michael they were stalled completely. Mateus told them that they were entering the rainy season when no one traveled. They must wait there for the return of the messengers he had sent to Queen Helena and to the Patriarch. Time dragged. Quarrels broke out. Many Portuguese were ill. Mestre João was so sick himself he couldn't attend to the purging and bleeding.

Mateus set off with his attendants and all his goods for Bisao. He promised only to delay the embassy a few days while he dispatched his business. "He stayed there forever because he died there," wrote Padre Alvares dryly. When Mateus took sick again at a halfway house where the monks of that mountain monastery kept their cows, the padre hurried to him. He heard his last confession and gave him absolution before he gave up the ghost.

They buried him up at the monastery of Bisao which was on a very high peak. "Looking out," wrote Padre Alvares, "it was like the depths of hell all around." The monastery was handsomely built with three great naves and arches painted "so that you couldn't tell whether they were wood or stone." Around the body of the church there were two stories of vaulted cloisters "painted with figures of apostles, patriarchs and prophets and many symbols out of the Old Testament, lots of angels and St. George on horseback who is in all the churches in this country."

The embassy was stranded without a guide. The monks kept telling the Portuguese that if they waited until their bishop arrived he would furnish animals and guides for the journey upcountry to the court of Prester John, but nothing happened. Dom Rodrigo lost patience and sent his interpreter with a couple of other men to remind the Barnagash of his promises of help. At last a man came from the Barnagash announcing that oxen and mules were on the way. The monks produced nothing.

After weeks of delay some oxen appeared and Negro slaves to carry the rest of the baggage. They would only carry it just so far and trooped off leaving the baggage out in the rain in an open field. Eventually, after continual nagging delays the embassy reached the Barnagash's provincial capital but found that dignitary had managed to absent himself. The ambassador and Padre Alvares tracked him down. They found him in another of his chief towns in a large one-story house—there were no upper stories in the country—reclining on a sort of bedstead hung with cheap curtains. He was suffering from an infection in his eyes. His wife was seated at his head.

After they had made their bows the ambassador offered to send him Mestre João to care for his illness but he said rather tartly that it wasn't necessary. Then the ambassador demanded in the name of Prester John that he be furnished with proper transportation for his journey upcountry. The Portuguese king and his governor of India would see to it the Barnagash was well paid for his services and he himself would speak well of him to Prester John. He asked for oxen and asses for the baggage and mules for the Portuguese. The Barnagash answered that if the Portuguese wanted mules they would have to buy them, but that he would furnish other pack animals and send his son to show them the way.

After they had taken their leave, the Barnagash's people took them to another house where they offered them a great platter of barley flour barely mixed with water and an oxhorn full of mead. "As it was the first time we saw this food," wrote Padre Alvares, "we didn't want to eat it; but once we caught on to the customs of the country we ate it perfectly well."

So, without eating, they set off for the place where they had left their caravan. After they had covered about half a league a man came running after them and said to wait. The Barnagash's mother was sending them food. She couldn't have them leave without eating. They waited and in a little while a man appeared with five great loaves of wheat bread and a horn of mead. "Don't be surprised when I speak of a horn of mead," wrote Alvares, "because for the great lords and Prester John horns are the drinking vessels: there are horns that hold fifteen or eighteen pints . . . This mother of the Barnagash sent us some more of this kneaded flour and this time we ate it. It was made of toasted barley and mixed with very little water, the way they do it in Alentejo."

The country was densely populated. In spite of that game was unimaginably abundant. There was plenty of good fish in the rivers. In a single morning the Portuguese could catch twenty or thirty hares in a net, and this without dogs. There were three kinds of partridges, one kind as large as a capon, and quail and swarms of doves and wild pigeons, and wild pig and deer and antelope and gazelle. "You will ask how can there be so much game on the land and so much fish in the streams in such a populated country?" The answer was that nobody hunted or fished. They didn't have the skill or the desire to do it. They were much afraid of the lions and tigers and panthers but they never bothered them any way.

In spite of the fine hunting the Portuguese were impatient to be on their way to the court of Prester John. One fine morning toward the end of June men and animals arrived from the Barnagash. The Portuguese set out all happy and singing at the thought of being on their way again but the people who were transporting their baggage unloaded it after about a half a league saying that they would go no farther. After endless journeys back and forth to the Barnagash's quarters, they managed to move the expedition a few more leagues to a market town. There the Barnagash made a great stir of getting ready an army to attack the Nubians on the borders of Egypt to the North, because they had killed a son of his. On this pretext he inveigled Dom Rodrigo into giving him two fine swords. The Portuguese had been assigned a house without doors. One night a thief crept in and stole two swords and a helmet. From then on they were plagued by the continual thievery of the natives.

There was no coined money in the country. The Portuguese were ready to pay with gold dust for mules but, at first, the Barnagash let it be known that if people took gold dust in exchange he would confiscate it. After long delays the Barnagash finally let the Portuguese buy mules and even gave them three camels.

Although it was the middle of the rainy season they made their way through thunderstorms and cloudbursts to a place called Temei which was under a different feudal lord. There they found the country laid waste by a great plague of locusts. The croplands were yellow with them. They ate every green thing. The Portuguese joined the natives in a procession through the fields imploring divine intercession. According to Alvares such a storm of wind and rain came up from the sea that next morning there was not a locust to be seen. The flooded watercourses were heaped with their dead bodies. The countrypeople said the Portuguese had practiced witchcraft. From then on they were pestered by people coming to beg them to drive the locusts away from their crops.

This was the territory of a chief named Tigremahom. They crossed a great river which flowed toward the Nile and entered a region of high peaks "that rose to the sky and all of them had hermitages on the heights mostly dedicated to Our Lady but we couldn't imagine how people reached them."

That night they slept in a village near a handsome church. The central nave was raised above the others, the windows well constructed and the whole church vaulted. This was a type of architecture they had not seen in this country before. It was like a monastery in northern Portugal. Beside it rose a tower of fine squared stones, somewhat ruined, and all about handsome houses in the same style, "like some great lord's dwellings." These were surrounded by irrigated fields watered by wellmade ditches that came down from the mountains. "We saw wheat, barley, beans, chickpeas, peas, garlic, onions, rue and mustard and along the watercourses first-rate parsley and watercress."

The clergy here were well dressed and had a substantial air. Even the laymen wore some clothes, the men belted jerkins of cloth or leather pleated like kilts but so short that sitting down or in a wind they showed their shame. The women wore very little more than beads. The married women wore the beads round their necks but the unmarried girls wore them round their middle with a mass of trinkets and often little bells over their private parts. Some of them wore a sheepskin tied by the feet over one shoulder. To the Portuguese this hardly seemed like Christian garb.

East of these peaks was the great ruined city of Aquaxuma. Some Catalans and Genoese sailors who had escaped from the Turkish galleys in the Red Sea and had joined up with the Portuguese for protection told Padre Alvares that its ruins were grander than the ruins of Troy or of Joseph's granary in Egypt. When he himself visited Aquaxuma in later years, he was shown in a most noble church a chronicle which was first written in Hebrew and then translated into Greek and then from Greek into Chaldean and from Chaldean into the Abyssinian tongue. Padre Alvares quoted from it the story of the Queen of Sheba's journey to Jerusalem to see the great works of Solomon and how she had a son by Solomon and returned to her realm from which she sent much gold and ebony to decorate Solomon's buildings. The boy was raised among the sons of Solomon. By the time he was seventeen he had become so overbearing that the children of Israel cried out to their king to send him back to his mother. On his return he made himself such a great lord that he ruled the land "from sea to sea" and outfitted sixty ships on the Indian Ocean.

Aquaxuma was the seat of that Queen Candace who introduced Christianity into Abyssinia. The Apostle Philip had first converted the queen's majordomo, a eunuch who managed her lands in Gaza which Solomon had given to his son by the Queen of Sheba. When the eunuch returned to Ethiopia he converted the queen and all her household. So the Abyssinians claimed to be the first Christians in the world. The queen built the first church which was named Our Lady of Zion because the altar stone was sent by the apostle from Mt. Zion. Padre Alvares described the great church and its painted vaults and the fine houses of squared stones embellished with carvings of lions and dogs and birds and the huge monoliths that had framed fallen buildings enscribed with lettering that none of the local people could read which he figured must be Hebrew.

The Portuguese embassy had already been four months on the road. Now they had a monk for a guide. At night they put up in empty hospices where the doors were always open which were called the Negus's houses. Prester John, they were discovering, was known as the Negus to his subjects. Where there was no hospice the natives who carried their baggage made enclosures of thorns round them and their baggage animals to keep out the wild beasts. The natives of these parts used salt for money. In another region they used iron.

In a place called Agro they saw the first of the churches cut out of the solid rock which they found to be characteristic of the upland country. They had left the rich farmland and entered a wild and wooded region. All the same churches abounded. They were lost one night in a deep forest. Tigers followed them so close that they were only a lance's length away.

Another month went by and they were still toiling through alternate barren mountains and populated valleys. In a principality known as Angote they were assailed by a hail of stones from the height above the trail. Of the forty persons accompanying the caravan hardly a man escaped injury. Mestre João got a broken head.

The local ruler—known as the Ras—made it up to the ambassador and to Padre Alvares by plying them with excellent mead out of four great jars. They drank out of clear glass goblets. According to Alvares the Ras had the air of a terrific drinker and his wife too. Finally the Portuguese escaped from the drinking bout by explaining that they had to relieve themselves.

They met this Ras again in a church the following Sunday. He questioned Alvares closely about the life of Christ and was so delighted by his answers that he invited him and the ambassador to dinner. For their own dinner the Portuguese had already prepared two fat roast chickens and a fine piece of beef. These the ambassador fortunately ordered brought along. They sat on mats on a dais around two great round trays. Water was brought to wash their hands but no napkins to wipe them with or to set their bread on. Before eating the Ras ordered up a number of loaves of ordinary bread with lumps of raw meat on them which he sent out to the beggars waiting at the gate. For his guests bread was brought in made of a variety of different grains. Padre Alvares then said grace. The main dish turned out to be a soup that looked like the kind they make at Palmela with a clove of garlic; but this soup turned out to be flavored with cow manure and gall, highly esteemed in these parts and only eaten by people of distinction. The soup came in small casseroles of black terra cotta very well shaped. The Ras and his attendants crumbled in bread and butter. "We didn't want to eat these messes so the Ambassador sent for our food which had been very well prepared, but our hosts wouldn't taste it. There was wine in abundance. . . . The Ras's wife ate behind a curtain beside us."

The Portuguese sent her some tidbits. They couldn't tell whether she ate them, on account of the curtain, but she certainly did her part with the wine. "To top the meal off they brought in a breast of raw beef and the Ras ate it for dessert the way we would marzipan." To Padre Alvares and his friends these hardly seemed Christian victuals.

On leaving the Ras's house they had to pass through another

hail of stones from the natives. They had reached the vicinity of the mountain where the sons of Prester John were confined behind a great wall that ran up the mountain until it seemed to disappear into the sky—all except the heir apparent who remained with his father. From every village people rushed out to throw stones at the strangers.

One night the stones came so thick they almost met their deaths. The ambassador who was in the rear turned back but Alvares and Lopo da Gama were so far ahead they couldn't turn back. Alvares climbed off his mule. It was so dark "it was as if one didn't have eyes" and the stones kept raining down. Thanks to God an honest man came out of a house and asked Padre Alvares who he was. Padre Alvares answered that he was one of the king's strangers. This was a very tall man and he took the padre's head under his arm, "the way a piper would a bagpipe," and led him with his slave and his mule into a garden where long poles were stacked in such a way as to make a sort of little cabin. Alvares felt so secure in his hiding place that he lit a light. Immediately the stones began falling again until he put out the light. Eventually Lopo da Gama found his way to the shelter and their host appeared and killed two chickens and brought them bread and wine and entertained them as best he could. In the morning he showed them his house and beside it a gate in a thicket of trees blocked up with rubble. The gate led up into the mountain where the exiled princes were confined. Their host, who was one of the guards of the mountain, told them that, on peril of his life, if one of them dared to pass through that gate he would have to cut off his feet and hands and to pluck out his eyes and to leave him lying there.

The two Portuguese mounted their mules and rode off in a hurry to find the rest of the caravan. It was evening before they joined their friends. Next day they rode up a cultivated valley until, after crossing a steep pass, they found themselves in a region of forests and stony outcroppings. They were told that they were entering the kingdom of Amara. They passed a large lake. In the midst of it was a monastery dedicated to St. Stephen on an island planted with oranges and lemons and citrons. To reach it the monks used a raft of reeds held up by great gourds. They did not know how to build boats.

From the lake the Portuguese made their way into the kingdom of Xoa through a slit in the mountain so narrow that the mules' saddles scraped the rock on either side. They had to pay the keepers of the pass to let them by. The day was the first of October. They had been six months on the road.

After a tortuous climb down the mountain they traveled for six days through a level land sown with wheat and barley. There were great herds of every kind of livestock, but all they could get to eat was badly made barley bread. The people were dirty and miserable and suffered from fevers and other illnesses. The only cure they knew was to bleed the head if the head hurt or if the belly hurt to apply hot irons "the way we do to animals in Portugal." For fevers they had no remedy.

At last they were approaching the court of Prester John. In the afternoon of October 11 they caught sight of his tents in the distance. It had been explained to them that the Negus had no fixed abode. He lived in a tent in a great armed camp, which he moved according to the exigencies of war or politics or of his personal whim. Their hearts leaped up.

The monk who was their guide made them camp for the weekend beside a new church which hadn't been painted yet which they were told was the Negus's own private chapel. The monk rode off to visit the patriarch, whom the Abyssinians called the Abuná, who resided in a church less than half a league away. He came back with a basket of raisins and a jar of excellent grape wine. Three sailors who had deserted from the fleet at Massawa turned up. When the monk saw them talking to the ambassador he flew into a rage and would have had them put in irons if the other Portuguese hadn't forcibly prevented him. The monk claimed that no newcomer had the right to speak to anyone before he had spoken to the Negus.

Another week went by. At last on October 17 the Portuguese were full of hope that that day they would be received by Prester John because they were told to move their tent to a distance of a league from the imperial camp. Instead a great lord appeared, said to be the chief of all the majordomos, who made them backtrack through a region of rough escarped hills. The majordomo told them not to worry. Prester John was about to move his camp to near where they would be. He pitched his tent and the Portuguese pitched the sorry little tent they had brought all the way from Massawa beside his. Next day his men brought them a fine large round tent saying that Prester John sent it and that no one else had such a fine tent as that except the Prester himself. The captain of the majordomo's guard and the monk who had been their guide both warned them to look out for thieves. There were many thieves in this land, particularly Franks who hung around the court. They were organized. There were captains of thieves who paid part of their take to the Negus's officers.

At last on a Friday, October 20, the Portuguese were sent for by Prester John. They dressed in their best, and "thanks to God," wrote Padre Alvares, managed to put up a pretty good appearance. They rode forth in orderly files until they reached a portal from which they could see white tents pitched in a great field and in front of them a huge red tent, which they were told was only pitched for great festivals and receptions. In front of the tents were two rows of arches draped with alternate red and white cloths. In front of the arches was a crowd of people. There must have been twenty thousand. These people were drawn up in ranks into two groups. Men with scourges ran about keeping them in order. Among the best dressed who were ranged nearest to the arches were many ecclesiastics with mitres on their heads that had peaks of dyed silk and cochineal red. In front of the best-dressed people were ranged four horses, two on one side and two on the other, saddled and hung with trappings of brocade. These horses had diadems on their heads with great plumes that hung down as far as their bits. Beyond on either side there were other fine horses, saddled but not harnessed, all standing in order like the people and beside them the fidalgos of the court, all stripped to the waist as men had to be who were about to make their obeisances to the Prester.

About sixty men, doormen and mace bearers, advanced toward the Portuguese at a dogtrot "as men had to do who carried messages from the Prester." They were dressed in shirts of silk and each wore a lion skin over one shoulder. Over the skins they wore necklaces of crudely worked gold. Around their necks there was a glitter of gems which Alvares figured were probably false. They wore colored silk sashes with long fringes that reached the ground.

As the Portuguese advanced toward the red tent they were

greeted by dignitaries who accompanied them without speaking a word. Before reaching the arches they passed between four lions, two on the one hand and two on the other. The lions were held back by heavy chains. Among the fidalgos Alvares noticed an old cleric who was the Prester's confessor and said to be, after him, the most powerful man in the realm. This man who was known as the Cabeata stood a few paces from the ambassador and asked him in formal style where he had come from.

Rodrigo de Lima answered that he was sent by the governor of India for the King of Portugal. The Cabeata retired into the red tent and then came out twice more to ask the same question. Then he told the ambassador to say what he had to say and that he would repeat it to the Prester.

The ambassador replied that he could only discharge his embassy to his Highness in person. The Cabeata disappeared again and came back telling the ambassador to send in all the gifts he had brought the Prester from the governor of India. After some consulation among themselves the Portuguese decided to send in the bales of goods with the addition of four sacks of pepper which they had kept for their own use.

Everything was unpacked while they stood there. The tapestries were hung up on the arches for all to see. The people were ordered to be quiet and the chief justice of the court described each article in a loud voice and cried out that everyone should thank the Lord God for this reunion of Christians. If anybody regretted it let him weep; if anybody rejoiced let him sing. At that the people gave a great shout which lasted a long time and the Portuguese took their leave and, having fired a slavo of musketry, retired to their tents.

There they found that one of their servants had been robbed of a number of cooking pots and wounded in the leg by the thieves for good measure. Meanwhile messengers arrived with three large loaves of white bread and many jars of mead and a cow. They told the Portuguese that the Prester was about to send them fifty cows and as many jars of mead. Next day the Prester's servants brought many cooked dishes including an entire veal roasted in a pasty but the cows and the mead never appeared. The monk now told them that if they would turn over all the pepper they had to Prester John he would promise to furnish them with supplies all the way back to Massawa. When they demurred they were told that none of the Franks were to be allowed to speak to them and that they were not to be allowed to leave their tents until they had been received by the Prester. The food stopped coming. A Portuguese who had been put in irons for trying to speak to a member of the embassy sought refuge in the tent. When Dom Rodrigo complained of their ill treatment to the chief eunuch who came to fetch the man, the chief eunuch said he didn't know why the Portuguese had come. Mateus had never been commissioned an ambassador by Queen Helena or by the present Negus.

Days dragged on. They had very little to eat. They could get no news of the Queen Helena Mateus had promised would receive them. They learned that the Prester had moved his camp to a distance of three leagues. The monk came to tell them that they had permission to buy mules to move their merchandise if they wanted to follow the camp. He had obtained leave for them to buy and sell their merchandise as they would. Dom Rodrigo answered haughtily that they were not merchants. They had come to serve God and their king and to affirm the unity of the Christians of all faiths.

Two days later Dom Rodrigo sent Padre Alvares and the interpreter to court to try to talk the chief eunuch into arranging an interview with the Prester. The chief eunuch suggested that they make their demands in writing.

Dom Rodrigo insisted he must be allowed to see the Prester in person. There followed an uneasy wait. Several of the escaped Frankish galley slaves who spoke Portuguese came in secret to the tent and told Dom Rodrigo that Prester John thought the Portuguese were holding back on the presents the governor of India had sent. They would never be allowed to leave unless they turned over all their goods, particularly clothing—in Abyssinia woven goods were more esteemed than cities. Dom Rodrigo decided to give up four chests of clothing and all the pepper they had left, saving out only one bale to cover their expenses.

The following Monday, October 30, the Franks arrived with a train of mules to carry the merchandise. Padre Alvares, who was developing a knack for dealing with the Abyssinian officials, and the secretary were sent along to prepare the way for the ambassador who would ride over to the camp a little later with the rest of his staff. On the way a messenger met them with orders for the ambassador to come at once. Alvares explained that the ambassador was on the way and that he was going before him with the merchandise. At last they came to a new camp surrounded by a great hedge. Inside were many tents and a long one-story house thatched with straw where the guides said the Prester at present was. At a little distance from the entrance the Portuguese were told to dismount from their mules. An official advanced toward them asking angrily why the ambassador hadn't come. Alvares explained that he had thought best to let his gifts go before him. Then it came out that the Prester wasn't in the long house at all but at another camp some leagues away.

Back at their tent the Portuguese learned from the Franks, who now came and went fairly freely, that the Prester was being advised not to see the ambassador and not to let the embassy leave the country. This was what had happened to numerous other Europeans, notably to Pedro de Covilhã who had been sent by John II. When the Portuguese asked why Covilhã hadn't come to greet them it was explained that he was at his house near the mountain passes.

The days dragged on. Messages went back and forth each with more unsatisfactory results than the last. Once in the middle of the night they were told the Prester wanted to see them. They had barely dressed in their best finery when a messenger told them not to come. "There we were," wrote Alvares, "like the peacock who spread out his tail so happily, but was heartbroken when he looked at his ugly feet; so happy to be going but so sad because we couldn't go."

Next night, on the first of November, they were sent for again. They found the enclosure circled by men with lighted torches in their hands. After waiting for an hour in the cold two of the Portuguese shot off their muskets. The Prester sent out a message asking them why they hadn't brought more muskets up from the sea. Dom Rodrigo answered with dignity that they came on a mission of peace. Only three or four had brought muskets for their own entertainment.

This time they were let into a thatched building of rough hewed beams crudely painted. From behind a curtain the Prester sent them another message. He had never commissioned Mateus. Further he wanted to know what happened to all the merchandise Mateus had reported the embassy was bringing from the King of Portugal. Dom Rodrigo tried to explain the difficulties the Portuguese encountered in the Red Sea. He was merely a forerunner sent to find the way. With Massawa in Portuguese hands a real embassy would be sent direct from Lisbon. No decisive answer came that night. The Prester did send out bread and wine and meat. The men who brought the food assured Dom Rodrigo that they were instructed to furnish the Portuguese with all the food they needed every day. Nothing more came of that promise.

The next time they were sent for was a Saturday. After the usual wait they were ushered in through various gates and draperies until they came to a curtained dais ornamented with bands of brocade. In front of the dais stood richly dressed men with swords in their hands posed as if they were about to slash at each other. The place must have been illuminated by two hundred torches.

Immediately messages began popping back and forth through the curtains. The first question was how many Portuguese there were in the embassy and how many muskets they had brought. Right on its heels came another: Who taught the Moslems to make guns and muskets? The ambassador replied that the Moors and Turks had as much ingenuity as other men. The Turks made as fine cannon as anybody. What they lacked was the True Faith. Then the Prester said he wanted to see some Portuguese sword play. The ambassador ordered two men out with sword and buckler and they performed tolerably but not as well as the ambassador wished so he stepped out himself with Jorge d'Abreu and they performed "as well as one could expect of men brought up in the science of arms."

The ambassador took the opportunity to urge the Prester to let him dispatch his business and return to Massawa in time to meet the fleet which was coming to fetch him. The Prester replied that he wanted the Portuguese to know the immensity of his realm so that they would establish fortresses at Massawa and Suaquem and Zeila. Then he asked the Portuguese to play on the spinet and to dance. After they had sung and danced awhile the ambassador asked permission for them to perform the mass after the custom of the Roman Church. The Prester answered that since he allowed the Moslems to perform their rites he would certainly do the same for Christians. When they reached their tents the Portuguese found waiting for them three hundred large loaves of bread and twenty-four jars of wine. They were told that the Prester had sent thirty but that six had somehow disappeared on the road.

The next day was Sunday. Messages kept coming with questions as to the number and quality of the arms that the King of Portugal would send to Prester John. Monday at the hour of vespers the Prester sent for Padre Alvares and asked to be shown how the Roman Catholics made the Host and all their apparatus of the mass. Standing on a carpet at two arms length from where the Prester sat behind the curtain, Padre Alvares showed him the vestments and the furniture of the altar and explained the meaning of each piece as he brought it out. For the first time the Prester addressed the Portuguese with his own voice. The interpreters told Alvares he was saying that the Portuguese were good Christians. Padre Alvares was asked to go through his whole performance again. There followed a long cosy conversation through the curtain in which the Prester and Alvares compared the Roman and the Abyssinian rites.

At the very time when Padre Alvares was discussing the sacraments with the Prester thieves were breaking into the ambassador's tent. From his baggage they carried off two capes and two embroidered coats and seven shirts, an expensive cap and a portmanteau belonging to one of his attendants with all this man's clothing and seven pieces of linen that had been placed in his custody. The value of the thefts that night amounted to two hundred cruzados. When they went to complain to the Prester, a woman rushed in claiming that the Portuguese had despoiled her of her daughter. Nothing came of either plea.

Next day the Prester sent the Portuguese a heavily decorated tent to say mass in, which, noted Alvares in his dry way, would have been a fine tent had it been new. Thefts and demands from the Prester for more swords and for all sorts of articles of clothing continued daily. But now the Prester was sending the embassy gifts which somewhat made up for the thefts and for the arms which he had requisitioned. He sent four fine horses and a gilt goblet and some articles to adorn the tent which the Portuguese used as their chapel.

317

It wasn't until November 19 that Prester John allowed the curtains to be opened so that the Portuguese might see him face to face. As usual they were waked up in the middle of the night and kept waiting for three hours outside his tent in the cold and the wind. When the ambassador and the padre and seven other Portuguese were let in through the curtains of the tent they found many more people and many more torches than they had ever seen before. They hurried through various sets of curtains till they came to a dais hung with tapestries more ornate than any they had seen.

The hangings parted and there sat Prester John on a richly carved throne, six steps in height. He wore a gold and silver crown on his head and carried a silver cross in one hand. A scarf of blue taffeta covered his mouth and beard. It was only when he let it drop that his whole face appeared. He was a young man of medium height with a round face, very large eyes and an aquiline nose. His color was more chestnut than black, somewhat the color of a russet apple. The Portuguese had been told he was twenty-three years old and he looked about that age. His beard was just beginning to grow. There was a look of breeding about him. He wore a brocaded mantle and under it silk shirts with ample sleeves. From the knees down he was draped in what looked like a bishop's vestment which billowed about him like the draperies of a God the Father painted on the wall.

A page stood by him holding a crucifix worked with human figures. Another held a naked sword. Others held torches at the four corners of the dais.

The conversation was carried on through the Portuguese interpreter and the Cabeata. At last Dom Rodrigo was able to present his credentials and to deliver his messages from the governor of India. He told of Portuguese plans to build fortresses against the Turks in the Red Sea ports which would be used as bases for an attack on the holy cities of the Moslems. The Negus promised to furnish all the supplies needed for these fortresses.

Nothing came of these promises. Procrastination was the rule at the court of the Negus of Abyssinia. Five years went by before the Portuguese, somewhat disillusioned by all they had learned of the strange laws and customs of the Abyssinians, reached the Red

Sea coast and were picked up by a Portuguese fleet. With them they took letters to the pope and a fresh ambassador from the Negus to the Portuguese king. In Portugal there was no more loose talk of Prester John. Reality had taken the place of legend.

5

THE MARCH OF
THE FOUR HUNDRED

Padre Alvares and Rodrigo de Lima reached Lisbon in July of
1527. Dom Rodrigo was escorting a swarthy gentleman named
Zagazaab who came as ambassador from the Negus to the Portuguese king. The letters he bore were addressed to King Manoel.
The news of the death of the Fortunate King had not reached the
Abyssinian highlands at the time when the court scribes, with the
tactful assistance of Padre Alvares, were sweating over the compilation of these epistles. Padre Alvares was charged with letters
to the pope and with a gold cross entrusted to him by the patriarch as a personal gift to His Holiness. The diplomats were arriving full of hope for the speedy establishment of an understanding
between the two churches. Negus and the patriarch had declared
themselves ready to receive instruction in the Roman Catholic
dogma. Padre Alvares' last promise had been to send a mission
back immediately for the enlightenment of the Abyssinian
churches.

The news which greeted the Portuguese ambassadors when they
stepped ashore in Lisbon was appalling. In a culmination of the
disorders set off by the war between Charles V and Francis I for
the domination of Italy, Rome had been taken by storm and sacked
by a motley army of Spaniards, Flemings and Lutheran Germans
nominally in the service of Charles V. Giulio de' Medici, who,

after a lifetime of intrigue to restore the family fortunes, had assumed the pontificate as Clement VII upon the death of Adrian of Utrecht, was a prisoner in his own castle of Sant'Angelo. The king's nephew Dom Martim, his ambassador to the papal see, had just arrived back in Portugal to try to raise money for the pope's ransom. His suite brought tales of the sacking of palaces and churches, of the massacre of the citizenry, of outrages against priests and nuns. According to Andrade, the royal chronicler, so many high ecclesiastics were held for ransom in Rome that "a canon was bringing less than a mule."

John III, in the company of his two brothers, the lively Dom Luis who was proving to be the most lettered member of the family and an intelligent patron of the arts and sciences, and devout Dom Henrique who at sixteen had taken Holy Orders and been created a bishop, greeted the ambassadors with effusive cordiality in his great hall at Coimbra. He stepped down from his dais to salute the Abyssinian ambassador and to receive from his hands a gold and silver crown similar to the crown the Negus wore on state occasions.

The king and his ministers had to explain to the Abyssinian envoy that unfortunately the papacy was in no position right then to consider the complicated problems of reconciling the two churches. While waiting for a more propitious season Zagazaab was housed at the royal expense and Padre Alvares was endowed with a benefice in Braga, where he found the leisure, with the encouragement of the scholarly bishop, to put down the narrative of his Abyssinian adventures.

Five years went by before the roads were considered safe enough for Padre Alvares and Zagazaab to proceed to Italy. The war between the French king and the emperor had been brought to a temporary lull by the intervention of two sensible women, Francis I's mother and Charles V's aunt, Margarite of Austria. The French called it *La Paix des Dames*. The pope, whose family had for a third time been expelled from the government of Florence, made the best of a bad business and crowned his old enemy emperor in Bologna in 1530. It was in Bologna three years later that Padre Alvares introduced Zagazaab to the papal consistory. His speech, in Portuguese, translated by one of the best Latinists of the day, was highly applauded, but that was all. The pope and the curia were engrossed in more pressing problems.

The Turks, emboldened by the religious schisms and royal quarrels of Europe, were making fresh advances through Hungary. Their fleet and the pirates they encouraged, were terrorizing the Mediterranean. Henry VIII of England was clamoring for a divorce from his Aragonese wife and letting it be known he might become a Protestant if it were denied him. Germany, only nominally under allegiance to the emperor, was dividing into Lutheran and Catholic leagues. Francis I confused every issue by diplomatic flirtations with the Turks and with the Protestant heretics. Even after the pope moved back to Rome nothing was done about a mission to Abyssinia. Padre Alvares died there, a frustrated and disappointed man, in 1535.

No more than the pope did John III have the time to worry about reconciling the Abyssinian church. During the uproar of reformation and counterreformation he was kept busy trying to carry out the basic foreign policy of the House of Avis, which was to steer clear of European entanglements and to join only in wars against the infidel. The most immediate problem he had to solve was how to counter the growing depredations of French pirates on his fleets coming home from India laden with gold and spices. Many of these raiders out of La Rochelle, Rouen and Dieppe were manned by French Protestant crews, Huguenots as they were coming to be called, which made them particularly detestable. Often they were navigated by renegade Portuguese pilots. These were bold navigators. As early as 1527 a ship out of Dieppe was captured in the vicinity of Diu on the east coast of India. During the first ten years of John III's reign something like three hundred Portuguese ships, including small coastal vessels, were lost to French freebooters.

The Portuguese diplomats collected clear evidence that some of them carried letters of marque from the French Crown by which Francis I, always desperate for cash, shared in the loot.

Instead of declaring war or joining in the many coalitions against the French rigged by the imperial court, John III tried to buy his way out. When Francis I was released from the imprisonment in Madrid which followed his capture in the battle of Pavia he had to leave his two young sons as hostages. John III arranged through his emissaries in France to advance him a hundred thousand cruzados toward their ransom. At the same time he tried to buy off the leading French shipowners and to bribe the French Admiral Chabot who was involved in outfitting the pirates.

When these measures failed he was forced to establish a convoy system of fast caravels to protect the heavy-laden naos. The Azores, where the naos and galleons, battered by their long sea journey, often had to refit before attempting the stormy crossing to Lisbon, had been a favorite cruising ground of the French. Now a fortress was built on Terceira and heavily armed caravels were commissioned to patrol the islands during the season when the India ships were expected.

The first permanent settlements in Brazil resulted from this campaign against the French. Since King Manoel's day Portuguese squadrons had tried to protect the tiny plantations where sugar was beginning to be grown in the hinterland of a scattering of safe harbors from Pernambuco to Guanabara Bay. Now John III placed one of his most competent captains, Martim Afonso de Sousa, in command of a large fleet to clear the Brazilian coast of interlopers and to set up pillars with the royal arms proclaiming Portuguese sovereignty over the entire region that stretched from the eastern bulge of the South American continent to the Rio de la Plata. While his brother Pero Lopes explored the lands to the southward, Martim Afonso established the town of São Vicente on an island near the present port of Santos and, in the brisker air of the tableland above, an outpost on the Pirinatinga River which later grew into the city of São Paulo. While the Sousas were still engaged in this work messages from John III reached them with orders to survey the whole vast stretch of coast, so that it could be divided into capitancies, each based on fifty leagues of shore, which the king was planning to grant outright to such of his fidalgos as would develop the country independently and without expense to the Crown.

The revival of this plan at this time, which was the same plan used by Prince Henry in settling Madeira and the Azores, has been attributed to the advice of one of the king's most influential correspondents, Diogo de Gouveia. Born in Beja in 1471 Gouveia, one of the great teachers of the age, was for many years the principal of the College of Santa Bárbara in Paris which was the chief resort of Portuguese in search of higher learning. John III established fifty scholarships there for Portuguese students. At a time when the Sorbonne harbored such disparate characters as François Rabelais and John Calvin, Gouveia served for a while as rector of the entire university. Renowned all over Europe as a humanist and theologian no one could be in a better situation to keep the Portuguese court informed of the vagaries of French policy.

Gouveia's teaching not only stimulated plans of reform within the structure of the Catholic Church but it liberated some of the wildest enthusiasms of the counterreformation. At the end of a letter written in February of 1539, dealing with the charges and countercharges that arose from Portuguese attempts to put down French piracies in Brazil, Gouveia announced the formation of the dedicated band which was to become the Society of Jesus. A French priest, a Portuguese named Simão Rodrigues, a tawny-haired young Basque named Francisco Xavier and three others had joined with Ignacio de Loyola, in a vow taken in the pilgrimage church on Montmartre, to devote their lives to the propagation of the Faith.

Loyola, much older than his companions, had found the College of Santa Bárbara a haven of refuge after a stormy career. Like Xavier he was of Basque origin. After studying for the priesthood, he had thrown up the church to become a soldier. Returning home to nurse a wound received at a siege of Pamplona he had decided at the age of thirty-one to reform his life. He made the pilgrimage to Jerusalem and then drifted from university to university preaching asceticism and dedication. At Alcalá de Henares he was imprisoned for heresy and again at Salamanca. He moved to Paris and there, in the atmosphere of free discussion which amounted to a last afterglow of the humanist renaissance, he applied himself to theological studies, earning the degrees of bachelor and master of arts. By this time he was forty-three. The experiences of an agitated and wandering life had convinced him that only a group of newly dedicated men could save Christianity from the corrosion of heresy and indifference. He had seen enough of armies to appreciate the value of military discipline. Perhaps it was from Gouveia that he imbibed his enthusiasm for learning.

He was to incorporate a practical system of education into the organization of the Jesuit order. At this point, wrote Gouveia, these pupils of his thought only of securing papal approval for their plans for missionary work among the heathen. He recommended them warmly to John III as men who wanted nothing for themselves, the sort of men the king had been looking for, to bring about the conversion of the gentiles in India.

Clement VII had been succeeded by Alessandro Farnese who, as Paul III, when he wasn't too busy advancing the fortunes of his own family, took measures to reform some of the abuses of the church. He appointed serious men of learning as cardinals and made the first moves toward calling the Council of Trent which was to establish the principles of the counterreformation. In 1540 after considerable hesitation he approved the foundation of the Company of Jesus.

Some years before, he had granted to the Portuguese Crown the right to establish an inquisition similar to the inquisition in Spain. Throughout the papacy of Clement VII, John III had been trying to convince him that such a tribunal was needed in Portugal to expose the sins of new Christians who had relapsed to judaism and were making a mockery of the royal ordinances. Uppermost in the king's mind, too, was the damaging effect on the royal revenues of the operations of certain exiled Jewish financiers who, with the collusion of correspondents in Portugal, occasionally cornered the spice market in Antwerp. A king, John III explained almost tearfully in a letter to the pope, who had no power to root out heretics was no king at all. Even after he reluctantly assented to the Portuguese inquisition, the pope, to avoid the excesses committed under Torquemada in Castile, tried to keep the right of review in the hands of a papal legate. In the end Paul III so far succumbed to the fever of intolerance that was sweeping Europe as to set up his own inquisition in Rome.

A tribunal was established in Lisbon. Censorship of the press was placed in its hands. John III decided to send no more students to Paris where their souls' salvation might be jeopardized by northern heresies and the relaxed morals of the court of Francis I. He transferred his subsidies to the University of Coimbra. Soon eager disciples of Loyola were arriving in Portugal with plans for indoctrinating these students with the True Faith. Xavier, their leader saw much farther. He was bent on converting the whole Portuguese Orient to Christianity.

The enthusiasms of the counterreformation found more positive aims than the persecution of backsliding New Christians. In 1535 the king raised an armada to join with the emperor in an expedition to destroy the pirate fleet of the two Barbarossas in Tunis. Prince Luis and the flower of the young courtiers went along. Two years later the king at his own expense equipped a force of four hundred and fifty volunteers to go to the aid of the Negus of Abyssinia, now hardpressed by a Moslem invasion from Somaliland.

News of the disasters suffered by the Christian kingdom was brought to Lisbon by a member of the first embassy who had remained behind when Padre Alvares and Rodrigo de Lima came home. This was Mestre João, the Gallego who had sailed to India as barber and bleeder. He arrived in Lisbon claiming to be the ambassador of a new Negus. He further claimed that he had been consecrated Patriarch of Abyssinia by the old abuná on his deathbed and that his title had been recognized by the Roman curia. His first act was to put the original ambassador, Zagazaab, under arrest for inattention to his duties.

The tale he told was that the Abyssinian kingdom had been cut in two by an invasion by a Somali chief known as Granye the Left-handed. Armed with matchlocks his army had routed the Abyssinians, who had none, so decisively that many of the chieftains deserted the Negus and swore fealty to the Moslem. To make things worse the Turks were furnishing Granye with musketeers and artillery. Mestre João, now known as João Bermudes, had escaped overland and made his way through Egypt to Rome and, after receiving the blessing of Pope Paul, had journeyed to Lisbon.

The reappearance of the unknown Gallego as a high ecclesiastic must have somewhat strained the credulity of John III's court, but Bermudes succeeded where Padre Alvares had failed. Immediate arrangements were made for him to sail back to India with the contingent of men-at-arms who became known as the Four Hundred. There were the usual delays. Bermudes sailed for India with the fleet commanded by Pero Lopes de Sousa in 1539 but two more years went by before the Portuguese relief expedition was assembled at Massawa by the governor of India, who was now old Vasco's son, Estevão da Gama. He gave command of the Four Hundred to his youngest brother, Christóvão.

Christóvão was twenty-four. He proved such an energetic leader that, traveling at night on account of the exhausting heat, in six days the troops reached the cool mountains, where they could take advantage of the abundant game for food. There they began to see the results of the Somali invasion. Every church had been pillaged. The holiest monasteries had been stripped of their wealth, the villages ravaged and burned. In eleven days they reached Debarwa, where the rivers were so full of fish and where the earlier embassy had met so many delays. There they learned that the widow of the last Negus, whom the Portuguese had called David, was in hiding in a mountain fastness and that her son, the new Negus known to the Portuguese as Claúdio, was hiding out in another.

Messengers were dispatched to the queen dowager. She showed herself a woman of spirit and rode down from her mountain top to the Portuguese camp. She appeared with a suite of thirty women and fifty men. One of Christóvão's lieutenants, Miguel de Castanhoso, who kept a diary of events, described her as a beautiful woman "in the oriental style." She wore fine white Indian cloth under a black cloak trimmed with gold. Her hair "was dressed in the Portuguese manner," and a silk umbrella was held over her head.

The young Negus remained in hiding. Word came from him that this was the wrong season for a campaign and that he didn't have enough troops to venture down from his mountain.

Somewhat dismayed by the lack of support from the Abyssinians the Four Hundred set out in search of Granye's army. They celebrated Christmas in the high mountains. After New Year's Day they crossed a peak so high that, wrote Castanhoso, "we thought we should all die of the cold." By the first of February they had reached Basanete, the first Moslem strong point. In spite of the misgivings of the queen and of their native guides they stormed the place in a few hours with only the loss of two Portuguese killed and a number wounded.

As a result of their success at Basanete native contingents began to swell the queen's forces. The Four Hundred were further cheered by the arrival of messengers from Massawa reporting that five Portuguese ships lay in the harbor, laden with supplies for the expedition and were awaiting instructions as to how to send them upcountry. Christóvão sent off forty men on mules to collect the munitions which he much needed.

Without waiting for their return he started toward Wajarta where Granye's army was reported to be assembling to receive him, this in spite of messages from the Negus begging him not to risk an engagement. By the beginning of April the armies were in contact. The Muslims attempted to storm the Portuguese camp. Christóvão was wounded. Things were going badly when a Portuguese fidalgo managed to shoot Granye through the leg with a musketball which then went on to kill his horse under him. When their leader was carried off the field the Somali tribesmen fled. Eleven Portuguese had been killed and about fifty of the enemy.

The Portuguese celebrated with hearty hallelujas at their Easter service. A few days later, in a fresh engagement, a charge by five hundred Somali horsemen was routed by the accidental explosion of a powder magazine. It seemed a miracle. Many claimed they had seen São Tiago on a white horse in pursuit of the infidel. The Portuguese suffered fourteen killed and sixty wounded.

Their jubilations were interrupted by the return of the messengers from Massawa. The news they brought was grim. The Portuguese ships had been forced out by a superior force. Turkish galleys were in full command of the Red Sea.

The rainy season began, giving the men of both armies a chance to recover from their wounds. Granye, who was an able commander, spent the wet months training his men in the use of their Turkish muskets. Christóvão kept his men busy capturing a hill village occupied by black Jews known as Felasha which the Moslems had taken. In the village they found eighty much needed horses and three hundred mules as well as horned cattle. According to Castanhoso, the leader of these villagers was so impressed with the valor of the Portuguese that he became a Christian overnight. Strategically the capture of this fortress opened a path for the Negus to bring his small force down out of its hiding place to join the Four Hundred. He delayed too long.

Instead of a friendly Abyssinian army, it was Granye, cured of his wound and reinforced by Arab horsemen and ten Turkish field guns, who appeared in martial array before the Portuguese camp. Desperately outnumbered, the Portuguese made the first onslaught. Christóvão, in the front rank as always, had his leg smashed by a musketball and was wounded in both arms. Nothing to it but to retire into the mountains. The queen and Bermudes were sent off with a guard under Castanhoso's command.

Christóvão was carried away on a stretcher by the men of his bodyguard. He was in agony from jolting over the stony trail. Since the Moslems were in hot pursuit he ordered his men to hide him in a thicket and to get away as best they could. The Somalis found him still living and carried him off to be tortured to death in Granye's camp.

The Portuguese retired to the hill village of the Felasha. When all the stragglers were in they still amounted to three hundred men. When the Negus joined them with a pitifully small contingent, he proved to be of very little help. First thing he declared he had no intention of giving up the Abyssinian ritual for the Roman and denied that Bermudes' investiture as patriarch had any validity.

Disputes arose about who should command. Morale was low until a troop of a hundred and twenty Portuguese, supported by some eight thousand terrified Abyssinians, met Granye in a fresh engagement on Shrove Tuesday of 1543. Granye had lost the support of his Turkish musketeers. One of Christóvão da Gama's old bodyguard had the immense pleasure of shooting him through the chest when he led the attack with a contingent of cavalry. The Somali tribesmen galloped away in confusion. Granye's camp was captured, so was one of his sons. Only forty Turks escaped alive. To celebrate the victory Claúdio had Granye's head exhibited on a pike in the four corners of his kingdom.

There was peace for a while until the Galla, a group of Bantu tribes from East Africa, began to occupy the country ravaged by the Somalis. Many of the Portuguese married Abyssinian wives and settled down in the country.

Castanhoso and some fifty fidalgos declared that they had accomplished their mission and wished to return home. The Negus who was trying to carry on the traditional policy of never letting a foreigner leave, gave his consent with very ill grace. Bermudes stayed on until he was displaced by an ecclesiastic named Joseph whom Claúdio imported from the Coptic partiarchate of Alexandria. Bermudes had lost his authority though he continued to perform religious services for the Portuguese settlers. He had to keep out of the way of the Negus and his court.

He was living in hiding at Debarwa when Padre Gonçalo Rodrigues arrived there in 1555 as the forerunner of a Jesuit mission. The Abyssinian clergy was thrown into an uproar by the prospect of new missionaries who they felt were bound to undermine their power over the people. Claúdio declared that no matter what letters his father had written he had no intention of giving up the traditions of his nation. Since Massawa was again open to Portuguese shipping, more eager Jesuits appeared. Some converts they did make but even when they imported a bishop named Oviedo, who engaged in endless controversies with the Abyssinian monks, the Roman Catholics remained a small sect in the crumbling empire of the successors of Prester John. Bermudes himself managed on various pretexts to sneak down to Massawa. In spite of a guard dispatched to detain him he managed to get himself and his slaves and considerable treasure aboard a ship bound for Goa. There he was hospitably received by the Jesuits at the College of São Paulo. Eventually he returned quietly to Portugal where he settled down to write a book about his experiences.

6

THE EVANGEL IN JAPAN

If the Jesuits failed to make many converts among the Abyssinians, in Japan they were unexpectedly successful. This was partly due to the curiosity and the openness of mind of the sixteenth-century feudal rulers of Japan and partly due to the extraordinary qualities of the tawny-haired Basque who was Loyola's secretary, who has been immortalized by the church as St. Francis Xavier.

Xavier's mission to Japan was the result of a series of accidents. About the time when Loyola's plans for the establishment of his Society received the papal blessing, the man who was to set up a teaching and proselyting center in Lisbon became ill, so Loyola reluctantly sent his bosom friend and secretary in his place.

With the help of Simão Rodrigues, who was the only Portuguese among the founders of the order, and of an Italian priest, Xavier organized a teaching seminary in Lisbon. The response was immense. Eager young Portuguese flocked to the Jesuit order. From that time on Jesuit influence was paramount in Portuguese education and Jesuit priests became the confessors and the confidential advisers of the king and his brothers.

Xavier himself must have been a man of immense personal charm. The king was so taken with the disciple that he wrote Loyola himself begging him to come to his court and offering to finance his whole undertaking. Loyola, whose ambitions comprised all Christendom, tactfully refused.

Xavier displayed such a burning desire to preach to the heathen that it was arranged that Rodrigues should conduct the seminary in Lisbon which would prepare priests and laybrothers to spread the word of God throughout the Portuguese world. Xavier would be left free to conduct missions in the Orient.

He sailed for India in the spring of 1541 with the fleet that crossed the bar of the Tagus under the command of Martim Afonso de Sousa, the first colonizer of Brazil. Only two assistants could be found to go with him. So that he should have authority in dealing with other clerics, at John III's request, the pope conferred on Xavier the dignity of apostolic nuncio. The journey took eighteen months because the fleet arrived in Moçambique too late for the southwesterly monsoon and had to winter there. Xavier was kept so busy ministering to the sick Portuguese in the hospital that he had no time to preach the word to the natives. When he finally arrived in Goa in May of 1542 his first impression was that the place was, as he put it, "a pestilential slough."

Though there were plenty of churches, and priests and friars enough, he found the Portuguese of all classes living with harems of native women. In spite of the efforts of various governors to have them marry their favorite concubines and bring up their children in Christian homes they kept relapsing into the heathen customs of the polygamous natives. Goa was the greatest mart in the Orient. Bribery and corruption oiled the wheels of trade. People seemed to think of nothing but amassing wealth and of the pleasures of the belly and the bed.

The practical operations of such organizations as the Santa Casa de Misericórdia with branches in all the oriental ports, which attended to the wants of destitute widows and orphans and cared for the needy without regard to caste or creed, had little appeal to the religious enthusiasm of Xavier and his companions. They had no interest in material goods. To save men's souls in this world and the next they must be made total Christians immediately. To attain this aim the Jesuits had at their hand all the techniques of humanist scholarship that had been accumulated in Europe during the last century and a half. They were the first of the religious orders to foster a consistent study of the manners and traditions, and of course the languages, of the populations they hoped to convert.

Xavier's first business in Goa was to found a college for the instruction of missionaries. Wherever he went he was accompanied by young pupils in white surplices intoning canticles. It wasn't enough to teach the young Goans. He had come to preach to the infidel. He carried his mission to the pearl divers of the Palavá coast. These naked fishermen, leading precarious and impoverished lives, had applied for Portuguese protection against exploitation by the native rajahs, and had shown a certain aptitude for Christianity. Xavier spent fourteen months among them and returned to Goa refreshed and invigorated by the conviction that he had saved many souls from damnation.

From Goa he sailed to the Moluccas. On Amboina, where the natives had been converted before but had relapsed to their primitive superstitions, whole villages ran off into the bush in terror at the holy man's approach. Xavier patiently traversed the island, scrambling up impossible trails in the deadly heat, accompanied only by an acolyte carrying a cross. The two of them sang hymns as they strode along. Gradually the villagers came out of hiding and listened to Xavier's preaching. He visited other islands. He made little impression on the headhunters and cannibals, but among the less aggressive agricultural peoples he found some acceptance. Still he was not satisfied. He must find a people who once Christianized would propagate the faith themselves.

Already in the Moluccas he was hearing rumors of the high state of civilization of the Japanese. The first Europeans to land in Marco Polo's Cipangu were three Portuguese traveling in a Chinese pirate junk which took refuge in a port on the small island of Tanega-shima. They were hospitably received and almost immediately a brisk trade began between populous Kiushiu and the Portuguese trading posts. These were establishing a precarious foothold in small ports round the mouth of the Pearl River, which was the commercial thoroughfare into the Chinese heartland. The Portuguese found themselves in control of a lucrative monopoly because the Ming emperors had forbidden Chinese ships to visit foreign ports.

By 1548 Xavier was back in Goa. He spent most of that year

there reorganizing the College of São Paulo which the Jesuits were taking over. Their special style of education was not introduced without opposition from the Franciscans and Dominicans who had been in the field long before. The Jesuits, brimful of the vision instilled in them by their founder, tended to run rough-shod over the other orders. Xavier's plan was to make the college a seminary where young men from all the tribes and castes of India and Ceylon, Javanese, Burmans, Chinese and Abyssinians should study for the priesthood. They would be sent home under the discipline of the Society to evangelize their own peoples. Yet even among his own companions there were doubts about the practicability of making Jesuits out of Hindus.

The following year he shook the dust of godless Goa from his sandals. "I see what goes on here," he wrote John III. "Your Highness will send out orders and regulations for the good of the Christians. I have no hope of seeing them complied with. That is why I am fleeing to Japan. I have already wasted too much time. I do not want to waste more." The years were passing. His health was precarious. "I am going to Japan," he wrote the Jesuit fathers in Rome. "There at least I will not find Moslems or Jews, only pagans open to things new to them about God and nature. There I believe the natives will be capable of perpetuating for themselves the benefits those of the Company will bring to them."

Xavier wrote with such confidence because, in the wake of a request for missionaries by a Japanese feudal lord which had reached the governor at Goa, there had appeared in Malacca a Japanese whose name was known to the Portuguese as Anjiro, asking for instruction in the faith. Anjiro had been a sort of bandit chief and had committed so many crimes and stirred up so many blood feuds that he feared for his salvation in this world and the next. Fleeing his native land on a Portuguese ship he had learned enough Portuguese by the time he was taken to Father Master Francis, as Xavier was known in the Orient, to act as interpreter for the Jesuit mission. He was promptly baptized under the name of Paul.

Led by Anjiro, Father Master Francis and two companions landed on Tagoshima and were hospitably received by the chiefs of the Satsuma clan. The Japanese leaders were eager for a revival of the once profitable trade with the China ports. Encouraging the Portuguese clergy seemed to them a way of encouraging the Portuguese merchants. Then they were genuinely "open to things new to them about God and nature." In a short time Father Master Francis, through the mouth of Anjiro, had made a hundred and fifty converts.

In spite of occasional reverses the Jesuits were so encouraged by their reception that they determined to build a church and a house for the Company. In search of funds Xavier turned to one of the Portuguese skippers anchored in the port for a loan of three hundred cruzados.

This shipmaster, Fernão Mendes Pinto, was almost as vivid a character as Father Master Francis himself. The son of a poor and possibly a New Christian family in Montemór-o-Velho he arrived penniless in India in 1537. Immediately he took service under the most notable captains. He served in the siege of Diu, and took part in one of the expeditions to the Red Sea to succor the embassy to Abyssinia. There he made his first successful commercial venture and suffered his first captivity at the hands of the Turks. Somehow he was ransomed and joined the captain major of Malacca, the very aggressive Pêro de Faria. For Faria he undertook embassies and commercial ventures that led him through Sumatra and Burma and Siam and finally into China. There he visited the Great Wall and Tartary beyond and the forbidden cities of Nanking and Peking, suffered all sorts of mischances and captivities, was shipwrecked and joined the coastal pirates. Somehow he returned to Malacca with cash in his pocket. He left China full of admiration for the civilization of the Chinese and for the smooth administration of their government.

It is possible that Mendes Pinto was one of those three Portuguese who had turned up in Tanega-shima in 1542. Anyway he told a plausible story of their reception by the Japanese. One of his companions went hunting on the island one morning and came back with his two coolies loaded with game. The Japanese had never seen a musket. The local daimyo immediately sent for the Portuguese and asked to be shown how the machine worked. The Portuguese promptly shot him two wild pigeons and a hawk.

It seemed enchantment but the Portuguese explained it was merely the effect of gunpowder. The daimyo bought the musket for a thousand taels of silver and made the Portuguese promise to teach him how to make gunpowder. The daimyo had his armorer copy the musket. When, at the end of four months, the Portuguese and their Chinese friends departed, wrote Mendes Pinto, there were six hundred muskets on the island.

Mendes Pinto was shipwrecked again. After breathtaking adventures he reached Malacca. He made and lost fortunes, but when a few years later he first met Father Master Francis, he owned his own ship and was one of the most prosperous merchants in the Malacca trade.

These two dissimilar individuals seem to have been immediately attracted to each other. One of Xavier's great gifts was his ability to communicate simply and directly with all sorts of conditions of men. Mendes Pinto immediately recognized that he was dealing with a saint. He called him "the slave of God." They seem to have been together in a storm on a ship bound for China. In a lull the ship's boat was launched to help cut away the wreckage of a fallen mast. A fresh gust of wind carried the boat away and out of sight. Everyone aboard gave the men in it up for lost. Father Master Francis insisted that they were safe. After the wind began to moderate the ship's boat reappeared. When, years later Mendes Pinto wrote up his adventures he devoted a chapter to describing the eerie feeling it gave him when he discovered that "the slave of God" had performed a miracle.

At the end of the year 1552 Mendes Pinto was in Goa winding up his affairs before returning home to Portugal. He was a rich man, worth nine or ten thousand cruzados. He had deserved well of the Crown. He was looking forward to a life of ease and luxury and possibly to a title of nobility.

Meanwhile he had been writing letters to Father Master Francis giving information about the manners and customs of the Chinese to whom Xavier was preparing to preach the gospel. Mendes Pinto first visited the college of São Paulo in Goa, when his letters remained unanswered, to get news of Father Master Francis. The Jesuits crowded around him when they learned from a brother recently returned from Malacca that Mendes Pinto had

been one of Father Master Francis' closest friends. It was there
that Mendes Pinto learned of the saint's death on the island of
Sanchao while waiting for a ship to take him to China.

The provincial, Father Belchior, on his way to meet a vessel
bringing the body back from the Straits invited Mendes Pinto
to board the galley the viceroy had put at his disposal.

They met the vessel at a point about twenty leagues south of
Goa. The Jesuits and the "children of the doctrine" they had
brought with them went aboard with garlands and flowery boughs
in their hands singing "Glory be to God in the Highest." The
sailors had decked the vessel with banners and pennants and awnings and when the body was transferred to the galley many
rounds of artillery were fired.

Father Belchior said, "Look, here is our great friend Master
Francis whom we have come to seek." The saint was in a coffin
lined with damask and covered with a surplice of white brocade
which, "although it had been long time under the lime" was
fresh enough for Father Belchior to wear it months later when
he went to talk to the Emperor of Japan. Master Francis' face
was covered. His hands were crossed and held together by a
cord as fresh and new as if it had just left the cobbler's shop.
He had light slippers on his feet. "When I saw him thus whole
I kissed his feet with many tears remembering the many things
we had gone through together."

When the body was carried to the Jesuit College, accompanied
by ninety "children of the doctrine" in white surplices carrying
lighted candles, all the bells rang. The street was perfumed with
incense from the silver censers swinging on each side of the
coffin. "There were so many people in the streets and windows
and on the walls that in my day I never saw anything so marvelous." Father Master Francis lay in state for three days and
nights in the college. People crowded round to kiss his feet or,
for all the brothers could do, to touch beads and reliquaries to
his body. The body was eventually placed in a silver sepulcher in
front of the altar in the Jesuit church.

Mendes Pinto lived through this time in what he described as
a vast confusion of spirit. He was so torn between his desire
for wealth and the need for his soul's salvation that for days

on end he lay groaning on the ground. The conviction grew within him that he must win forgiveness for his sins by helping complete Father Master Francis' work of preaching the gospel to the people of Japan.

Mendes Pinto was admitted as a novice into the Jesuit order. A few days later he sailed for Japan with Father Belchior and six priests and five "children of the doctrine." To facilitate the work the viceroy appointed him ambassador to the ruler of Bungo. There the record stops. Possibly because he was suspected of being a *marrano*, of having Jewish blood; or more likely because this satirical-minded adventurer just did not have the vocation for the religious life, Mendes Pinto was either expelled or asked to resign from the Society of Jesus. Scraping together some remnants of his fortune he returned to Portugal where he settled near Almada in the estuary of the Tagus.

There he set to work to write one of the most extraordinary books in Portuguese. *Peregrinação*, "pilgrimage," is not only the sole Portuguese picaresque novel, but it is a compendium of information, in which travelers' tales are interwoven with acute ethnographical and historical observation, about the countries he visited. What Padre Alvares did for Abyssinia Mendes Pinto did for the Extreme Orient. He painted an indelible picture of Japan, China and the various kingdoms of Indo-China as first seen through Portuguese eyes. The book is full of the sardonic humor and the earthy self-criticism which characterized so much of sixteenth-century Portuguese writing about the East. Though many of the descriptions of events are those of an eyewitness, nobody has been able to disentangle Mendes Pinto's own adventures from the stories other people told him or the tales he merely made up.

In the end the firearms the Portuguese introduced had more influence on the course of Japanese history than their religion. Though the number of Christians rose by the end of the century to somewhere between three hundred thousand and half a million, the free-wheeling regime of the feudal lords was brought to an end by the dictatorship of Hideyoshi. Hideyoshi's well-disciplined troops armed with muskets made short work of the samurai with their sacred swords. After twenty years of hesitation Hideyoshi decided that Christianity was detrimental to the centralized order he was determined to establish. The Christians were exterminated.

Priests were crucified if they refused to leave the kingdom, churches were demolished. Tens of thousands met a martyr's death. His successor, Iyeyasu, inaugurated the Takugawa regime with its policy of complete isolation from the rest of the world. The Japanese were no longer "open to things new to them about God and nature."

7

THE FADING OF
A GOLDEN AGE

The intellectual ferment which accompanied the great discoveries continued on late into the sixteenth century. The dogmas of the counterreformation had not yet become so rigid as to stifle curiosity about the natural world. A careful sifting of reports to establish the true facts had been inherent in the researches of Prince Henry. A flair for something very like the nineteenth-century style of scientific investigation characterized the early pilotbooks, such as Duarte Pacheco's *Esmeraldo*. As late as the middle of the century while John III was welcoming the Jesuits to his realm, he was also establishing a school at Coimbra for the teaching of the classical humanities, and inviting to Portugal foreign scholars whose speculations were soon to be considered heretical. The early Jesuits themselves seem to have seen no discrepancy between the objective study of the peoples they were trying to convert and the religious discipline they were determined to enforce.

Even after the establishment of the Inquisition in Goa, as late as 1563 one of the first essays in scientific botany was published there: "Dialogues on the Herbs and Drugs and Medicinal matters of India and Certain of its Fruits," by Garcia da Orta. This first edition had another claim to fame. The introductory poem is considered to be the first printed work of a frustrated exile named Luis de Camões.

Garcia da Orta was the family physician and confidential friend of Martim Afonso de Sousa. He studied medicine in Salamanca and Alcalá de Henares. He accompanied Martim Afonso on his journey to Brazil and sailed with him to India when he was appointed captain major of the fleet which left the Tagus in 1534. Wherever he went he made notes on the medicinal plants. On the African coast he complained about his inability to learn anything from the natives at Sofala and Moçambique. The Arabs he dismissed as dreamers. He listened more carefully to the Brahmin doctors in India. "There is no man so ignorant," he wrote, "that he does not know something good."

The bulk of his book was dedicated to Indian plants. He made a point of describing them at each stage of their growth from the seed to the fruit. Of course he was most interested in their medicinal properties. He tried to put down only what he knew from experiment and direct experience. He was suspicious of many of the theories of Galen and Avicenna, which he attributed to legend and hearsay, on the efficacy of various herbs and simples in medicine. According to Orta the Greeks were great writers, but they were also the inventors of many lies. "I bow to myself," he wrote, "where I have seen things with my own eyes rather than to all the Fathers of Science when they are misinformed."

His work was immediately translated into Latin and pirated and epitomized throughout Europe. It became one of the bases from which rose the new science of botany coming into existence in France and Italy.

Orta did come a cropper when he failed to apply his own principles, as in his famous debate in Goa with an apothecary from Moçambique as to whether black and white pepper came from separate trees or from the same tree. Orta declared there were two different species and that he had it on the authority of the Rajah of Cochin, on whose lands the bulk of the pepper grew. The apothecary claimed that white pepper was just black pepper with the husk rubbed off. That the debate was held at all shows how little the Portuguese or the Indian natives knew about the origins of their chief stock in trade. This debate took place at the court of the highly knowledgeable fidalgo, himself a practical botanist, who had taken Martim Afonso's place as governor of India.

João de Castro was brought up at the court of King Manoel. His father was governor of Lisbon, a stern disciplinarian who threw him out of doors for some youthful prank at the age of eighteen. He enlisted for service in Morocco and within a few years had made such a name for himself that he was knighted by Duarte de Meneses, then governor of Tangier. At court he had the friendship of Dom Luis, King John's learned younger brother. Both were interested in geography and navigation and were pupils of Dr. Pedro Nunes, author of a treatise on charts and the most expert theorist in the maritime mathematics of the time. When the joint Castilian and Portuguese expedition to Tunis was organized Castro went along with Dom Luis as a member of his staff. After the successful conclusion of that enterprise against the Barbarossa pirates Castro retired to his estate called Penha Verde near Sintra. There he spent his time planting a botanical garden where he acclimatized plants and trees imported from Brazil and the Orient, and in studying trigonometry and navigation. In 1538 the king lured him out of retirement by giving him the command of the ship *Gryfe* in the great fleet being assembled to convoy the elderly Garcia de Noronha to his post as third viceroy of India.

As soon as he got to sea Castro began checking Nunes' theories with practice. He wanted to discover the cause of the variations of the magnetic needle. There was a theory abroad that longitude could be measured by noting these variations. Castro discovered on the journey from Brazil to the Cape of Good Hope that these variations had other causes than differences in longitude. By the time he anchored in the roads off Moçambique he had found that the most puzzling variations in his compass were caused by the iron in a large cannon near the binnacle. When he moved his compasses—he used several—to another part of the ship he got a truer reading. This discovery of Castro's was the first step toward the invention of the nineteenth-century ship's compass where all such influences were neutralized.

Further he was at work on the sort of chart where a ship's course could be reduced to a straight line which a few years later was standardized as Mercator's Projection. In the notes he compiled for Nunes he made the first careful description of a waterspout. Many of his observations were incorporated by Nunes in the second edition of his treatise.

The climate of Goa made short work of Garcia de Noronha. Estevão da Gama became governor. Right away he organized a flotilla to destroy the Turkish galleys based in the Red Sea which were again becoming a threat to the Portuguese strong points around the Indian Ocean. For Castro that expedition was the occasion for the compiling of a logbook of the coasts between Goa and Suez. Castro's *Roteiro* has been the basis of the geography of the Red Sea ever since.

He looked into the old problem of why the Red Sea was called red. He noted that the water there was of the same color as other sea water only clearer. Geographers had written about red dust. He found no red dust. In fact the arid mountains that bordered the Red Sea seemed to him to be gray to dark gray in color or even black as if scorched by fire.

He did find a type of tree coral that imparted a red color to the water. On the shallows and reefs this coral showed green where it was mossy and otherwise white and red. He sent down divers to bring up hunks of it so that he could see for himself. The water was so clear that he could see the bottom at twenty fathoms. He concluded that it was occasional glimpses of these red corals at the upper end of the great inlet that gave travelers the idea that the sea was all red. The Arabs he pointed out didn't call it the Red Sea at all. They called it the Sea of Mecca.

After completing this exploration Castro sailed home to write up his notes in the quiet of Penha Verde. In 1545 he was brought out of retirement again by royal appointment as governor of India. During his tenure he performed the great military exploit of the relief of Diu which was suffering its second siege by the Turks. All India rang with this exploit. The chroniclers told the story that when he was trying to raise funds to rebuild the shattered fortifications of Diu the merchants of Goa complained they had no security for a loan. "Here's their security," cried Castro and pulled a hair out his beard. The hair was dispatched to Goa. The loan was forthcoming, John III was so pleased with him he sent out an appointment for a second three year term, this time as viceroy, but Castro died, although he was barely forty-eight, four-teen days after the arrival of the messengers.

Dom João de Castro was the last of the governors in the great tradition of da Gama and Albuquerque. To Camões he was one of the supreme heroes. Punning on his name the poet called him Castro Forte in *The Lusiads*.

It was Camões' fate to live in the period when Portuguese ex-pansion began to falter. His poetry accomplished the apotheosis of the enterprise of the Indies. In some ways he can be said to have written its epitaph. As Dom João de Castro's all too short career illustrated the glories and successes of that enterprise, Camões' life illustrated its frustrations and failures. History has crowned both men with laurel.

Luis de Camões was probably born in Lisbon in 1524, the year Vasco da Gama died. He came of a family of lesser gentry with origins in Galicia. His grandfather had married into the da Gama clan. His father, of whom he saw very little, is said to have been a sea captain and to have died in Goa from exposure when his ship was wrecked off the bar. There was learning in the family. Luis's uncle Bento de Camões, long a teacher at Santa Cruz, became chancellor of the university of Coimbra when it was re-established by John III. Luis was sent to study there at the age of thirteen.

The Portuguese renaissance was in its heyday. In transferring his subsidies from the Sorbonne to Coimbra and importing such foreign scholars as James Buchanan and Nicholas Claenarts, John III, perhaps all unwitting, opened the college town on the Mon-dego for a short space to all the liberal culture of Europe. Sá de Miranda, a few years before, had brought home from Italy a taste for Petrarchian sonnets and for the grandiose epic style of Ariosto. An eager pupil, brimming with poetic talent, young Camões be-came imbued, not only with fads and fashions of the classical style but with its prevailing passion for the heroic aggrandisement of the human figure. It is likely that he started while still a student at Coimbra to compose the lyrics where, as in his magnificent sonnets, he managed to inject into Italianate forms the freshness and the direct simplicity of early Portuguese poetry.

Camões was a man of bravado. All his life he showed a genius for getting into scrapes. Lacking any knack for accumulating money he remained dirt poor while some of his companions were filling their pockets. Through a career of almost continual misadventure he was kept going by his devotion to the art of poetry, and the deep religious fervor of his love of country.

In his very early twenties he left Coimbra and went back to Lisbon to seek his fortune. His first writings were comedies. His farce taken from Plautus' *Amphitryon* may well have been performed by students at the university. Perhaps he felt that there was an opening for a new playwright in Lisbon. Gil Vicente, the court dramatist, had stopped writing. It has been suggested that he was silenced by fear of the Inquisition. Vincente's reformist ideas were becoming dangerous. Friends may have told Camões that a youth of irreproachable orthodoxy, steeped in the fashionable Greek-Roman lore, might well take Vicente's place. Though the chief characters of Camões' *Amphitriões* are based on Plautus they are Portuguese in Roman dress. The rustic interludes have a strong flavor of Vicente's dialogue.

In Lisbon Camões was employed as a tutor in the household of a member of the Noronha family who had been ambassador to France. A fresh *auto* called *King Seleucus* was produced in the household of one of the king's grooms at the celebration of the engagement of some member of the family. The young poet was for a while well received in court circles. This was the period of his most fervent love poetry always directed at some unattainable mistress.

Meanwhile he gained a reputation for riotous living in the company of more easily attainable charmers. He was known as one of the most reckless of the young bloods on the town in the gang of a hare-brained satirist named Ribeiro, who for his malicious verses was nicknamed O Chiado, and who left such a legend behind him that a section of Lisbon still bears his name. Some scandal suddenly closed all doors at court to Camões.

To wash out his disgrace he enlisted for service in Morocco under another member of the Noronha family who was governor of Ceuta. There has survived a sarcastic letter written from Ceuta to a friend in Portugal. It is the letter of a truculent and frustrated man. The striking thing about it is that young Camões couldn't write a paragraph without breaking into verse, remembered quotations in Spanish or Portuguese, or improvisations of his own. The man's mind overflowed with poetic fancy.

He lost his right eye in an engagement with the Moslems, whether on land or sea we don't know. Back in Lisbon, with a wound in the king's service to his credit, he would have been in line for a pension if he had not cut off all hope of preferment at court by getting into a brawl during the Corpus Christi procession. To make it worse the man he wounded with a sword thrust was a gentleman of the court. Camões was sentenced to nine months in prison. After serving most of his term he was pardoned by the king at the request of the very gentleman he had wounded. There must have been a feeling in court circles that they were dealing with no ordinary man. The terms of the reprieve were that he should depart from Portugal immediately to serve the king in India.

Somehow he put off his departure for a year. In 1553 he sailed on the great galleon *São Bento*. The Cape was at its stormiest. Of the four ships that left Lisbon for India that year *São Bento* was the only one to arrive. Though she was described as the biggest and the best Portuguese vessel afloat she too was lost on the return trip. Portuguese seamanship had deteriorated since the days of the caravels.

Prince Henry's caravels were swift and seaworthy, but they rarely displaced more than two hundred tons. With the growth of the spice trade great carracks or galleons of eight or nine hundred tons displacement were thought to be more profitable. Everything was sacrificed to carrying capacity. Captains and pilots relied on the established routes and steady winds of the long loop, south to Brazil and east to India. Workmanship and the quality of the spars and sails and rigging deteriorated as the shipyards in Oporto and Lisbon vied with each other as to who should produce the biggest ship fastest. The ships were so stuffed with men and cargo that often they were in an unseaworthy condition before they left port. While Camões was at work celebrating the triumphs of Portuguese seamanship, shipwreck became the nightmare of the India trade. Long before *The Lusiads* left the press, stories of drowning and disaster were being put on paper that made such gruesome reading when they were later collected in the *História Trágica Marítima*.

In Goa Camões found plenty to occupy him. He took part in expeditions to quell risings on the Malabar Coast, and probably went along with Francisco Barreto's excursion to the Red Sea. He seems to have found a friend in Barreto. When that captain celebrated his accession as governor in 1555 a third *auto* called *Filomena* was performed in the palace at Goa. Soon after Camões was appointed Trustee for the Dead and Absent in the new colony of Macao recently established by permission of the Ming emperor at the mouth of the Pearl River.

Things went wrong in Macao. After a couple of years Camões was recalled to Goa. On the way his ship was wrecked in the estuary of the Mekong River. Out of whatever cash or goods he may have accumulated in Macao all he saved was a bundle of manuscript. Already he was working on the epic which would describe in heady rhythms and chiming rhymes the exploits of the first adventurers.

Whatever accusations there were against him seem to have been dropped, but he lingered on in Goa, penniless and discredited, until a friend appointed to the captaincy of Sofala gave him a lift to Moçambique. There he spent two miserable years trying to borrow the money for his passage home. Diogo de Couto, the historian, who saw him there in 1569 reported a further misfortune. Somebody stole the volume in which he had collected the bulk of his lyric poetry. Couto and other friends chipped in for the poet's passage to Lisbon.

Nothing could have been worse than the situation that met Camões when he landed. Lisbon was barely recovering from a visitation of the plague. A hundred years of neglect of agriculture and the draining off of men to India had left the kingdom dependent on imports of grain and salt meats and cured fish from Flanders. Since John III's death in 1577 Portuguese finances had been in such confusion that there was rarely enough revenue to pay for these imports. Taxes, from which nobles and clergy were exempt, crushed all initiative in the peasantry. Famine was widespread even in the richest farmlands of the Minho. Portuguese laborers were fleeing to Spain in search of work and food.

A stroke had carried off John III without warning. He left no will to guide his executors. The great line of the House of Avis had petered out. All the king's sons had gone before him. The last surviving prince, the sickly Dom João, did manage to engender a son on a Spanish princess before he died. This boy, Sebastião, was born posthumously and recognized by the nobles and the Cortes as heir to the throne. Until he should grow up the royal council appointed John III's widow, an Austrian princess who was the Emperor Charles V's sister, to serve as regent. Finding the duties too hard she resigned the regency in favor of John III's younger brother, the cardinal Henrique, who as Grand Inquisitor was the chief advocate of the Holy Office in Portugal.

Cardinal Henrique surrounded himself with Jesuit advisers. He founded the Jesuit university of Evora. The handsome Italianate courtyards testify to this day to a certain elegance in Jesuit scholarship. He managed to effect economies. He obtained papal consent to a project, which had been long pending, of taxing the clergy and the religious foundations to pay for a crusade in Morocco. John III's policy of abandoning half the fortresses there for economy's sake had proved self-defeating. Each time a strong point was evacuated the rest proved harder to hold and more expensive in men and treasure. Two years before Camões reached home Dom Sebastião, amid scenes of considerable popular enthusiasm, had assumed the throne. He was all of fourteen.

He proved a flighty and capricious youth. Though he dedicated his life to reviving the old glories of his house as a crusading knight, he lacked the sober common sense that had served his ancestors so well. He was never able to develop a consistent policy in any direction. His wild aspirations kept blowing up in fits of petty temper. When Camões arrived in Lisbon the city was buzzing with the young king's plans to reconquer Morocco.

Camões at forty-six was a worn-out man. He was a stranger in the city he had known so well. Most of his friends were dead. His aged mother was his only human tie. The wits and satirical versifiers that had made Lisbon so amusing in his youth had been driven into the shadows. Intellectual life was at a dead end. Prosecution by the Holy Office had scattered the humanist scholars at Coimbra. James Buchanan, that tough Scot, to be sure had survived his interrogation and gone home to Edinburgh where he defiantly avowed himself a Protestant.

Spanish influence was paramount at court. Even in retirement after his abdication as emperor, Charles V was busy with plans to enforce his family's claims to the Portuguese throne when this young addlepate should run his course. His agent in Portugal was none other than the very eminent Commissary General of the Jesuit Order, Francisco de Borja, later canonized by the church. The ex-emperor freely admitted that the only thing that stood in his way was the passion for independence of the Portuguese people.

Maybe it was from the Lisbon commoners, the lowlives and tavern brawlers with whom Camões spent his leisure, that the poet absorbed the courage to finish his poem. He shared the passionate patriotism of the Portuguese people as well as that spirit of personal bravado which ran like a scarlet thread through all the exploits of the great discoverers.

In a year he had his book ready for the printer. In a rousing epilogue addressed to the young king he offered, in return for some slight recognition, to celebrate Dom Sebastião's coming deeds in Morocco as lustily as he had celebrated the conquests of Vasco da Gama. The censor who passed on *The Lusiads* for the Inquisition found "nothing scandalous in the poem, on the contrary faith and good morals," but he wrote that he should warn the reader against the poet's use of fictitious gods and goddesses: "This is all poesy and fiction and the author as a poet pretends to nothing but to ornament the poetic style."

It is this heavy incrustation of renaissance ornament which tends, in these later ages when classical mythology has lost the glamor it had for men of the sixteenth century, to throw the reader off. Thought of as a counterpart of the decoration furnished by classical motifs in the plateresque or manueline styles of architecture, the mythological framework becomes part of the surge and bombast inseparable with ottava rima. Read aloud the stanzas, with their steady beat, pile up an oratorical effect like Handel's music two centuries later. Like the *Odyssey* the poem is an epic of the sea, full of the smell of pitch and creaking timbers and the spray screaming off the caps of the ocean waves. The pompous rhythms are embroidered with an abundance of naturalistic detail so that gradually the real scenes of the great enterprise, the braggadocio, the bloodshed, the lust for gold and precious stones, the delight in discovery, the exultation of empire burn through the formal framework. For better or for worse *The Lusiads* remain the outstanding literary expression of Portugal's golden age.

The year the book was published the last of the Portuguese humanists was hauled into the prisons of the Inquisition. Damião de Góis, after being employed on many diplomatic missions by John III, had served as official chronicler at the Tôrre do Tombo. Cardinal Henrique himself had commissioned him to write the lives of King Manoel and John II. Now an old accusation filed by Simão Rodrigues, the first Jesuit provincial of Portugal, with whom he had had some kind of academic falling out at an Italian university many years before, was suddenly revived. He was indicted for heresy. The proofs were his friendship with Erasmus and Melanchthon. He had met Martin Luther. He had written about the rites and beliefs of the Abyssinians without denouncing their heresy. He defended himself manfully. He was an old man and ill. His family abandoned him. He never got out of the clutches of the Holy Office and died in its custody at the monastery of Batalha a few years later.

Camões' own orthodoxy was never questioned. He even achieved a modest recognition from Dom Sebastião. "For the sufficiency he showed in the book he wrote concerning the affairs of India," he was endowed with a tiny pension from the Crown which was to be extended after his death for the support of his mother.

Most likely it was never paid because Dom Sebastião was squeezing every cruzado to raise funds for a vast expedition he was equipping for the reconquest of Morocco. He had mortgaged the profits of the India trade to German bankers for three years. He had even promised the New Christians to exempt them from prosecution for heresy for four years in return for a gift of two hundred and fifty thousand cruzados.

The expedition was hopelessly mismanaged from the start. The king's troops were never properly provisioned. One crack-brained decision after another led the Portuguese forces to an appalling defeat in the vicinity of Alcácer Kebir.

Camões lived long enough to learn of his king's death and the slaughter of eight thousand troops by the Moors. What was worse fifteen thousand men allowed themselves to be taken prisoner. They were sold in the African slave markets. A fresh outbreak of the plague the following year found the poet with no more resistance left to disease and misfortune. "And so I shall end my life," he had written to a friend, "and all will see that I loved my country so that not only was I content to die on her soil, but to die with her."

He died in the hospital. There being nobody to claim his body he was buried in a pauper's grave. He was spared the final humiliation. In March 1581, his way well-prepared by the Duke of Alba's disciplined troops, Charles V's son, Philip II of Spain, was declared king of Portugal by a carefully packed assembly meeting in the convent at Tomar.

8

TO RENOUNCE THE WORLD

On the flank on the high ridge of the Serra da Arrábida that rises like the scaly back of some extinct saurian between the estuaries of the Tagus and the Rio Sada, above a lovely sheltered bay called the Portinho, stands a small abandoned convent. It was established in the middle of the sixteenth century by two noble Spaniards and Frei Francisco da Cruz, a Portuguese, as a retreat from the world under the most rigid discipline of the Capuchin order. Most likely the wild stretch of scrubby mountainside, the immensity of blue ocean rimmed under beetling hills by a curve of white beach, which seems so breathtakingly beautiful to us, seemed to them—like the view from his first Abyssinian mountaintop to Padre Alvares—"the depths of hell all around." The agony of renunciation still hangs over the crabbed cells encrusted haphazard into the rocky ledges. A trickle of water springs from under the cliff but there is no other human amenity. In the narrow court squeezed in between cruel rock walls the presiding genius of the place hangs beside the entrance. The custodian calls it São Martinho: dear little Saint Martin.

It is the figure of a coarse-looking man with a black spade beard hanging from the cross. A bandage covers the eyes. The ears are stopped up. The mouth is sealed by a padlock through the lips. There is a keyhole in the chest, perhaps in case the Holy

Ghost should care to unlock the erring heart. The arms are lashed to the arms of the cross. One hand holds up a candle, the other a scourge. Under the crude feet writhes a small Satan wincing under the weight of holy abnegation.

The flesh creeps at the sight. The brutal symbols say to the humanist: "This is the man you thought to raise up equal to God. Only by becoming blind and deaf to the sights and sounds of the world, and by macerating the eager curiosities of the flesh, and by locking the lips that might speak blasphemy can you attain salvation."

This, pushed to its ultimate extreme, was the counterreformation's answer to the sensual pride and the scientific curiosity and uninhibited inventiveness of the enterprise of the Indies.

PART FIVE

Portugal in America

I

THE YEARS OF SHIPWRECK

During the sixty years when Portugal was under the domination of the Spanish Hapsburgs the seaborne empire disintegrated in the Orient. At the same time in Brazil, almost ignored by the home government, foundations were being laid for a type of colony quite different from most of the colonies which resulted from the sudden domination of the world by the peoples of Western Europe.

Despite assurances to the contrary when Philip II of Spain assumed the crown as Philip I of Portugal, the country became involved in Hapsburg quarrels and in the wars against English and Dutch heretics which brought the century to a gory close. It was the end of the policy of neutrality in Europe maintained so stoutly by the great men of the House of Avis. The immediate results were the interruption of Portugal's profitable trade with England and the Netherlands.

As heir to the Burgundian line the Emperor Charles V had in 1548 inherited feudal sovereignty over the seventeen provinces of the Netherlands. Life in these provinces was centered in self-governing towns. Their population, part Dutch, part Flemish and part French-speaking, amounted to something over a million, about equal to the Portuguese population at the time. They were

357

manufacturers, farmers, fishermen and seamen trained on the stormy North Sea. They were a stubbornly independent, hard-headed and industrious people. For years they had dominated the trade in textiles. They were Portugal's main source of food. Lisbon had long since lost the primacy of the traffic in spices to Antwerp. Amsterdam was becoming the banking center of Europe.

When Charles V tried to reduce the Netherlands townspeople to the position of subjects in his motley empire he found it hard going. They stood up for their ancient rights and charters. The provinces had already been in intermittent revolt for twelve years when his son Philip assumed the Portuguese throne. An absolutist in politics as in religion, Philip tried to put the Netherlands down by force. His best general, the Duke of Alba, though he won military victories and succeeded in sacking Antwerp and Ghent and in executing a number of leaders, wore himself out trying to suppress the rebellion. More than sixty years were to go by before the Dutch Republic was formally recognized but, after the signa-ture of the pacts of Ghent and Utrecht in 1576 and 1579, by which the leaders of the various provinces agreed to subordinate religious differences to the national cause, eventual independence became a certainty. Calvinists and Catholics alike united to fight the spread of despotic rule and of the Inquisition. After the second sacking of Antwerp by Spanish forces, Elizabeth of England entered the war on the Protestant side.

The towns and hamlets of the West of England were breeding a race of daring seamen. In Devonshire ports on the Channel shore they built sturdy swift-sailing ships. For some years John Hawkins, a West Country skipper, had been poaching on the Portuguese slave trade. In 1577 his nephew, Francis Drake, brazenly sailed down the South American coast, negotiated Magellan's straits and, provisioning his cruise from the spoils of Spanish forts and Spanish galleons, followed Magellan's course to circumnavigate the globe. During the same years Frobisher was exploring the Labrador in search of a Northwest passage to India and Gilbert was taking possession of Newfoundland, which had been discovered but never formally settled by the Portuguese. In 1587 the indefatigable Drake sailed into the harbor of Cádiz and destroyed a Spanish fleet at anchor there. On the way he made a landing at Sagres and wrecked Prince Henry's ancient fortifications. Historians conjecture that many valuable records of the early navigators were lost in the burning of the prince's village; but by an odd chance the only picture we have of the famous arsenal is a sketch made by one of Drake's officers before his jolly tars burned the place to the ground.

It was to avenge these insults that Philip lavished every resource of his kingdoms on the great fleet he sent north the following year to teach the upstart English a lesson. Drake's smaller, trimmer and more maneuverable ships battered the armada in the Channel and a storm in the North Sea did the rest. The following year Philip forbade the Portuguese to trade with England. In 1594 he forbade any trade or intercourse with the Netherlands. In 1599 he died, full of remorse and frustration for having made so little headway against the heretics, in his great monastery palace of the Escorial. The year after his death London merchants organized the East India Company to take over the oriental trade from the Spanish and Portuguese. Two years later the Dutch East India Company was formed for the same purpose.

The next few years were a race between the Protestant allies to see who could fastest despoil the Portuguese of their trading posts in the Orient. This was not accomplished without a fight. The Portuguese showed their mettle in the defense of their strong points and in many a stiff naval engagement.

At sea they were at a disadvantage. Portuguese seamanship was bogged in precedent and routine. Their great square-rigged ships of up to sixteen hundred tons were lightly gunned and mostly manned by crews of Lascars or Negro slaves. In spite of their breadth of beam they easily capsized. With three or four flush decks and high poops and forecastles they wallowed in cross seas and formed a poor platform for the gunners. In spite of a horrifying record of shipwrecks that often interrupted communications between Lisbon and Goa for many months, the Portuguese shipyards kept building larger and larger ships which set out recklessly packed with passengers and cargo. The only exception was during a number of years under Dom Sebastião when a limit of a thousand tons was set by royal decree. One historian has remarked that this was about the only sensible measure promulgated during that unfortunate young man's reign.

There was no proper sanitation on these great ships. Each passenger was supposed to bring along his own food. Water was insufficient or putrid. Out of six to eight hundred passengers and men-at-arms crowded aboard half would die before they reached India. Out of twenty-two ships that left Lisbon between 1590 and 1593 only two returned safely. Out of thirty-three ships, in the period between 1606 and 1608, only three were ever seen again in the Tagus. That doesn't mean that they were all wrecked. Some were retained for the Malacca trade or pulled to pieces at Goa as unseaworthy. Still the odds were all for shipwreck. If Camões' *Lusiads* was the supreme expression of the well-directed bravado of the enterprise of the Indies in the fifteen hundreds, the keynote to the years of decline was struck by the anthology of shipwreck tales collected toward the beginning of the eighteenth century by Bernardo Gomes de Brito under the title of *História Trágica Marítima*.

In spite of their many disasters the Portuguese galleons remained the monarchs of the seas for their size and carrying capacity. When in 1592 *Madre de Deus* was captured in the Azores by six English raiders she was taken into Dartmouth and was the wonder of all seafaring England.

The English and Dutch sailed small sharp ships manned by crews of freemen greedy for prize money. Their skippers kept improving their sailing qualities, trying new types of gear and new shapes of sails. They had the advantage of coming fresh to the game, always ready to turn new tricks. The remarkable thing is not that the Portuguese were driven out of the Orient but that they held on so long.

The Dutch made a start by sending four ships to Java in 1598. The voyage was profitable. During the next three years twelve other ships from the Netherlands invaded the eastern trade routes. After the foundation of the East India Company Dutch penetration was carefully organized. In 1619 they founded the fortress of Batavia on the Java coast thereby interrupting the course of the annual galleon the Portuguese sent from Goa to Macao to Nagasaki. Except for Timor where the Portuguese held on, they took over the Spice Islands. They expelled the Portuguese from Ceylon and in 1652 established a settlement on the Cape of Good Hope. In 1666 Malacca fell to them. During the same decade they supplanted the Portuguese in Coromandel and in the smaller trading posts along the Malabar Coast. Goa held firm until, late in the century, peace terms were arranged between the newly independent Bragança government and the Dutch Republic.

The British East India Company meanwhile centered its attention on Northern India and the Persian Gulf. In 1612 they established a post at Surat. With the help of Portugal's old allies the Persians they took Ormuz in 1625. A few years later their armed trading posts were doing business in Madras, Bombay and Calcutta.

In spite of invasions from the Dutch and English East India Companies and the closing of Japan to all Europeans, except for the foothold the Dutch managed to retain under humiliating conditions at Nagasaki, Goa and Macao remained flourishing centers of oriental trade. The passage to Lisbon lost its importance for them.

Portuguese influence lingered long in the oriental trade routes. Wherever they set up strong points they had introduced cattle and sheep and goats. They had diffused the cultivation of the clove tree and of oranges, lemons and tobacco. Through the Jesuit missions a measure of Portuguese culture had spread into Japan and even as far as Peking. For a century Portuguese was the trading language of the China Sea. In his *Dialogue in Praise of Our Language*, published in 1540 in Lisbon, João de Barros, the historian of India, declared with pride: "The coats of arms and the monumental pillars which the Portuguese set up in Africa and in Asia and in so many thousand islands outside of the divisions of the three parts of the world are material things and time can destroy them: but time cannot destroy the Doctrine, the way of life and the language which the Portuguese left behind them in those lands."

2

THE JESUITS IN BRAZIL

While Portuguese power waned in the East fresh waves of colonization and expansion flowed into Brazil.

Before sailing home from São Vicente Martim Afonso de Sousa had sent four Portuguese inland from the Bay of Guanabara, which he named River of January because he entered it the first day of the year 1531. These men came back in sixty days reporting that they had crossed the steep mountains of the coastal range and found an Indian king in charge of the level lands beyond who treated them well and gave them crystals brought from the interior to present to their captain. Furthermore, so the explorers reported, he told them that along the Paraguay River in the interior could be found plenty of gold and silver. On the strength of these unsubstantiated reports Martim Afonso sent out an expedition of some sixty armed men to search for the great river. They were never seen again. An exploratory cruise by Martim Afonso's brother Pero Lopes up the estuary of the Rio de la Plata in search of the silver it was named for proved equally fruitless. When Martim Afonso sailed home to continue his career in India, he left his brother Pero Lopes in charge of their captaincies.

Martim Afonso had established an incorporated town on the island of São Vicente and the Piratininga outpost up on the Rio

Tietê. This river though it had its source only a few miles from the sea in the mountain wall that towered over São Vicente, by one of the many freaks of Brazilian geography, flowed inland toward the basin of the Paraguay. As soon as he received his grant as hereditary captain of the region south of his brother's captaincy, Pero Lopes founded the village of Santo Amaro. These small settlements along the shore of what is now the State of São Paulo were made easy by the influence over the Indians exercised by an outcast Portuguese named João Ramalho. This man, stranded on the coast either by desertion or shipwreck established himself as a sub-chief in one of the Indian tribes. He collected a harem of Indian women and in a few years produced a large clan of half-breeds. He had daughters married to most of the chief men of the region.

The Portuguese patriarch dominating the Indians by sexual prowess, by strength of character, by the possession of firearms and the knowledge of how to make gunpowder, became a prime factor in the colonizing of Brazil. When Francisco Pereira Coutinho landed in Bahia de Todos os Santos to establish his settlement he found a noble Portuguese living in the neighborhood with a family of half-breed descendants. This fidalgo was known as Caramuru, "man of fire," to the Indians. In spite of Coutinho's mistaken policy of trying to impose on the warlike Tupinambá tribes methods of despotic rule he had learned in the East Indies, his hamlet of Vila Velha, with Caramuru's help, was eventually made secure.

The captaincies suffered various fortunes. At Ilhéus a colony was set up without difficulty by treaty with the local Indians. In Espírito Santo the settlers were driven from the coast and had to build their town of Vitória on an island. After a long struggle with the Indians and French interlopers a precarious settlement was established at Olinda in Pernambuco. The colonists who tried to plant a town near the mouth of the Northern Paraíba River were driven off. The historian, João de Barros, with two associates equipped a great fleet to occupy the captaincy of Maranhão. The fleet was wrecked on the coastal shoals and the region was left open to penetration by the French a few decades later. In spite of the very partial success of the captaincies the Brazilian settlements were already producing enough sugar to yield an income to the royal exchequer in Lisbon.

With the dwindling of profits from India the Crown needed to foster these imports from Brazil, but Portuguese possession, even of the regions claimed under the treaty of Tordesillas, was still precarious. French interlopers continued to infest the coast. The Indians, who at first had seemed so submissive, were proving unruly. The Spaniards, stimulated to fantastic efforts by the immensity of the treasure plundered off the Incas and the Aztecs, and the seemingly inexhaustible mines of gold and silver that had fallen into their hands, were scouring the continent for new Potosís. In 1541 Orellana accomplished his journey from Peru to the mouths of the Amazon and sailed home to claim the whole Amazon basin for Spain. Spaniards were already established in Asunción and were working their way up toward the headwaters of the Paraguay and its tributary the Paraná.

John III and his advisers decided that a central government was needed to protect the sugar plantations along the coast. In 1549 he sent out Dom Tomé, a younger member of the Sousa family, to Bahia as Governor General. With him in a squadron of six great galleons were three hundred men-at-arms, about as many free colonists and four hundred degredados.

With the help of Caramuru Tomé de Sousa built the city of Salvador on the heights overlooking the bay and surrounded it with a mud wall for protection. Four hundred houses are said to have gone up in four months. With the governor had come judges and commissioners of finance known as *ouvidors* who were to represent him in the various captaincies. A militia was set up for local defense and frontier wars. Every able-bodied man had to serve. Education and religion were to be cared for by six members of the Jesuit order.

These fathers and laybrothers, men of courage and sense and first rate ability tried to provide a disciplined framework for the development of colonial civilization in Brazil.

Father Manoel da Nóbrega's first report from Bahia to his provincial in Lisbon sets the stage. He thanks God for having arrived safely after a voyage of eight weeks. He found the settlement at Vila Velha to consist of some forty-five Portuguese living in peace with the neighboring Indians. The Jesuits' first work was to arrange a hut for use as a church and then housing for themselves. In the church they reaffirmed their own vows and heard the confessions of the settlers. A father went aboard ship to confess such members of the crews as could not come ashore.

As the new town progressed on the hill Father Nóbrega preached to the governor general and his suite up there, while Father Navarro preached to the settlers in the hamlet below. These were all living in mortal sin, wrote Father Nóbrega, not one of them was without a flock of native women by whom they had children galore. A school was already in session where Brother Vicente Rijo taught the Doctrine and reading and writing to the children. "I feel that this is a good way to attract the natives of this land who show a great desire to learn."

The brothers taught them their ABCs and how to make the sign of the cross. In return they wanted it understood that the Indians must eat no more human flesh and marry only a single wife. Unfortunately, noted Father Nóbrega, the Indians had to wage war against enemy tribes and to capture hostiles to serve them and to sell as slaves. It was these captured enemies they were accustomed to eat.

One local chief was already a baptized Christian. The fathers had given him a red sailor's stocking cap left over from their sea voyage and a pair of breeches. He, in return, with every evidence of affection, furnished them with fish and with products of the soil. Father Nóbrega found the Indians eager for conversion. What worried him most was the bad example set by the Christians "whose whole happiness seemed to be in having as many native concubines as possible."

As he traveled up and down the coast, preaching, setting up schools, organizing resistance against the French heretics in Rio, trying to argue the settlers out of following the native custom of capturing hostiles for slaves, the problem of how to regularize people's matrimonial affairs came up again and again. From Piratininga, where he was organizing the primary school which was later to become the College of São Paulo, he wrote asking the provincial to send some one to João Ramalho's home town of Vousela to find out if the wife he abandoned there forty years before was still living. Ramalho and his family, through his intimate connection with the Indian chiefs, would be of the greatest help in obtaining their conversion. He was willing to marry the wife who had borne him his favorite children if some legal way could be found. Furthermore, Father Nóbrega asked the provincial to obtain a dispensation from the pope, so that as many unions as possible among Christians and gentiles could be legally blessed, without too many complications, by the sacraments of the Church.

As more missionaries arrived the Jesuits multiplied their mission schools. Their colleges in Rio, São Paulo, Salvador da Bahia and Olinda in Pernambuco became the nuclei around which these outposts developed into cities. By 1580 the college at Salvador had reached the university level and was awarding bachelors' degrees.

The Jesuits housed their institutions in handsome buildings. They imported architects and stonemasons and Portuguese painted tiles. They encouraged painters and woodcarvers. They laid the foundations for a Brazilian theater by performing devotional autos in the style of Gil Vicente on church steps or in town squares, in Portuguese, Castilian or Tupi according to the needs of the audience. Their colleges trained the first students in the Indian languages. Padre Anchieta at São Paulo in his grammar of Tupi-Guarani invented the first written language for the forest peoples. The Jesuits organized hospitals and gave what medical assistance they could during epidemics. Every hamlet had a Jesuit pharmacy where such medicines as were available were at the disposal of any one in need.

Perhaps the greatest boon the Jesuits conferred on the Brazilians was that, partly through their efforts, no Inquisition was established in the New World. Their experience at Goa had been that the appearance of the Holy Office scared off converts among the native peoples.

As more and more Indian tribes accepted Christianity the Jesuits collected their converts into villages for protection against the savage heathen and against the slave-raiding half-breeds. These villages, which first appeared in the hinterland of Bahia, were ruled paternally by Jesuit priests. The most extensive of these governments was, of course, the Spanish Jesuit "republic" of Paraguay. The settled Indians practiced, as had been the habit of most of the tribes, communal agriculture, food gathering and hunting. Far from evil influences the Fathers patiently instructed children and adults in reading and writing and in the Doctrine. The Fathers tried to accustom the Portuguese plantation owners to paying a wage to the Christian natives instead of seizing them for slaves.

On this question of slavery the Jesuit enterprise ran into a blank wall. Though under Dom Sebastião Father Nóbrega managed to procure a royal edict severely limiting the enslavement of Indians, the ever-increasing importation of black slaves from Africa to work the sugar plantations made the whole effort nugatory. Some Jesuits even found themselves encouraging the importation of blacks to lessen the peril for their Indian converts.

3

RANSACKING
HALF A CONTINENT

The central government in Bahia had barely begun to link up the plantations scattered down the enormous extent of coast, before, the year after John III's death, a formidable attempt was made to create a French colony in Brazil. The French called it *la France Antarctique*. A dashing seaman named Villegagnon, a veteran trader on that coast, obtained the support of Admiral Coligny, who led the Huguenot faction in France, and landed a contingent of Protestants on a peninsula in the bay of Guanabara. For defense he built a fort on an adjacent island which he named Fort Coligny. La France Antarctique was to be a refuge for oppressed Protestants in America. For a while the Portuguese settlers were driven out of the bay, until, possibly on account of some change in the fortunes of war between the factions in France, supplies ceased to reach the colony. Villegagnon, who had been a Catholic all along, turned on the Huguenots.

The colony was in confusion when Mem de Sá, a brother of the great humanist, Sá de Miranda, appeared in the bay with a powerful Portuguese fleet. Mem de Sá was an active commander. After some skirmishing he was able to dislodge the French, with the help of Father Nóbrega and his converts who were in the forefront of the fight, and to regroup the scattered Portuguese.

'Another brother, Estácio de Sá, credited with the actual foundation of the city of Rio, was killed in the final assault.

For the next century Portuguese Brazil was continually on the defensive. Incursions from European powers reflected the ebb and flow of the religious wars.

By the early sixteen hundreds, the French, all schisms temporarily healed by the acceptance of Henry of Navarre as their king and his promulgation of religious toleration by the edict of Nantes, found fresh leisure to realize their dream of empire in America. Though the scheme for *La France Equinoctienne* was launched during Henry's lifetime, it wasn't until two years after his murder that a fleet set sail to establish a colony on the island of São Luís do Maranhão where French freebooters were already trading with the Indians for dyewoods and forest products. The first reaction from Bahia was to build the Fortaleza dos Reis Magos in what is now the State of Ceará. After two difficult campaigns in 1613 and 1615 Alexandre de Moura invested the fort of Saint Philippe de Maragnon and forced the French to capitulate. The next step in defense of the northeast was to build a strong point at Belém do Pará to protect at least one great waterway among the intricate channels through which the Amazon poured its flood of fresh water into the sea. At the same time Moura dispatched a vessel to inform the reigning Philip (the third of Portugal and the fourth of Spain) that even with the French eliminated there was a danger that English and Dutch interlopers might take over the mouths of the Amazon.

The answer came that the protection of the Amazon was up to the Portuguese. As a result the royal council in Lisbon set up a new and separate State of Maranhão to include the Amazon and the north shore of the eastern bulge. The chief reason was that because of adverse winds round Cape São Roque and the strength of the Caribbean current it was almost impossible for Maranhão to communicate with Bahia by sea.

Portuguese exploration of the Amazon began in 1623 but it wasn't until 1629 that Pedro Teixeira, doggedly cruising against the current of the great river, reached the Rio Tapajós and founded Santarém. Teixeira was a dour and indefatigable adventurer of the old school. Nine years later with a flotilla of canoes paddled by reluctant Indians he penetrated to the headwaters of one of the westernmost tributaries of the vast river system and almost scared the wits out of the Spanish authorities by suddenly turning up in Quito. He started back downstream in the company of two adventurous Spanish Jesuits. On the bank of a river where he had left his Indians and his canoes, with the two Spanish Jesuits as witnesses, he formally took possession of the Amazon basin for the crown of Portugal.

An unexpected advantage was accruing to the Portuguese from the union of the two crowns. For sixty years nobody remembered the provisions of the Treaty of Tordesillas. Teixeira never gave a thought to the old line barring Portuguese expansion to the west when he drew up his document deep in the rainforest at the base of the Andes.

The explorers of the *sertões*, the hinterlands back of the coastal ranges, were equally uninhibited. All through the fifteen hundreds occasional expeditions, *entradas* they were called, from Salvador and Pôrto Seguro and Vitória traveled inland in search of gold and emeralds. Though some gold dust was placered out of the rivers, most of their efforts were fruitless and a number of them vanished forever. It wasn't until the very distinctive migrations of the mixed peoples who became known as *Paulistas* that the interior was thoroughly explored to the Andes in the West and to the Rio de la Plata in the south.

The Paulistas were everything the Jesuit fathers most deplored. Each chief was the master of a troop of Indian concubines. They were slave raiders. Captained by immigrant Portuguese or native half-breeds they respected no man-made law. Their indefatigable marches were motivated by greed for slaves and later for silver, gold and precious stones. They were held together, if not by the Doctrine, by a sort of frontier Christianity, by the Portuguese language and by rough loyalty to the Portuguese way of life. They traveled in bands which became known as *bandeiras*, from a Portuguese military term for a group of men enlisted behind some leader's flag.

The first bandeiras went out from Santo Amaro and São Vicente, but soon the tableland of São Paulo became the center from which these movements flowed into the four corners of the continent. The Rio Tietê offered easy access to the basin of the Paraguay River.

Most of the *bandeirantes* were stock herders. As much as they needed slaves sugar mills needed oxen and horses. By 1580 coastal Brazil had become the chief supplier of sugar to Europe. One document lists three hundred and sixty-three *engenhos*, as they called the sugar mills, operating during that year. Oxen turned the great cylinders that crushed the cane. Oxen and horses hauled the carts that brought the cane in from the fields. One writer estimated that if a Brazilian mill employed a hundred slaves it would need fifty yokes of oxen and a hundred horses. The slaves, after the Indians had been discovered to be unsuited to bondage, were imported from Africa. The cattle had to be raised in Brazil.

So, on the tablelands beyond the coastal ranges, a race of cattlemen grew up. These were the ancestors of the rural Brazilian population of the twentieth century. Driving their herds and their slaves before them in search of water and pasture they scoured the arid tablelands and the fertile river valleys of the interior. Organized in bandeiras they became ferocious raiders. They dislodged the wild Indians who for years had menaced Rio. They attacked the villages of converts the Jesuits so diligently fostered on the Paraná River.

In 1628 a bandeira under Antonio Raposo Tavares seized the whole province of Guairá. In 1633 they overran a Spanish outpost in what is now the State of Mato Grosso, and prepared the way for the founding of the mining towns of Cuiabá and Goiás. In 1637 the Paulistas were reported to have carried off sixty thousand Indian converts to sell into slavery. Two years later a ravaging bandeira was repulsed by an army of Guarani Indians led by the Spanish governor of Paraguay. In 1641 the Paulistas suffered another defeat, but even after their raids into the Paraguay region petered out, they firmly held for Portugal the fertile territory between the Paraná and Uruguay rivers and the South Atlantic shore which now forms the State of Rio Grande do Sul.

While the Paulistas were infiltrating the interior the sugar producing region of Pernambuco was invaded by a Dutch fleet. This was a more serious threat to Portuguese America than English raids or the precarious footholds attained by the French. Encouraged by the success of their East India Company the Dutch in 1624 founded a West India Company. The same year a fleet of twenty-six Dutch ships appeared before Salvador, stormed the city and captured the governor general. The Dutch were shut up behind the mud wall by forces of militia and Indians hastily assembled by Bishop Teixeira of Bahia, but a year went by before the appearance of a combined Portuguese and Spanish fleet of overwhelming power forced them to let go their hold on the Brazilian capital.

The Dutch were obstinate people. Five years later they arrived in Pernambuco with a still larger armament and landed at Recife, where there was no force available to resist them. Count Maurice, an able member of the House of Orange, was sent out to organize a sugar producing colony on a permanent basis. Though a fresh attack on Bahia was a failure he occupied the eastern bulge as far south as the Rio São Francisco. It was twenty-five years before his Dutch were expelled from Pernambuco. They reorganized the sugar trade, which they found immensely profitable, and greatly extended the plantations. Feeling a need for more slaves to work them they coolly, in 1640, sent a fleet to occupy Luanda in Portuguese Angola.

Ousting the Dutch was a complicated business. They had shrewdly gauged the moment for their enterprise. The Spanish empire, under the least competent of the Hapsburg Philips, was in confusion. Philip's prime minister the Conde-Duque de Olivares faced revolts at home and abroad. At home the Catalans and the Portuguese were in arms against heavy taxation and impressment for foreign wars. Abroad the British and Dutch were whittling away at his overseas possessions. In 1640 the Portuguese renounced their allegiance to Philip and elected as their king an amiable but somewhat lackadaisical Duke of Bragança. For many years the Dukes of Bragança, descended from John of Avis' bastard son, as Portugal's most powerful and richest family, had enjoyed half-royal status. At the same time the Catalans threw over the traces. Olivares admitted he didn't have enough troops to quell both revolts. He decided to keep Catalonia and let Portugal go free.

In Portugal the restoration of the native monarchy proceeded fairly smoothly. The townspeople and the lettered middle class were still passionate nationalists. One of John IV's first acts was to send ambassadors to Holland. Since Portugal was free from Hapsburg overlordship there seemed no sense in continuing the war with the Dutch. Negotiations dragged on. The Dutch were reluctant to give up Pernambuco.

Eventually a number of factors combined to restore Pernambuco to Portuguese sovereignty. The severe discipline the Dutch tried to impose made them unpopular with the population of mixed breeds accustomed to the easygoing methods of the Portuguese. There was continual guerrilla warfare in the backlands. The native-born plantation owners rose in revolt. By that time the Dutch were involved in a war with England; the two Protestant powers were quarreling over the spoils of the Catholic empires. When that seasoned campaigner, Francisco Barreto, arrived from Lisbon with a well-equipped army the Dutch had no choice but to capitulate. They left many traces behind them. Up to the middle twentieth century the old houses in Recife still had a Netherlands look.

Brazilian historians have made much of the fact that the force which twice defeated the Netherlanders in Pernambuco was led by three men. One, André Vidal de Negreiros was born in Brazil of Portuguese parents. The other was an Indian named Felipe Camarão and the third, Henrique Dias, was a Negro. The union of the three races in the war against the Dutch foreshadowed the beginnings of Brazilian nationality.

4

THE BRAZILIANS

In India and the Orient Portuguese governors had encouraged the colonists to marry into the native populations. In Brazil intermarriage became not so much a policy as a fact of nature. That these intermarriages did not result in the complete dilution of "the Doctrine, the way of life and the language" which Barros was so proud of his people for having left behind them in Asia, was very largely due to the integrating power of the Portuguese family.

The family in Portugal, possibly as a result of Moslem and Semitic influences, had always been patriarchal. More than by individuals the penetration of India was carried on by great clans, the da Gamas, the Albuquerques, the Meneses, the Noronhas, the Sousas. Launched among the neolithic peoples of the forests and backlands of Brazil, the patriarchal family succeeded the Indian tribe as the chief social bond. The country was so enormous, such great extensions of land were needed for stock raising and agriculture—which was carried on by the old Indian system of burning off the forest or scrub, planting a crop or two of maize or manioc and, as the soil became exhausted, moving on to another virgin tract—that the settlers left behind by the restless bandeiras were thrown on their own resources. Colonial organization hardly touched them. The royal governor and his ouvidores could only reach them after weeks of travel over rough trails or by dugout canoe through the wilderness.

Even on the coastal sugar plantations, linked by water with the centers of government, the patriarchal family was the prevailing unit of society. The father lived in the great house with his official wife, who often in a quiet way exercised more power than he did. They presided over a tightly knit group of sons and daughters, daughters-in-law and sons-in-law, children and grandchildren. At a lower level the half-breeds, part Indian or part Negro, still belonged to the family group. The patriarch recognized his bastards. No obstacles were placed in the way of their rising to any situation they were capable of. The slaves were at the bottom of the heap but their lot was often alleviated by the fact that they too were thought of as relations.

The patriarch had the power of life and death over every member of his family, and sometimes exercised it. Family cohesion was unquestioned. When a conflict of interest arose with the church or the army or the government bureaucracy, the only other coherent organizations in the colony, it was family interests that prevailed.

The great families occupied *fazendas* of enormous extent and developed into a vested aristocracy roughly analogous to the medieval military aristocracy of Portugal in the days before the ascendancy of the House of Avis. The Portuguese strain was dominant. Subordinate to the patriarchs were the mixed breeds who cared for the stock, furnished the skilled and semi-skilled labor and the overseers and the minor officials. These were the heirs of the bandeirantes.

In the independent bandeiras that conquered the hinterland still burned the adventurous spirit, the savage acquisitiveness, the indomitable bravado that motivated the sailors and the men-at-arms who accomplished the enterprise of the Indies. Though suffering abject poverty for generations the rural classes of Brazil never quite fell into the subjection to the landowners which was the fate of the Portuguese peasantry. If a man didn't like it where he was he could disappear into the backlands. Often he could take his family with him. During the boom years of the eighteenth century he could prospect for gold and silver. There was always the hope of finding that one diamond in a muddy river bottom, which, in spite of the claims of the *regalia,* could raise a poor family to riches.

The royal prerogative in this case amounted to a fifth of the profits from the mining of gold and precious stones which reverted to the exchequer in Lisbon. The Braganças adhered strictly to the mercantilist theory in their dealings with their colonies. Trade with Brazil could only be carried on through special monopolies under royal charter and was restricted to Lisbon and Oporto. Immigration was controlled. The manufacture of machinery and household equipment was forbidden. Everything must be imported from Portugal. Printing presses were banned. After the expulsion of the Jesuits in 1759 higher education was discouraged. The business of a colony was to furnish materials cheap to the metropolis and to pay the highest possible price for the manufactured goods shipped back in exchange.

Mercantilism didn't work according to the book any more than any other economic theory. In Brazil distances were immense, transportation hazardous. Royal officials could be bribed. Sugar production was enormously profitable. The planters had plenty to bribe them with. Cotton became another lucrative monopoly. With profits from India dwindling to nothing the royal officials were so happy in the uninterrupted flow of specie from Brazil that they didn't ask too many questions. Sometimes the intermediaries got the lion's share. A class of Brazilian-Portuguese magnates grew up whose wealth and prodigality dominated the social scene during the eighteenth century.

As soon as the bandeirantes turned from slave-raiding to prospecting for precious stones and metals they developed another class of newrich miners. As often in mining booms purveyors and outfitters made the biggest fortunes. The word *brasileiro* began to connote affluence. Immigration from Portugal increased. By eighteen hundred the population of Brazil counting Negroes, Indians, whites and mixed breeds was reckoned at three million. This was considerably more than the population of the mother country.

This gold rush prosperity was accompanied by a burst of architectural invention. The design of churches and convents had tended to freeze, in Brazil and the Indies and in the home country, into the standardized solemnity of the seventeenth-century Jesuit styles. To be sure the dogmatic forms of the Italian baroque had all along been enlivened by the pictorial skill of the Portuguese tile makers. Large-scale decoration with blue and white tiles came to approach in scope the fresco-painting of the Italians. Now, particularly in the mining regions of Brazil, architectural inventions began to appear that matched, in Portuguese terms, the exuberance of the rococco of Northern Europe. Styles of building and decoration appeared which were in their own way as original as the manueline.

Ouro Preto, "Black Gold," the old mining capital, remains a museum of architectural achievement. From Ouro Preto emerged that strange genius known as Aleijadinho "the little cripple." His late sculpture, best represented by the Michelangelesque assembly of saints and prophets that loom above your head in pale soapstone as you climb the steps past the Stations of the Cross that lead up to the elegant hilltop church at Congonhas do Campo, may have a morbid intensity related to his physical disabilities; but his architecture, of which the great example is the church of the Third Order of Franciscans at São João d'El Rei, shows a sober skill in balancing plane surfaces against ornate decoration unsurpassed by any of the masters of European baroque. In the old gold-panning center of Sabará, there is a modish little church, Nossa Senhora do O, which embodies the most effervescent mixture of Portuguese and Chinese decorative styles. The heavy lacquered doors of the nearby parish church are reputed to have been brought from Macao. They testify to the amount of communication that still existed in the middle eighteenth century between outposts, half a world apart, of the Portuguese empire.

In Portugal itself, virtually the only source of wealth, apart from the gold and diamonds that came into the royal coffers from Brazil, was the wine trade with England. During a century after the breakaway from Spain, the country was administered by the church and the court bureaucracy. At the top a series of Bragança kings and queens were alternately profligate and conscientious. They ruled as absolute monarchs. The last Cortes met in 1697.

In spite of the stagnation of enterprise public and private, the Portuguese managed to hold on to such possessions in the Orient as Timor and Macao and Goa which had survived the depredations of the English and Dutch and to their posts in Angola and Moçambique. From the time of the Methuen treaty with England in 1703, which exchanged most favored nation treatment to Portuguese wines for the free import of British textiles, the country had become politically and economically a British satellite. Architecture and sculpture, pottery and tilework, became almost the only expression of the national personality. As attested by church exteriors and palace façades in every Portuguese town the baroque style kept developing until it culminated in such extravaganzas as the pink palace at Queluz and the whimsical mansion designed for a family of noble winegrowers at Mateus. The irrepressible inventive fantasy of stonemasons, carvers and artisans became a last manifestation of the vigor and energy of the early explorers.

The Enlightenment in Portugal took the form of the cruel but intelligent dictatorship of the Marquis of Pombal who ruled as prime minister during most of the long reign of addlepated Joseph I. It was Pombal who rebuilt Lisbon after the earthquake. He curtailed the privileges of the nobility and the church hierarchy. He reorganized the finances, drove out the Jesuits and made every effort to modernize the administration according to the views of the rational eighteenth century. The American and French revolutions found their echo in a malaise among the literate class in Portugal and in the uprising of the *Inconfidentes* in the mining country in Brazil.

It was Napoleon Bonaparte, on the rampage in Spain, who caused the Portuguese empire to break in two. He had long dominated the Spanish government under the distracted Carlos IV with whom Goya's portraits have made us so intimate. Feeling his oats as First Consul he fomented a small war between Madrid and Lisbon, now under a John of Bragança who ruled as regent on account of the insanity of his mother Maria, which resulted in the Portuguese having to renounce their treaties with England and pay an indemnity. A few years later, after being crowned emperor, he decided to add Spain and Portugal to his domain. He forced the abdication of the Spanish Bourbons and placed his brother Joseph on their throne. When the Portuguese regent got news that the French general Junot was advancing with his troops to enforce the partition of his country as part of Napoleon's plan for fitting it into his continental system, John and his whole court embarked on a fleet, sometimes described as consisting of a thousand ships, for Brazil. The crossing was made under the protection of an English admiral.

Rio de Janeiro suddenly found itself the capital of the Portuguese world. At the insistence of the English, royal decrees established free trade and removed restrictions on industry. A national bank was established and a royal printing press. English officers helped organize a Brazilian navy and built land defenses in the principal ports. When, upon his mother's death, the regent was crowned John VI in 1815 he pronounced himself ruler of the united kingdom of Portugal, Brazil and the Algarves.

Brazil was already showing all the symptoms of independence. Feeling that Brazil was getting out of hand John VI returned to Lisbon in 1821 to try to restore the family fortunes in the home country. Since the fall of Napoleon the regency he had left there had fallen under the thumb of the English.

John left his son Pedro I as prince-regent in Rio. Efforts of a new Portuguese government to restore Portuguese control of Brazil brought the independence movement to a head and in 1822 young Pedro was proclaimed constitutional emperor of an independent Brazil. His son Pedro II, brought up with a strong addiction to English constitutional principles, became one of the most successful of nineteenth-century monarchs. Dom Pedro introduced the amenities of the English nineteenth century. Even so Brazil remained a strip of inhabited coast backed by an unfathomable hinterland. Only gradually did successors of the old bandeirantes penetrate and settle the back country. Even in the latter half of the twentieth century that penetration is far from completed.

The traveler in twentieth century Brazil can still appreciate, in the migrations of the common laborers, something of the personal hardihood and the sheer bravado which inspired the bandeirantes of the sixteen hundreds and the Portuguese explorers of the preceding centuries. When in 1948 Bernardo Sayão, the great road builder, who lost his life in the moment of triumph when his Anápolis-Brasília-Belém highway was at the point of completion, was organizing an agricultural colony at Ceres in the western part of the central State of Goiás, settlers turned up from all over

Brazil. There were people from São Paulo and Paraná and Minas Gerais and Pernambuco. This was before the era of the blacktopped roads which Sayão did so much to inaugurate. Public officials traveled by air but the working farmer sort of people traveled by truck, jolting over endless miles of wilderness trails. These were the trucks called *pau d'arara:* parrot perches, because to keep from being jolted out you had to hold on to poles slung overhead. People who could not raise the truck fare had to walk. At Ceres there was a couple eagerly planting upland rice who had walked in from Ceará in the far eastern bulge. They worked their way as they came. In all they must have walked a thousand miles with their poor possessions on their heads, through tropical rain and scorching sun.

These were the *candangos* who furnished the labor for the building of the new capital at Brasília, who appear for a while at each new construction site or each new agricultural colony opening in the west, and then, after a few years move on.

By 1966 the report was that almost all the first settlers at Ceres had sold out to land speculators. Much as the Jesuits deplored the bad morals and the brutal aggressiveness of the bandeirantes, the twentieth-century engineers and administrators deplore the incurable nomadism of the candangos and their weakness for *cachaça,* the national brew of raw cane spirits; but even the most casual traveler in inland Brazil can note their slow irresistible penetration of the remotest corners of the land.

In August 1966 a tourist enterprise ran a houseboat down the Araguaia River, a tributary of the Tocantins which forms the border between the states of Goiás and Mato Grosso. The houseboat slid smoothly day after day down the glass-clear swift stream. Below the small settlement of Mato Verde there were no more launches, no Indian villages. The houseboat tied up for the night against a sandbank empty except for turtlecrawls and the circling river gulls and flocks of every conceivable variety of heron perching among the yellow flowering *ipê*.

Just before the boat made its landing the travelers had noticed a dugout on the river. A couple of them walked up the beach to see where the canoe was going. They found it pulled up on the beach in front of a small promontory. On the rise, in an open space under the shade of great trees, there were traces of a camp. The place was airy and cool. Upstream and downstream you could see long reaches of silent sheening river. Pitched between two trees hung a large hammock, what they call there a married couple's hammock. It was draped with mosquito netting. Near it were some charred sticks where a fire had been.

The couple quietly made themselves visible from among the dense foliage, a slender brown man and a slender brown woman. They both looked younger than they probably were. They were smiling. They were pleased to receive visitors. They were so completely at their ease that the travelers immediately felt at their ease too.

The man said he had come from the Northeast. He had worked on a construction job in Goiânia, the booming state capital. Then he'd worked for the great fazenda that occupied hundreds of square miles west of the river. He'd saved some money to buy cattle of his own but finding cattle too high he had decided to plant beans. He and his woman had come downriver to fish. They would smoke the fish to take back to Mato Verde for the winter when the rains came and the river would rise eighteen feet and it would be hard to get food.

While they talked the travelers made a mental inventory of the couple's possessions: the hammock, a light blanket, a battered cooking pan, a gun and a fishhook on a handline. Besides they had the dugout and two paddles.

The travelers reluctantly wished them good evening and walked back toward the houseboat for supper. There was such serenity about this man and this woman alone and at home in the enormous wilderness that it was a wrench to leave them. It was people like these, the travelers told each other, men and women at home wherever they found themselves, who had explored the four corners of the world and the American continents. Now they were peopling Brazil.

Next morning the man turned up under the stern of the houseboat in his canoe with a medium-sized *pirarucú*. This is the giant lungfish which is the most important source of food for the dwellers on these waters. He wanted to trade it for fishhooks, because fishhooks, he explained, were almost unobtainable on the Araguaia River.

A NOTE ON SOURCES AND
BACKGROUND READING

Up to the last twenty years the best books in English on Portuguese history and literature have come from scholars working in the British universities. Many of the classics of Portuguese discovery were translated and annotated in the irreplaceable series of volumes brought out by the Hakluyt Society. The full set is in every well-furnished public library. There you will find translations of part of Azurara's chronicles, the original first hand accounts of da Gama's and Cabral's voyages, Cadamosto's explorations of the West Coast of Africa, Duarte Pacheco Pereira's *Esmeraldo in Situ Orbis*, Duarte Barbosa's pilotbook for the coasts of East Africa and Malabar, the *Verdadeira Informação* of Father Francisco Alvares and a second volume on later Portuguese penetration into Abyssinia; and João de Castro's famous geography of the Red Sea. Another Hakluyt volume is the most available source for Pigafetta's salty narrative of Magellan's ill-fated cruise to the Philippines and Elcano's completion of the first circumnavigation of the globe aboard *Victoria*.

Among other English writings probably the most useful is Edgar Prestage's *Portuguese Pioneers*. K. G. Jayne's *Da Gama and His Successors* is full of information. H. V. Livermore's *New History of Portugal* is the best available. There is Aubrey FitzGerald Bell's *History of Portuguese Literature* and his excellent short monographs on Gil Vicente and Gaspar Correa. Professor C. R. Boxer has produced a series of studies that throw light into some dark corners of Portuguese colonial history. I found P. E. Russell's *English Intervention in Spain and Portugal in the Time of Edward III and Richard II* an invaluable source book for the period of the

Plantagenet alliance. Walter Crum Wallace's *Portuguese Architecture* is good. The Rev. Sidney R. Welch's three volumes published in Cape Town: *Europe's Discovery of South Africa, South Africa Under King Manuel* and *South Africa under John III* I found refreshing because the position of the observer is so different from that in works by Europeans or Americans.

In recent years American scholars and aspirants for PhDs have begun to show interest in Portuguese history. Samuel Eliot Morison's magnificent biography of Columbus, *Admiral of the Ocean Sea* (much better in the original two volume edition), may have opened up the field. After all, Columbus's background was more Portuguese than Castilian. Morison's *Portuguese Voyages to America*, though I think he is a little dogmatic in his refusal to admit any secret or unpublicized voyages prior to the official ones, is essential to the understanding of Atlantic exploration in the fifteenth century. Charles Wendell David's text and translation of *De Expugnatione Lyxbonensi* is a model of historical scholarship. Bailie M. Diffie's *Prelude to Empire* is first rate as is Dan Stanislawsky's *The Individuality of Portugal*. Francis M. Rogers in his *The Travels of the Infante Dom Pedro of Portugal* has rescued a historical personage from the realm of myth. His *Quest for the Eastern Christians* is a good introduction to the legend of Prester John and its ramifications. Frederick J. Pohl's *Amerigo Vespucci: Master Pilot* rescues another historical character from an imbroglio of forgeries and misunderstandings. J. Duffy's *Shipwreck and Empire* offers an excellent summary of the decline of Portuguese seamanship in the seventeenth century. There is a useful doctoral dissertation by Elizabeth Feist Hirsch on the life of Damião de Góis, the humanist and Abyssinian scholar who chronicled the reign of Manoel the Fortunate.

The reward for research into the period of the Portuguese explorations is a real bonanza of personal records, letters, chronicles and down-to-earth descriptions of the joys and pains undergone by the adventurers who discovered three continents barely known to Europeans. Unfortunately very little of this material has been translated into English and much of it is hard to come by even in the original Portuguese.

The chronicles of Fernão Lopes, Azurara and Rui de Pina contain episodes of a vividness unique in historical literature. The more sophisticated narratives of Garcia de Resende and João de Barros and Damião de Góis still remain close to the original eye-witnesses who poured their stories into the chroniclers' ears. Francisco Alvares' account of the first Portuguese embassy's trials and tribulations in Abyssinia and Mendes Pinto's picaresque *Pilgrimage* are masterpieces of narrative in their own right besides being the depositories for an immense amount of ethnographic information. Vaz de Caminha's account of the first glimpse of Brazil and Alvaro Velho's account of Vasco da Gama's rounding of the Cape of Good Hope are among the great autobiographical fragments of world literature. The letters of the first Jesuits in Brazil are packed with carefully observed anthropological data about the Tupi-Guarani Indians. Gaspar Correa's *Legends of India* detail events so vividly from the point of view of the average man that you feel you have talked with and rubbed shoulders with the people he tells about. And these are only a few. It would take a lifetime to work your way through the contemporary literature of the great enterprise. Dr. Manoel Cardozo of Catholic University in Washington has touched pleasantly on the atmosphere of these chronicles in a short paper: "The Idea of History in the Portuguese Chronicles of the Age of Discovery" in the *Catholic Historical Review* for April 1963.

INDEX

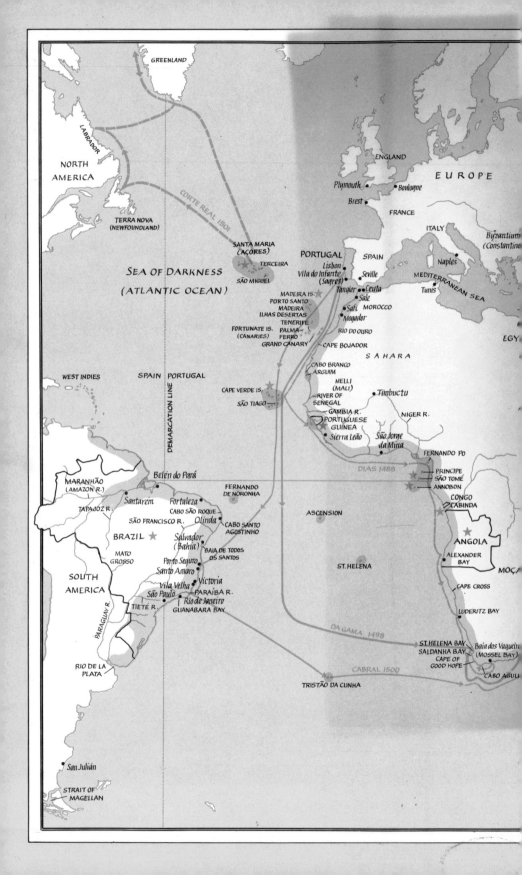